1–2 PETER AND JUDE

PREACHING THE WORD
Edited by R. Kent Hughes

1–2 PETER AND JUDE

SHARING CHRIST'S SUFFERINGS

DAVID R. HELM

R. Kent Hughes
Series Editor

WHEATON, ILLINOIS

Hardcover ISBN: 978-1-4335-5016-4
ePub ISBN: 978-1-4335-5019-5
PDF ISBN: 978-1-4335-5017-1
Mobipocket ISBN: 978-1-4335-5018-8

Library of Congress Cataloging-in-Publication Data

Helm, David R., 1961–
   1 and 2 Peter and Jude : sharing Christ's sufferings / David R.
Helm; R. Kent Hughes, general editor.
      p.   cm. — (Preaching the word)
   Includes bibliographical references and index.
   ISBN-13: 978-1-58134-960-3 (hc)
   1. Bible. N.T. Peter—Commentaries. 2. Bible. N.T. Jude—
Commentaries. I. Hughes, R. Kent. II. Title. III. Title: First and
Second Peter and Jude. IV. Series.
BS2795.53.H45   2008
227'.92077—dc22   2007031316

Crossway is a publishing ministry of Good News Publishers.

VP		28	27	26	25	24	23	22	21	20	19	18
14	13	12	11	10	9	8	7	6	5	4	3	2

From *1–2 Peter*:

In thanksgiving to God for my dad,
Richard Helm, who models gospel stability
and who along with my mom taught me true grace
and the importance of finishing well.

From *Jude*:

In memory of my father-in-law,
Theophilus Schmid, a faithful husband and a man of few words,
whose charge to me remains an encouragement:
"Contend for the faith."

Contents

A Word to Those Who Preach the Word

There are times when I am preaching that I have especially sensed the pleasure of God. I usually become aware of it through the unnatural silence. The ever-present coughing ceases, and the pews stop creaking, bringing an almost physical quiet to the sanctuary—through which my words sail like arrows. I experience a heightened eloquence, so that the cadence and volume of my voice intensify the truth I am preaching.

There is nothing quite like it—the Holy Spirit filling one's sails, the sense of his pleasure, and the awareness that something is happening among one's hearers. This experience is, of course, not unique, for thousands of preachers have similar experiences, even greater ones.

What has happened when this takes place? How do we account for this sense of his smile? The answer for me has come from the ancient rhetorical categories of *logos*, *ethos*, and *pathos*.

The first reason for his smile is the *logos*—in terms of preaching, God's Word. This means that as we stand before God's people to proclaim his Word, we have done our homework. We have exegeted the passage, mined the significance of its words in their context, and applied sound hermeneutical principles in interpreting the text so that we understand what its words meant to its hearers. And it means that we have labored long until we can express in a sentence what the theme of the text is—so that our outline springs from the text. Then our preparation will be such that as we preach, we will not be preaching our own thoughts about God's Word, but God's actual Word, his *logos*. This is fundamental to pleasing him in preaching.

The second element in knowing God's smile in preaching is *ethos*—what you are as a person. There is a danger endemic to preaching, which is having your hands and heart cauterized by holy things. Phillips Brooks illustrated it by the analogy of a train conductor who comes to believe that he has been to the places he announces because of his long and loud heralding of them. And that is why Brooks insisted that preaching must be "the bringing of truth through personality." Though we can never perfectly embody the truth we preach, we must be subject to it, long for it, and make it as much a part of our ethos as possible. As the Puritan William Ames said, "Next to the Scriptures, nothing makes a sermon more to pierce, than when it comes out of the inward affection of the heart without any affectation." When a preacher's *ethos* backs up his *logos*, there will be the pleasure of God.

Last, there is *pathos*—personal passion and conviction. David Hume, the Scottish philosopher and skeptic, was once challenged as he was seen going to hear George Whitefield preach: "I thought you do not believe in the gospel." Hume replied, "I don't, but he does." Just so! When a preacher believes what he preaches, there will be passion. And this belief and requisite passion will know the smile of God.

The pleasure of God is a matter of *logos* (the Word), *ethos* (what you are), and *pathos* (your passion). As you preach the Word may you experience his smile—the Holy Spirit in your sails!

R. Kent Hughes
Wheaton, Illinois

Acknowledgments

I am grateful to Crossway Books, especially Lane Dennis, for his vision and long-standing commitment to bring sermonic material into printed form. Further, I am indebted to Kent Hughes for the opportunity to contribute this volume to his Preaching the Word series. Having collaborated in gospel ministry with Kent in one way or another for over twenty years, I know firsthand his aim for this series. On more than one occasion while laboring over the task of turning my preaching into something that might be readable as well, I have wondered just how he did this for all those years! And while at times I felt as if I were "going to work in another man's boots," I trust that this volume will both meet his standards and feed his soul.

To the two congregations who first heard these chapters as sermons, Holy Trinity Church in Hyde Park and Chicago Business Focus, my continuing gratitude. For your salvation I labor, and in your love for Christ I am constantly refreshed. I would be remiss if I did not thank Ted Griffin at Crossway Books for his careful editing of the text of this book. To my colleague at the Charles Simeon Trust, Robert Kinney, whose attention to the manuscript ensured proper form and accurate footnotes, my appreciation for your shared commitment to biblical exposition. In addition, thanks to my good gospel friends Jim and Sue Bowen for providing the ideal place to escape when I needed to write.

Lastly, to Lisa, you have my constant love. You know me best, and yet you encourage and support me better than anyone. In printing these manuscripts, may God alone receive all the praise and glory that is due his name. And may those who read this volume be strengthened in Christ to continue following in the obedient way of grace.

1 PETER

1

Reading 1 Peter

LIFE IS DIFFICULT. But this harsh truth has not always been understood by those following Jesus Christ. Many Christians today have trouble sorting out the complexity of their identity and calling in Christ. They were reared to believe that a Christian should only experience the joys of being one of God's elect. They have been taught nothing of our exilic state. With three simple words in the opening of this letter, Peter gives us the biblical corrective—a profound clue for finding life's true horizon. We are the "*elect exiles* of the *dispersion*" (1:1).

How did this phrase come to describe the true state of Christians in every age? "According to the foreknowledge of God the Father, in the sanctification of the Spirit, for obedience to Jesus Christ and for sprinkling with his blood" (1:2). Our soul rises in praise and falls in sorrow on the same afternoon "*according to the foreknowledge of God the Father.*" We are God's beloved, and yet we are carried off into exile like Daniel of old "*in the sanctification of the Spirit.*" We remain on the outside of the world in which we live "*for obedience to Jesus Christ.*" And we are all these things as a fragrant offering in Christ's "blood." According to Peter, we owe our full identity as "elect exiles" to the mysterious plan of God.

Throughout the Scriptures, the way up comes by going down; restoration comes after trials (5:10). It is this inversion in attaining glory that marks Peter's theme throughout this letter. Christians' future inheritance and exaltation—our eternal share in the glory of Christ—will be awarded to us on the day of his appearing (1:13; 2:12; 4:13; 5:1, 4, 10). But that promised day only comes *after* this brief season of present-day sufferings. For suffering always precedes subsequent glories. As it was for God's Son, so it will be for all of us who are in him.

This bringing together of two seemingly incompatible truths—our status in Christ *and* our sufferings on earth—is how Peter's letter begins (1:1, 2). And in the body of the letter these incompatible ideas are continually joined to one another. In 1:3–12 we see that an eternal inheritance is linked to various trials. In other words, salvation's future goal (vv. 3–5) is built upon the present trials (vv. 6–9) as well as the past glories (vv. 10–12).

Beginning with verse 13, Peter begins to establish answers to some pending questions. In light of these present trials, how are Christians supposed to bear witness to Christ's glory? How are we to live in this wilderness world? Peter's prescriptive answer centers on the Christian's *conduct* (v. 15). The word translated "conduct" in this verse is used only twenty-four times in the entire New Testament. And yet nearly half of those come from Peter. He uses it eleven times (see 1:15, 17, 18; 2:12; 3:1, 2, 16; 2 Peter 2:7, 18; 3:11). In essence, Peter's strategy for Christian conduct, rooted in a settled hope, comes from a focus on:

- Sanctification (1:13–21)
- A sincere love for others both in and out of the church (1:22—2:12)
- Submission to unjust leaders out of a love for Christ (2:13—3:7)
- A willingness to suffer (3:8—4:6), and
- Service to God's new family (4:7—5:14)

These are the elements of Christian conduct.

Peter goes on to develop this theme of Christian identity and conduct in light of a settled hope. Reaching a turning point in 2:11, 12, we find a concise *exhortation* to live lives worthy of our unique calling. *Examples* of what this looks like abound (2:13, 18; 3:1). And in case Peter's early readers have trouble grasping this gracious truth, he will go so far as to argue that Jesus Christ was the supreme *example* of this teaching (2:21–25). Aware of the high demands this will place upon his readers, Peter encourages them by setting forward the exilic-like wandering years of King David, the anointed one who suffered, in an effort to help them press on (3:9–17). Finally, in 3:18–22, he returns to Christ and grounds the irony of his divine logic in the demonstration of Christ's ultimate vindication as proof of our future hope and present calling (4:19).

In these later chapters Peter continues to encourage his readers with the example of Christ overcoming extraordinary trials. He concludes by making an appeal to the elders specifically (5:1–5) and then to everyone more generally (5:6–14) to fulfill their unique callings in humility and grace. The divine principle of "true grace" (5:12) is this: God has established our salvation, given us our identity, confirmed our present-day calling, and secured our future inheritance by means of an inverted irony—namely, the death, resurrection, and ascension of Christ. Therefore, just as the exaltation of Jesus followed a season of humiliation, so too our share in his eternal glory will appear after we have learned to follow in his true and gracious ways.

Peter, an apostle of Jesus Christ, To those who are elect exiles of the dispersion in Pontus, Galatia, Cappadocia, Asia, and Bithynia, according to the foreknowledge of God the Father, in the sanctification of the Spirit, for obedience to Jesus Christ and for sprinkling with his blood: May grace and peace be multiplied to you.

1:1, 2

2

A Letter to Elect Exiles

1 PETER 1:1, 2

IF YOU WERE TO WALK home with me from work, you would travel a few short blocks—down an alley, through an iron gate, and up seven or eight stairs to a landing. Then, with a turn of the key and a push of a door, you would find yourself in one of Chicago's throwback, turn-of-the-century, southside six-flats, standing in my kitchen. Once the door was shut behind us (no small task given the number of shoes that seem to collect there), you would see me greet Lisa and the kids, and then, on a normal day, you would hear me ask, "Any good mail?"

Two things constitute a "good mail" day in the Helm household. First, good mail is that which comes from a friend or family member. No bills! And second, good mail means that the note was not only handwritten but written well. Well, although you didn't walk home with me, you have nevertheless found your way to this book; you have come in through the door, so to speak, and have gotten yourself situated. And, yes, it is a very good mail day.

The Author

A letter has arrived, and it is from one of the members of God's family. According to verse 1 it claims Peter, the great and gregarious follower of Jesus, as its author. It is signed "Peter, an apostle of Jesus Christ." Later on, as if to leave no doubt as to his identity, the writer confirms himself as Peter the Apostle by stating, "I exhort the elders among you, as a . . . witness of the sufferings of Christ" (5:1). So, from the opening words to the final chapter internal testimony supports the notion that the letter we are studying is from none other than Peter, a disciple of Jesus, an elder in the early church, an apostle, and a witness of the death and resurrection of Jesus.

Of course, there are, and forever will be, melancholy Eeyores standing around, many who are prepared to pour rain on a good mail day. When it comes to reading 1 Peter, learned detractors intrude into our kitchen and say, "Are you so sure, simpleminded pastor? Is the letter actually from the hand of Peter? After all, it might not be, you know. In fact, many of us don't believe in the notion of Petrine authorship. For proof we make our appeal to your own criteria on what constitutes a good mail day. This letter is simply too well written to come from Peter the Apostle."

So we arrive, even before we begin, at a contemporary charge against this piece of divine mail. There is nothing to be gained by hiding this from you. A veritable gaggle of scholars feel that the Greek used in this letter is too elevated for Peter—the vocabulary too rich and uncommon—the engaging rhetorical flow too far above the intellectual capacity of an uneducated first-century fisherman like Peter. Our very own Eeyores shake their heads from side to side as if to say, "I am so sorry to disappoint you, but this letter was written later in time. It comes from the hand of one well acquainted with the literary tools necessary for this kind of ascendant discourse." To support their claim, they appeal to Acts 4 where Peter is referred to as an "uneducated [and] common" man.[1]

The effect, of course, is devastating. Our initial excitement over a good mail day begins falling to the ground like a balloon losing the air that once kept it afloat. Well, don't be overly discouraged just yet. There is a great irony in the charge, and like a knife, it cuts both ways.

> Now when they saw the boldness of Peter and John, and perceived that they were *uneducated, common men,* they were astonished. And they recognized that they had been with Jesus. (Acts 4:13)

The charge that Peter and John were "uneducated, common men" can certainly be perceived as a derogatory one. Yet, and this is important, these words were not used by the biblical scholars of Peter's day to level a negative verdict on whether or not the man standing before them was actually Peter the Apostle. Rather, these precise terms were the only ones available to adequately express their astonished surprise at the superior ability and elevated style of *this man,* Peter. In other words, these men were amazed that one so ordinary could also be one so well-spoken.

Now, with that knowledge in place, the irony of the contemporary charge leveled against apostolic authorship for our letter is unmasked. If the terms *uneducated* and *common* were the ones employed by the elite of Peter's day to support—not to deny—his person, then certainly the pundits of our day should be willing to consider that this same Peter could possess the ability to write well. In fact, if we are honest, all of us should be willing to admit that someone who is so well-spoken might also have the capability of becoming so well-written.

And what is it that makes good writing? Well, C. S. Lewis, in correspondence with a young American girl on June 26, 1956, wrote:

> What really matters is:
>
> Always try to use the language so as to make quite clear what you mean, and make sure your sentence couldn't mean anything else.
>
> Always prefer the plain direct word to the long vague one. Don't "implement" promises, but "keep" them.
>
> Never use abstract nouns when concrete ones will do. If you mean "more people died," don't say "mortality rose."
>
> Don't use adjectives which merely tell us how you want us to feel about the thing you are describing. I mean, instead of telling us a thing was "terrible," describe it in such a way that we'll be terrified. Don't say it was "delightful," make *us* say "delightful" when we've read the description. You see, all those words, (horrifying, wonderful, hideous, exquisite) are only saying to your readers "please will you do my job for me."
>
> Don't use words too big for the subject. Don't say "infinitely" when you really mean "very"; otherwise you'll have no word left when you want to talk about something *really* infinite.[2]

Isn't that great? Good writing, after all, is clear, simple, and direct. It contains what Lewis called "concrete" nouns. As we make our way through this letter, we will see Peter put all of Lewis's dictums into practice. This letter is good because it is clear, simple, direct.

The Audience

Peter doesn't waste any time in utilizing concrete nouns to identify the ones to whom he is writing. In verse 1 he writes:

> To those who are elect exiles of the dispersion in Pontus, Galatia, Cappadocia, Asia, and Bithynia.

He uses three strong nouns to describe his audience: "*elect exiles* of the *dispersion*." In time you will see that these three words function as floor joists to the book. They undergird and support everything Peter wants to say. Like flowers in a garden, the ideas and concepts hidden in these strong nouns will open in full bloom. In fact, one could argue that everything in 1 Peter flows from the force of these three simple words.

The Elect

The word translated "elect" simply means "chosen." Throughout the Bible *chosen* is the intimate term most often used to speak of those whom God loves. To grasp the relational intimacy behind the term, consider the exalted picture Ezekiel paints when speaking of God's electing choice of Israel:

> And as for your birth, on the day you were born your cord was not cut, nor were you washed with water to cleanse you, nor rubbed with salt, nor wrapped in swaddling cloths. No eye pitied you, to do any of these things to you out of compassion for you, but you were cast out on the open field, for you were abhorred, on the day that you were born. And when I passed by you and saw you wallowing in your blood, I said to you in your blood, 'Live!' I said to you in your blood, 'Live!' I made you flourish like a plant of the field. And you grew up and became tall and arrived at full adornment. Your breasts were formed, and your hair had grown; yet you were naked and bare.
>
> When I passed by you again and saw you, behold, you were at the age for love, and I spread the corner of my garment over you and covered your nakedness; I made my vow to you and entered into a covenant with you, declares the Lord GOD, and you became mine. Then I bathed you with water and washed off your blood from you and anointed you with oil. I clothed you also with embroidered cloth and shod you with fine leather. I wrapped you in fine linen and covered you with silk. And I adorned you with ornaments and put bracelets on your wrists and a chain on your neck. And I put a ring on your nose and earrings in your ears and a beautiful crown on your head. Thus you were adorned with gold and silver, and your clothing was of fine linen and silk and embroidered cloth. You ate fine flour and honey and oil. You grew exceedingly beautiful and advanced to royalty. And your renown went forth among the nations because of your beauty, for it was perfect through the splendor that I had bestowed on you, declares the Lord GOD. (16:4–14)

What a special picture describing God's electing love! Israel became God's chosen. They were his elect. Although born helpless and vulnerable, they were given life through God's electing love. Do you see the comfort associated with this word *elect*? The term *elect* is meant to encourage the church. It is to remind the people of God of his great love. It is not a term to be waved in front of those who don't yet know God.[3] It should be used to bring comfort for those in the faith. Peter intended to assure his early dispersed readers of God's steadfast love. And certainly they would have basked in the reassuring strength of the word.

Exiles of the Dispersion

We have already seen that the term *elect*, in all its grandeur, was given to the entire household of Israel. Unfortunately, history shows that Israel began to presume upon God's good grace. As special objects of his love, they believed they would always know his goodness. Over time their familiarity with God worked against them. They felt that they were entitled to the good life even when their affections for God fell off. Presumptuous sin became the unfortunate companion of God's elect. During the days of the kings, they turned away from God and forfeited the glory of his approval. As a result, the great nation was carried off into *exile*; they were *dispersed* by God. The term *exiles of the dispersion* was now, for the first time, joined to the term *elect*. In Shakespeare's *Henry VI* we read of the tragedy of glory dispersed.

> Glory is like a circle in the water,
> Which never ceaseth to enlarge itself
> Till by broad spreading it disperse to naught.
> With Henry's death the English circle ends;
> Dispersed are the glories it included.[4]

Israel knew something of lost glory. They knew, all too well, that the term *elect* does at times stand beside the phrase *exiles of the dispersion*—beloved by God, yet seemingly left alone in the world. In this letter Peter does not hesitate to place these terms alongside one another to identify his readers. They are called the "elect exiles of the dispersion." How strange. One would have thought that putting these words together would be like mixing oil with water. Yet for Peter, it is no trouble at all.

There is one major difference, however, in the way Peter uses the terms. As the letter unfolds, it will become clear to us that Peter believes that his readers are exiles of a different sort. Their exilic identity has nothing to do with ancient Israel's sin—or their own. Their *exilic* state is not the result of disobedience to God. In fact, all the evidence in the letter demonstrates that they were living faithful and fruitful lives in obedience to Christ (1:2). For Peter then—and this is most important—the phrase "exiles of the dispersion" depicts the normative state of any follower of Jesus, so long as he or she remains in this world.[5]

In this sense Peter's early readers were not very different from you and me. They were men and women who had come into a relationship with God through faith in Christ and as such remained on the outside of everything in this world. C. S. Lewis stated the normative condition of the Christian as *elect exiles* this way:

At present we are on the outside of the world, the wrong side of the door. We discern the freshness and purity of morning, but they do not make us fresh and pure. We cannot mingle with the splendors we see. But all of the leaves of the New Testament are rustling with the rumor that it will not always be so. Some day, God willing, we shall get in.[6]

So we have established this much: we have a lot in common with Peter's first readers. In Christ we are God's chosen, his elect in all the earth. And yet we are living our lives out in a complex and often confusing context. We are capable of waking up each morning in joyful praise *and* going to bed dejected in spirit.

Toni Morrison closes her gripping novel *Sula* with an emotional scene depicting both love and loss. Two women, Sula and Nel, had been friends. But now Sula has passed away, and Nel is forced to come to grips with her equal sense of loss and feeling alone in the world.

Suddenly Nel stopped. Her eye twitched and burned a little.

"Sula?" She whispered, gazing at the tops of trees.

"Sula?" Leaves stirred; mud shifted; there was the smell of overripe green things. A soft ball of fur broke and scattered like dandelion spores in the breeze . . . the loss pressed down on her chest and came up into her throat. "We was girls together," she said as though explaining something.

"O Lord, Sula," she cried, "girl, girl, girlgirlgirl."

It was a fine cry—loud and long—but it had no bottom and it had no top, just circles and circles of sorrow.[7]

Who doesn't know that wrenching sense of isolation and sorrow? In getting to know Peter's audience, know this—they were men and women of faith who knew it too. They knew what it was to have "a fine cry—loud and long," one without bottom or top, "just circles and circles of sorrow."

An Opening Word of Encouragement

Many Christians today have trouble sorting out the complexity of their identity in Christ. They were reared to believe that a Christian should only experience the joys of being one of God's elect. They have been taught nothing of our exilic state. With three simple words in the opening of this letter, Peter has given us the biblical corrective. We are "the elect exiles of the dispersion."

How did this phrase come to describe the true state of Christians in every age? Peter tells us.

According to the foreknowledge of God the Father, in the sanctification of the Spirit, for obedience to Jesus Christ and for sprinkling with his blood. (v. 2)

Our soul rises in praise and falls in sorrow on the same afternoon "according to the foreknowledge of God the Father." We became God's beloved and yet are carried off into exile like Daniel of old "in the sanctification of the Spirit." We remain on the outside of the world in which we live "for obedience to Jesus Christ." And we are all these things as a fragrant offering in Christ's blood.

According to Peter, we owe our full identity as *elect exiles* to the mysterious plan of God. It is no accident that the three concrete nouns Peter used to identify his readers in verse 1 are followed by three descriptive phrases explaining how this came to be. To ensure that his readers don't misunderstand him, Peter plants his thoughts in the soil of a Trinitarian formula.

- "According to the foreknowledge of God the *Father*,
- in the sanctification of the *Spirit*,
- for obedience to *Jesus Christ* and for sprinkling with his blood."

In the strongest way possible, Peter has told us: The Lord God, the Creator of the heavens and the earth, is behind all of this. The hidden counsel of the Eternal Trinity has planned for us to be known as his "elect exiles." And he has done all of this through the sprinkling of the blood of Jesus. So take heart. Be encouraged. Christians are those who are chosen by God *and* called to live in this world. There is something in this letter for every Christian. This is a fine mail day. As you read on, Peter's desire is that you would experience God's grace and know his peace. In fact, verse 2 says that he wants them to be yours in abundance ("May grace and peace be multiplied to you").

Dear Father, Son, and Holy Spirit, we thank you for this letter of 1 Peter. We thank you for clarifying our identity in this world. We praise you that you have called us for obedience to Jesus Christ. May his eternal glory be ever before us. May his season of earthly humiliation guide us. And may his vindication inspire us to press on through this wilderness world. It is in Jesus' name that we pray. Amen.

Blessed be the God and Father of our Lord Jesus Christ! According to his great mercy, he has caused us to be born again to a living hope through the resurrection of Jesus Christ from the dead, to an inheritance that is imperishable, undefiled, and unfading, kept in heaven for you, who by God's power are being guarded through faith for a salvation ready to be revealed in the last time.

1:3–5

3

Salvation's Future Goal

1 PETER 1:3–5

EARLY IN THE TWENTIETH CENTURY there was a young Welsh boy by the name of Jones. In search of a better education, his parents sent him away to boarding school—far from home. Years later the boy, Martyn, would reflect on his experience:

> I must add that I suffered at that time from a—sickness—which has remained with me all along life's path—and that was hiraeth [the Welsh word for longing or homesickness].—Hiraeth is an awful thing, as also is the feeling of loneliness, of being destitute and unhappy which stem from it. It is difficult to define hiraeth, but to me it means the consciousness of [a person] being out of his home area and that which is dear to him.—My three years at [boarding school] were very unhappy and that was only because of this longing. I had bosom companions there—and I enjoyed the lessons . . . but! I remember as if it were yesterday sitting in [church on Sunday night when I had come home for the weekend] and suddenly being hit by the thought—"This time tomorrow night I shall be in my lodgings [at school]"—and all at once I would be down in the depths.[1]

Every Christian experiences something analogous to what Jones called *hiraeth*. In fact, *hiraeth* might be the perfect word to describe the spiritual constitution of Peter's early readers. The metaphor in the opening verse that likened them to "elect exiles of the dispersion" gave us a hint of this very thing. For everyone unfamiliar with Old Testament history, the "elect exiles of the dispersion" were by nature a scattered and conflicted people. As God's *elect* they wrestled with what it meant to be the object of his affections, yet seemingly abandoned to out-of-the-way places. As *exiles* they struggled with questions of cultural engagement—of what it meant to conduct themselves as God's people living under an ungodly rule.

At this point in our study it is not beyond reach to surmise that Peter takes up his pen to take on questions brought on by *hiraeth*—"the consciousness of [a person] being out of his home area and that which is dear to him."

Peter's Introduction

In this light I simply love how Peter chooses to begin his letter.

Blessed be the God and Father of our Lord Jesus Christ! (v. 3a)

Significantly, before Peter does anything else, he rises to pronounce a *blessing* on God. Notice: he doesn't immediately write about difficult circumstances—there will be time enough for that. Neither is he compelled to begin by telling them how to conduct themselves while living in an evil world—evidently there will be enough time for that later on as well. What he does is this: he calls upon his readers to make a decided and determined prayer of praise. We know this because Jewish prayers most often opened with the time-honored word *blessed*. In particular, "Blessed be God."

Peter's introductory prayer of praise sounds strikingly close to the ancient Hebrew prayer called *Shemoneh 'Esreh*—The Eighteen Blessings. The Eighteen Blessings were recited three times each day in the synagogue, and each one ended with the refrain, "Blessed be Thou, O Lord." Just imagine the words "Blessed be Thou, O Lord" cascading no fewer than fifty-four times a day from the house of God.

In our text Peter calls upon his early readers, wherever they may be, to stand and praise God—to bless God, as it were, with eighteen blessings. The subtle aim beneath Peter's choice of opening words would not have been lost on his first readers. Peter knows that when their echoes of *blessing* are made in response to his call, their hearts and minds will be transported across the rugged terrain that separates them from their spiritual homeland. This word, "blessed," alone has the strength to bring them in spirit to Jerusalem and to the temple. And thus with one phrase, even a single word, Peter gathers a distant and scattered people on his wings and in mutual prayer carries them all the way to the throne room of Heaven.

What an encouragement this introductory call must have been to Peter's first readers. While they may have been tucked away in remote, out-of-the-way places, they have now been reminded that with a decided and determined prayer they can stand in the presence of all that is dear to them. And so can you! When you bless God in Christ, you come home. You enter into his very presence. And as we see next, when weary followers of Jesus begin blessing and praising God, encouragement is sure to follow.

Words of Inspiration and Hope

Peter writes:

> According to his great mercy, he has caused us to be born again to a living hope through the resurrection of Jesus Christ from the dead. (v. 3b)

This next sentence is meant to move the affections of the readers to ascendant heights. With the words "he has caused us to be born again to a living hope," Peter soars high above all the difficult circumstances of life. It is as if by verse 3 Peter is flying at an altitude of 30,000 feet and is encouraging those of us yet stationed on the ground. He reminds us that our ability to arrive safely at God's home is rooted in God's mercy and is grounded in one great truth—we are "born again to a living hope through the resurrection of Jesus Christ from the dead."

The remedy for humanity's *hiraeth*—the soul's homesickness—is found only in the resurrection of Jesus from the dead. Jesus, the elect and chosen one of God who voluntarily left his home and descended to an exilic-like existence on this earth, has returned to Heaven. It is through his resurrection from the dead and his ascension into Heaven that we who go by his name have been "born again to a living hope."

The idea of finding the cure for your spiritually homesick soul in the resurrection of Jesus from the dead may be an entirely new thought for you. You have felt the homesickness of soul that accompanies every person. You have sensed that you were born for a purpose but are not quite sure you will discover it in this world. Peter would urge you to consider Jesus and his resurrection. Could it be that he willingly bore the weight of your separation from your Father in Heaven, your *hiraeth*, on the cross? If so, hope abounds.

Do you see what Peter has done in these few short verses? He has moved his readers from the *hiraeth* of exile (v. 1) to the hope of an eternal inheritance (vv. 3, 4). And he has done so by the power of the resurrection of Jesus from the dead. In showing the activity of God in the past, he helped his early readers regain hope for the future.

An Eternal Inheritance

What is the "living hope" to which we have been "born again" going to look like? Verse 4 reads: "to an inheritance that is imperishable, undefiled, and unfading, kept in heaven for you."

Our hope consists of the "inheritance" that is being "kept" for us "in heaven." Evidently Peter finds it difficult to find words that do justice in capturing the greatness of this future inheritance. In describing it, he can do no better than use three words that tell us what it is not.

- "imperishable"
- "undefiled"
- "unfading"

These three words are put forward by way of contrast, to help us get our minds around the magnitude of our inheritance. These words are not merely synonyms. Peter is not some long-winded preacher who has hit upon identical terms and piles them on top of one another for rhetorical effect. Rather, each word has a distinct meaning, and each is specially chosen. Further, each one comes with a nuanced purpose.

- "Imperishable" means "not able to be destroyed."
- "Undefiled" means "not polluted."
- "Unfading" means "not subject to decay."

Such is Peter's way of describing the Christian's inheritance. He can't tell us very much about what it will be like, but he helps us, nonetheless, by revealing what it is *not* like.

Imperishable

Given the apparent transience of the human condition and the seeming permanence of creation, it is good to be reminded that we shall outlive it all in a place that can never be destroyed. Robert Louis Stevenson's poem "When the Stars Are Gone" states it well:

> The stars shine over the mountains,
> The stars shine over the sea,
> The stars look up to the mighty God,
> The stars look down on me;
> The stars shall last for a million years,
> A million years and a day,
> But God and I will live and love
> When the stars have passed away.[2]

Undefiled

From our vantage point it is hard to even imagine a world undefiled by sin. A world without locks or alarms. Cities where keys would be unnecessary, for theft is obsolete. A world where every woman sleeps without fear, every man is honorable, and every child is cherished. No jails. No need for police. No sin—none at all. When speaking of the next world, Peter says that it will be without stain or blemish. It will not be morally compromised or sinfully polluted. It will never be defiled. It will be unlike anything we have ever known!

This present world is fallen and defiled. Our hearts are corrupt and deceitful. Our hands are stained with the indelible ink of pride. We are all, to some degree, like Shakespeare's Macbeth. In the classic midnight scene, murderous Lady Macbeth is found out by the doctor and woman in waiting. The two had been standing in the shadows in hopes of observing Lady Macbeth sleepwalking and talking in the pitch of night. And on the third night their hopes are realized. Lady Macbeth enters, and the woman in waiting whispers to the doctor:

> *Woman:* Lo you! Here she comes. This is her very guise; and, upon my life, fast asleep. Observe her: stand close.
> *Doctor:* You see, her eyes are open.
> *Woman:* Ay, but their sense are shut.
> *Doctor:* What is it she does now? Look, how she rubs her hands.
> *Woman:* It is an accustom'd action with her, to seem thus washing her hands. I have known her continue in this a quarter of an hour.
> *Lady Macbeth:* Yet here's a spot.
> *Doctor:* Hark! She speaks. I will set down what comes from her, to satisfy my remembrance the more strongly.
> *Lady Macbeth:* Out, damned spot! Out, I say! . . . Hell is murky.—Fie, my Lord, fie! . . . who would have thought the old man to have had so much blood in him?
> *Doctor:* Do you mark that?
> *Lady Macbeth:* . . . What, will these hands ne'er be clean? . . . Here's the smell of blood still: all the perfumes of Arabia will not sweeten this little hand. Oh! oh! oh! . . . Wash your hands, put on your nightgown; look not so pale—I tell you yet again, Banquo's buried; he cannot come out on's grave. . . . To bed, to bed: there's knocking at the gate. Come, come, come, come, give me your hand. What's done cannot be undone. To bed, to bed, to bed. [Exit]
> *Doctor:* Will she now go to bed?
> *Woman:* Directly.
> *Doctor:* Foul whisp'rings are abroad. Unnatural deeds do breed unnatural troubles: infected minds to their deaf pillows will discharge their secrets.[3]

This is the defilement our world knows. We know it all too well. In an age of existentialism, French playwright Jean-Paul Sartre gave us another picture of this world's moral and ethical pollution. In 1948 he came out with his play *Dirty Hands*. In this play, a man named Hugo emerges as an idealist—a man who refused to dirty his hands in political backroom deals. Hoederer, however, the antagonist, functions as the pragmatist. He would strike any kind of a deal if it would keep him at the center of influence. Not surprisingly, the two clashed over how to use power:

> *Hugo:* For years you will have to cheat, trick, and maneuver; we'll go from compromise to compromise. . . . We shall be contaminated, weakened, disoriented. . . . I beg you: don't sacrifice it with your hands. . . .
>
> *Hoederer:* But we have always told lies, just like any other party. . . . I'll lie when I must.
>
> *Hugo:* All means are not good. . . .
>
> *Hoederer:* How you cling to your purity, young man! How afraid you are to soil your hands! All right, stay pure. . . . Do nothing. Remain motionless, arms at your sides, wearing kid gloves. Well, I have dirty hands. Right up to the elbows. I've plunged them in filth and blood.[4]

By the end, surprisingly, it will be the idealist, the pure-minded Hugo, who takes the life of Hoederer in cold-blooded murder. The point Sartre was making is unmistakable. We are all defiled, polluted. Every one of us is contaminated. No one is pure. No one is clean. The world is filled with people who have dirty hands.

In contrast, Peter tells us that our inheritance is unlike the world we live in. It is unlike the world we know. In the book of Revelation we get a glimpse as to why this is and how this can be so. In Revelation 5 John is shown a vision of our future home where no one is worthy to take the scrolls of God's good plan for our inheritance and bring it to completion. So discouraging was this fact that John wept over humanity's universal unworthiness. But then one does at last come forward. It is none other than Jesus, the Christ, the Lamb of God, who comes to the rescue of a polluted, defiled, and unworthy world. He alone is pure. His character alone is spotless and without blemish. Jesus, the undefiled! Through him alone are we able to enter into God's presence and receive an inheritance as glorious as the one Peter calls "undefiled."

Unfading

Peter next describes our inheritance as "unfading"—that which is not subject to fading or decay. Having come to middle age, I am learning that the human body fades. Presently mine is falling fast into a state of decay. Gravity is taking over. My skin is no longer taut. The inevitable descent toward the earth from which it came is noticeably underway.

In contrast, the inheritance toward which Christians are said to be moving is said to be "unfading." It will never be subject to decay. What good news! When our own bodies, long since expired, are reunited with Christ on that final day, we will be made incorruptible forevermore, restored, new, complete. This is the inheritance that awaits all who are in Christ.

An Invincible Power

Peter closes his look into salvation's future by assuring us that what God has promised rests secure.

> ... who by God's power are being guarded through faith for a salvation ready to be revealed in the last time. (v. 5)

This inheritance is said to be "kept in heaven" for us even as we are being "guarded" through faith for a salvation that will be "revealed in the last time." Doesn't that just sound almost too wonderful? This great promise is being *kept* for us through God's eternal power. And all of it will be revealed in its fullness on the day that Jesus returns!

Can you imagine the effect these words had upon Peter's first readers? The dispersed and small Sunday gatherings of Christians in what is now modern-day northern Turkey and elsewhere were a spiritually tired lot. Through the preaching of the gospel they had come to know God's favor. But for some time now they had found life difficult. They were filled with a sense that perhaps God had forgotten about them. They were in the throes of *hiraeth*. And knowing their discouragement, Peter writes of their future salvation. He fills them afresh with hope.

Within the first five verses he has set them on their feet and told them what they need to do. They need to rise up and bless God (v. 3). They need to pull again on the anchor of their living hope—namely, the resurrection of Jesus from the dead (v. 3). They need to be reminded that the inheritance they are going to receive is so extraordinary that there are not words to describe it (v. 4). Peter can only tell them that it will never be destroyed, it will never be polluted, it will never be subject to decay. Finally, Peter affirms that this great future is kept for us by the power of God. Nothing on earth can shake it loose from those who are in Christ (v. 5).

Our Heavenly Father, blessed is your name! The inheritance you have planned astounds us. Help us, even before we receive it in full, to live lives that are undefiled. It is in your Spirit and the power of the resurrection of Jesus from the dead that we place our hope. Amen.

In this you rejoice, though now for a little while, if necessary, you have been grieved by various trials, so that the tested genuineness of your faith—more precious than gold that perishes though it is tested by fire—may be found to result in praise and glory and honor at the revelation of Jesus Christ. Though you have not seen him, you love him. Though you do not now see him, you believe in him and rejoice with joy that is inexpressible and filled with glory, obtaining the outcome of your faith, the salvation of your souls.

1:6–9

4

Salvation's Present Trials

1 PETER 1:6–9

THE CELEBRATED POET William Blake is buried in London's famous Bunhill Cemetery. Close by are the graves of other luminaries such as John Bunyan, Susannah Wesley, John Owen, and Daniel Dafoe. A friend who was present with Blake on the day of his death wrote that he died

> in a most glorious manner. . . . He said he was going to that country he had all his life wished to see & expressed himself happy hoping for salvation through Jesus Christ—Just before he died his countence became fair—His eyes brighten'd and he burst out in singing of the things he saw in heaven.[1]

What an exalted exit from life's stage. Imagine bursting forth in joyful song as the fullness of salvation approaches. For William Blake, the "living hope" described in Peter's opening verses as "imperishable, undefiled, and unfading" on that day became his own enduring and unending inheritance.

Yet, in life Blake experienced difficulty as well. He was acquainted with more than the joyful prospect of an eternal inheritance. He had firsthand knowledge that the road to Heaven is marked out by earthly sorrow. It was Blake who penned:

> Joy and woe are woven fine,
> A clothing for the soul divine,
> Under every grief and pine
> Runs a joy with silken twine.
> It is right it should be so;
> Man was made for joy and woe;

And when this we rightly know,
Through the world we safely go.[2]

"Joy and woe are woven fine." How true. And yet somehow suffering still catches us by surprise. That God's elect, his chosen and beloved, should experience trials and the weight of exile is perplexing. In some measure, Peter is writing to remind us of this very thing. He now asks his readers to consider salvation's future glory (1:3–5) in light of present-day adversity (1:6–9).

Therefore, the verses before us (6–9) lend balance to the Christian's delightful anticipation of Heaven (vv. 3–5). We are reminded that the inheritance will not be won without enduring myriad difficulties first. To put it differently, after bursting forth in a joyful song on Heaven (vv. 3–6a), Peter now turns to compose a sonnet uniting woe to joy (vv. 6b–9). To use his exact vocabulary: "rejoice" is coupled to "grieved by various trials." In full, verse 6 reads:

> In this you rejoice, though now for a little while, if necessary, you have been grieved by various trials.

Various Trials

Getting a precise handle on what Peter means by "various trials" is important. After all, the entire letter is ensconced in this theme. Clarity on Peter's intended use, however, has kept more than one commentator awake at night.[3] And yet progress can be made. The word *trials* has a rich biblical history, and it can have an especially wide meaning. The phrase has more elasticity in it than one might at first expect.

Hebrews 3:7, 8

In the book of Hebrews we read:

> Today, if you hear his voice, do not harden your hearts as in the rebellion,
> on the day of *testing* in the wilderness.

The writer of Hebrews is quoting from a time in Israel's history when God's people were without a home in the world. They were wanderers, sojourners—exiles if you will—people trying to make their way through the wilderness of life. As such, they were marked by a lack of position, power, and provision. They were without human protection and awoke every day to the reality that their life lacked permanence of any kind.

These are the kinds of trials Peter's readers were experiencing as well.

They knew a thing or two about being exiles—strangers, sojourners in a foreign land (1:1; 2:11). They were familiar with navigating life without position, power, or any sense of political permanence (2:13–17).

Luke 8:13

Luke uses the term *trials* with even greater particularity. In the Parable of the Sower, Jesus said:

> And the ones on the rock are those who, when they hear the word, receive
> it with joy. But these have no root; they believe for a while, and in time
> of *testing* fall away.

Two observations help us get a sense of the word Peter is using in our text. First, like Peter, Luke uses it in close proximity to the word "joy." In Luke's Gospel, however, instead of joy and trials being united in the heart and mind of those who finish well, they are wedded in the soul of those who fall away. The initial joy of Christian faith abates in some and, sadly, is spoken of as being altogether lost when encountering life's trials. What a warning! Enduring during trials is an important indicator of our true status in Christ. The second observation we can make from Luke's use of the term, and more importantly for our understanding of Peter, is his connection between trials and verbal and physical persecution. In fact, in Matthew's parallel telling of this parable, the term *trial* refers specifically to the kinds of tribulation or persecution that arise "on *account of the word*" (13:21). Young followers find this kind of early verbal assault on their faith difficult to endure. As we work our way through 1 Peter, the same connection is going to be made. Peter gives examples of trials that refer to verbal and physical abuse on account of the Word (see 2:12, 18–20, 23; 3:16; 4:1–6 [esp. v. 4], 12–14).

Galatians 4:13, 14

A third use of the term *trials* in the New Testament can be found in Paul's letter to the church at Galatia. There we read:

> You know it was because of a bodily ailment that I preached the gospel to
> you at first, and though my condition was a trial to you, you did not scorn
> or despise me, but received me as an angel of God, as Christ Jesus.

Galatia was one of the geographic regions Paul covered on his first missionary journey, and it was while there that he was dragged out of the city, stoned, and left for dead. Paul survived the ordeal, but he was left bloodied, disfigured, and in great pain. Seeing him in that state proved to be a great trial for the saints.

In this instance, the term *trial* is used in reference to the angst suffered by those Christians whose loved ones are undergoing physical suffering and pain. This trial was also the lot of some of Peter's readers (2:18–20).

Matthew 26:41

The final use we turn to for our purposes here is found in Matthew 26:41. At this point in the narrative, Jesus is in the Garden of Gethsemane, and the author of our letter, Peter, is with him. On this night, the intensity of the conflict between Jesus and the devil was so severe that elsewhere we are told that Jesus began to sweat blood (see Luke 22:44). Meanwhile, as Jesus battled against his own trials and temptations to flee from the cross, Peter and the others slept. Jesus awakened them and then said to Peter:

> So, could you not watch with me one hour? Watch and pray that you may not enter into *temptation*. The spirit indeed is willing, but the flesh is weak. (Matthew 26:40, 41)

The word translated "temptation" is the same word Peter uses in the text before us. Various trials can refer to direct attacks from the evil one. Strikingly, later in Peter's letter we will find him making use of this very imagery and language:

> Be sober-minded; be watchful. Your adversary the devil prowls around like a roaring lion, seeking someone to devour. Resist him, firm in your faith, knowing that the same kinds of suffering are being experienced by your brotherhood throughout the world. (5:8, 9)

So there you have it. Peter's use of the words "various trials" matches exactly the wide-ranging use of the term elsewhere in the New Testament. As a result we *can* say a few things about what Peter means by "various trials." He is not speaking here of a localized trial or a season of suffering. Rather, he means:

• There will be seasons in life when you will lack provision, power, position, protection, and a sense of permanence.

• At times you will become the recipient of verbal or physical persecutions that arise on account of the Word.

• This includes the pain experienced by those who have loved ones whose bodies appear to be wasting away before their very eyes.

• This includes the dark moments in life when we are asked to fend off the prowling attacks of Satan.

These difficulties may be temporal, occasional, and spasmodic (after all, 1:6 adds, "if necessary"), but in the end Peter wants his readers to know that for anyone who takes up with Jesus, trials of some size and stripe are inevitable. We must go through the waters of tribulation if we are to arrive at our rightful inheritance, for wandering and woe are the earthly lots of any who desire to enter into an eternal rest characterized by joy.

What Purpose Do Trials Serve?

Trials Prove the Genuineness of Our Faith

Hearing that Heaven's joys are intertwined with earthly trials—and this by divine design—must have raised many questions in the minds of early followers of Jesus—questions like, "What function do trials serve?" or "What ultimate purposes will trials accomplish?" From our text it appears that Peter intends to provide an answer. No sooner does he connect joy to woe than he begins explaining the purpose of life's trials.

> . . . so that the tested genuineness of your faith—more precious than gold that perishes though it is tested by fire—may be found to result in praise and glory and honor at the revelation of Jesus Christ. (1:7)

Trials come for testing, and testing, like putting gold into the fire, is meant to prove the genuineness of one's faith. To put it differently, trials are the proving ground for our faith. Others in church history understood this well. It is to John Rippon, the pastor of the Metropolitan Tabernacle in London prior to Charles Haddon Spurgeon, that we owe the famous verse,

> When through fiery trials thy pathway shall lie,
> My grace, all sufficient, shall be thy supply:
> The flame shall not hurt thee; I only design
> Thy dross to consume and thy gold to refine.[4]

Rippon's words sound as if they were birthed in the soil of Peter's text: "your faith—more precious than gold that perishes though it is tested by fire."

A picture from ancient Roman times shows the method by which grain was threshed. One man can be seen stirring up the sheaves, while another rides over them in a crude dray equipped with rollers instead of wheels. Attached to the rolling cylinders are sharp stones and rough bits of iron. As they grind over the recently tossed sheaves, the stones and iron help separate the husks from the grain. The simple cart was called a tribulum.

This agrarian piece of farm machinery is the object from which we get our word *tribulation*. Do you ever feel as if you are under the inescapable weight and force of the tribulum? If so, Peter wants to remind you that no thresher ever operated his tribulum for the purpose of tearing up his sheaves. The thresher's intentions were far more elevated than that. The farmer only wanted to cull out the precious grain. And as it is with the ancient farmer, so it is with God.

Understanding that God's purposes for us include various trials is important, for by them we are tempered. The extracts of this world are removed from us, and we are made fit for Heaven. A simple bar of iron ore, pulled from the earth, might be worth $5.00. However, that same bar, when made into horseshoes, would be worth $10.50. If the owner decided to make the bar into needles for sewing, it could be worth as much as $3,285. And if he turned it into springs for watches, its value could jump as high as $250,000. What made the difference? Simply the amount of heat by which the iron bar was tempered and honed.

What Peter is saying is that our faith is far more precious to God than a bar of iron. According to the text it is even more precious than gold! So be encouraged. You may find yourself on the anvil of suffering, but God is at work. He is testing the genuineness of your faith. And for him, that faith has eternal value.

The Importance of Our Response to Trials

Our willingness as Christians to endure earthly affliction says a lot about our trust in God. He is fashioning us into praiseworthy and honorable vessels for his glory. Malcolm Muggeridge, having come to Christ late in life, understood this well. His ability to embrace life's woes was never put more succinctly than when he wrote:

> I can say with complete truthfulness that everything I have ever learned in my seventy-five years in this world, everything that has truly enhanced and enlightened my existence, has been through affliction and not through happiness, whether pursued or attained. In other words, if it ever were to be possible to eliminate affliction from our earthly existence by means of some drug or other medical mumbo jumbo, as Aldous Huxley envisaged in *Brave New World*, the result would not be to make life delectable, but to make it too banal and trivial to be endurable. This, of course, is what the Cross signifies. And it is the Cross, more than anything else, that has called me inexorably to Christ.[5]

It was this same belief—that God is at work in the muck of life—that enabled Dietrich Bonhoeffer to write the final stanza of his poem "New Year 1945."

That day was a mere three months and nine days before he was executed by Hitler at the close of World War II:

> Should it be ours to drink the cup of grieving
> Even to the dregs of pain, at thy command,
> We will not falter, thankfully receiving
> All that is given by thy loving hand.[6]

The Temptation to Flee Trials

The responses of Muggeridge and Bonheoffer are only made possible by embracing Peter's words as divine truth. For without a deep and abiding trust in God's words, we will try to flee trials at all costs and will miss out on the very lessons God has for us.

In this respect I am reminded of the biblical character Joseph. Joseph knew what it was to be the elect one, the favored one. The many colors of his coat served as vivid reminders that God was good and had special plans for him. They appeared on his frame as if taken from the very palate of Heaven. Yet Joseph knew exile too. He was well-acquainted with various trials. He was sold into slavery and was without protection, position, or power.

Thomas Mann, in his masterpiece *Joseph and his Brothers*, captured with imaginative force what must have been Joseph's very real temptation to escape suffering. Mann writes of Joseph's journey toward Egypt after being sold to Ishmaelites:

> He knew that he was taking . . . the same journey which he had covered [but now in reverse] to meet his brothers. He was going toward if also past his home. . . . Therefore, his heart beat so anxiously as temptation knocked. . . . Could it be, up there Jacob was sitting? How near lay the thought of flight. How the urge pulled and tugged at his limbs. How his thoughts worked in him. . . . The boy who had been ravished away was ravished anew by longings to be off. Up the orchard clad hills in the dark. On over heights and gullies eight miles and furlongs of ground. For more it probably was not. Joseph would easily find the right direction as he climbed on into the mountain land. Into Jacob's arms to dry his fathers' tears with the words, 'Here I am!'
>
> But did he carry all this out and flee? We know that he did not. . . . He put away temptation. Gave up the idea. Stopped where he was. His renunciation of the violent temptation came from a point of view quite peculiar to Joseph. Put into words, it was something like this: 'How could I commit such a folly and sin against God'. In other words he had insight into the mad and sinful error that would lie in escape. The clear and intelligent perception that it would have been a clumsy blunder to try to destroy

God's plan through flight. For Joseph was penetrated by the certainty that he had not been snatched away to no purpose. That rather, the planning intelligence which had rent him away from the old and led him into the new had plans for him in one way or another. . . . To shrink from the affliction would have been a great sin and error. Escape would be distinctly evil. It would, "literally," wish to be wiser than God, which according to Joseph's shrewd insight was quite simply the height of folly.[7]

The world needs men and women like Joseph—followers of Jesus who refuse to take themselves out of harm's way lest God's work in them be left incomplete. Remember, God uses our sufferings to assist us in obtaining the outcome of our faith, namely, the salvation of our souls. For Peter, these present-day sufferings only heighten our awareness of the separation we feel from the presence of Jesus. Thus he concludes:

> Though you have not seen him, you love him. Though you do not now see him, you believe in him and rejoice with joy that is inexpressible and filled with glory. (1:8, 9)

I like that. "Inexpressible" joy is said to be the handmaiden to the suffering Christian. Interestingly, when Peter closed his thoughts on Heaven in verse 5 he wrote, "in this you rejoice" (v. 6). But here when he finishes his thoughts on suffering, he says that our rejoicing is largely "inexpressible." In other words, think about Heaven and you will have something to say. But while you endure various trials, know that the joy they produce in you will be a quiet sort, a nonverbal kind, an "inexpressible . . . joy." The strange truth of the gospel is this: salvation's future inheritance is gained during this season of present sufferings.

May joy rise in your heart, for various trials are producing within you the outcome of your faith, nothing less than the salvation of your soul.

Dear Lord, we desire to be found faithful until you are revealed from on high. Help us be a joyful people in the midst of our present sorrows and sufferings. We do love you. We do believe in you. And we long for the day when we shall both see you and dwell with you forevermore. Lord, have mercy. Amen.

Concerning this salvation, the prophets who prophesied about the grace that was to be yours searched and inquired carefully, inquiring what person or time the Spirit of Christ in them was indicating when he predicted the sufferings of Christ and the subsequent glories. It was revealed to them that they were serving not themselves but you, in the things that have now been announced to you through those who preached the good news to you by the Holy Spirit sent from heaven, things into which angels long to look.

1:10–12

5

Salvation's Past Glories

1 PETER 1:10–12

IN 1925 T. S. ELIOT GAVE the world his poem "The Hollow Men." In it
he forces us to face down the angst and despair that so often accompanies
human existence. The poem begins:

> We are the hollow men
> We are the stuffed men
> Leaning together
> Headpiece filled with straw. Alas!
> Our dried voices, when
> We whisper together
> Are quiet and meaningless
> As wind in dry grass.[1]

Eliot's metaphor for humanity is especially haunting—"as wind in dry
grass." We are spoken of as being arid and hot; our voices are dried up, and
we merely whisper. We are incapable of great usefulness, except perhaps in
starting a fire. Eliot wants us to see ourselves as being without water—incapable of bringing refreshment, let alone life to anything. All of humanity
is depicted as nothing more than "stuffed men/leaning together/headpiece
filled with straw." Like scarecrows we are hollow men without life or hope
or connection to the source of blessing.

Where We Are in the Letter

Eliot's image is a good one to describe Peter's readers before they ever
heard gospel preaching that filled their lives with good news. After all,

before coming to know faith in Christ their circumstances were as dry as their souls. By and large they were a people who lived far off the beaten path. Together they shared the unhappy distinction of being dispersed in arid and out-of-the-way places. For the most part, his readers spent their lives away from the refreshing centers of culture.

Spiritually they had been dry too. Souls parched. Longing for life. But then, through Peter or someone else, we simply are not told, they got wind of the source of all life. They heard about Jesus and the gospel. And as their faith attests, they drank deeply. They were born again. They had gone from being hollow men to holy saints—"born again to a living hope" and an eternal "inheritance" (1:3, 4).

In coming to Christ, they exchanged Eliot's lines for the verse of another poet—one named Isaiah. First Peter 1:23–25 reads:

> . . . since you have been born again, not of perishable seed but of imperish-
> able, through the living and abiding word of God; for

> "All flesh is like grass
>   and all its glory like the flower of the grass.
> The grass withers,
>   and the flower falls,
>   but the word of the Lord remains forever."

> And this word is the good news that was preached to you.

These are the words of the poetic prophet at his best. For they remind us that it is the word of the Lord that makes all the difference in this world of hollow men. No longer were these first-century men and women like wind in dry grass. Instead they were new creatures. Waters flowed from within. They flourished as plants growing in God's eternal kingdom.

And yet by the time Peter picked up his pen to write, it appears that sagebrush of the soul had swept through their towns. Their rising life in Christ had been eclipsed with difficulties. Trials had been their lot. Some were despairing. Most were feeling as if they had lost their way in the world. Collectively, the *elect* of God were again succumbing to *exilic hiraeth*—the longings and homesickness brought on by feeling out of sorts and away from all that was dear to them. Simply put, they were discouraged.

And so Peter writes to them. In part we have asserted that he writes to shore up distant and sparsely populated groups of believers who were trying to faithfully live out the conflicted and fragile existence we call the Christian life. I don't know where you would have begun with these elect exiles, but it appears that Peter was given divine insight on what would be most helpful. With his introduction to the letter, Peter encouraged them with an exhortation on salvation's fullness:

• 1:3–5: Salvation's Future Reward (see v. 5—"a salvation ready to be revealed at the last time")

• 1:6–9: Salvation's Present Adversity (see v. 9—a salvation only won by present trials)

• 1:10–12: Salvation's Past Glories (see v. 12—a salvation with a rich prophetic past)

Peter stood his readers on their feet by pronouncing a blessing on God. Next he poured the refreshing waters of "a living hope" (v. 3) over them. And then he carried them heavenward by speaking of a future "inheritance that is imperishable, undefiled, and unfading" (v. 4). Certainly there are present trials of various kinds, but even these produce joy and warm the hearts of his readers as they consider the outcome of their faith—namely, "the salvation of [their] souls" (v. 9).

In the verses before us now (1:10–12), Peter will bring his introduction to a cascading close. He will unfurl three truths from salvation's past in hopes of stirring their souls to restored gratitude toward God. And in the end he is making them ready to press on in the ongoing work of gracious gospel living (1:13ff.).

Encouragement from the Prophets (vv. 10, 11)

To see the force of the final verses of Peter's dramatic introduction, consider verse 10:

> Concerning this salvation, the prophets who prophesied about the grace that was to be yours searched and inquired carefully.

For the first time, Peter formally introduces us to past Hebrew prophets. He writes of "prophets who prophesied." The prophets were some of Israel's ancient officeholders, beginning with Moses. The institution of the prophetic office can be found in Deuteronomy 18. At that point in the narrative of God's grace, the writer is recounting the period when God's people reached Mt. Sinai after the exodus from Egypt. Initially God spoke to them in the hearing of all the people. But the people were afraid of God's voice, and they asked if God would speak to them through the voice of Moses instead. God condescended to their request and in doing so instituted the prophetic office.

All of Israel's prophets, from Moses onward, *stood* in the presence of God in order to receive God's word and then *spoke* that word in the presence of all the people. What Peter is telling his readers in the verse before us is that the prophets' best days were spent searching out salvation's fulfillment. They were men who studied long and hard. They pored over God's word as he was giving it to them. And what were they inquiring about in particular? Peter tells us in verse 11. They were searching

> carefully, inquiring what person or time the Spirit of Christ in them was indicating when he predicted the sufferings of Christ and the subsequent glories.

In essence, these words show us that the prophets were given a particular insight into salvation's mystery—that the Christ would be a *suffering* Christ—and that only after suffering would he be given "*subsequent*" glories. For the typical first-century religious Jew, this thought was simply unacceptable. They wanted a Christ of glory. They had no time for a Messiah given over to suffering. Yet Peter's early readers had been saved by just such a gospel. For the discouraged believer in Peter's audience, this reminder would have been greatly encouraging. The life they were living, filled as it was with trials and difficulties, mirrored the life of the Messiah, in whom they had put their trust.

The encouragement Peter has already given them would only continue to swell as they read the opening line of verse 12:

> It was revealed to them that they were serving not themselves but you.

These words did more for Peter's early readers than we can possibly imagine. Upon hearing them for the first time in church on Sunday, we can envision someone interrupting the reading with, "Wait. Stop for a minute. Would you please read that last line over again? Did he say that the prophets knew that they were not serving their own generation but ours? Did he imply that they were aware that God had put them to work on our behalf?"

As the reader for that day would have recited it over again, the hearts of those collectively gathered would raise up in praise to God. Any earlier signs of self-pity were left behind. Any thoughts that God didn't care about them or that they had never been a part of anything great were now quieted. For Peter had shown them that the prophets were the true outsiders, not themselves. The prophets of the past were the ones kept from seeing salvation's fullness. The prophets had been relegated to serving God by serving a distant generation rather than their own. In fact, for the most part the prophets outdid them all in having to endure rejection and loss.

In addition, every early reader of Peter also would have recognized that the prophets had a far rougher go of it in life than they did. Anyone who had ever read the ancient prophetic writings knew that this careful inquiry into and searching out the sufferings of Christ was brutal and exhausting work. We get a hint of how draining the prophetic work was through the words of Daniel. Of the sufferings he had to behold he writes:

My spirit within me was anxious, and the visions of my head alarmed me. (Daniel 7:15)

And I, Daniel, was overcome and lay sick for some days. Then I rose and went about the king's business, but I was appalled by the vision and did not understand it. (8:27)

When he had spoken to me according to these words, I turned my face toward the ground and was mute. And behold, one in the likeness of the children of man touched my lips. Then I opened my mouth and spoke. I said to him who stood before me, "O my lord, by reason of the vision pains have come upon me, and I retain no strength. How can my lord's servant talk with my lord? For now no strength remains in me, and no breadth is left in me." (10:15–17)

Such is the reward of the prophet. They were largely rejected in their own day. They served another time. They couldn't understand salvation as clearly as they desired. And they were often physically impaired due to the nature of their work.

Peter's first readers would have been deeply humbled by this fresh consideration of salvation's past glories. The extent that God went to in securing their salvation was borne with a cost, not only to himself, not only to his Son—it cost the prophets as well.

It should humble us too. We know nothing of this kind of suffering. There is a vivid picture in contemporary literature that sympathizes with the idea of having to see Christ's sufferings. Marilynne Robinson's penetrating novel *Gilead* tells the story of a young boy who learns about life from letters his father had written to him while he was dying. The boy's father recounts an incident from his own childhood that involved his preaching grandfather:

My grandfather told me once about a vision he'd had. . . . He had fallen asleep by the fire, worn out from a day helping his father pull stumps. Someone touched him on the shoulder, and when he looked up, there was the Lord, holding out His arms to him, which were bound in chains. My grandfather said, "Those irons had rankled right down to His bones." He told me that as the saddest fact, and eyed me with the one seraph eye he had, the old grief fresh in it. . . . When I spoke to my father about the vision he had described to me, my father just nodded and said, "It was the times." He himself never claimed any such experience, and he seemed to want to assure me I need not fear that the Lord would come to me with His sorrows. And I took comfort in the assurance.[2]

At this point we might rightly ask, what enabled God's prophets to go on? Verse 11 in our text reveals the answer. It was "the Spirit of Christ in them."

This phrase is an especially beautiful and comforting one. In Greek mythology, Aeolius was the wind god who purportedly lived on a floating island with six sons and six daughters. Homer writes of Aeolius in *The Odyssey*.[3] The wind god summoned the breezes to help Odysseus on his way. From this myth we have a musical instrument called the aeolian harp. It is not played by human touch. Instead, the wind blows through taut strings that have been intricately strung over a sounding board. Something very much like this must have been at work in the prophets. It was "the Spirit of Christ in them" who kept them going.

In the verse before us, Christ himself is depicted as wind blowing gently through the prophets as they told about the coming Christ. It was the Spirit of Christ who enabled the prophets to pore over their own sermons and visions. It was Christ in them who kept them reading the scrolls of other prophets who had gone before.

In one sense you could say that in this first chapter Peter has moved his readers from Eliot's wind as through dry grass to the Word and the Spirit's breadth, and then to Christ who brings life to all. What an encouraging word. Imagine, the prophets were put to work by God for you!

Encouragement from Past Preachers

In Peter's attempt to refresh the beleaguered saints, he adds an additional word of encouragement beyond the role of the prophets. He writes of past preachers. Verse 12 reads:

> It was revealed to them that they were serving not themselves but you, in the things that have now been announced to you through those who preached the good news to you by the power of the Holy Spirit sent from heaven. . . .

Did you catch how Peter builds upon the prophets? He introduces for the first time those who preached the gospel to his early readers. He wants them to know that God sent more than Spirit-filled prophets to them. He sent preachers too. Never again could these churches wander off into dejection without having the Word of God in their midst to shore them up during difficult days. God had sent prophets to them. God sent preachers too. Beyond a shadow of a doubt, Peter is proving God's love for them.

Encouragement from the Angelic Host

Because he cannot contain himself, Peter throws a third encouraging word to his readers about salvation's past glories. Not only did God put prophets and preachers to work for them, but he did so with a message so great that it had the angelic host standing at rapt attention as they watched it unfold. These are three encouraging truths.

• Prophets labored their entire lives to present the true gospel to us.

• Preachers have traveled around the globe to ensure that it has gained a hearing before us.

• Angels would like nothing better than to gaze into what God has done for us.

"Surprise!" says Peter. "This is how much God cares for you." I can almost hear the shouts of joy rolling across the rugged topography of Pontus, Galatia, Cappadocia, Asia, and Bithynia. This is amazing love. Ancient prophets, itinerant preachers, and exalted angels have for ages stood in service to this salvation that has come to us! The fullness of your salvation has been the joyful business of God's servants over the centuries.

Knowing this, I hope you have a surge of spiritual fortitude to remain faithful wherever God has placed you. Hearts were made to rise in worship. And looking ahead, our minds are to be made ready for action.

Our Heavenly Father, these words have brought us much needed encouragement. We are amazed at the majestic history of our salvation. We thank you today for prophets and preachers of old, and we thrill at the notion of the faithful service of your heavenly host. May we live in this present day with full recognition of the past. And may we forever be cured from the sin of self-pity as a result. In Jesus' name, amen.

Therefore, preparing your minds for action, and being sober-minded, set your hope fully on the grace that will be brought to you at the revelation of Jesus Christ. As obedient children, do not be conformed to the passions of your former ignorance, but as he who called you is holy, you also be holy in all your conduct, since it is written, "You shall be holy, for I am holy." And if you call on him as Father who judges impartially according to each one's deeds, conduct yourselves with fear throughout the time of your exile, knowing that you were ransomed from the futile ways inherited from your forefathers, not with perishable things such as silver or gold, but with the precious blood of Christ, like that of a lamb without blemish or spot. He was foreknown before the foundation of the world but was made manifest in the last times for your sake, who through him are believers in God, who raised him from the dead and gave him glory, so that your faith and hope are in God.

1:13–21

6

A Settled Hope

1 PETER 1:13–21

The Importance of Hope

Viktor Frankl has written powerfully on the importance of maintaining hope. After enduring an exilic-like existence in a German concentration camp during the Second World War, Frankl, in his book *Man's Search for Meaning,* told the true but tragic tale of a fellow prisoner who lost all hope:

> A fairly well-known composer and librettist confided in me one day: . . .
>
> "Doctor, I have had a strange dream. A voice told me that I could wish for something, that I should only say what I wanted to know, and all my questions would be answered. What do you think I asked? That I would like to know when the war would be over for me. You know what I mean, Doctor—for me! I wanted to know when we, when our camp, would be liberated and our sufferings come to an end." . . .
>
> "What did your dream voice answer?"
>
> Furtively he whispered to me, "March thirtieth."
>
> When [he] told me about his dream, he was still full of hope . . . but as the promised day drew nearer, the war news which reached our camp made it appear very unlikely that we would be free on the promised day. On March twenty-ninth, [he] suddenly became ill. . . . On March thirtieth . . . he became delirious and lost consciousness. On March thirty-first, he was dead. To all outward appearances, he had died of typhus.
>
> [But] those who know how close the connection is between the state of mind of a man . . . and the state of immunity of his body will understand that the sudden loss of hope . . . can have a deadly effect. . . . Any attempt to restore a man's inner strength . . . had first to succeed in showing him some future goal.[1]

From what we know of 1 Peter so far, it appears that the apostle not only comprehended Frankl's truth centuries earlier but wrote of hope on an exalted plane—of something fixed and permanent—a hope far above what Frankl believed could ever exist. Peter's hope was "a living hope" (1:3), and it was "living" because it was grounded in the resurrection of Christ. Peter spoke of nothing less than the hope of a real Heaven. And for his early readers this message could not have come at a better time.

You see, the spiritual "exiles" of verse 1 had come to a faith in Christ that believed his return was very near. But now much time had passed. Those early Christians were now adrift in difficult days. They were confined to the hull of an out-of-the-way existence. Their promised port of freedom was nowhere in sight. So hope sagged, and the winds of spiritual vigor had died down.[2]

Like the sailor perched high above a ship's decks—the one charged with keeping his eyes on the horizon—Peter sees the distant land, and with his introduction (1:3–12) he calls to the beleaguered ones below, "Get your head up! Your future goal is real. From where I sit, your hope is alive." In fact, by the time Peter finishes his opening cry in verse 12, everyone below will have heard of the fullness of their coming salvation.

We can only imagine the effect of Peter's introduction. It must have washed over those early exilic saints like the warmth of the summer sun. They must have felt as if they were standing barefoot on white sand again.

A Call to Set Your Hope

Knowing that his readers are spiritually refreshed, Peter now sets out to make them ready to live obedient lives for Christ. For with a change in grammar, it appears that he is convinced they are ready to respond. He heralds:

> Therefore, preparing your minds for action, and being sober-minded, set your hope fully on the grace that will be brought to you at the revelation of Jesus Christ. (v. 13)

The response that Peter is looking for is hidden right in the middle of the verse. The command here is to "set your hope fully on the grace that will be brought to you." As we will see, the tasks of "preparing [our] minds, and being sober-minded" are the first ways in which we fulfill our calling. Grammatically, however, the center of gravity for the entire opening section of 1 Peter is the phrase, "Set your hope fully on the grace" that will be yours. That is what Peter commands his readers to do. If we miss this imperative, we will miss Peter's point altogether.

From the opening words in verse 3 Peter has been moving toward the command to set our hope on the grace that will come. It is a topic he will return to again when he closes out this first part of the letter in 1:21.

In between them we find the command of 1:13. Contextually it looks like this:

- 1:3: "He has caused us to be born again to a living *hope*."
- 1:13: "Set your *hope* fully on the grace that will be brought to you."
- 1:21: "Your faith and *hope* are in God."

Think of Peter's arrangement this way: Have you ever watched as Canada geese fly high overhead? Seldom are they alone. Instead, they seem to glory in forming a majestic and powerful V. One goose is at the head. He is pumping his wings for all they are worth. Trailing on either end are two other geese. These provide cohesion and symmetry to the whole flock. The opening segment of Peter's letter possesses something of that beauty. At one end flies the phrase "[Since you have] *a living hope*" (v. 3). At the other end we find, "*your . . . hope . . . [is] in God*" (v. 21). And between them both, out in front, cutting through the air with powerful strokes, is the key verse, 13, which says "Therefore . . . set your hope fully." Thus, we have arrived at the verse that holds Peter's thoughts in formation. If verse 3 is Peter's theme, his bold truth, then verse 13 is Peter's aim or striking application.

The call for struggling Christians is this: set your hope fully on the future coming of Christ. That is what Peter commands us to do. If any of us is to do more than simply outlast life's exilic weight—if we are to move beyond melancholy endurance and into positive engagement with the world, let alone enjoyment in it, we must become a people who know what it is to comprehend a decided hope in life's eternal future. Certainly church history gives us plenty of examples to emulate in this task. Part of John Owen's epitaph reads, "While on the road to heaven, his elevated mind almost comprehended its full glories and joys."[3] Another exemplar of decided hope was C. S. Lewis. Of Heaven, he wrote:

> Our lifelong nostalgia, our longing to be reunited with something in the universe from which we now feel cut off, to be on the inside of some door which we have always seen from the outside, is no mere neurotic fancy, but the truest index of our real situation. And to be at last summoned inside would be both glory and honour beyond all our merits and also the healing of that old ache.[4]

The question for us, then, is not, can this be done? but rather, how can we follow the flight of these exhilarating and heroic exiles of an earlier time? How do we go about maintaining hope? More especially, how do we maintain it while living in this foreign world? Fortunately for us, Peter tells us how. In these verses he gives us two marks that distinguish those of decided hope and three motivations to keep at it.

• The two marks of decided hope: A healthy mind and a holy life (1:13–15)

• Three motivations to stay at it: God's character, God's judgment, and Christ's sacrifice (1:16–19)

Two Distinguishing Marks of Decided Hope (vv. 13–15)

A Healthy Mind (v. 13)

In anticipation of setting our hope fully on the grace that is to be ours, Peter writes:

> Therefore, preparing your minds for action, and being sober-minded . . .

That first little phrase about preparing the mind for action is an especially vivid one. Literally, it reads, "Gird up the loins of your mind." As one commentator put it, this is

> an almost unintelligible phrase for modern readers unfamiliar with the ancient Oriental custom of gathering up one's long robes by pulling them between the legs and then wrapping and tying them around the waist, so as to prepare for running, fast walking, or another strenuous activity.[5]

Those who distinguish themselves with a set hope are those who have learned to cultivate a healthy mind. To put it simply, if God is to have your heart, he must first have your mind.

In the day in which we live, this will prove challenging. These are dark days for the disciplined mind. Thomas Cahill, writing on the shortcomings of the Dark Ages, said something that could easily apply to our time:

> The intellectual disciplines of distinction, definition, and dialectic that had once been the glory of men like Augustine were unobtainable by readers of the Dark Ages, whose apprehension of the world was simple and immediate, framed by myth and magic. A man no longer subordinated one thought to another with mathematical precision; instead, he apprehended similarities and balances, types and paradigms, parallels and symbols. It was a world not of thoughts, but of images.[6]

And so it is in our day as well. We think with our eyes. And as a result, our minds are never made ready for running, let alone for this exilic race called the Christian life. Martyn Lloyd-Jones, the twentieth-century preacher in London, expressed the disastrous results that occur when the intellect is left behind:

> No true Christian in his right mind will desire anything other than true holiness and righteousness. . . . But . . . if you want to be holy and righteous, we are told, the intellect is dangerous and it is thought generally unlikely that a good theologian is likely to be a holy person. . . . The apostles, who wrote 'stir up your minds', 'strive,' 'fight the good fight of faith,' and many such things, would be surprised to hear what some people now say about 'the higher life'. . . . If you teach that sanctification consists of 'letting go' and letting the Holy Spirit do all the work, then don't blame me if you have no scholars![7]

No wonder Harry Blamires opened his classic book *The Christian Mind* with the words, "Today there is no Christian mind."[8] Blamires's road map to recovery is entirely consistent with the Apostle Peter's emphasis on some future goal. The first step back for the Christian, says Blamires, is the recovery of the supernatural, complete with a view of another world and a heavenly destination.

Let me put the problem of acquiring the first distinguishing mark of decided hope this way: in our day the church is wearing her robes too long. Our minds have not been properly elevated. We must raise them and tuck them in. We must make ourselves ready for running. A healthy mind is the means by which we fulfill Peter's command to be known for decided hope. He calls us to it. Gird up the loins of your mind. Be sober-minded.

Holy Living (vv. 14, 15)

Immediately following the command to *set our hope fully on the grace that will be ours* is the second mark of decided hope. Take a look at verses 14, 15:

> As obedient children, do not be conformed to the passions of your former ignorance, but as he who has called you is holy, you also be holy in all your conduct.

Holy conduct is the second distinguishing mark of those who set their hope on the grace to be revealed at Christ's coming. When we live lives that are modeled on God's holy character, we demonstrate that we have internalized the call to set our hope on our eternal inheritance. Conversely, whenever we find ourselves trapped and enslaved to sin—when all we can do is continue grasping for the pleasures of the world—we reveal to the world, and to God, that we place too little value on the grace that is to be ours with the coming of Christ. By wallowing in the husks of earthly pleasure we are saying, in effect, that we despise the better wheat and rewards of the next world.

There are two more observations to make from this text about holy living, and the first is this: holy living, or the Christian's *conduct*, becomes the subject matter for the rest of Peter's letter. He uses it seven times (see 1:15, 17, 18; 2:12; 3:1, 2, 16). In essence, one could make the argument that the entire letter is given to explaining what this distinguished mark of decided hope looks like. We will see in coming chapters that holy living looks like:

- sanctification (1:13–21)
- a sincere love for others both in and out of the church (1:22—2:12)
- submission to unjust leaders (2:13—3:7)
- a willingness to suffer (3:8—4:6)
- service to God's new family (4:7—5:14)

The second observation from this text about holy conduct is this: it is the mark of being a member of God's family. Take a look at the familial nature of Peter's terms—verse 14: "As obedient *children*" and verse 17: "And if you call on him as *Father*." That God puts the mark of his holiness into the lives of his children is nothing less than what Peter trumpeted back in verse 3: "Blessed be the God and *Father* of our Lord Jesus Christ!"

What does this mean for us? Simply this. If God is not your Father, living a holy life will be impossible because holy conduct is the fruit of being a member of his family. We simply don't possess the power to do so from our own genes or heritage. That is why Peter will say in verse 18, by way of contrast, "you were ransomed from the futile ways inherited from your *forefathers*." Understanding God as your Father will be pivotal to your ability to live as a worthy member of his family. The theologian J. I. Packer underscored this when he wrote:

> If you want to judge how well a person understands Christianity, find out how much he makes of the thought of being God's child, and having God as his Father. If this is not the thought that prompts and controls his worship and prayers and his whole outlook on life, it means that he does not understand Christianity very well at all. For everything that Christ taught, everything that is distinctively Christian . . . is summed up in the knowledge of the Fatherhood of God. "Father" is the Christian name for God.[9]

If we are in Christ, we are born into a new family. We now have God as our Father. Ironically, this truth should be a great encouragement to those who had poor models for earthly fathers. Of all people, these, more readily than most, should be drawn to the idea of having God, in all his love, as Father. Here is one who gives and gives and gives again. He never takes or abuses.[10]

Three Motivations (vv. 16–19)

Peter puts forward three motivations to get us out of our chairs and heading in the right direction.
- God's holy character (v. 16)
- God's impartial judgment (v. 17)
- Christ's precious sacrifice (vv. 18, 19)

God's Character (vv. 15, 16)

The first motivation Peter gives us to live honorable lives is God's holy character. Take a look again at verses 15, 16:

> But as he who called you is holy, you also be holy in all your conduct, since it is written, "You shall be holy for I am holy."

Peter motivates us toward a life of holiness with a quote from Leviticus 11:44. In doing so he selected an ancient text in which God commanded his people to be separate from the world. They were to be distinct. His family was to act differently from unbelieving nations. After all, they were to be his people, possessed with his good character. As his children, should we not want to grow up to be just like him? Christians ought to be motivated in holiness by the desire and opportunity to reflect God's character.

God's Judgment (v. 17)

Peter goes on to advance a second motivation for holy living. If God's character isn't enough to move us into the way of obedience, perhaps his impartial judgment will. Take a look at verse 17:

> And if you call on him as Father who judges impartially according to each one's deeds, conduct yourselves with fear throughout the time of your exile.

Each of us in God's family needs to be careful how we live because we all have a Father who is absolutely impartial in his judgments. This truth alone ought to protect us against presumptuous sin. Let me put it to you this way: whenever we begin thinking, *Oh, I can do this and get away with it. God will forgive me. After all, God is my Father and therefore my friend*, we are on dangerous ground.

The idea of having God as Father leads Peter to the exact opposite conclusion. God is impartial. The fact that we are called his children testifies to this very fact. Thus, instead of presumptuous sin, which is always the result of taking his grace for granted, Peter motivates us to live out our days in fear because of his impending and impartial judgment.

Christ's Sacrifice (vv. 18, 19)

But Peter isn't finished motivating us yet. If God's character won't capture us for holiness, and if God's impartial judgment won't scare us into the pursuit of holiness, perhaps a reflection on the preciousness of Jesus' sacrifice will compel us to live lives worthy of our calling. Take a look at verses 18, 19:

> . . . knowing that you were ransomed from the futile ways inherited from your forefathers, not with perishable things such as silver or gold, but with the precious blood of Christ, like that of a lamb without blemish or spot.

Don't you love how Peter elevates the work of Christ? I especially love the irony in the precious metals he chooses to call perishable—the earthly metals of silver and gold. These, above all others, are earth's most precious metals, the most lasting. But Peter makes them look like little more than fruit left too long on the table. The precious blood of Christ is precious indeed. Truly we were bought with a price. Our salvation was costly. It is as costly as the blood of Christ. Honestly, ask yourself, do I really need any other motivation for holy living?

Conclusion

Peter's cry from high above the ship's decks now comes to rest. He has finished his early call. He wants us to do one thing: set our hope on the grace that is to be brought to us at the revelation of Christ. He has shown us the two distinguishing marks of those who are doing so—a healthy mind and a holy life. And he put forward three reasons to motivate us to it—God's holy character demands it, his impartial judgment warns us to it, and Christ's sacrifice compels us in it.

There is a little character in C. S. Lewis's *The Voyage of the Dawn Treader*, a mouse named Reepicheep. Little Reepicheep sailed the seas of this life in pursuit of Heaven's shore. In every respect he is one that we should follow. The narrative of his arrival in Heaven should encourage us to continue setting our hope on the distant horizon of Heaven:

> The current drifted them steadily to the east. None of them slept nor ate. All that night and all the next day they glided eastward, and when the third day dawned—with a brightness you or I could not bear even if we had dark glasses on—they saw a wonder ahead. . . . What there was—eastward, beyond the sun—was a range of mountains. And the mountains must have

really been outside the world. These were warm and green and full of forest and waterfalls however high you looked.

And suddenly there came a breeze from the east, tossing the top of the wave into foamy shapes and ruffling the smooth water all round them. It brought both a smell and a sound, a musical sound. No one in that boat doubted that they were seeing Aslan's country. At that moment, with a crunch, the boat ran aground. The water was too shallow now even for it. "This," said Reepicheep, "is where I go on alone."

They did not try to stop him, for everything now felt as if it had been fated or had happened before. They helped him into his little coracle. Then he took off his sword ("I shall never need it no more," he said) and flung it far away across the lilied sea. . . . Then hastily he got into his coracle and took his paddle, and the current caught it and away he went, very black against the lilies. The coracle went more and more quickly, and beautifully it rushed up the wave's side. For one split second they saw its shape and Reepicheep's on the very top. Then it vanished, and since that moment no one can truly claim to have seen Reepicheep the Mouse. But my belief is that he came safe to Aslan's country and is alive there to this day.[11]

Do you long for Reepicheep's reward? Don't be discouraged during these drifting days of exilic existence. You have been born again to a living hope. And your hope is in God. Therefore, set your hope fully on the grace to be brought to you on that day. May the bow of your ship always be pointed for the port of Heaven, where warm mountains await your eternal exploration.

O Lord, help us to set our hopes not on what we can do, but on what Christ has already done in redeeming us by his blood; not on our own agendas but on your plans for us; not on what we think we deserve but on your grace, your unmerited kindness to us. This we pray in Jesus' name, amen.

Having purified your souls by your obedience to the truth for a sincere brotherly love, love one another earnestly from a pure heart, since you have been born again, not of perishable seed but of imperishable, through the living and abiding word of God; for "All flesh is like grass and all its glory like the flower of grass. The grass withers, and the flower falls, but the word of the Lord remains forever." And this word is the good news that was preached to you. So put away all malice and all deceit and hypocrisy and envy and all slander. Like newborn infants, long for the pure spiritual milk, that by it you may grow up into salvation—if indeed you have tasted that the Lord is good.

1:22—2:3

7

A Sincere Love

1 PETER 1:22—2:3

A Love That Lives

The Vietnam War was mercifully drawing to a close during my middle-school years. And that meant that young men who had been sent over to fight were now returning to the States. Each one needed a fresh start on life. For one man that meant enrolling at Judson College. I never knew the man by name, but I regularly saw him from a distance of a hundred yards.

Judson College is on the Fox River in Illinois; my dad's office in the Athletic Department was a wedge shot from its banks. I could see the river from the gym. During the frigid winter months the man stood alone along the river's frozen edge, tending a covey of ducks. He fed them. He cut through the ice to open up an area of water for them. In short, he met their every need during the cold season. Every day.

I asked my dad why the man cared so much about the ducks. I will never forget the story he told: "He has just returned from the war in Vietnam. The story is that ducks saved his life. His unit had been ambushed. Many of his friends had been killed, and while he hadn't been shot, he lay down to look like he had. He hoped they would go away. But they didn't. The enemy kept coming. Through the fields they came. They'd put one more shot in every fallen man to ensure that he was dead. But suddenly a covey of ducks flew overhead, and the attention of the soldiers was diverted. In their excitement they began running after the ducks to shoot at them instead. In the end, they stopped checking the field for men and left. That's how the man down by the river escaped. And now he has a special love for ducks. He loves because he lives." The call of our text conveys something similar.

Having purified your souls by your obedience to the truth for a sincere brotherly love, love one another earnestly from a pure heart, since you have been born again, not of perishable seed but of imperishable, through the living and abiding word of God. (vv. 22, 23)

A sincere and earnest love, a life given over to the genuine care of others, is the natural result of being born again. To highlight the command in the text simply notice the phrase, "love one another earnestly." To see why we love simply note, "since you have been born again." To put the force of Peter's thought as clearly as possible: when you get a fresh start on life (see 1:3 and its connection to 1:23), love should happen (1:22—2:3).

The Logic of Love

The mark of the Christian life is love. And according to the text, our love is to be *sincere* and *earnest*. By that Peter means genuine. It must come from the heart. We must give ourselves fully to it. Most of us don't have difficulty understanding the idea that our love for one another is the natural result of being born again. After all, when someone gets a fresh start on life, love happens. The tough part to untangle is in the logic of what Peter says next. Peter claims that love not only comes from being born again, but from being born again *through* the imperishable Word of God. Look at the intricate links Peter puts forward in verses 22, 23:

Love one another earnestly . . .

Since you have been born again . . .

through the living and abiding word of God.

Figuring out exactly how sincere love is the natural consequence of God's imperishable Word is not easy. When we ask Peter, why must we love? he responds with, we love because of the imperishable nature of God's Word! Well, that leaves us scratching our heads a bit. How exactly is sincere love the natural consequence of the living and abiding Word of God? For that question, we will need to explore the logic of love.

Seeds Possess the Power to Bring New Life

First, begin with what you know about seeds. Seeds possess within themselves the power to bring forth life. For instance, we know that the perishable seed of an oak tree, after falling into the ground, possesses the power to bring forth new life. In essence, the sapling emerges because all of the necessary life-giving properties were present in the seed from the beginning.

And so it is with God's Word. Like a seed, the Bible is alive. It contains within itself everything necessary for life. The faithful and rigorous preacher John Piper recounts a story that bears witness to the life-giving power of God's Word. He writes:

> Consider the story of "Little Bilney," an early English Reformer born in 1495. He studied law and was outwardly rigorous in his efforts at religion. But there was no life within. Then he happened to receive a Latin translation of Erasmus's Greek New Testament. Here is what happened:
>
>> I chanced upon this sentence of St. Paul (O most sweet and comfortable sentence to my soul!) in 1 Timothy 1: *"It is a true saying, and worthy of all men to be embraced, that Christ Jesus came into the world to save sinners; of whom I am the chief and principal."* This one sentence, through God's instruction and inward looking, which I did not then perceive, did so exhilarate my heart, being before wounded with the guilt of my sins, and being almost in despair, that . . . immediately I . . . felt a marvelous comfort and quietness, insomuch that "my bruised bones lept for joy." After this, the Scriptures began to be more pleasant to me than the honey or the honeycomb.[1]

Notice: it was simply raw exposure to God's Word that brought "Little Bilney" to life. He simply read a sentence in the Word of God, and life entered into his soul. The Word of God contains within itself all the properties necessary for life. And that ought to revolutionize our understanding about the power of God's Word to bring forth life.

Seeds Come with Fullness of Purpose

But we can say more. Life isn't the only natural result of God's Word. Peter is arguing here that love is as well. How is it that the gospel brings forth both life and love? For an answer we turn to the prophet Isaiah who tells us:

> For as the rain and the snow come down from heaven and do not return there but water the earth, making it bring forth and sprout, giving seed to the sower and bread to the eater, so shall my word be that goes out from my mouth; it shall not return to me empty; but it shall accomplish that which I purpose, and shall succeed in the thing for which I sent it. (55:10–11)

Isn't that great? The Word of God has intentions beyond giving life. God says, "It will accomplish that which I purpose, and shall succeed in the thing for which I sent it." And what is the full intention of God's Word? Isn't it that he would be made known in all his fullness? God, we know, is love. Therefore, the imperishable seed not only gives us life but gives us love. The activity of God's Word brings life. And the full intention of God's Word brings love. And all of this is because within the Word of God we gain Christ, who is both life and love.[2]

Therefore, the logic of love rests in this: God is life, and God is love. Thus, if God sent his Word into our hearts to give us life, then we have tasted of his fullness and will make manifest the fruit of his character. It is for this reason that Peter says:

Love one another earnestly . . .

Since you have been born again . . .

through the living and abiding word of God.

The Brevity of Life

It is interesting to note that Peter grounds his argument for love on a quote from Isaiah 40. Contextually, Isaiah 40 comes on the heels of a prophecy that said God's people would go into exile. God's people were in need of comfort. Peter chose this portion of Isaiah to bring comfort to his own exilic community of Christians.

"All flesh is like grass and all its glory like the flower of the grass. The grass withers, and the flower falls, but the word of the Lord remains forever." And this word is the good news that was preached to you. (vv. 24, 25)

For Peter, this quote is a proof text for his point. He has been arguing that God's Word is eternal and capable of bringing forth life. And thus he turns to Isaiah to prove it. The reference does more though. It contrasts our inability to *live and love* with that of God's ability to do both. While God's Word may be eternal, our flesh is not. We are temporal. We are here today and gone tomorrow. And as Psalm 103:16 reminds us, after we are gone, this place will remember us no more.

This is a good reminder for us all. You and I will not be remembered within two generations of our death. Think about that for a minute. Each of us can remember back one generation—we know our parents' names. We can recall the place of their birth and the resemblance of their face. We can even hear the sound of their voice—and at times we hear it in our own. But what can you recall of the second generation? How much do you know about your grandparents? Do you know all their names? What about their place of birth? Can you speak at length of their vocation or interests? And beyond them, what do you know about your great-grandparents? Anything at all? Yet, they are separated from you by only two generations. No wonder John Wesley linked the brevity of life to our need for the imperishable Word:

> I am a creature of a day. I am a spirit come from God, and returning to God. I want to know one thing: the way to heaven. God himself has condescended to teach me the way. He has written it down in a book. Oh, give me that book! At any price give me the book of God. Let me be a man of one book.[3]

In God's "book" we have found life. Through it, then, let us express love. Peter wants Christians everywhere to be a people known for living lives that demonstrate God's love. The time is short. All flesh *is* like grass. Get about the business of growing up in love.

The Look of Love

Peter wastes no time in applying the logic of his thought. Chapter 2 begins:

> So put away all malice and all deceit and hypocrisy and envy and all slander. Like newborn infants, long for the pure spiritual milk, that by it you may grow up into salvation—if indeed you have tasted that the Lord is good.

There is nothing sentimental here. There is no sense that love is an entirely emotional thing. Our "grow[ing] up to salvation" demands a love that is known for "*put[ting] away*" some things while "*long[ing] for*" others. The things we are to "put away" have one thing in common. They all undo other people. They destroy relationships. In contrast love builds others up; love strengthens relationships. Twentieth-century theologian H. Richard Niebuhr has written a beautiful definition of love that unfolds this putting away and longing for:

> Love is rejoicing over the existence of the beloved one; it is the desire that he be rather than not be; it is longing for his presence when he is absent; it is happiness in the thought of him; it is profound satisfaction over everything that makes him great and glorious.

Love is gratitude; it is thankfulness for the existence of the beloved; it is the happy acceptance of everything that he gives without the jealous feeling . . . it is a gratitude that does not seek equality; it is wonder over the other's gift of himself in companionship.

Love is reverence; it keeps its distance as it draws near; it does not seek to absorb the other in the self or want to be absorbed by it; it rejoices in the otherness of the other; it desires the beloved to be what he is and does not seek to refashion him into a replica of the self or to make him a means to the self's advancement. . . . In all such love there is an element of that "holy fear" which is not a form of flight but rather deep respect for the otherness of the beloved and the profound unwillingness to violate his integrity.

Love is loyalty; it is the willingness to let the self be destroyed rather than that the other cease to be; it is the commitment of the self by self-binding will to make the other great.[4]

What great phrases to describe what love looks like. Love rejoices over another, is thankful for the other, reverently respects and demonstrates loyalty to the other. You could say that our earnest love resembles a strong, healthy family. Indeed, Peter intends for us to see it this way. Notice the familial terms given to us: In 2:2 we are likened to "*newborn infants.*" This idea goes all the way back to 1:3 where we are said to be "*born again.*" And in 1:22 we are called to relate to one another as *brothers.*

The point is this: Peter wants us to grow up into Christ as members of his family. He is longing for the church to be mature, adult-like, strong. Newborn infants are not to remain that way. We should all be striving—through love—to grow up, for that is what God wants from us. In the novel *Gilead* the main character, John Ames, wonders about the age and maturity his son will be when they meet again in Heaven. His reflections put forward a powerful picture of Peter's desire for a love that is all grown up:

Sometimes now when you crawl into my lap and settle against me and I feel that light, quick strength of your body and the weightiness of your head—when you're cold from playing in the sprinkler or warm from your bath at night, and you lie in my arms and fiddle with my beard and tell me what you've been thinking about, that is perfectly pleasant, and I imagine your child self finding me in heaven and jumping into my arms, and there is a great joy in the thought.

Still, the other is better, and more likely to be somewhere near the reality of the situation, I believe . . . I believe the soul in Paradise must enjoy something nearer to a perpetual vigorous adulthood than to any other state we know. At least that is my hope. . . . I certainly don't mind the thought of your mother finding me a strong young man.[5]

May it be so for all of us. May we be known for our earnest love. May we grow up strong and vigorous in the family of God.

Dear God, we praise you for your Word. We thank you for your love. As your children we pray that we might grow up in both. May your Word be ever open before us, and may your love be ever growing within us. We pray that by the power at work within us you might make us into mature family members and followers of your Son. In his name we pray, amen.

As you come to him, a living stone rejected by men but in the sight of God chosen and precious, you yourselves like living stones are being built up as a spiritual house, to be a holy priesthood, to offer spiritual sacrifices acceptable to God through Jesus Christ. For it stands in Scripture:

"Behold, I am laying in Zion a stone,
a cornerstone chosen and precious,
and whoever believes in him will not be put to shame."

So the honor is for you who believe, but for those who do not believe,

"The stone that the builders rejected has become the cornerstone,"

    and

"A stone of stumbling, and a rock of offense."

They stumble because they disobey the word, as they were destined to do. But you are a chosen race, a royal priesthood, a holy nation, a people for his own possession, that you may proclaim the excellencies of him who called you out of darkness into his marvelous light. Once you were not a people, but now you are God's people; once you had not received mercy, but now you have received mercy.

2:4–10

8

A Spiritual House

1 PETER 2:4–10

ON THE DAY when the young Hebrew exile Daniel entered the throne room of Nebuchadnezzar, king of Babylon, the lives of many hung in the balance. The king's sleep had left him, and his spirit troubled him on account of a terrifying dream. The king had threatened to take the lives of all his counselors if they could not make known to him his dream and its interpretation. But to Daniel—the exile—God made everything known. So he entered the throne room, and said in effect:

> You saw, O King, a great image, and its appearance was frightening. The head of the image was of fine gold. Its chest and arms were of silver. Its middle and thighs were of bronze. Its legs were of iron, and its feet partly iron and clay. Then a stone was cut out of a mountain not made with hands, and the stone struck the image and broke it into pieces. The interpretation, O King, is this: the precious metals are all kingdoms—and you are the head made of fine gold. The stone, however, is the coming kingdom of God. And it shall stand forever, and of its increase there shall be no end. (see Daniel 2:31–45)

Daniel was not the only one in Israel's history who spoke of God's kingdom as a stone. Isaiah had seen a stone in a vision God had given to him years before.

> Behold, I am laying in Zion a stone, a cornerstone chosen and precious. (v. 6; see Isaiah 28:16)

The psalmist also spoke of a *cornerstone* that would bring salvation to all who believed as well as *a stone that would be a stumbling-block* for those who reject it (v. 7; see Psalm 118:22). And so, deeply imbedded in the strata of Israel's rich history was the conviction that she was God's promised kingdom—that Jerusalem was God's saving city and that the temple stood at the center of God's activity in the world.

Centuries later a young, impoverished itinerant preacher from Galilee named Jesus would come along and take all the imagery of the stone passages in the Hebrew Scriptures and commit the unpardonable sin of applying them to himself instead of to Judaism, the city, or the temple. Luke records the day when Jesus came through the stone gates of Zion, that great city, and stood in the temple teaching with authority. When the religious leaders asked him, "By what authority do you do this?" he responded by telling a parable of wicked tenants who rejected the authority of the vineyard owner's son. The leaders knew, of course, that the story had been directed against them, and they took issue with it (Luke 20:9–18).

In defending himself, Jesus provoked them further by quoting from the psalmist about the rejected stone of God. And then, most amazingly of all, Jesus alluded to the prophet Daniel and took upon himself the stone not made with hands—the one that would come from Heaven and replace all the kingdoms of the world.

On that storied day Jesus of Nazareth stole all of Israel's strong poetic and prophetic stone imagery and called it his own. In essence he proclaimed that in him all the promises of God are being fulfilled.

A Spiritual House

It is in the light of all this rich and contested history regarding Israel's religious identity that Peter—the one whom Jesus called the "rock [upon whom] I will build my church"—writes in 2:4, 5:

> As you come to him, a living stone rejected by men but in the sight of God chosen and precious, you yourselves like living stones are being built up as a spiritual house, to be a holy priesthood, to offer spiritual sacrifices acceptable to God through Jesus Christ.

These are stunning words, and elevating beyond measure. In one sentence Peter grasps the entire wealth of Israel's identity and applies it not to Jesus alone, but to any man, woman, or child who comes to faith in Christ!

• When we come to Jesus—not the city of Jerusalem—we come to the "living stone."

• When we come to Jesus—not to Judaism—we come into God's kingdom.

• When we come to Jesus—not the ornate temple—we become God's "spiritual house" and "holy priesthood."

These phrases, applied metaphorically here to Peter's early readers, represent the most exalted ideas within all of Judaism. After all, the spiritual house was the temple. If God was going to dwell anywhere in the world, certainly his presence would be there. In addition, the royal priesthood consisted of those honored ones who had the privilege of standing in the very presence of God. Yet now, following Jesus' example in usurping these ideas, Peter claims that in Christ these truths are likewise transferred over to every follower of Jesus. In essence the church has become God's people and God's place in the world. Truly, with these phrases "a spiritual house" and "a royal priesthood," Peter is raising the identity of his early readers to storied and unimaginable heights.

With these words Peter cements his thought in an architectural metaphor. Notice: he is moving beyond the idea of the church being God's family (1:1—2:2). Further, he will leave to the Apostle Paul the metaphor of the church as Christ's "body." What he takes for himself, though, is the architectural metaphor of the church as God's building.

Kyle Dugdale, in his Master of Architecture thesis for the Harvard Graduate School of Design, has written powerfully on the role that architecture plays in our post-Edenic world. He makes special note that ever since humanity was forced to leave the garden, we have been busy constructing buildings. In making this observation he argues that as architecture rises, it is in some measure an attempt to replace the sense of being at home, a feeling that has seemed to elude us east of Eden. He writes:

> Architecture has struggled to mitigate the effects of the fall. But the city is a poor substitute for the Garden of Eden. Architecture performs, at best, the role of a fig-leaf, covering humanity's exposure. In the end, it is, perhaps, not so much a cure as it is an expression of humanity's homesickness.[1]

Keeping Dugdale's astute insight in view, can you begin to see the impact this metaphor of God's *spiritual house* would have on those early readers? Remember, by and large they were followers of Jesus living in out-of-the-way places. They were off the beaten path; they were geographically removed from Jerusalem's great stone temple, the place of culture and religious action in the world. They were the dispersed ones, some of them far from home—not merely from Heaven.

But now, by way of a single metaphor, Peter proclaims that they are at the very heart and center of God's activity in the world. They are God's building, and in Christ they are being built up into a residence intended for God's very presence. To put it as simply as I can, they must have been thrilled to learn that their identity was secure. They were God's special building project. How inspiring to be reminded by Peter that if you have come to Jesus as God's "living stone," you are at the center of what God is doing in the world. We are God's spiritual house.

No Sacred Space

Other implications can be drawn from Peter's metaphor of a spiritual house. First, his teaching cuts directly across the contemporary notion that we need sacred space. People are God's sacred space. The New Testament does away with the idea of being at home anywhere outside of faith in Christ. His Spirit dwells within us. There is no need for us to lean on brick and mortar in an effort to get close to God. In fact, we can't get any closer to God than through faith in Christ.

Second, in light of Jesus' claim that he fulfills the Hebrew Scriptures' promise of a house, the notion that some of God's promises to Israel still need to be fulfilled should be questioned. There is no need to rebuild the temple in Jerusalem. And in this sense contemporary Zionism, as well as blind support for Israel in all things political, especially among evangelicals, might be, in some ways, misguided. After all, the apparently unfulfilled rebuilding of the temple, as put forth in a text like Haggai 2:6–9, has already found its fulfillment in Christ and the church, as proven by Hebrews 12:18–29.

A Royal Priesthood

The second new identification tag Peter bestows on his readers is the priesthood. Peter mentions it in verse 5 as well as in verse 9. The priesthood, of course, began with Aaron. And it was Aaron who stood before a holy God on behalf of a sinful people. In some respects he functioned as an intermediary between God and the world. As such the priests were the ones most intimately acquainted with God.

Now consider the impact of this verse in light of Israel's priestly history. Peter calls all believers a "*holy*" (v. 5) and "*royal*" (v. 9) "priesthood." This means that every Christian is the ultimate insider. We are not merely representative of God's place in the world; we serve as God's priests before the world. No wonder Peter closes verse 10 with the words,

> Once you were not a people, but now you are God's people; once you had
> not received mercy, but now you have received mercy.

What an encouraging word for those who were identified in 1:1 as "exiles." The ones who struggled with the sense of being outsiders now see in a fresh way that they are very dear to God indeed.

A New and Honored Identity and Calling

I hope that these awesome truths put forward by Peter encourage you in your faith. Your identity in Christ is an exalted one. And how did these things come to be bestowed on you? The closing words of verse 6 and the opening words of verse 7 read:

"Whoever believes in him will not be put to shame." (v. 6)

So the honor is for you who believe. (v. 7)

This new and exalted identity is held out for all who come to believe that Jesus is God's Ruler. Conversely, anyone who rejects Jesus as God's cornerstone shall stumble and fall. Put simply, what you and I do with Jesus will mean everything to our standing and identity before God. Jesus alone is the full expression of God in the world, and by his sacrifice he has brought us close to God. What will you do with Jesus? The Bible says that when he stood outside Jerusalem, he wept for the people of his own day. From the distance he could see the stone city gates. He also saw the temple mount. And yet he knew that he would be rejected by many. May it not be so for you. May you come to Jesus as God's "living stone." And may you experience in fresh ways your new and treasured identity in Christ.

When a person comes to faith in Christ, his or her identity is not the only thing that changes. Our text says that one's calling in life does too. The latter half of verse 9 says all this occurs so "that you may proclaim the excellencies of him who called you out of darkness, into his marvelous light." Wow! What an exalted calling! We now exist to proclaim the excellencies of God. Could anything be better? Precisely what this new calling entails and how we are to go about it is what Peter will begin to tell us next (2:11—3:7).

Dear Lord, we come to you. And though the world may reject you, we receive your rule with humble thanksgiving. We are honored to be called your people, and we ask that our lives would proclaim the excellencies of your name, amen.

Beloved, I urge you as sojourners and exiles to abstain from the passions of the flesh, which wage war against your soul. Keep your conduct among the Gentiles honorable, so that when they speak against you as evildoers, they may see your good deeds and glorify God on the day of visitation.

2:11, 12

9

Good Deeds

1 PETER 2:11, 12

Beloved

I like to imagine Peter's early readers, spread as they were across the isolated terrain of modern-day Turkey, pausing for a moment, nearly lost in wonder after coming to the end of 2:10 for the first time:

> Once you were not a people, but now you are God's people; once you had
> not received mercy but now you have received mercy.

In that brief silence they must have felt as if they were breathing privileged and rarefied air. After all, Peter has dazzled them with fresh and invigorating reminders that *they* have been "born again to a living hope" (1:3). To *them* belongs "an inheritance that is imperishable, undefiled, and unfading" (1:4). *They* are the recipients of God's prophetic promises. *They* are the people of God, the ones who will inherit Heaven. Not since the day they first became followers of Jesus had they been so filled with the sensation of how much God loved them.

If human language retains within her possession a word better suited to follow 2:10 than the one Peter chose, I can't think of it. "*Beloved.*" They were God's beloved. *Beloved* is precisely how they felt. This particular word, and it alone, captures the ascendant affections now rising within the hearts of Peter's readers. *Beloved* is the honored title that accompanies everyone whose spiritual identity and eternal destination are wrapped up in Christ.

And so Peter, having now written for them in plain language the very word that was rising within them, is free to turn his attention away from things like where they are going and to whom they belong. And in their place—from 2:12 all the way through 4:19—he will urge his freshly believing beloved to live in this wilderness world as those who are worthy to inherit all the wonders and relationships that belong to the next. Do you see the force of his pen in verse 11, "Beloved, I *urge* you . . ."?

Where We Are in the Letter

In a very real way these two verses function as the threshold to the remainder of the letter. Enter through them and you enter fully into the home of 1 Peter, where rooms upon rooms explore how the beloved are to live. From here on we learn of true grace (5:12) in action—what it looks like to stand firm while living far from our heavenly home.

Verses 11, 12 clearly form an *exhortation* to good and honorable gospel living. In subsequent chapters we will find specific *examples* of the gracious life expressed in the vast array of contexts in which every follower of Jesus must walk. Peter will take us into the rooms of the Christian's relationship to society and government (2:13–17), employment (2:18–25), and marriage (3:1–7). However, in these two verses we arrive merely at the threshold of Peter's home.

A Call to True and Gracious Living

To highlight the central teaching of this text, consider this question: What is required of us, the beloved, to live in *this* world as citizens worthy of all the wonders and relationships belonging to the *next*? Peter gives us his answer in two simple words:
- Verse 11: "abstain."
- Verse 12: "keep."

As people marked by the grace of God, we must refrain from some things while at the same time giving ourselves to other things. In verse 11 the "how to" of gracious Christian living is stated negatively, while in verse 12 we find it expressed positively. Thus, in the end, true and gracious Christian living means that we will become men and women who are known for being *this* and not *that* kind of people.[1]

Abstaining from the Passions of the Flesh

Peter's first admonition comes in verse 11: "Beloved . . . *abstain* from the passions of the flesh." To live in *this* world as citizens worthy of all the wonders and relationships belonging to the *next*, we must refrain from acting upon the impulses and desires of the flesh.

To understand what Peter has in mind when he exhorts us to "abstain from *the passions of the flesh*" we must reach all the way back to what he wrote in 1:14:

As obedient children, do not be conformed to *the passions of your former ignorance*, but as he who called you is holy, you also be holy in all your conduct.

Peter then went on to define what those passions were. He listed them as "malice," "deceit," "hypocrisy," "envy," and "slander" (2:1). These are the things a person in Christ puts away. These are the vices from which we abstain. They are the attitudes, actions, and way of life in which we once walked. They speak of the season when we were tethered to this world without God's indwelling power to resist.

To further understand what Peter means one can reach beyond our text in the letter as well. In 4:2, 3 Peter will write:

Live for the rest of your time in the flesh no longer for *human passions* but for the will of God. The time that is past suffices for doing what the Gentiles want to do, living in sensuality, passions, drunkenness, orgies, drinking parties, and lawless idolatry.

Peter calls us to renounce *all* these things as well. These are the activities we participated in when we were still attached to this world.

To catch the force of his appeal, we need to remember that he is urging us to it: "Beloved, I *urge* you . . . to abstain." To put it simply, if Peter was alive and preaching today, each of us would sense the angst in his appeal and the emotion in his voice. Even now, in his words he is yet rising in our midst and calling us to abstain.

We must abstain from the malicious desires of our mind that would feast on others as carcasses to be devoured, and we must renounce our tongue when it brings forth the dead wood of slander (2:1). Further, we must learn to cover ourselves when tempted to go nakedly into the presence of the illusion that physical pleasure is the end of all things. To "abstain from the passions of the flesh" requires us to live with a renewed mind, a disciplined tongue, and a controlled body. For in Christ we are tethered to Heaven and are merely wanderers on earth.

Interestingly, it was Plato, long before Peter, who first joined the three words *abstain*, *passions*, and *soul* in an effort to help people live honorable lives. In his work *Phaedo*, he narrates with picturesque imagery what occurs to people who fail to guard themselves against the passions of earthly impulse.

Plato brings his readers into a graveyard, and there we behold the souls of some of the departed, still visible after death. These ghost-like souls left on the earth are said to "flit about the monuments and the tombs." And according to Plato, our ability to see them rests upon the notion that during life they were tied too much to this world. They were a passionate people. They were tethered to this world and this world alone. They had led impure lives. As a result, their passions had stained their souls. And the earthly impulses that governed them in this life now made communion with the gods in the next life impossible.

> And this corporeal element, my friend, is heavy and weighty and earthy, and is that element of sight by which a soul is depressed and dragged down again into the visible world . . . and these must be the souls, not of the good, but of the evil, which are compelled to wander about such places in payment of the penalty of their former evil way of life; and they continue to wander until through the craving after the corporeal which never leaves them, they are imprisoned finally in another body.[2]

For Plato, then, the stubborn man in this life may return as a donkey in the next. For Plato, humanity needs a cure for human passions. And we must find it while we are still in the land of the living. In putting forth his own cure, Plato, long before Peter, brings together the three words of 1 Peter 2:11, 12.

> The true votaries of philosophy *abstain* from all **fleshly lusts**, and hold out against them and refuse to give themselves up to them . . . they who have any care of their own *souls*, and do not merely live moulding and fashioning the body.[3]

Plato's words "*abstain* from all fleshly lusts, and hold out against them . . . they who have any care for their own *souls*" are the very words that Peter utilizes when he calls us to "*abstain* from the *passions* of the flesh, for they wage war against your *soul*." Could it be that Peter, while rejecting Plato's rank dualism and the sense that the human body is base, nevertheless won't reject the overlapping ideas and vocabulary in order to make his point?

Perhaps the common ground between the two accounts for Peter's belief that the unbelieving world will "see your good works and glorify God" (2:12). You see, implicit in Peter's argument is that believers—and nonbelievers alike—have a *shared* sense of what is good and honorable and right. The ancient Greeks and Peter alike would both say, "Abstain." Don't succumb to the contemporary idea that what you think with your mind or say with your mouth or do with your body can be thought or said or done without doing damage to your own soul!

I hope you can now see that the logic of Peter—and Plato—shows us just how far our world has fallen from the commonly shared morals of the past. In our day there is little shared understanding of honorable conduct. We have lost the vital connection between the body and the soul. We live in a day that has not only loosened itself from biblical moorings but from the ancient Greek classical ones as well. The sad truth is this: we live in a day that is more earthbound and passion-driven than even the unbelieving ancient world. And this is all the more reason to heed Peter's call. "Abstain."

Two Motivating Ideas

You Are Now Sojourners and Exiles

Peter goes on to give his readers two motivations to abstain. The first is found in the words immediately following: "Abstain *as sojourners and exiles.*" To put it simply, your commitment to abstain from the impulses and desires of the flesh is based upon your true identity in Christ (2:4–10). You are a sojourner here. You are an exile. Your true identity is tethered to Heaven. Its pull upon you should be irresistible. You don't belong to this world anymore.

Thus we need to remember that every time we run headlong into fulfilling the passions of the flesh, we show the world and God that we have forgotten that something far greater than earthly pleasures exists. Pleasure is not all there is to life. We are travelers. As the old bluegrass gospel song goes, "This world is not my home, I'm just a passing through." If it helps put a face on what Peter is after here, think of Abraham. The Hebrew Scriptures use *sojourner* when speaking of his time wandering in Egypt (cf. Genesis 23:4). "Christian," Peter cries, "abstain." "Why?" you ask. "Sojourner!" he proclaims.

Human Passions Wage War against the Soul

If our identity in Christ is not enough motivation to move us, Peter has more to say. His second motivation to abstain from the passions of the flesh is found at the close of verse 11:

> Beloved, I urge you as sojourners and exiles to abstain from the passions
> of the flesh, *which wage war against your soul.*

We would expect Peter to say that the passions of the flesh wage war against our body. That, after all, is as far as our world goes today. But Peter goes further. He says there is an intimate relationship between what we do in the body and what happens to our soul. Literally, the human passions are said to be *serving as soldiers* against your soul. They are fighting men, and they intend to keep you tethered here. Disaster awaits those who fail to win this war. The Bible teaches that something far worse than Plato could have ever dreamed up awaits those who die without God's cure for human passions. You and I won't be hovering over this world in search of another body to possess. No; we will be cast into the outer darkness of the next, and that without hope.

Imagine never having the opportunity to be born again to a living hope that comes through faith in Christ. Imagine forfeiting the chance of eternal communion with the true God. Does this not motivate you to abstain? Remember, the impulses of the flesh are fighting men. And the war they are waging is not against your body but your soul. How do we live in this world in a way that shows we are waiting for the next? Thus far Peter has told us, "Abstain."

Keep Your Conduct Honorable

Interestingly, 1 Peter 2:11, 12 are two sentences in English. In the original, however, they are only one. Verse 12 is a continuation of verse 11—we live well not merely by those things from which we abstain, but by the host of things we choose to embrace. Peter says:

> Keep your conduct among the Gentiles honorable, so that when they speak against you as evildoers, they may see your good deeds and glorify God on the day of visitation.

Our lives are to be filled with good works. Notice: the "*honorable . . . conduct*" of the first half of the verse is connected to the "*good deeds*" of the second half. In other words, we are called to honorable conduct, which is nothing less than doing good deeds. It is nice to know that Christianity is more than a call to abstain from a list of activities. We are to be people who are busy filling our lives with good things as well. The ironic tragedy, however, is that Protestantism, after the Reformation, most often refers to good works solely in a negative fashion. This is, of course, because of its insistence on justification by faith.

In my office I have a sermon illustration file. In it are nearly 3,000 illustrations on a variety of topics. In my attempt to illustrate the value of honorable conduct—of the rightful place of good works—I searched and searched for even one among my thousands. All to no avail. For some reason I filed nothing along the way except those stories, anecdotes, and quotes that denounce good works in favor of justification by faith![4]

In contrast, take a look at the apostles' files. The New Testament epistles are filled with this idea of good works as an expression of our calling:

• Ephesians 2:10 states, "For we are his workmanship, created in Christ Jesus for *good works,* which God prepared beforehand, that we should walk in them."

• Titus 2:7 reads, "Show yourself in all respects to be a model of *good works.*"

• Titus 2:14 declares that Jesus redeemed us "to purify for himself a people for his own possession who are zealous for *good works.*"

• In Titus 3:8 Paul concludes his charge to Titus by saying, "I want you to insist on these things, so that those who have believed in God may be careful to devote themselves to *good works.*"

Therefore, having been convinced by the apostles about the rightful place of good deeds, we ask, what constitutes good works? Thankfully, just as we were able earlier to define what Peter meant by *abstain from human passions* by reaching backward and forward in this letter, we can do the same for *good works.*

• 1:15: " . . . *as he who called you is holy, you also be holy in all your conduct.* "

• 2:15: "For this is the will of God, that by *doing good* you should put to silence the ignorance of foolish people."

• 2:20: "But if when you *do good* and suffer for it you endure, this is a gracious thing in the sight of God."

• 3:6: "And you are her [Sarah's] children, if you *do good.*"

• 3:11: "Turn away from evil and *do good.*"

• 3:13: "Now who is there to harm you if you are zealous for what is *good?*"

• 3:16: "so that . . . those who revile your *good behavior* in Christ may be put to shame."

• 4:19: "Therefore let those who suffer according to God's will entrust their souls to a faithful Creator *while doing good.*"

This is what honorable conduct looks like. And yet the greatest text of all is taken from Matthew 5:16. Here we find the dominical words of Christ:

> In the same way, let your light shine before others, so that they may see your good deeds and give glory to your Father who is in heaven.

Peter appears to have intentionally borrowed the words of Jesus, for verse 12 is a very close paraphrase of what Jesus had taught him long ago. He is staying close to his Lord. Let us therefore do likewise. Let us seek to live lives that model the mature honorable conduct for which Peter is calling. May it be rooted in our knowledge of his love. And may we be faithful until Christ's return. Indeed, Peter closes out this section by affirming that our works will on that day be seen for what they are and shall give God great glory.[5]

We have come under the lintel of Peter's door. He has greeted us with a strong exhortation to live lives that are worthy of the billing we have been given as Christ's beloved. Next we will see what that looks like in a variety of contexts.

Our Heavenly Father, we thank you for the strong word from these verses. Indeed, you have called us to good deeds and honorable conduct. Forgive us for feeding for too long on the passions of the flesh. Return our hearts, our minds, and our wills to you. May we sojourn well, that the world might see and glorify you. Grant us the strength of your Holy Spirit. In Jesus' name we pray, amen.

Be subject for the Lord's sake to every human institution, whether it be to the emperor as supreme, or to governors as sent by him to punish those who do evil and to praise those who do good. For this is the will of God, that by doing good you should put to silence the ignorance of foolish people. Live as people who are free, not using your freedom as a cover-up for evil, but living as servants of God. Honor everyone. Love the brotherhood. Fear God. Honor the emperor. Servants, be subject to your masters with all respect, not only to the good and gentle but also to the unjust. For this is a gracious thing, when, mindful of God, one endures sorrows while suffering unjustly. For what credit is it if, when you sin and are beaten for it, you endure? But if when you do good and suffer for it you endure, this is a gracious thing in the sight of God. For to this you have been called, because Christ also suffered for you, leaving you an example, so that you might follow in his steps. He committed no sin, neither was deceit found in his mouth. When he was reviled, he did not revile in return; when he suffered, he did not threaten, but continued entrusting himself to him who judges justly. He himself bore our sins in his body on the tree, that we might die to sin and live to righteousness. By his wounds you have been healed. For you were straying like sheep, but have now returned to the Shepherd and Overseer of your souls.

2:13–25

10

Honorable Living

1 PETER 2:13-25

A HUMOROUS STORY is told of a certain twentieth-century member of Parliament whose rhetorical flair was often accompanied by a complete disregard for facts. Other members came to know by experience that while he might stand and speak well on an issue, the force of logic necessary to convince others of his point of view might be absent entirely. One contemporary, fed up with this man's blatant disregard for things as they were and his incessant practice of saying whatever he pleased, finally rose and complained, "He uses facts the way a drunk uses a lamppost—more for support than illumination."[1]

The Preacher's Temptation

As we come to this new section of Peter's letter (2:13—3:7), we realize that a similar temptation arises for the preacher. For instance, take the verses before us outlining Peter's directive regarding the relationship that the Christian community is to have with the authority vested in the state. Contemporary readers find Peter's unqualified call to submission so unilateral, so unsettling, so startling and surprising that the preacher is tempted to lean upon this text for what he thinks Peter should have said instead.

Indeed, in many respects it would be quite easy to prepare a sermon from these verses entirely on the subject of civil disobedience. All the preacher would need to do is turn up some of the great biblical passages that deal with this theme. He could tell of the Egyptian midwives who rightly disobeyed Pharaoh out of their fear for God; the gallant Shadrach, Meshach, and Abednego who doggedly refused to worship Nebuchadnezzar's statue out of reverence for Yahweh; Daniel, who faithfully refused to follow legislation that prohibited prayer to the Most High; finally, the preacher could wax eloquently on Peter and John, who stood defiant in the face of authorities when ordered to stop preaching in Jesus' name.[2]

Not surprisingly, when the preacher treats his task in this way he is just as likely to receive affirmation from his congregants as dismay. After all, most churchgoing people today are happy to attend a church where issues of social justice form the sole substance of pulpit discourse.

The problem, of course, in doing this kind of thing *from this text* is that it is absolutely silent on anything advocating civil disobedience. In fact, what Peter does have to say is something quite different. Peter's word here is nothing short of an unabashed emphasis on civil obedience—an obedience that extends even to times when the ruling authorities are ungodly. Many pastors don't want to touch civil obedience with anything shorter than a ten-foot pole, and so such a pastor decides, long before Sunday, to become an inebriated preacher, so to speak. That is, in the language of the opening illustration, he leans upon the text the way a drunk leans upon a lamppost— more for support than for illumination. The result? Peter's voice is rendered silent, the Spirit who gave us this text is unable to shed any light upon us, and the church is never taught to think clearly about what kind of response we are to make before a watching world.

When preachers succumb to this particular temptation in preaching, they show their inability to take God at his word. We end up preaching by way of qualification rather than explication.[3] We blunt the edge of the text in front of us from having any real force.

The Parishioner's Temptation

Interestingly, preachers are not alone in their temptation to avoid portions of the Word of God. People in the pew must fight temptation too. There will always be people on the fringes who will deconstruct the Bible's message in its call for godly conduct. For example, take the text in front of us. Some Christians in our country represent the far pole of conservative political thought. And within that stream are a few who take the law into their own hands when it comes to following leaders and laws that they feel are ungodly. The fact that someone is willing to bomb an abortion clinic is evidence enough.

On the other religious political pole are a few who would deconstruct verses 18–21 of any meaning whatsoever. Instead of Jesus' willingness to suffer being lifted up as an example to follow, the force of the text is turned on its head to mean that Christ's work is really only manifest in the world when and where the oppressed are being liberated.

In light of this, how should we proceed? How can we approach this text as Peter would want us?

• We should first see Peter's *intention*.

• We can then explore his *instruction*.

• Finally, we can highlight the example of the one put forward for *imitation*.

Peter's Intention

If we were right in arguing that 2:11, 12 serve as Peter's general exhortation to good works, then his intention in 2:13—3:7 is to provide particular examples of what Christian good works look like in society, at work, and in the marital union.

Further, a quick glance at the same verses reveals Peter's intent to deal with only one side of these relationships: he wants to talk about good works from the vantage point of the one most likely to be mistreated. In other words, he doesn't intend to write a full treatise on the responsibilities of all parties involved in these relationships.

This is a striking feature when compared with other New Testament *haustafel* texts.[4] The passages in Ephesians and Colossians that speak of husbands and wives and servants and masters are much more balanced. They put forward a code of conduct that is more comprehensive than what Peter intends to do here. In those texts the one in authority is told how to act as well. Paul has a lot to say to husbands and masters. Peter, on the other hand, is unconcerned about writing exhaustively. In fact, he omits parents and children altogether, replacing them with political leaders and citizens.

This is a very important thing to take note of. Peter's intention is highly specific and limited in scope. He desires to provide examples of good works done by the one most likely to be mistreated in the world's institutional economy. And as we will see, they are the good works to be done even when rulers are less than good in return.

Peter's Instruction

What is the content of Peter's instruction? In one word it is *submission*. Submission is the word that unfolds what Peter is looking for when he writes about honorable conduct and good deeds. The idea of submission is found in the opening verse of each setting of relationships:

• 2:13: "Be *subject* for the Lord's sake to every human institution."

• 2:18: "Servants, be *subject* to your masters with all respect."

• 3:1: "Likewise, wives, be *subject* to your own husbands."

For people in our day this is nothing short of startling. It is as counter-cultural as one can get. Yet, for Peter the good and honorable work of the Christian community is nothing if it is not submission to authority. Now, before exploring this theme of submission any further, we need to stop and consider something important. True, Peter appears to be arguing that *submission* is the preeminent mark of Christian grace and goodness. Could this be true? Does the sum and substance of one's Christian life—one's good works before a watching world—come down to some blind adherence to a principle called *submission*? The answer of course is no. And we need to get this straight at the outset.

The principle of submission in this section (see 2:13, 18; 3:1) is not our foundation. Instead, *submission* defines the Christian's ways because "being like the Savior" describes the Christian's goal. Take note, the gravitational center of this part of the letter is the meekness and submissiveness of the Lord Jesus Christ (2:21–25). The one we are to imitate stands in the middle of it all. In essence, Peter wants us to follow in the footsteps of the Prince of Peace. It is for this reason that Christian men and women gladly and voluntarily put on the garments of submission. We are not operating out of some blind adherence to a rigid principle but rather out of love for the *one* with whom we have a relationship. At the end of the day, Christians willingly submit themselves to people in authority because we desire our lives to be pleasing to someone, not something!

Keeping that important point in mind we are now prepared to look at the instructions given in the first two of these relationships (human institutions and masters). The next chapter will be devoted entirely to the third in sequence, namely, the relationship of husband and wife.

Submission to Those in Political Office[5]

Peter writes:

> Be subject for the Lord's sake to every human institution, whether it is to
> the emperor as supreme, or to governors as sent by him to punish those
> who do evil and to praise those who do good. (2:13, 14)

The extent and force of Peter's words on this point only grow in stature when one considers that the emperor in Peter's day was none other than Nero. Nero was the Roman ruler who led a great persecution against the Christians in the first century. In fact, historians tell us that it was under Nero that Peter was martyred. Other authorities of this time included governors Pontius Pilate and Felix. The one, Pilate, handed Jesus over to death while Peter stood off in the shadows, while the other, Felix, played with his power in the case of Paul. All three of these men lived in the time of Peter's letter. Each of them was calloused in life and friendless to those in the Christian faith. Yet Peter tells us to submit to such rulers as these. Why? Verse 15 gives us the answer:

> For this is the will of God, that by doing good you should put to silence the ignorance of foolish people.

Our motivation rests in this: submission to authority is the strongest apologetic against the view that Christians are never up to any good. Certainly the first century showed that the bad behavior of some resulted in Christianity getting a bad name. One of Jesus' own disciples was called "the Zealot" (Luke 6:15). Some went as far as sedition. In regard to morality, perhaps the word had spread about the one in Corinth who was involved in an incestuous relationship. Whenever the nonbelieving world picks up the newspaper and is confronted with Christian leaders acting badly, it assumes that all Christians are just like them. Our goodness will be our greatest apologetic for the gospel. Good works silence false accusations. We ought to be throwing ourselves into good things. Submission is the great apologetic for the gospel.

Learning this lesson didn't come overnight for Peter. Do you remember the night Jesus was betrayed in the garden? Peter brought a sword that night. He thought this was the hour for action, and he cut off the ear of one who had come to arrest his Lord. But now, decades later, as an older and wiser man, Peter says to us in essence, "I have put that sword away." God has given a sword to the state, but except for the Word of God, "the sword of the Spirit" (Ephesians 6:17), the church is to keep hers sheathed. For Peter, preaching from the Bible was enough. It cut to the bone and marrow of the harshest in authority. Peter has learned his lesson. He is now free to submit. And so he writes:

> Live as people who are free, not using your freedom as a cover-up for evil, but living as servants of God. Honor everyone. Love the brotherhood. Fear God. Honor the emperor. (vv.16, 17)

These verses are positioned beautifully. Freedom is for serving. In verse 17 Peter puts four short sentences together that rise in distinction. He begins with 'honor *everyone*" and then, on an elevated plane, "Love the *brotherhood*." Following this he ascends to the heavens with the words, "Fear *God*" before finally coming back to the playing field on which he began, "honor the *emperor*." Show proper respect for all rulers.

Submission to Those over You in the Workplace

Peter now moves on to give instructions to a second set of relationships. He writes:

> Servants, be subject to your masters with all respect, not only to the good and gentle but also the unjust.

For those of us who live in North America it is impossible to read these verses without the history of our country's horrific commitment to slavery coming to mind. In this respect, our own past is appalling. And at first glance these verses appear inappropriate. They seem to accept the very thing we have now come to disdain. And some question aloud, "Why doesn't the Bible speak out against slavery? Why doesn't Peter reject the institution outright?"

A doctoral candidate in political philosophy at the University of Chicago, who is working on some of these questions in their American historical context, points out the key differences between the Biblical practice and the American counterpart as a means of answering these questions. "The Biblical injustice of American slavery comes down to two things, working in tandem: its permanence (complete legal barriers to manumission) and its purely racial basis. Even ancient Hebrew slaves enjoyed periodic jubilee. Certainly New Testament slaves had various means to earn their freedom, depending on context. This much can be said: God never permits his people to use slavery as a means of permanent exploitation, the gluttonous feeding off of others and their children, generation after generation."[6]

In actual fact the Bible does condemn, and in no uncertain terms, the slavery practiced in North America. In 1 Timothy 1:8–11 the Apostle Paul makes a list of activities that are "contrary to sound doctrine" (v. 10)— behavior that is against the glorious gospel (v. 10). One activity in the list is the noun translated "enslavers" (v. 10). This word refers to those who would take a person captive in order to sell him or her into slavery. Paul condemned this as contrary to sound doctrine and against the glorious gospel. The Bible is clear on North American slavery. It is against it. It abhors it. It is a sin and as such is reprehensible. In fact, Paul lists those who practice it as "ungodly," "unholy," and "profane" (v. 9).

Interestingly, the word translated "servants" in Peter's text comes from the Greek genre of household terms. Some distinctions from its North American counterpart are in order. In the ancient Roman world there were three classes of people: the Roman citizen who had full rights and protection under law; the freedmen who had restricted protections but still enjoyed a great deal of autonomy; and the servant class. These were the men and women largely employed as managers and helpers in the home. They ran the agrarian workplace. This servant class is the one Peter is writing about at this point in his letter.

So, while we bring North American slavery to the text, in reality Peter is writing about something with significant differences. A closer modern-day parallel might be someone who received their college education for free in exchange for serving five years in the armed services upon graduation. Or medical school students and residents who receive a wage but are nonetheless "owned" by the institution who has agreed to pay for their training.

These modern-day examples much more closely approximate the subjects mentioned by Peter in this text.

These servants are to be subject to their masters with all respect—even to those who according to verse 18 are "unjust." The word "unjust" can be more literally rendered those who are "crooked." They cheat. These masters cook the books. Peter says, "Do you have an employer like that? Well, do them all the good you can, even if it leads to suffering." For an example of what such service looks like without compromising your integrity, we need only look at Joseph in the Old Testament. He did Potiphar good all the days of his life, and we are told that God was with him. The promise of God's presence in the midst of suffering is for us as well.

We are involved in a great work when we do good while suffering. Peter writes:

> For this is a gracious thing, when, mindful of God, one endures sorrows while suffering unjustly. For what credit is it if, when you sin and are beaten for it, you endure? But if when you do good and suffer for it you endure, this is a gracious thing in the sight of God. (vv. 19, 20)

Did you catch the repeating word "gracious"? When you endure unjust hardship, you are doing "a gracious thing" (v. 19), and this gracious thing is such in the sight of God (v. 20). Your goodness is displaying true graciousness to the world. And here we stumble upon something at the very core of Peter's mind. In 1 Peter 5:12 he writes, "I have written briefly to you, exhorting and declaring that this is the true grace of God. Stand firm in it." In other words, "the true grace of God" is revealed in the world when Christians who are treated unjustly nevertheless act honorably and good. This is what the world needs to see from us. Our submission is not only within the will of God—it is a gracious thing in the sight of God. In submission you gain God's smile.

Peter's Example for Imitation

Peter doesn't leave us on our own to figure out what our submissions looks like. He provides an example for us to follow.

> For to this you have been called, because Christ also suffered for you, leaving you an example, so that you might follow in his steps.

There is perhaps nothing more beautiful in the English language than Milton's depiction of the moment God's Son stood upon the rim of the universe in *Paradise Lost*. Seeing our need for a Savior, he said to the Father, "I will go." So the eternal Word of God took on flesh. And this one, Jesus, the one who possesses all authority and all power—this one humbled himself and became a servant.

Peter, knowing just how difficult our sojourning in this world will be, says in essence, "I have an example for you to imitate. I have an exile for you to follow. The one who flung the stars into space—this one shall lead you!" We are to imitate the one of whom Peter says:

> He committed no sin, neither was deceit found in his mouth. When he was reviled, he did not revile in return; when he suffered, he did not threaten, but continued entrusting himself to him who judges justly. He himself bore our sins in his body on the tree, that we might die to sin and live to righteousness. By his wounds you have been healed. For you were straying like sheep, but have now returned to the Shepherd and Overseer of our souls.

Isaiah's Influence on Peter

Numerous passages throughout the New Testament make reference to Isaiah's writings, especially with reference to Christ's suffering. Without question, Jesus recognized himself to be in Isaiah 53's description of the Suffering Servant (see Matthew 12:15–21). Peter also here, in verses 21–25, is either quoting or alluding to Isaiah 53. This connection is important enought to quote Isaiah's passsage in full.

> Behold, my servant shall act wisely; he shall be high and lifted up, and shall be exalted. As many were astonished at you—his appearance was so marred, beyond human semblance, and his form beyond that of the children of mankind—so shall he sprinkle many nations; kings shall shut their mouths because of him; for that which has not been told them they see, and that which they have not heard they understand.

> Who has believed what he has heard from us? And to whom has the arm of the LORD been revealed? For he grew up before him like a young plant, and like a root out of dry ground; he had no form or majesty that we should look at him, and no beauty that we should desire him. He was despised and rejected by men; a man of sorrows, and acquainted with grief; and as one from whom men hide their faces he was despised, and we esteemed him not. Surely he has borne our griefs and carried our sorrows; yet we esteemed him stricken, smitten by God, and afflicted. But he was wounded for our transgressions; he was crushed for our iniquities; upon him was the chastisement that brought us peace, and with his stripes we are healed. All we like sheep have gone astray; we have turned—every one—to his own way; and the LORD has laid on him the iniquity of us all. He was oppressed, and he was afflicted, yet he opened not his mouth; like a lamb that is led

to the slaughter, and like a sheep that before its shearers is silent, so he opened not his mouth. By oppression and judgment he was taken away; and as for his generation, who considered that he was cut off out of the land of the living, stricken for the transgression of my people? And they made his grave with the wicked and with a rich man in his death, although he had done no violence, and there was no deceit in his mouth.

Yet it was the will of the Lord to crush him; he has put him to grief; when his soul makes an offering for sin, he shall see his offspring; he shall prolong his days; the will of the Lord shall prosper in his hand. Out of the anguish of his soul he shall see and be satisfied; by his knowledge shall the righteous one, my servant, make many to be accounted righteous, and he shall bear their iniquities. Therefore I will divide him a portion with the many, and he shall divide the spoil with the strong, because he poured out his soul to death and was numbered with the transgressors; yet he bore the sin of many, and makes intercession for the transgressors. (Isaiah 52:13—53:12)

The structure of Isaiah 53 consists of three basic elements. First, in 52:13–15 we have an introductory appraisal of God announcing the exaltation of his Servant who will come and receive the worship of the nations. The second unit is a confessional statement of the people of God. No longer is God the one who is speaking. Rather, the people contrast their past rejection of Christ with the true meaning of His death (53:1–9). The final unit of the passage returns to the great theme of exaltation (53:10–12). God is again the speaker. Christ is promised to be exalted because of his work as a guilt offering.

A 52:13–15 (Exaltation of Christ)
B 53:1–9 (Humiliation of Christ)
A' 53:10–12 (Promised Exaltation of Christ)

The contrast between the humiliation and the exaltation of Christ in this passage should be clear. This is certainly the theological theme of the song. The entire poem is dominated by it. There are "many" transgressors, but "one" Servant. He is the one who has come from on high to deliver his people. And the literary style of Isaiah provides for us further insight into the meaning of this passage, 52:13—53:12, as it relates to Jesus Christ. Indeed, Peter's adoption of this passage makes the relationship clear.

In Peter's words: the King of Glory enters into a state of suffering. We can almost see him standing before the earthly governor, Pilate, and not reviling in return. When he suffers at the hands of the officer who flogged him and beat him, he did not threaten in return. How did he do it? He entrusted himself to the one who judges justly.

With Peter's dependence on Isaiah now in place, we are ready to assert that the humility of Christ—his own earthly season of suffering—is the gravitational center of this section of the letter. As such, we've moved past the "thing" to the "person" of our Lord and Savior. We submit to ungodly authorities out of a desire to please him and emulate his life. Thus, we are now ready to put this language of commitment and submission into its proper context: a relationship with Jesus Christ. In so doing, we can cease being the sheep that strayed in Isaiah's chapter and in Peter's. We can be exalted with Christ. We can live in righteousness. Our wounds can be healed. In him we can entrust ourselves to the one who judges justly. And in him we will have the strength we need to walk in this world, for God will be the shepherd and guardian of our souls.

Our Heavenly Father, today we thank you for Jesus, your Suffering Servant and King. Having come today to the center of this text, with Jesus' example before us, help us to live in such a way as to please you. Indeed, may all our submissiveness be rooted in love to you. May our obedience to these verses stem from our desire to grow in our relationship with you. For pleasing you is all we want to do. In Jesus' name, amen.

Likewise, wives, be subject to your own husbands, so that even if some do not obey the word, they may be won without a word by the conduct of their wives—when they see your respectful and pure conduct. Do not let your adorning be external—the braiding of hair, the wearing of gold, or the putting on of clothing—but let your adorning be the hidden person of the heart with the imperishable beauty of a gentle and quiet spirit, which in God's sight is very precious. For this is how the holy women who hoped in God used to adorn themselves, by submitting to their husbands, as Sarah obeyed Abraham, calling him lord. And you are her children, if you do good and do not fear anything that is frightening. Likewise, husbands, live with your wives in an understanding way, showing honor to the woman as the weaker vessel, since they are heirs with you of the grace of life, so that your prayers may not be hindered.

3:1–7

11

Internal Adornment

1 PETER 3:1–7

IN THE YEAR AD 397 an aging saint in the Christian faith wrote what would become one of the most compelling autobiographies ever published. When the book was finally finished, he titled his own tale *The Confessions of Saint Augustine*. Buried in this celebrated narrative is the moving tribute Augustine gave his mother, Monica, on the influence she had in bringing her unbelieving husband, Patricius, to personal faith in Jesus. Augustine described his mother's role with these words:

> She served her husband as her master, and did all she could to win him for You, speaking to him of You by her conduct, by which You made her beautiful. . . . Finally, when her husband was at the end of his earthly span, she gained him for You.[1]

It doesn't take much for us to envision Augustine's mother, hard-pressed for years in a difficult marriage, looking for strength to go on in the quiet words and understated promises of 1 Peter 3:1, 2. Perhaps she even had them committed to memory:

> Likewise, wives, be submissive to your own husbands, so that even if some do not obey the word, they may be won without a word by the conduct of their wives, when they see your respectful and pure conduct.

One could say that Augustine's mother received the full outcome of what Peter promised back in 2:12: "Keep your conduct among the Gentiles honorable, so that when they speak against you as evildoers, they may see your good deeds and glorify God on the day of visitation." One result of a Christian's doing good works is that some unbelieving people will, in the end, give God unending glory. With that encouragement before us, our text emerges within its context.

The force of 3:1, 2 shouldn't be lost on us. Some men entering Heaven—giving glory to God on the day of Christ's final visitation—will owe their very salvation to the honorable conduct and good deeds of a wife who determined to live out her days in real, costly, and faithful submission. Such earthly, worldly husbands were saved through the example of women who powerfully, mysteriously, and without fear learned to entrust themselves to God's promised care. I can't think of a more encouraging word for many women today who are giving everything they have to follow Christ in difficult circumstances.

However, while Augustine's mother received the best possible outcome, I also want to acknowledge that the upside of our text isn't going to make life any easier for Christian women living in the worst of marital situations. Compounding matters, Christian women, regardless of their marital status, have too often been subjected to degrading explanations and abusive applications from this very text.

Therefore, given the pain that can be evoked by this text, I want to say a few things about what Peter's call to submission does *not* mean for Christian wives. It does not mean that if your husband asks you to abandon your faith in Christ, you should do so. It does not mean that if your husband asks you to sin, you should do so. It does not mean that you must always agree with him and never present a differing view. It does not mean that if he is unfaithful to you, you are left without Biblical recourse. It does not mean that if he abuses you physically or abandons you through incessant verbal humiliation, you must remain quietly in the home and accept the daily cruelty of that relationship at all costs.

I have wrestled with why Peter says so little by way of qualification. Clearly, Peter isn't concerned to show us how God's Word might be applied to someone's personal situation. Perhaps he felt that if he had to outline all the possible exceptions to the principle, it would have taken him fifty pages. And even then there is no guarantee that he would have covered every particular situation. So he leaves that to the work of the pastor. But let me say to the many women who are experiencing trying times and are asking questions around the edges of this text, get help from trusted people in an effort to think clearly about your situation. To do that is always appropriate, honorable, Biblical, and wise.

The Principle of Submission

What Peter *does do* in this text is to lay down a single principle. It is the same principle of submission that we looked at in the last chapter (2:13 said, "Be *subject* for the Lord's sake to every human institution"). We find the Biblical principle of submission throughout Peter's letter. It extends to how we treat elected officials and unjust employers and, in the text before us, how wives relate to their husbands.

Again we've come to an important theme of this letter, perhaps its gravitational center. The principle of submission directly relates to the example and the person of Christ in 2:21–25. The *submission* of which Peter speaks is not adherence to a principle but recognition of the person who compels us to submit in order to live lives of godly obedience.

In all three cases (2:13—3:7) Christians are to present themselves before a watching world as people who emulate Jesus. We are to pattern our lives on his example. For in doing so we present the world fresh and vibrant pictures of living hope. Clearly, that is the logic of our opening verses. Equally clear are Peter's desires that his words apply to all Christian wives, not just those who are married to unbelieving husbands, for the text says, "even if *some* do not obey the word." So the force behind the words we are looking at in 3:1–6 are intended for all Christian wives.

External Adornment

So, what does this living hope and soul-winning conduct look like in Christian wives? Peter begins his answer, just as he did when describing our eternal inheritance (1:4), by way of contrast. He tells us what good deeds and honorable conduct *do not* look like in Christian wives.

> Do not let your adorning be external—the braiding of hair, the wearing of gold, or the putting on of clothing—but . . . (3:3, 4)

Peter's culture, like our own, had an obsession with external adornment. Women were under enormous pressure to look beautiful. They were fixated on their hair, the wearing of jewelry, and clothing. In response, Peter wants Christian women not to be overly concerned about external beauty. Only the famed children's book character Amelia Bedelia could misunderstand the meaning of this verse. Amelia was a household servant for Mr. and Mrs. Rogers, and Amelia took everything she was told to do literally—woodenly. So she would put real sponges in the sponge cake she was baking or pitch a tent by throwing it into the woods. An Amelia Bedelia interpretation of this verse would leave women without *any* braiding of hair, wearing of jewelry, or wearing of clothing. Peter is not advocating any such thing. His concern is one of emphasis, as any discerning reader will understand. The pressures placed on Christian women by today's culture are nothing short of oppressive. Women today can't walk into a store without being bombarded with shelves devoted to hair products. They can't walk down the street without being overwhelmed by the need for more jewelry. Women cannot open a magazine without being assaulted by the sense that their own closets are threadbare of anything worth wearing.

This passion for external adornment comes at a terrible cost for today's women—the sense of never looking good enough, never being pretty enough, never measuring up. Women are made to feel inferior, ugly, and unlovable. And the consequences are mounting.

It is with a sense of irony then that we recognize that the Bible leads the way against such oppression and that Peter thinks more highly of women than does the culture in which we live. Peter wants to free women from the obscene obsession of looking good.

Internal Adornment

What are Christian women to be concerned about instead?

> But let your adorning be the hidden person of the heart with the imperishable beauty of a gentle and quiet spirit, which in God's sight is very precious. (3:4)

Peter calls upon Christian wives and women to adorn themselves with the *"imperishable beauty"* located in *"the hidden person of the heart."* Literally, he asks wives to be concerned to dress "the inner man." Peter tells Christian women to pay attention to the adornment with which they are dressing the interior of their souls. "Arise, put your feet on the ground, and get dressed from the inside out." Further, he desires that they cultivate *"a gentle and quiet spirit."* By way of application, women should consider how much time it takes to prepare getting ready in the morning, then see that Peter is urging them to take time to adorn the inner person as well. Christian women ought to be known for putting on the clothing of Christ. After all, he was gentle and meek.

The motivation for women taking the time to adorn their souls is now put forward by Peter. The later half of verse 4 says that in doing so they become *"precious"* in the sight of God. In other words, when God looks upon them, he is glad to have them for his bride. Men and fathers, is this the kind of woman we are teaching our sons to look for in a wife? Is this what we ourselves appreciate most in women? Are our hearts in tune with the heart of God concerning what is considered precious?

The Principle of Submission in the Life of Sarah

Peter doesn't stop at simply giving women instruction and motivation. He goes on in this text to provide an illustration, an example, for every woman to follow.

> For this is how the holy women who hoped in God used to adorn them-
> selves, by submitting to their husbands, as Sarah obeyed Abraham, calling
> him lord. And you are her children, if you do good and do not fear anything
> that is frightening. (3:5, 6)

When Peter went looking for a woman whose life modeled good works,
he chose Sarah, the wife of Abraham. When he wanted to put forward someone with "a gentle and quiet spirit," he selected Sarah. And we can all thank
Peter for doing so. After all, Sarah wasn't a wallflower woman. Sarah wasn't
weak. She was real. And the Scriptures portray her faith and life as precious
and beautiful.

Sarah is the perfect choice. When Christian women hear preachers call
upon them to put on "a gentle and quiet spirit," the culture will bombard
their minds in an effort to convince them that God's Word is asking them to
be weak. Our culture is constantly trying to make women think that applying this principle will in the end be a setback to women everywhere. But
Peter says, "No. No. No. Look at Sarah!" Sarah was a woman who got into
her husband's face a time or two—and he needed it a time or three more.
(In some ways Sarah did have it easier than women today. Concerning this
calling to "a gentle and quiet spirit," my wife, Lisa, has reminded me that
Sarah had many servants.)

The Befuddled Laughter of Sarah

Why does Peter draw our attention to Sarah? It is because she lived out
God's principle of submission by calling Abraham, "lord." I looked back
in the Old Testament narrative to see the precise time when Sarah called
Abraham that and found that it was at the time of her laughter. This "lord
and laughter" day in her life is recorded in Genesis 18:9–14, and it is worth
reading.

> They said to him, "Where is Sarah your wife?" And he said, "She is in
> the tent." The LORD said, "I will surely return to you about this time next
> year, and Sarah your wife shall have a son." And Sarah was listening at
> the tent door behind him. Now Abraham and Sarah were old, advanced in
> years. The way of women had ceased to be with Sarah. So Sarah laughed to
> herself, saying, "After I am worn out, and my lord is old, shall I have plea-
> sure?" The LORD said to Abraham, "Why did Sarah laugh and say, 'Shall I
> indeed bear a child, now that I am old?' Is anything too hard for the LORD?"

Interestingly, Sarah's laughter betrayed her sense of disbelief—her ner-
vous, verbal wonderment at the idea that God could fulfill his promise of a
son. And God replied in effect, "Is anything impossible with God?"

The Laughter of Today's Women

The laughter of Sarah can still be heard behind the curtain of our tents today. The voices of many women who hear these words on submission are likely to exclaim, "You have got to be kidding me. That's absurd. God will keep his promises to me? He will keep me safe in this relationship?" And Peter says, "Yes. God can be trusted." Women who give themselves to this pattern of life, though it is "frightening" (v. 6), will be those whom God meets in their hour of need. Those who entrust themselves to God will find that he will keep his word to them. And what was his promised word? "You have been born again to a living hope, and you shall receive an inheritance that is imperishable, undefiled, and unfading" (see 1:3, 4). You can trust God to keep his word. That is what Peter has been saying throughout this letter. Entrust yourself to God, and God will go with you.

So whatever your situation—an unjust official, an overbearing employer, a difficult husband—Peter wants you to know that God will deliver you. He can be trusted. And not only that, he wants you to know that when you live according to this pattern of submission, when you entrust yourself to God's Word, you show yourself to be living a life modeled by Jesus and righteous Sarah. Concerning Jesus, Peter has already shown us that he walked this "entrusting" way before he was honored by God (2:23). Concerning the righteous, Peter is about to quote Psalm 34:15 (in 3:12), which promises that "the eyes of the Lord are on the righteous, and his ears are open to their prayer." Later in 4:19 Peter will say concerning the righteous, "Let those who suffer according to God's will entrust their souls to a faithful Creator while doing good." So Peter could not be any clearer. The woman living out the pattern of submission through proper adornment of the soul will herself be like Jesus and the righteous.

The Laughter of the Proverbs 31 Woman

Sarah reminds me of the Proverbs 31 woman. There verse 10 reads, "An excellent wife who can find? She is far more precious than jewels" (a connection to 1 Peter 3:3, 4). "The heart of her husband trusts in her, and he will have no lack of gain. She does him good [there is our word from 1 Peter 3:6], and not harm, all the days of her life" (vv. 11, 12). Proverbs 31:25 will go on to assert, "Strength and dignity are her clothing." Isn't that great? When Christian wives adorn themselves with gentleness and quietness, what do they get? They get strength and dignity!

Now, the dilemma for so many today is the view that *power* is the end of all things. But the Bible says that strength and dignity should be our end. And this alone allows godly women to do something spectacular. Look at the later half of Proverbs 31:25, "She laughs at the time to come." Isn't that beautiful! She laughs the laughter of entrusting faith.

So we have seen the befuddled laughter of Sarah who questioned God's ability to keep his word. We have heard the incredulous laughter of women in the modern era who disbelieve God's Word. And we have seen that Christian women gain irrepressible encouragement at the laughter of the wonderfully righteous woman in Proverbs. And what is her reward? Verses 28, 31 of Proverbs 31 read, "Her children rise up and call her blessed; her husband also, and he praises her. . . . Give her of the fruit of her hands, and let her works praise her in the gates." Men, husbands, if the call upon the Christian wife is as strong as Peter claims, then surely she deserves your praise, your devotion and adoration, your care and abiding love. Rise up! Give her the fruit of her hands. Praise her all the days of your life.

A Word to Husbands (v. 7)

Peter also has something to say to husbands. He writes briefly:

> Likewise, husbands, live with your wives in an understanding way, show-ing honor to the woman as the weaker vessel, since they are heirs with you of the grace of life, so that your prayers may not be hindered.

According to Knowledge

The husband is called upon to live with his wife "*according to knowledge*" (v. 7, KJV; ESV, "in an understanding way"). The word used here for "knowl-edge" is used throughout the Bible in reference to sexual intercourse.[2] A man knows a woman. Peter wants husbands to live out this aspect of the one-flesh relationship with intimate concern and care. In the next verse he will give the reason for his concern: in regard to her physical frame she is "the weaker vessel."

Therefore, husbands know this: your wife deserves nothing less than your most elevated and intimate care, concern, love, and honor. Is it any wonder that Christian women today are so frightened in this area of life? Too many men are only fixated on their needs and desires. Too many are not living according to knowledge. Too many are bringing into the marriage bed a view of sex that is borrowed from the world, a view that is base and unlovely. Peter provides a well-placed corrective, "showing honor."

The Husband's Twofold Motivation

Sadly, Peter needed to remind husbands that their wives are *fellow heirs* with them of the grace of life. They are equal partners and partakers of the glory that is to be revealed on the last day. As such, they should be treated with respect and dignity. After all, they are, like you, the very bride of Christ. They too have been bought with his blood. They also are the majestic ones in whom is his delight. Therefore, men, take care. Your charge is of eternal value and is priceless in the sight of God.

A second motivation for careful stewardship of your marriage is found at the end of verse 7: "*so that your prayers may not be hindered.*" Interestingly, the word translated "your" is plural. This implies that married couples will be praying together. The act of praying together is one of the most difficult things for a husband to cultivate. For some reason most of us have trouble going before the throne of grace in the presence of our wife. Yet, if we consider how great and glorious this is—namely, the two standing together in his presence—we will begin afresh in this endeavor. If a man does not honor his wife and live according to knowledge with her, his prayers will be hindered.

In the text of 1 Peter 3:1–7 we have seen *one* overriding principle—namely, submission. We have seen Peter's *twofold* plan: women, do not let your adorning be external, but let your adorning be the adorning of the hidden person of the heart. We have seen the woman's *threefold* reward: the possible salvation of her spouse, her preciousness in the sight of God, and her reward for entrusting herself to God. In addition, we have heard the call for husbands to live godly lives in the home.

Much more could be said. But wives especially, and those in difficult circumstances, can be encouraged by God's grace as seen in this text. In closing, in my personal correspondence I have the testimony of how God was active in the life of one Christian woman who entrusted herself to God in a difficult marriage. Her daughter writes:

> When my mother and dad were married she was a new believer and he had recently gone forward in a church service to receive Christ as his Savior. It became evident, however, that my dad had no interest in anything spiritual. So through the years he would drive us to church and some years attend at Christmas. My mother faithfully lived for the Lord and taught us from the Word.
>
> When I was thirteen she found out that my dad had been unfaithful. I can still remember a few days later sitting at the kitchen table as she read to me from 1 Corinthians 7:13 (in the KJV), "If the unbelieving husband wishes to remain, let him remain." That settled it for her. Theirs was not a "happy" marriage, but we were a family. Twenty-nine years later in a morning service in a small church on his 72nd birthday my dad stood at the invitation and truly accepted Jesus as his Savior! (We were all there, and Kleenex was passed up and down the row.) He was a changed man. He prayed, they had a Bible study in their home, and six years later he went

to be with the Lord he loved, joined five years later by my mother. I praise the Lord for His faithfulness and for my mother's obedience to Scripture and faithful witness through the years."[3]

Our Heavenly Father, help every man and woman, husband and wife to live in a way that pleases you. In this fallen world, where distortion of your Word and ways abound, have mercy. Where wicked acts against women are still being perpetuated, bring relief, healing, and judgment. In Jesus' name we pray, amen.

Finally, all of you, have unity of mind, sympathy, brotherly love, a tender heart, and a humble mind. Do not repay evil for evil or reviling for reviling, but on the contrary, bless, for to this you were called, that you may obtain a blessing. For

*Whoever desires to love life
and see good days,
let him keep his tongue from evil
and his lips from speaking deceit;
let him turn away from evil and do good;
let him seek peace and pursue it.
For the eyes of the Lord are on the righteous,
and his ears are open to their prayer.
But the face of the Lord is against those who do evil.*

Now who is there to harm you if you are zealous for what is good? But even if you should suffer for righteousness' sake, you will be blessed. Have no fear of them, nor be troubled, but in your hearts regard Christ the Lord as holy, always being prepared to make a defense to anyone who asks you for a reason for the hope that is in you; yet do it with gentleness and respect, having a good conscience, so that, when you are slandered, those who revile your good behavior in Christ may be put to shame. For it is better to suffer for doing good, if that should be God's will, than for doing evil.

3:8–17

12

Encouragement to Continue

1 PETER 3:8–17

IN 1965 BOB DYLAN came out with the runaway album *Highway 61 Revisited*. On it was his incendiary "Ballad of a Thin Man." Its aggressive and toxic refrain fueled a movement while at the same time it haunted an established generation.

> Because something is happening here
> But you dont know what it is
> Do you, mister jones?[1]

With those words Dylan uncovered the discomfort of his age. A shift had taken place; things were no longer what they once were. The clear lines and markers that once provided everyone with a sense of where they stood were now erased. Overnight, they were simply gone, like footprints when waves wash over them. One minute they are all there, and the next they are not. It can be a discomforting thing to feel, all of a sudden, as if you've lost your way, no longer sure of where you are or how you even got there.

On a smaller scale, something like discomfort happens to the readers of 1 Peter somewhere in the middle of chapter 3. One moment everything is clear. The structure is sound. The markers are all within view. Peter is writing about our "good deeds" in 2:11, 12, and as such he gives us a clear theme. From there he spells out *good conduct* for us, and while the nature of that conduct may have surprised us, there can be no doubt as to its content—God's new community will be known for *submission*. He formerly announced as much in 2:13. He continues with the same term in 2:18. And he shows it to us again in 3:1, 2.

But then imperceptibly, beginning with 3:8, something begins to change. A shift takes place; and by the close of 3:17 we suddenly find ourselves standing on untried ground. Our reading slows, our eyes stand fixed, and we pull up from the text searching for familiar landmarks. But unfortunately there are none in sight. The literary framework that has carried us from 2:13 is suddenly gone. Submission has receded with the tide, and in its place *suffering* is about all there is to see.

If you read the commentators, as I do, you will find that at this point in the letter, they too appear glassy-eyed and lost. "Because something is happening here but you dont know what it is, do you, mister jones?" I suppose this is what accounts for the wide discrepancies on where to break the text. Luther felt that Peter's words on submission carried through to 3:16. Some place the shift at 3:17, while others recognize it to be underway after 3:18. Some go so far as to say that a change can be seen only after 3:22. But clearly, any way that you cut it, by the time you find yourself reading about Noah and the ark in 3:20 you are forced to admit that something has happened.

For what it's worth, I chose to end this section at verse 17. In some measure that's because I see the structure like this:

• Peter's threefold *exhortation* to submission as the mark of good conduct is now complete (2:11—3:7).

• The *example* for us to follow in Christ has been given (2:21–25).

• *Encouragement* to submission in a difficult day is what is still needed (3:8–17).

The Need for Encouragement

My dad was a basketball coach for over forty years. Good coaches have an intuitive understanding of when their players need to be pushed, prodded, and encouraged. Vince Lombardi, the famed coach of the Green Bay Packers, is said to have been one of the best in knowing when to do what. Once he decided to encourage his troops at a surprising time. They had just suffered a difficult road game loss on Sunday. The team fully expected Lombardi to take it out on them during the plane ride home. But his biographer records:

> Instead of lambasting his players for their mistakes (two fumbles and a punt blocked for a safety), he let them drink two beers on the flight home, spoke spiritedly to them about how they would right themselves for the rest of the season, and later that night brought them all downtown to the

Elks Club with their families for a turkey dinner. The Old Man could be gruff, awkward, unrelenting, but now he showed another side.[2]

In like manner, Peter shows himself in this text to be an excellent coach. Having finished his demanding section on the difficult work of submission, he is keenly aware that his early readers will need encouragement. So in this text he encourages Christians to get on with the difficult work of gracious living. He knows his early readers will need cheering on if they are to battle with the world week after week. To accomplish this goal Peter finds the perfect phrase, the ideal biblical reference, and the precise words needed to stimulate the church toward godly submission.

The Encouraging Phrase: Called to Be a Blessing

Peter will claim that our ability to continue living graciously rests in a proper understanding of our calling. And our calling, he says, is to be a blessing. Peter huddles the family and introduces his encouraging phrase.

> Do not repay evil for evil or reviling for reviling, but on the contrary, *bless*, for to this you were called, that you might obtain a *blessing*.

We are called to bless. Shockingly, the uniqueness of Peter's thought in this section isn't that we are called to bless God (1:3) but rather that we are called to bless those who persecute us. We are to bless the ungodly ruler, the unjust employer, the difficult husband. He wants us to bless those who are in authority over us. A Christian community, says Peter, is a community that *blesses*.

My great-grandfather, A. E. Mitchell, was an artist. He made plaques of plaster and metal with Biblical references on them. They were beautifully done, hand-painted, and adorn the walls of many in my family. One of his most famous plaques simply says "Bless." He wanted his family to be known for blessing others. For the church, Peter's word hangs artistically upon the wall of our souls. And it does so to encourage us in our work of submission by reminding us that we have been called to a life of blessing.

Thankfully, the text goes on to show that when we live in the world in this way, our actions will be rewarded. The text says we will "obtain a blessing" (v. 9). Isn't that encouraging? When we bless, we will receive a blessing. Interestingly, that blessing will come at times from God and at other times from man. Certainly verse 9 indicates that it is God who blesses us. Take note then: without blessing others there is no guarantee that any of us can obtain the approval and smile of God. Can there be any higher motivation for us to bless than to obtain a blessing *from God*? Evidently Peter has not forgotten the day when Jesus taught his disciples about those who are *blessed* by God (Matthew 5:2–11).

But Peter also implies that there may come a time when we receive a blessing from members of the world after some come to faith in Christ. According to 2:12, on the day when Jesus returns, some will give glory to God. Imagine arriving in Heaven and hearing from those who have been won to Christ through your faithful, submissive service and "Bless you!" (see 3:1, 2). Don't be mistaken: it will be through blessing that the world will be both silenced and saved (see 2:15 for the first and 2:12; 3:1 for the second). All of this should encourage us. Be encouraged to bless. It is a matter of calling.

The Ideal Biblical Reference: Psalm 34

When Peter arrives at verse 10, he makes an appeal for encouragement from Psalm 34. This particular Psalm is the ideal reference to encourage Christians to get on with the difficult task of godly living.

> Whoever desires to love life and see good days, let him keep his tongue from evil and his lips from speaking deceit; let him turn away from evil and do good; let him seek peace and pursue it. For the eyes of the Lord are on the righteous, and his ears are open to their prayer. But the face of the Lord is against those who do evil.

When we turn to Psalm 34 we find that it comes with a heading—a historical context to mark the period in which it was written. Literally it reads:

> Of David, when he changed his behavior before Abimelech, so that he drove him out, and he went away.

This Psalm, then, was written when David was under great duress. It was the season of his life when, although anointed by Samuel as king, he was nevertheless forced into hiding from Saul. Saul had become an unjust ruler, an authority figure who actively persecuted submissive and righteous David. After David had gone to the priest, he retreated to the caves. David, the elect of God, was forced to suffer on the earth as an exile.

Yet, Psalm 34 begins:

> I will *bless* the LORD at all times; his praise shall continually be in my mouth.

What an incredible line. David, the humble follower of the Most High God, submitted himself to God's timing and continued to bless God (and

Saul) in the most difficult times and under the most unfair circumstances. Clearly this is why Peter picks this Psalm to support the point he has been making on submission, suffering, and blessing.

Twice during those sojourning years David had the opportunity to take Saul's life. On the first occasion David cut off a corner of Saul's robe when Saul had come unknowingly into the cave where David was hiding (1 Samuel 24). After Saul arose and left, David called to him from the opening of the cave, and Saul replied:

> Is this your voice, my Son David? . . . You are more righteous than I, for you have repaid me *good*, whereas I have repaid you *evil*. . . . So may the Lord reward you with good for what you have done to me this day. (1 Samuel 24:16, 17, 19)

On the second occasion (1 Samuel 26) David spared Saul's life while he slept in his own camp. He refused to be the one to undermine Saul's God-given authority, taking his spear and helmet instead. After returning to a safe distance David again called out, and Saul replied:

> "The Lord rewards every man for his righteousness and his faithfulness. . . . *Blessed be you*, my son David." (1 Samuel 26:23, 25)

This was the real-life situation of a man who gave his life to submission. What an encouragement to Peter's early readers who were troubled by the call to submit to ungodly rulers and unjust leaders. In David's obedience, Peter has found one who prefigured Christ in his sufferings. He has found one who emulates the point he has been making. And the church now has proof that God does reward the righteous. So we press on in doing good because we have seen again that God is trustworthy. Not only will God bless us, but we have hope about hearing the words "Blessed be you!" from our enemies. Be encouraged.

The Precise Words: Fear and Blessing

Fear

Two particular words run freely between Psalm 34 and 1 Peter 3. They are the words *fear* and *blessing*. The linguistic connection is not only intended by Peter but is meant to encourage his readers to continue in submission. In 1 Peter the Christian is told to have a proper fear of God (1:17; 2:17) without succumbing to an unhealthy fear of human authority (3:6, 14). Peter's concern, of course, is to show that a proper fear of God actually results in a proper respect for human authority. Interestingly, the same point was made in Psalm 34. There David uses the term at least five times (Psalm 34:4, 7, 9 [twice], 11). And the emphasis throughout is on proper fear. The one who *fears* the Lord will be delivered from his own fears. He shall be protected and have no lack.

Blessing

The second word is *blessing*. We have said much about it already. However, more might be said. This is the very word Peter chose to open his letter with as well: "Blessed be the God and Father of our Lord Jesus Christ!" Was this by accident or coincidence? I don't think so. This word, *bless*, is an especially important word for a beleaguered people needing encouragement to press on. Why else would it reappear in Peter's letter twice within the limits of this very text (3:9, 14)? Therefore, learn to take it up in practice. Bless God and others. It is the divine key that unlocks our ability to remain steadfast and joyfully submissive.

By the time Peter reaches verse 15, his early readers had, no doubt, found the encouragement they needed. All Peter needed to do now was to relay two results that arise from obedience. First, a submissive life affords many opportunities for God's people to make a defense for the hope that is in them. Look at verse 15:

> But in your hearts regard Christ the Lord as holy, always being prepared
> to make a defense to anyone who asks you for a reason for the hope that
> is in you.

One good thing that emerges from our obedience is that we will have plenty of opportunities to speak about Christ. Now, I know that many Christians point to this verse as a proof text for gospel witness and the need for apologetics. However, given the context that we have been exploring—namely, faithful submission in a hostile world—it is more likely that what Peter intends is that we will have a chance to explain why we are suffering. People will be wondering how we patiently endure the unjust decisions and treatment of those in authority over us. And when they ask, we can explain the reason for the hope that is in us. With all gentleness and respect (v. 15) we can tell others that we are looking for God to raise us up in his good time. As such, we don't expect to receive any better treatment than Jesus received.

The result of our obedience is reserved for what will occur on the last day. Verse 16 reads:

> . . . so that . . . those who revile your good behavior in Christ may be put
> to shame.

God will vindicate us on that day. So leave room for his judgment. Endure. Be encouraged. You have been called to be a blessing. The psalmist has confirmed it. And God's perfect words will enable you to do it.

Our great God and Father, blessed be your name. We choose to bless your name at all times. We thank you for the encouragement we can draw from the life of King David. Indeed, during his exilic years he nevertheless lived faithfully for you. May it be so for us too! Amen.

For Christ also suffered once for sins, the righteous for the unrighteous, that he might bring us to God, being put to death in the flesh but made alive in the spirit, in which he went and proclaimed to the spirits in prison, because they formerly did not obey, when God's patience waited in the days of Noah, while the ark was being prepared, in which a few, that is, eight persons, were brought safely through water. Baptism, which corresponds to this, now saves you, not as a removal of dirt from the body but as an appeal to God for a good conscience, through the resurrection of Jesus Christ, who has gone into heaven and is at the right hand of God, with angels, authorities, and powers having been subjected to him.

3:18–22

13

Encouragement in Christ's Victory

1 PETER 3:18-22

WHEN THE GREAT AND LEARNED Reformer Martin Luther put his thoughts on this text to paper he could only say:

> A wonderful text is this, and a more obscure passage perhaps than any other in the Testament, so that I do not know for a certainty just what Peter means. . . . I cannot understand and I cannot explain it. And there has been no one who has explained it.[1]

On verses 19, 20 a second commentator writes, "The meaning of this phrase is much disputed."[2] From a third we get, "His words were no doubt clear to those who first heard them, but they have been hard for later generations to understand."[3] A fourth commentator framed the problematic text this way: "The exegetical questions basically come down to these: Where did Christ go? When did he go? To whom did he speak? What did he say? Different answers to each of these questions can be found, resulting in a labyrinth of exegetical options, each of which has no clearly overwhelming claim to certainty, [with one] calculating 180 different exegetical combinations, in theory."[4]

Well, so much for today's working pastor getting insight from the learned divines! The complexities of the text have led me to approach this passage with three simple ground rules. First, we need to limit our reach. I have no intention of trying to settle centuries of mystifying debate. Second, we must refrain from reducing the preaching of God's Word to the mere rehearsing of the history of interpretation. After all, we need a living word from this text for our hearts. Third, we will present what *is* known in such a way that it will encourage and instruct us toward maturity in Christ. Simply put, we should want to feast on God's Word.

Detectives in Search of Meaning

How do we go about coming to grips with this tough text? For starters, there is a book that teaches us how to approach any text for better comprehension. It is the classic little volume written by Mortimer Adler and Charles Van Doren, *How to Read a Book.* In it Adler shares some tips about how to approach books generally that can help us with this text specifically. He writes:

> Think of yourself as a detective looking for clues to a book's general theme or idea, alert for anything that will make it clearer. . . . You will be surprised to find out how much time you will save, pleased to see how much more you will grasp, and relieved to discover how much easier it all can be than you supposed.[5]

We come to the text as detectives. And we begin by looking for clues. Does our paragraph have a general theme or idea? Is there something within its structure or flow of thought that lifts our understanding above its complexities? Let's take a look at its flow of thought. First, it begins with the sufferings of Christ. Verse 18 begins, "For Christ also suffered . . ." And a little later we read, Christ was "put to death in the flesh." But then notice, Peter immediately goes on to say that Jesus was "made alive in the spirit." Finally, Peter rises far above both death and resurrection in verse 22 to claim that this same Jesus has now "gone into heaven."

Jesus was put to death in the flesh but was made alive in the Spirit and has now gone up into Heaven. In the original Greek these three phrases possess a lyrical symmetry and beauty that the English hides. In fact, some writers go so far as to see a connection between them and the ancient hymn Paul made use of in his first letter to Timothy: "He was manifested in the flesh, vindicated by the Spirit . . . taken up in glory" (3:16).[6] This much has been established: Peter's main idea is about the victorious Christ, and it is captured in three ascending phrases.

Now that, believe it or not, is a very important discovery. Our text has a definite movement and flow of thought! It starts with Christ's sufferings but ends with his ascension. It opens with his willful submission to unrighteous rulers, but by the time it closes, a complete reversal has taken place. The submissive Son is, by the end, the ruling King seated at the right hand of God. And everything—all angels, authorities, and powers—are now subject to him. Our difficult text, which at first had enough complexities to make us think it was unintelligible, does seem to have a central theme after all.

In fact, the main idea is easily observable and readily seen—Jesus Christ was vindicated, and now he sits in Heaven victorious. With confidence we can now say that if this text is about anything, it must be about Christ's victory and ascendant glory. It is about his climbing supremacy and complete vindication.

More Clues from the Surrounding Context

With that much discovered, other clues will be needed to increase our understanding further. For help, we turn to another one of Adler's aids in reading for comprehension. He writes:

> Every book has a skeleton hidden between its covers. Your job as an analytical reader is to find it. A book comes to you with flesh on its bare bones and clothes over its flesh. It is all dressed up. . . . You must read the book with X-ray eyes, for it is an essential part of your apprehension of any book to grasp its structure.[7]

According to Adler the job of the reader is clear: find the *structural skeleton* hidden between the book's covers. Thus far in this study of 1 Peter, at least two structural or skeletal elements have been commented on. Each one is significant and should help us come to terms with this particular text.

A Particular Word: Subject

There is a repeated word in this section of 1 Peter. In Adler's vernacular, it is a *bare-bones* kind of word, hidden beneath all the clothing. The word is *subject*, and we find it here in the final verse of chapter 3:

> . . . [Jesus Christ] has gone up into heaven and is at the right hand of God, with angels, authorities, and powers having been *subjected* to him. (v. 22)

Clearly, this word has played a strong structural role for Peter up to this point in the letter. It appeared first in 2:13, "Be *subject* for the Lord's sake to every human institution." We saw it again in 2:18, "Servants, be *subject* to your masters." And it emerged a third time in 3:1, "Likewise, wives, be *submissive* to your own husbands."

The ironic use of it in our own text can hardly be missed. For nearly two chapters now Peter has been calling the church to the difficult work of submitting to ungodly authorities. But here the tables have been turned. All angels and authorities and powers have been *"subjected"* to Jesus. Christ has been victorious. It would appear that Peter intends in this text to refresh and encourage weary followers of Christ by showing them the final outcome. At present they were in danger of being lost in the fog, unable to see the victorious and distant shore. So it had been with the disciples of Jesus before them. It had appeared that Christ had lost the day when he suffered and died. What they needed was to see the risen and ascended Lord in all his glory. On the day after Good Friday, the full story had not yet been written. In the end, though, he would be vindicated, and they would be encouraged.

The Battle of Waterloo is one of the most famous battles in history. It occurred on the mainland of Europe on June 18, 1815. It pitted the French army, commanded by Napoleon, against the Anglo-German-Dutch forces led by the Duke of Wellington and the Prussian forces commanded by General Gebhard Blucher.

There is an interesting story about how the news about Waterloo reached England. News was carried first by a ship that sailed from Europe across the English Channel to England's southern coast. The news was then relayed from the coast by signal flags to London. When the report was received in London at Winchester Cathedral, the flags atop the cathedral began to spell out Wellington's defeat of Napoleon to the entire city: "Wellington defeated . . ." However, before the message could be completed, a good old-fashioned London fog moved in, and the rest of the message was hidden.

Based on incomplete information, the citizens of London thought Napoleon had won. That would have been a devastating defeat for England. Gloom filled the nation as the bad news quickly spread everywhere. But when the mist began to lift, the flags high up on Winchester Cathedral completed the news. The flags spelled out this triumphant message: "Wellington defeated the enemy!" The English fears had been unfounded. Joy immediately replaced the gloom. All over England people danced in the streets, rejoicing at this great victory over one of the most dangerous enemies the nation had ever faced.[8] In like manner, the resurrection and ascension of Christ gives us a certain hope that our own victory has been secured.

A Special Relationship: Jesus

Another structural element in 1 Peter that helps us make sense of the passage before us comes by way of relationship. Our passage marks the third time Peter has specifically and intentionally mentioned Jesus to his readers in a major way. Jesus is imbedded in the structure of the letter.

The first time he did so with special focus, he appealed to Jesus' costly death in order to motivate his readers to holiness. Peter said they had been ransomed from the futile ways inherited from your forefathers, not with perishable things such as silver or gold, but with the precious blood of Christ, like that of a lamb without blemish or spot. (1:18, 19)

In that part of the letter Peter was trying to impress upon his readers the importance of being holy. If Christ sacrificed everything for them, then surely, when they consider the cost of their salvation, they will be spurred on to holiness.

The second time we saw a relationship established between the readers and Jesus came in 2:21–25. There Peter wrote:

Christ also suffered for you, leaving you an example, so that you might follow in his steps. (v. 21)

Again, note the aspect of Christ's work that Peter is emphasizing. He appeals to his death. In fact, the entire language comes right out of Isaiah's classic Suffering Servant passage.

However, when Peter introduces Jesus for the third time (3:18–22), he appeals in large part to his resurrection and ascension.9 Jesus was "made alive in the spirit" (3:18), and this same Jesus has now "gone into heaven" (3:22).

How different this present emphasis is from the previous occurrences— and how important for us to make note of it. What do these insights on relationship teach us? They inform us that 3:18–22 are not concerned with the arduous task of submission, suffering, and death. Rather, this passage is about the final victory that is gained through them. Therefore, we can say that Peter wants to encourage us by lifting our hearts and minds to Heaven where Christ is already seated. In other words, "Take heart, you too shall one day win!"

Adler's admonition to look for structural clues has paid off. With the word *subject* we have seen that our text is about the great reversal that has taken place through Christ's victory. With the *relationship* of Jesus to Peter's audience we have seen that our text is about elevating our senses to our final destination. It appears that Peter has mastered the art of structure for this entire section of his letter:

- 2:11, 12: *Exhortation* to honorable conduct and good deeds
- 2:13, 18; 3:1: Three *examples* on submission: what good deeds look like
- 2:21–25: One person to *emulate*
- 3:8–17, 18–22: Two messages of *encouragement* (one from the victory of David, the other from the vindication of Jesus)

An Encouraging Conclusion to Our Pursuit

With that our detective work is done. We have heard from God on this text. We know what the text says: Jesus was victorious and completely vindicated. We know what the text is intended to do: encourage the reader with the certain and fixed truth that in the end those who are in Christ will win. In one sense I hope you go away from this chapter as if the great missionary Adoniram Judson's last words on this earth were your own:

> I go with the gladness
> of a boy bounding away from school,
> I feel so strong in Christ.[10]

We may never know exactly where Jesus went or when he went there. And we may not be any closer to understanding to whom he preached or what he said. We may not have satisfied our longing to know how baptism saves. But in the end that is okay.[11] The main thrust of the text is this: the faithful will get through the waters of this life. Indeed, like the eight who survived God's judgment back then, so, too, everyone in Christ shall be left standing on the last day.

Remember, minds more learned than ours have been stumped on the details surrounding these things for centuries. But as a friend of mine is fond of saying, "At least we know what we know!" Be encouraged with Christ's victory. Don't easily forfeit the gains you have made in your detective work on this text. It is God's living word to you. Sojourners and faithful ones who are living out life during these difficult days in tough out-of-the-way places, know this: you shall be vindicated for staying the course. Christ was vindicated, and you shall be too. Christ saw a great reversal of fortunes, and so shall you. Christ submitted himself to the Father, and now all things are subject to him.

Our Heavenly Father, gladly do we submit ourselves to the teaching of this text. Our hearts are filled with fresh wind for the journey. To know that Jesus was vindicated shall sustain us. To be reminded that all things are now subject to him encourages us. To consider that our own vindication awaits—what joy rises with us. To him be the glory, amen.

Since therefore Christ suffered in the flesh, arm your-selves with the same way of thinking, for whoever has suffered in the flesh has ceased from sin, so as to live for the rest of the time in the flesh no longer for human passions but for the will of God. For the time that is past suffices for doing what the Gentiles want to do, living in sensuality, passions, drunkenness, orgies, drinking parties, and lawless idolatry. With respect to this they are surprised when you do not join them in the same flood of debauchery, and they malign you; but they will give account to him who is ready to judge the living and the dead. For this is why the gospel was preached even to those who are dead, that though judged in the flesh the way people are, they might live in the spirit the way God does.

4:1–6

14

Embrace Your Calling
to Suffer in the World

1 PETER 4:1–6

SOME WOULD SAY that those who suffer most often suffer first from blind
naiveté. Albert Schweitzer thought as much about Jesus, claiming that his
cruel death on the cross was nothing more than the unfortunate result of
naiveté. According to Schweitzer, Jesus, the misguided visionary, never saw
the sufferings of the cross coming until it was too late:

> There is silence all around. The Baptist appears, and cries: "Repent, for
> the Kingdom of Heaven is at hand." Soon after that comes Jesus, and in
> the knowledge that He is the coming Son of Man lays hold of the wheel
> of the world to set it moving on that last revolution which is to bring all
> ordinary history to a close. It refuses to turn, and He throws Himself upon
> it. Then it does turn, and crushes Him. Instead of bringing in the eschato-
> logical conditions, He has destroyed them. The wheel rolls onward, and
> the mangled body of the one immeasurably great Man, who was strong
> enough to think of Himself as the spiritual ruler of mankind and to bend
> history to His purpose, is hanging upon it still. That is His victory and
> His reign.[1]

Peter, however, has been telling a different story. Jesus was vindicated
in death. He rose victorious in the spirit and now reigns eternally as the
Ascended Son at God's right hand. According to Peter, naiveté is set aside.
Jesus' suffering was not the unfortunate result of an impoverished itinerant's
idealistic fervor. Instead, his suffering was by divine initiative. Persecution
was the predetermined pathway for God's Son.

All the Gospel writers concur. The Jesus they present to the world is well aware that his unique work required suffering and service. Jesus believed it on the strength of the Hebrew Scriptures. And Jesus embraced it every step along the way of his earthly ministry. Repeatedly he told his disciples, "The Son of Man must suffer many things and be rejected by the elders and the chief priests and the scribes and be killed" (Mark 8:31; 9:31; 10:33). When Jesus stood before the Sanhedrin on the night of his betrayal, never once did he defend himself in hopes of avoiding the cross. In fact, when he did speak, he intentionally said what he knew would seal his fate (Mark 14:62).

Clearly, Jesus fully embraced his calling to suffer out of his desire to save us. As Peter argued in 3:18:

> Christ suffered once for sins, the righteous for the unrighteous, that he might bring us to God.

Now, with the opening phrase of our text, Peter again returns to Christ's sufferings, but this time with different intentions—he feels no need to further *encourage* us with Christ's triumphant vindication. He accomplished that in 3:18–22. Rather, he writes about Christ's suffering in this particular text to call us to *embrace* it as well. In 4:1 he says:

> Since therefore Christ suffered in the flesh, arm yourselves with the same way of thinking.

"Arm yourselves." Emulate Jesus. It is as if Peter has finally come to the place in the letter where he rises up to unashamedly proclaim, "Followers of Jesus, be prepared to embrace not only submission but suffering as an aspect of your calling! Get yourselves ready for suffering!"[2] The question of course is, how? How do we go about getting ready? What does a person need to know and do to prepare to embrace his or her calling in the world?

Fortunately for us, the structure of our text unfolds the answers to these questions with clarity and simplicity. If we intend to embrace this aspect of our calling, there are three gospel commitments we must be willing to make (4:1–3), two personal costs we should be ready to endure (4:4), and one encouraging reminder that a final accounting awaits all humanity (4:5, 6).

Three Gospel Commitments (vv. 1–3)

Become a Person of Resolve

How do we go about embracing our calling? First, by becoming persons of resolve. Take another look at verse 1. Peter writes, "arm yourselves with the same way of thinking." Notice, to embrace our calling in Christ initially requires the attention of our mind. We begin by *thinking* clearly. And for that we need to develop the mental disposition of Jesus.

Today, in the West at least, it is the church that suffers from a naiveté of the mind. It is difficult for Christians here to understand and embrace God's intentions in suffering. We prefer a gospel in which God gives us healthy bodies and bulging wallets. And we too readily think that material blessing is the entitled reward of the gospel. To put it bluntly, the democratized West expects Jesus, comfort, ease, and acceptance from the world.

Yet, in actual fact the life of Christ challenges all of this. Jesus resolved to live as a stranger in the world. He expected hardship. And when he read his own Hebrew Scriptures, they taught him that union with God culminates in mixed reviews here on earth.

In one sense, when Peter calls us to arm ourselves with "the *same way* of thinking," he is saying, "Beloved, grow up! Get the mind of Christ. Become a person of resolve. Be prepared. If you have been united with him by faith, you will need to identify with him in suffering."

The first gospel commitment Peter calls us to embrace closes with a phrase that needs some explanation. Look at the latter part of 4:1:

> Arm yourselves with the same way of thinking, for whoever has suffered
> in the flesh has ceased from sin.

The natural question this phrase raises is, what does it mean to "cease from sin"? Is the suffering person a sinless person? We ask this even though we know that such a wooden interpretation of the verse goes against all of Scripture and life experience. So what is Peter saying?

He is simply affirming that those who suffer for the gospel do, by their very willingness, demonstrate that they are done with sin. To put it as clearly as I can, everyone who suffers for Jesus first resolved, somewhere along the line, to cease from sinning. After all, the suffering they experience is a result of leaving off with sin. Thus, Peter says, "For whoever has suffered in the flesh has ceased from sin."

Live for the Will of God

In the next verse Peter puts forward the second and third gospel commitments that followers of Christ make as they embrace their calling in the world:

> . . . so as to live for the rest of the time in the flesh no longer for human
> passions but for the will of God. (v. 2)

The two commitments we are to make are spelled out by way of contrast:

• ". . . no longer for human passions
• but for the will of God."

Since the following verse is going to highlight the kinds of behavior the Christian leaves behind, let's look first at what we are to be about. Peter says we are to live "for the will of God." What does Peter mean by the phrase "the will of God"? And how are we to start living for his will? Fortunately we have already seen in 1 Peter the kinds of godly pursuits he wants us to pursue. And in fact, in each of those places he contrasted the things that God wills for us with the same phase he uses here—"human passions."

So by looking back in the letter for "*passions*" we will run headlong into what Peter means when he wants us to make a commitment to "*the will of God*." Look at 1 Peter 1:14, 15: "As obedient children, do not be conformed to the *passions* of your former ignorance, but as he who called you is holy, you also be holy in all your conduct."

If the will of God is found by way of contrast to human passions, then we can know for sure that we prepare our minds for suffering by giving ourselves wholly over to the pursuit of holiness. God wants us to make a commitment to holiness, to sanctification, to putting on the new man. This is how we prepare to embrace our calling.

Another text in 1 Peter that teaches us what the will of God is can be found in 2:11, 12:

> Beloved, I urge you as sojourners and exiles to abstain from the passions of the flesh, which wage war against your soul. Keep your conduct among the Gentiles honorable, so that when they speak against you as evildoers, they may see your good deeds and glorify God on the day of visitation.

We do the will of God when we "keep [our] conduct . . . honorable" by doing "good deeds." This, of course, will require us to be countercultural. We will always be swimming against the current of today's moral tide. We are to be known for doing good. And as we have seen in this letter, the supreme mark of goodness is our submission to difficult and ungodly people in authority.

Leave Human Passions Behind

I love the opening phrase in verse 3: "The time that is past suffices." It is as if Peter barks out, "Enough already. Put sin in your rearview mirror." And then he goes on to list the kinds of things that Christians are to put away. Look at how the verse finishes: "living in sensuality, passions, drunkenness, orgies, drinking parties, and lawless idolatry."

Be done. Enough. The past is sufficient. Life as an ongoing fraternity party is a major problem in the church today. If we are not there in person, we are all too often present through what we watch on television, see in the theaters, or watch on the Internet. For men, sensuality is an especially prevalent issue. Sex is the elephant in the room. Peter says that in this matter it is time to clean house. Until we wake up and tackle this area head-on and out in the open, we will only continue debilitating a generation and will keep them from being grounded in their faith, unable to fly unencumbered toward Heaven's delights.

The Danish philosopher Søren Kierkegaard tells a parable of the disastrous effects of not putting to death the desires of the flesh, of failing to leave a way of life behind. One springtime a duck was flying with his friends northward across Europe. During the flight he came down in a barnyard where there were tame ducks. He enjoyed some of their corn. He stayed for an hour, and then for a day. One week passed, and before he knew it a month had gone by. He loved the good food, so he stayed all summer long.

One autumn day, when the same wild ducks were winging their way southward again, they passed overhead, and the duck on the ground heard their cries. He was filled with a strange thrill and joy, and he desired to fly with them once again. With a great flapping of wings he rose in the air to rejoin his old comrades in flight.

But he found that his good fare had made him so soft and heavy that he could rise no higher than the eaves of the barn. He dropped back again into the barnyard and said to himself, "Oh well, my life is safe here, and the food is good." Every spring and autumn when he heard the wild ducks honking, his eyes would gleam for a moment, and he would begin flapping his wings. But finally the day came when the wild ducks flew overhead uttering their cries, but he paid no attention. In fact, he failed to hear them at all.

What an apt parable for the church in our time. As Christians, too many of us have feasted for too long on the pleasant fare this world has to offer. We too easily forget that the time past was enough. We forget that we are still far from home—we haven't arrived at our destination yet. Sadly, many go on day by day unfazed by the gospel thought that as we feed on the husks of this world we demonstrate that we think too little of the delights that await us in Heaven. Peter says to us, "Enough. Rise up, O men of God. Have done with lesser things."[3]

C. S. Lewis struggled with his own inability to grasp the gravity of his sin in light of God's clear teaching on the subject. He wrote:

Indeed the only way in which I can make real to myself what theology teaches about the heinousness of sin is to remember that every sin is the distortion of an energy breathed into us—an energy which, if not thus distorted, would have blossomed into one of those holy acts whereof "God did it" and "I did it" are both true descriptions. We poison the wine as He decants it into us; murder a melody He would play with us as the instrument. We caricature the self-portrait He would paint. Hence all sin, whatever else it is, is sacrilege.[4]

God has plans for your body, and they are plans for purity and for good. Don't cheapen life. Don't settle for distortion. Don't poison the wine God decants into you. Be done with "sensuality, passions, drunkenness, orgies, drinking parties, and lawless idolatry."

Make three gospel commitments that tell the world you are prepared to embrace this aspect of your calling in Christ.

- Become a person of resolve.
- Live for the will of God.
- Leave human passions behind.

Two Personal Costs (v. 4)

But as you do, know this: your newfound commitments come with a twofold cost. Consider verse 4:

> With respect to this they are surprised when you do not join them in the same flood of debauchery, and they malign you.

They Are Surprised at You

First, your friends and family will be surprised. You will be misunderstood. Remember, there are no categories for them to understand why you no longer grab all that you can in this life without regard for the next. "Come on," they will say. "What happened? Loosen up. Look out for your own happiness. Pursue some pleasure. Live a little!"

Malcolm Muggeridge articulates well how your new life in Christ will affect your relationship with former friends who are still pursuing only happiness and pleasure:

> Anyone who suggests that the pursuit of happiness—that disastrous phrase written almost by chance into the American Declaration of Independence, and usually signifying in practice the pursuit of pleasure as expressed in the contemporary cult of eroticism—runs directly contrary to the Christian way of life as conveyed in the New Testament is sure to be condemned as a life-hater.[5]

Over time their surprise will turn to ridicule.

They Malign You

Surprise evokes misunderstanding, and misunderstanding evokes a sense of being judged. And when the world feels that it has been judged by your way of life, those who are of it will condemn you as "a life-hater." They will malign you. Take a look again at the progression of behavior embedded in verse 4. "Surprised" gives way to the word "malign":

> With respect to this they are surprised when you do not join them in the same flood of debauchery, and they malign you.

R. C. Sproul, in his book *The Holiness of God*, tells of a time when Billy Graham was invited to play golf with President Ford and two PGA tour professionals. He writes:

> After the round of golf was finished, one of the other pros came up to the golfer and asked, "Hey, what was it like playing with the President and with Billy Graham?" The pro unleashed a torrent of cursing, and in a disgusted manner said, "I don't need Billy Graham stuffing religion down my throat." With that he turned on his heel and stormed off, heading for the practice tee. His friend followed. . . . His friend said nothing. He sat on the bench and watched. After a few minutes the anger of the pro was spent. He settled down. His friend said quietly, "Was Billy a little rough on you out there?" The pro heaved an embarrassed sigh and said, "No, he didn't even mention religion. I just had a bad round."

About the incident Sproul concludes:

> Astonishing. . . . Billy Graham is so identified with religion, so associated with the things of God, that his very presence is enough to smother the wicked man who flees when no man pursues. Luther was right, the pagan does tremble at the rustling of a leaf. He feels the hound of heaven breathing down his neck. He feels crowded by holiness even if it is only made present by an imperfect, partially sanctified human vessel.[6]

One Final Accounting (vv. 5, 6)

Peter closes our text with a reminder on the final judgment. It is meant as an encouragement to his readers. In verse 5 it appears that he is especially thinking of the judgment that awaits those unbelievers who choose to malign us.

> But they will give account to him who is ready to judge the living and the dead.

In one sense you and I do not need to judge the world. It already stands condemned. Entrust yourself to God, and wait for Jesus to set all things straight. The closing verse in our text is tricky to get hold of at first glance. It is especially hard to see how it functions as an encouraging word to Christians who await the final judgment.

> For this is why the gospel was preached even to those who are dead, that though judged in the flesh the way people are, they might live in the spirit the way God does. (v. 6)

What we need to remember is that the early church had many questions about their family members and friends who had died after coming to faith in Christ. They wondered what happened to believers after death. There was a concern for those who had already undergone the penalty of death. Peter wants to reassure his readers here with news that although believers are "judged in the flesh the way all people are," they need not worry about their future with God. He says they will still "live in the spirit the way God does."

We have nothing to fear in Christ! We have nothing to fear in embracing suffering in this life. Peter wants us to grasp this as part of our calling. To do so, we need to make three gospel commitments: become a person of resolve, live for the will of God, and leave human passions behind. We must be ready to incur two costs: the surprise of those with whom we once lived in sin and the inevitable maligning and slander that is sure to follow. In all this, though, Peter reassures us with one encouraging reminder: there will be a final accounting for everyone. As those who are in Christ, we shall live on in the Spirit forever.

Dear Lord, help us to truly embrace our calling to suffer in Christ. May we receive it with open arms. We know that everything we bear for you in this life will be nothing to compare with the glory we will share in with you in Heaven. Make us people of resolve. In your precious name we pray, amen.

The end of all things is at hand; therefore be self-controlled and sober-minded for the sake of your prayers. Above all, keep loving one another earnestly, since love covers a multitude of sins. Show hospitality to one another without grumbling. As each has received a gift, use it to serve one another, as good stewards of God's varied grace: whoever speaks, as one who speaks oracles of God; whoever serves, as one who serves by the strength that God supplies—in order that in everything God may be glorified through Jesus Christ. To him belong glory and dominion forever and ever. Amen.

4:7–11

15

Embrace Your Calling
in the Church

1 PETER 4:7–11

IN *PIGEON FEATHERS* John Updike presents a jarring description of what awaits us at the end of life. The view presented is rooted in Naturalism's belief that human history is accidental by nature and therefore without purpose, direction, or any ultimate goal. What will the end of life bring? He writes:

> Without warning, David was visited by an exact vision of death: a long hole in the ground, no wider than your body, down which you were drawn while the white faces recede. You try to reach them but your arms are pinned. Shovels pour dirt in your face. There you will be forever, in an upright position, blind and silent, and in time no one will remember you, and you will never be called. As strata of rock shift, your fingers elongate, and your teeth are distended sideways in a great underground grimace indistinguishable from a strip of chalk. And the earth tumbles on, and the sun expires, an un-altering darkness reigns where once there were stars.[1]

The Reign of Christ

Naturalism's harsh vision of the end is one of death, despair, and, in the words of Updike, "an un-altering darkness." The message that Peter has presented to his readers about the end is equally jarring, but everlastingly hopeful. This first-century fisherman-turned-preacher had come to believe that all of history is purposeful and that everything is heading toward God's intended goal. To state Peter's worldview simply, all of history is heading not toward an unaltering reign of darkness but toward the eternal reign of the risen and ascended Christ. The last verse of our text summarizes this well:

> . . . in order that in everything God may be glorified through Jesus Christ. To him belong glory and dominion forever and ever. Amen. (v. 11)

This is the Christian's majestic conception of what awaits the end of the earth: the glory of God, the dominion of the Lord Jesus Christ, and his reign forever and ever.

The Resurrection of Christ

We might ask, what caused this first-century fisherman to hold such an idea? What event in the life of this ancient, hard-working Palestinian caused him to lay hold of such a radical view? Peter's understanding of the end is rooted in what he witnessed in the death, resurrection, and ascension of Jesus of Nazareth. As he has already written, he holds to the reign of Christ "who has gone into heaven and is at the right hand of God, with angels, authorities, and powers having been subjected to him" (3:22). The Christian view, then, of an eternal reign rises from the ground of Jesus' resurrection. In Christ we see God's plan for both humanity and history. In him God has seen fit to give the world a king. And to him all authority has been given.

The Return of Christ

Peter not only holds to the *reign* of Christ but to his *return* as well! As we have seen, Peter holds that every nonbeliever "will give an account to him who is ready to judge the living and the dead" (4:5). And further, those who die in faith will "live in the spirit the way God does" (4:6). Therefore, Peter's preaching proclaims that due to Christ's resurrection, we shall be raised from the dead upon his return and shall reign with him forevermore.

This uniquely Christian conception of history is the most elevating and yet jarring teaching ever. It announces that in Christ, the end has come. He has already been crowned king. God's plans are now fixed. In fact, if Peter is correct, then the only thing keeping Jesus from returning today is God's gracious design to bring more men and women under the authority of Christ through repentance and faith.

By the time Peter comes to our text, then, his mind is full with these overwhelming truths. The end, or goal, of history has been made manifest to the world in Christ. Jesus reigns, on the basis of his resurrection, and will return in judgment to establish his dominion forever. No wonder Peter opens verse 7 with these words:

The end of all things is at hand.

According to the Bible, the end has already begun. It came with Christ's resurrection and will be fully consummated upon his return. Therefore, we are in the final stages of history. We are living in the last days. As Peter argued in his opening chapter, "He was foreknown before the foundation of the world but was made manifest in the last times for your sake" (1: 20). Indeed, the end is at hand.

Therefore, we should all be wrestling with what to do with the time we have left. We do not have the luxury of procrastinating our life away. Yet, many do this very thing. They keep looking to the future as the time when they will truly get moving. After school or marriage or after they buy their first home, they will begin investing in God's kingdom work and way of life. People while their life away. They draw back from relationships and productive work. They forget the Biblical truth that the end is at hand. How tragic. Thankfully, in this text Peter will point us in another direction. He will instruct us in the task of living well in these last days.

Peter presents four things to embrace, four marks to govern our lives in light of the end. Since the end is at hand we should:
- Verse 7: "Be . . . sober-minded."
- Verse 8: Show sincere "love."
- Verse 9: "Show hospitality."
- Verses 10, 11: "Serve one another."

What a contrast to the kinds of activities mentioned in the verses that precede this text. There Peter listed the kinds of things people give themselves to when they live as if God has no king in the world, no moral authority to uphold, and nothing beyond this life except the reign of eternal darkness.

- They give themselves to "drunkenness" (v. 3) rather than "sober-minded[ness]" (v. 7).
- They give themselves to "lawless" activity (v. 3) rather than sincere "love" (v. 8).
- They give themselves to "orgies" (v. 3) rather than "show[ing] hospitality" (v. 9).
- They give themselves to "malign[ing]" (v. 4) rather than "serving one another" (vv. 10, 11).

For the one who takes hold of Peter's teaching, the old has passed away because the end has come. Every man or woman who is following Jesus as King now has four new things to which to give themselves. The supremacy of Christ has altered what we do with our lives.

Self-Controlled and Sober-Minded (v. 7)

It has been said, "The difference between the Christian and the non-Christian is that the former controls his temperament, while the latter is controlled by it."[2] Peter might agree. Verse 7 reads, "Therefore be self-controlled and sober-minded." To put Peter's sentiment as clearly as possible, be clear-headed. Don't live like those in the world who are constantly looking for an escape. They look forward to the evening and the weekend when they can "turn off their minds." They desire an escape from reality. Yet, for the working Christian there is nothing further from the truth. We are to be different. We are to be clear-thinking men and women. We are to have our mental faculties with us at all times.

The value of this, according to Peter, is "for the sake of your prayers" (4:7). Our clear-headedness is for the sake of prayer. This is a convicting truth. Let me put it this way: the mark of a Christian at the end of the age is a person on his or her knees in prayer. Could it be that the strength of our private prayer life is an indication of our progress in self-control and sober-mindedness? If so, then most of us need to get busy before we are asked to meet and speak with Jesus face to face. We are to watch and pray. As Jesus said to his disciples, including Peter, in the garden, "The time is at hand." It is no accident that Peter uses the language of the garden. He connects the end of time to Christ's suffering, the subject of this entire section. The hour *is* evil. The devil *is* active. And our minds must get ready for the onslaught of the last days.

Sincere Love (v. 8)

Peter moves on: "Above all, keep loving one another earnestly, since love covers a multitude of sins." There are two observations to make about this verse. The first is the attending word "*earnestly*." Our love is to be real, sincere, genuine. Second, consider the words "*one another*." Love is by nature relational. This is something Peter has been driving at throughout. The words "one another" appear in the next verse and in verse 10 as well. What Peter wants in the last days is a *one another* kind of life.

In fact, when you consider that he is writing to a host of churches spread across the terrain of modern-day Turkey (see 1:1), it appears that Peter wants this truth to permeate entire geographic regions. Churches are called upon to love one another. In a multi-site church like the one that I serve in, this mark of mature end-times living becomes especially applicable. May all our neighborhood congregations feel as if we are one, for that is what we are; therefore, let us give ourselves to loving one another.

May we be known for our love. For indeed, as Peter goes on to say, "love covers a multitude of sins." There is certainly some debate in regard to what this phrase means. After all, the blood of Christ alone is what covers sins. What Peter is saying here might be understood by way of analogy. Love takes the oxygen out of sin the way a blanket chokes the air from one caught on fire. Similarly, as long as oxygen is present, forest fires rage. But if we could take the air away, the blaze would settle down, and great tracts of land would be saved. May we love in this way. May nothing evil be allowed to breathe for long. May we keep short accounts. The last days demand our sincere love.

Showing Hospitality (v. 9)

Peter is prepared to move on again. We are to be "self-controlled and sober-minded." We are to be known for a sincere "love." And, third, we are to be hospitable. Look at verse 9: "Show hospitality to one another without grumbling." Perhaps you are aware of the strategic importance of this for those traveling in the first century. Generally speaking there weren't hotels or motels in which to stay. A traveler would head to the town center in hopes of being invited home by a kind and gracious resident.

I was taught a great lesson in hospitality during the first six months of 1996. Lisa and I were living in London with our kids. We were in a foreign land, without friends or family, but the members of St Helen's Bishopsgate Church welcomed us as if we were some of their own. People knew that we were there for only a short time; nevertheless, they opened their homes and their lives to us. That experience had a profound impact upon us. In the world's great cities, people are constantly coming and going, and the temptation for us who live in them is to pull back from relationships. After all, the thought of investing in people who will be here for only a short time is draining.

No wonder Peter says, "show hospitality . . . *without grumbling*." While sitting in a neighborhood Bible study one day, my mind began to wander during a time of corporate prayer. *Who in this room will even be here next year? This one is moving. That couple is being transferred. This one is graduating.* Indeed, the entire room of people was going to be like a salad tossed to the four corners of the world within a few months. Then suddenly as I prayed I thought, *Give yourself to them!* Who knows, men and women might one day say, "It was while I was in one of the world's great cities, where I was for just a short time, that I first experienced Christian hospitality—authentic community that has shaped me ever since."

Jon Dennis, a dear friend and fellow-laborer in the gospel, when envisioning Holy Trinity Church at its outset wrote:

> The key with hospitality is to begin. It doesn't matter if you live in an
> apartment, a dorm, or a house. Once a week opening our home, baking a

few cookies, saying "hello" in the elevator, checking up on an older neighbor, and borrowing sugar from the next apartment. Yes, the city is a place of isolation. But it may be that through our doors all kinds will come, one who is hungry, an intellectual questioning, a colleague in crisis, a student from a far-off land. It may be that God's new people from the nations will sit around our table. It may be that having shared a meal, and having tasted of Christ, their own table will be open for the gospel in a country we would never reach.

Hospitality is not something we do overly pragmatically. We do not practice hospitality "to get conversions." We practice hospitality because it is right. We practice hospitality because we are God's people. We share God's goodness through our home because God has shown his goodness to us. His grace overflows the threshold of our homes.

Sometimes hospitality can be costly. Perhaps we don't think our home or apartment is large enough to host others. To meet this fear, consider a humorous but true story from the life of E. Stanley Jones. He was preaching an evangelistic service among the mountaineers of Kentucky, who were very poor people at that time. The meetings were held in a schoolhouse. Dr. Jones recounts his experience with their hospitality this way:

At the schoolhouse I was invited to stay with a man and his wife, and when I arrived I saw there was one bed. The husband said, "You take the far side." Then he got in, and then his wife. . . . I turned my face to the wall as they dressed, and they stepped out while I dressed. That was real hospitality! I have slept in palaces, but the hospitality of that one-bed-home is the most memorable and the most appreciated.[3]

May our lives be filled with the grace of hospitality. In this respect may the table grace of Brigid, who ran a medieval monastery, be ours in full:

I should like a great lake of finest ale
For the King of Kings.
I should like a table of choicest food
For the family of heaven.
Let the ale be made from the fruits of faith,
And the food be forgiving love.

I should welcome the poor to my feast,
For they are God's children.
I should welcome the sick to my feast,
For they are God's joy.

Let the poor sit with Jesus at the highest place,
And the sick dance with the angels.

God bless the poor,
God bless the sick,
And bless our human race.
God bless our food,
God bless our drink,
All homes, O God, embrace.[4]

Peter is so eminently practical! "The end of all things is at hand. Therefore, be sober-minded. Be known for your earnest and sincere love. Show hospitality."

Serving One Another (vv. 10, 11a)

Peter now turns to the fourth thing we ought to give ourselves to in light of the end:

> As each has received a gift, use it to serve one another, as good stewards of God's varied grace: whoever speaks, as one who speaks oracles of God; whoever serves, as one who serves by the strength that God supplies—in order that in everything God may be glorified through Jesus Christ. To him belong glory and dominion forever and ever. Amen.

Notice: he doesn't create a master list of spiritual gifts. He doesn't spell everything out in detail. Instead, he groups his directive to serving one another under two great headings.

Speaking

Those who serve the church by speaking and teaching are to speak as one who speaks the very "oracles of God." As one of my mentors in ministry, Kent Hughes, states:

> There are times when I am preaching that I have especially sensed the plea-sure of God. I usually become aware of it through the unnatural silence. The ever-present coughing ceases, and the pews stop creaking, bringing an almost physical quiet to the sanctuary—through which my words sail like arrows. I experience a heightened eloquence, so that the cadence and volume of my voice intensify the truth I am preaching. There is nothing quite like it—the Holy Spirit filling one's sails, the sense of his pleasure, and the awareness that something is happening among one's hearers. The

experience is, of course, not unique, for thousands of preachers have similar experiences, even greater ones.[5]

Those of us who preach and teach are to be mindful that at the end of the day, what we are engaged in is entirely beyond us. We are not fit for it. But by God's grace and out of concern for his body, our very words become his, for his Spirit is the one speaking.

Serving

For the second grouping Peter makes use of a first-century household word—*servants*. These were the men and women who gave themselves to the running of the home. They worked long and hard and ensured that the environment was conducive to healthy family life. And according to Peter, as with those who speak, they do so with "the strength that God supplies."

As Peter prepares to close this section, he is reminded of the ultimate goal of all things. He is thinking again of the end of all things. He closes in verse 11 where this section began: ". . . in order that in everything God may be glorified through Jesus Christ. To him belong glory and dominion forever and ever. Amen."

What a contrast Peter has put forward in these short verses. Since the end is at hand, we are to give ourselves to self-control and sober-mindedness. We are to be known for our sincere love. We are to show hospitality. And we are to be caught up in the power of the Holy Spirit in service to one another. These are the marks of Christian living for any who have given themselves to Jesus Christ.

The world can offer nothing better in its place. Abandon the teaching of Peter and you are left with Nevil Shute's 1957 thriller on the end of the world titled *On the Beach*. The novel unfolds the catastrophic results of accidental nuclear war and chronicles the ending of the world as we know it. The cover copy reads:

> In the Northern Hemisphere, the end had come suddenly, disastrously. . . .
> In the Southern Hemisphere, the end would come slowly, as radiation drifted in the wind. There would be time to prepare, time to seek solace in religion, or alcohol, or frenzied sex, or in the thing that one had always wanted to do. To drive a fast, expensive car. To buy some splendid object with one's life savings. To consume the best bottles of wine from the cellar of one's club.
>
> In the end, when the sickness could not be stopped, the government would issue cyanide pills to those who waited, hoping they would not have to use them, knowing they would.[6]

I won't ever forget reading the book for the first time. It was haunting. I vividly remember wrestling with the idea of the world ending. My mind raced with questions. What would I do if I learned that all of human history was drifting toward an inevitable ending? What would you do? How does one live when the end, the very end, is said to be at hand? What would you do with the time you had left? Peter has already given God's answer.

Dear Father, Son, and Holy Spirit, help us to do all things for your glory: be it self-control or sincere love, showing hospitality, serving or speaking. For indeed, your glory and dominion extend to eternity. Amen.

Beloved, do not be surprised at the fiery trial when it comes upon you to test you, as though something strange were happening to you. But rejoice insofar as you share Christ's sufferings, that you may also rejoice and be glad when his glory is revealed. If you are insulted for the name of Christ, you are blessed, because the Spirit of glory and of God rests upon you. But let none of you suffer as a murderer or a thief or an evildoer or as a meddler. Yet if anyone suffers as a Christian, let him not be ashamed, but let him glorify God in that name. For it is time for judgment to begin at the household of God; and if it begins with us, what will be the outcome for those who do not obey the gospel of God? And "If the righteous is scarcely saved, what will become of the ungodly and the sinner?" Therefore let those who suffer according to God's will entrust their souls to a faithful Creator while doing good.

4:12–19

16

Glory, Suffering, and Judgment

1 PETER 4:12–19

JUDAS GOT UP from the table quickly and prepared to leave. After closing the door upon his Lord, he made his way into the night. The hard stones on the streets received his heavy feet reluctantly. What he was thinking about we do not know; what he did we do. He made his way to religious leaders and sold out Jesus for thirty pieces of silver. Judas couldn't stomach the idea that the promised Messiah's glory would be attended by rejection and suffering.

Jesus, however, walked a different path. That very night he made it his special point to connect the hour of suffering with the coming of his glory. The climactic hour of the one provided him with the glory of the other. On the night of his betrayal he lifted his eyes up to Heaven and said, "Father, the hour has come, glorify your Son" (John 17:1). You see, somehow Jesus knew that the eternal glory of the Christ could be established only by suffering on the cross. Jesus was not surprised by this. He did not think it strange. So when the hour came for him to embrace it as his own, he was not ashamed.

Glory and Suffering (vv. 12–16a)

Peter would make the same connection, later. It would appear from the text that sometime after Jesus' resurrection and before the ascension Peter would learn his lesson. For when he arrives at the climactic moment in his letter, he too connects the coming of glory with the hour of suffering. The surprise in Peter's case though is this: the connection is made for the Christian, the follower of Jesus Christ. While Peter's doxology is emphatically Christ-centered, his exhortation is decidedly for the Christian. Concerning the centrality of Christ he writes in 4:11:

> . . . that in everything God may be glorified through Jesus Christ. To him belong glory and dominion forever and ever. Amen.

Then we see him applying suffering with glory to Christians:

> Do not be surprised. . . . But rejoice insofar as you share Christ's sufferings, that you may also rejoice and be glad when his *glory* is revealed. (vv. 12, 13)

> . . . as though something strange were happening to you. . . . If you are *insulted* for the name of Christ, you are blessed, because the Spirit of *glory* and of God rests upon you. (vv. 12, 14)

> If anyone *suffers* as a Christian, let him not be ashamed, but let him *glorify* God in that name. (v. 16)

This lesson is one that George Matheson, born in Glasgow, Scotland, in March 1842, put before us in elevated language. At birth Matheson's eyesight was poor. By age eighteen he had nearly lost it completely. Robbed of physical sight, he nevertheless recognized spiritual truths with penetrating clarity and insight. Take the role of suffering in the life of a believer, for example. It never caught him by surprise. He never thought suffering for his Christian faith strange. And when, according to God's will, he was asked to enter into it, he was never ashamed. He writes:

> There is a time coming in which your glory shall consist in the very thing which now constitutes your pain. Nothing could be more sad to Jacob than the ground on which he was lying, a stone for his pillow. It was the hour of his poverty. It was the season of his night. It was the seeming absence of his God. The Lord was in the place and he knew it not. Awakened from his sleep he found that the day of his trial was the dawn of his triumph.
>
> Ask the great ones of the past what has been the spot of their prosperity and they will say, "It was the cold ground on which I was lying." Ask Abraham; he will point to the sacrifice on Mount Moriah. Ask Joseph; he will direct you to this dungeon. Ask Moses; he will date his fortune from his danger in the Nile. Ask Ruth; she will bid you build her monument in the field of her toil. Ask David; he will tell you that his songs came in the night. Ask Job; he will remind you that God answered him out of the whirlwind. Ask Peter; he will extol his submersion in the sea. Ask John;

he will give the path to Patmos. Ask Paul; he will attribute his inspiration to the light which struck him blind.

Ask one more!—the Son of God. Ask Him whence has come His rule over the world; he will answer, "From the cold ground on which I was lying—the Gethsemane ground—I received my scepter there." Thou too, my soul, shall be garlanded by Gethsemane. The cup thou fain wouldst pass from thee will be thy coronet in the world by and by.

Isn't that spectacular? Ask the saints, any of them, and the response is the same. They never thought glory could be gained in any other way. Peter makes the point powerfully in verses 12, 13:

Beloved, do not be surprised at the fiery trial when it comes upon you to test you, as though something strange were happening to you. But rejoice insofar as you share Christ's sufferings, that you may also rejoice and be glad when his glory is revealed.

In these verses we see more than the connection between suffering and glory. Peter has three things to teach us about how to live our lives in the light of this knowledge.
- Verse 12: "Do not be surprised."
- Verse 12: Do not think it "strange."
- Verse 16: Do not be "ashamed."

Don't Be Surprised

Peter wants his early readers ready for what he calls "the fiery trial." What is this "fiery trial"? We know that Peter has used this term *trials* before. He opened his letter with it (1:6), and it appears that he could be returning to his starting point. The "various trials" in that chapter could be "the fiery trial" in this one. We noticed then that the general use of the word *trials* in the New Testament matches the internal evidence of Peter's letter with incredible precision. We mentioned then a few things about what Peter means by "trials."[1]

- He means there will be seasons in life when they will lack provision, power, position, protection, and a sense of permanence.
- He means that at times they will become recipients of verbal or physical persecutions that arise on account of the Word (2:12, 18–20, 23; 3:16; 4:1–6 [esp. v. 4], 12–16).
- He means to include the pain experienced by those who have loved ones whose bodies appear to be wasting away before their very eyes.
- He means the dark moments in life when we are asked to fend off the prowling attacks of Satan.

These trying difficulties may be temporal, occasional, and spasmodic (after all, 1:6 reads, "if necessary"). But in the end, for anyone who takes up with Jesus, Peter wants his readers to know that *trials* of some size and stripe are inevitable. We must go through the waters of woe if we are to arrive at our rightful inheritance; wandering and woe are the earthly lot of any who desire to enter into an eternal rest characterized by joy.

George Whitefield, the great evangelist of the Second Great Awakening, knew early that trials would become part and parcel of his experience. Therefore, when they came, and they did in abundance, he was prepared! Upon graduating from Oxford he wrote:

> I am now about to take Orders and my degree, and go into the world. What will become of me I know not. All I can say is I look for perpetual conflicts and struggles in that life and hope for no other peace, but only a cross, while on this side of eternity.[2]

What a good lesson for us to learn. We should expect difficulty. The fact that we don't only indicates how little we have learned of Christianity's true center. As our text will soon say, our sufferings come precisely *because we share in Christ's sufferings* (4:13). We should not be surprised, because we are with him.

Don't Think It Strange

The second "do not" in our text, by way of implication, is also found in verse 12: "Do not be surprised . . . as though something strange were happening to you." Suffering for the gospel is never to be thought of as strange. Many of us struggle with God during times of trials. We wonder where he has gone. We wonder if he still cares for us. We feel abandoned in our hour of need. Peter tackles this feeling with an incredibly comforting truth. Take a look at verse 14:

> If you are insulted for the name of Christ, you are blessed, because the Spirit of glory and of God rests upon you.

This is a timely word for us when we feel as if God's presence has left us. In actual fact, Peter claims that these seasons of difficulty are unique times when God's smile and approval are especially on us. The exalted truth in our time of testing is that God's glory is resting on us. He is covering us. He is guarding and guiding us. Be encouraged.

When reading verse 14 in our text, it would appear that Peter had committed Jesus' Sermon on the Mount to memory. For at that time, long before Peter would repeat it here, Jesus taught him:

> Blessed are you when others revile you and persecute you and utter all
> kinds of evil against you falsely on my account. Rejoice and be glad, for
> your reward is great in heaven, for so they persecuted the prophets who
> were before you. (Matthew 5:11, 12)

Two present-day examples ought to encourage us in this direction. The
death of Richard Wurmbrand in 2001 didn't attract a huge amount of attention, but back in the late 1960s and early 1970s, he was one of the better-
known dissidents in the Communist bloc. And unusually for a dissident at
that time, he was no intellectual but an evangelical minister in Romania
who was suffering for the gospel. He described the joy he possessed amid
persecution. He had been confined in solitary confinement. He had been
beaten and bore many scars. Yet he said that in it all there were times when
he was overcome with joy. In fact, he writes that he would actually stand up
in his weakened state and dance around his cell as if the angels were dancing with him. That is Beatitude-like rejoicing! That is the proper stance that
every Christian ought to have in the day of trial. We ought to be known for
dancing—as if all the host of Heaven are joining in.

Helen Roseveare was a Christian British medical doctor who served
more than twenty years in Zaire, Africa. In 1964 a revolution overwhelmed
the country. She and her coworkers were thrown into five and a half months
of unbelievable brutality and torture. For a moment she thought that God
had forsaken her, but then she was overwhelmed with a sense of his presence, and she records that it was as if God was saying to her:

> Twenty years ago you asked me for the privilege of being a missionary, the
> privilege of being identified with me. This is it. Don't you want it? This is
> what it means: These are not your sufferings, they are mine. All I ask of
> you is the loan of your body.

What an encouraging model for us all. Are you feeling forsaken? Peter
wants you to see that just behind the curtain, if you could pull back the veil,
is the presence of the God of glory and his Spirit resting upon you. So don't
be surprised, don't think it strange, and don't be ashamed.

Don't Be Ashamed

> Yet if anyone suffers as a Christian, let him not be ashamed, but let him
> glorify God in that name. (v. 16)

Suffering for the gospel where I live most often comes in the form of
verbal disdain. And when it happens, I am reminded of Peter's words, "let
him not be ashamed." Don't be afraid to identify with Jesus. Don't be afraid

to walk the road that Jesus trod. It would be a pity to meet him and not be able to say that we are suffering with him. The poet Ella Wheeler Wilcox penned these words:

> All those who journey, soon or late,
> Must pass within the garden's gate;
> Must kneel alone in darkness there,
> And battle with some fierce despair.
> God pity those who cannot say,
> "Not mine but thine," who only pray,
> "Let this cup pass," and cannot see
> The purpose in Gethsemane.[3]

Suffering and God's Judgment[4]

When Peter's text continues, we find what is perhaps the most surprising and intriguing moment in his entire letter:

> For it is time for judgment to begin with the household of God; and if it begins with us, what will be the outcome for those who do not obey the gospel of God? And "If the righteous is scarcely saved, what will become of the ungodly and the sinner?" (vv. 17, 18)

Embrace Your Suffering—It Is for Your Own Good

Notice: he is making a connection between our suffering and God's *judgment*. This is most surprising! To this point in the letter our suffering has always been at the hands of ungodly people. Yet here it appears to be the result of our own ungodly behavior. At times, then, our suffering comes to us because we deserve it. So God disciplines us. The text says that he begins with us. God will prune us like a tree that he desires to bear fruit. C. H. Spurgeon spun a story about the results of pruning.

> The apricot tree at 2828 Hill Heights Park was trimmed back so much I wondered if the branches and leaves would ever grow back, let alone the leaves. We ended up that next year having apricots coming out of our ears; Mom made apricot pie, jam, and we had it as fresh fruit, and there was still an abundance left for the birds.[5]

Take heart. If God is putting you through a season of suffering in connection with his concern for his glory, he has a desire for abundance in your future. And if you are still discouraged by this, take note of what Peter says about unbelievers and sinners. If sitting under God's judgment is difficult for us now, what will it be like for them when he stands before them at his return? Trust God. He knows what is best for you. Like Spurgeon, learn to say, "I have learned to kiss the wave that strikes me against the Rock of Ages."

Entrust Your Souls

Peter now comes to the one verse in his letter that most succinctly summarizes his theme.

> Therefore let those who suffer according to God's will entrust their souls to a faithful Creator while doing good. (v. 19)

Whether we are suffering for doing good or for sins we have committed, we are called upon to entrust our souls to God. George Matheson learned to entrust his soul to God on many occasions. June 6, 1882, was the day of his sister's marriage, and his family was staying overnight in Glasgow, Scotland. Something happened to forty-year-old George as he sat alone there in the darkness of his blindness, something known only to himself, something that caused him severe mental suffering. He never confided to anyone what the problem was, and yet his heart cried out to Christ. As his heart moaned, words welled up in his mind, words of comfort. "I had the impression of having it dictated to me by some inward voice rather than of working it out myself," he said later.

> O Joy that seekest me through pain,
> I cannot close my heart to thee;
> I trace the rainbow through the rain,
> And feel the promise is not vain,
> That morn shall tearless be.[6]

While Doing Good

The Christian must not be surprised when hardship comes. We must not think it strange. Certainly we must not be ashamed. In contrast, we are to entrust ourselves to God's eternal plan. And finally, we read that we are to do good to others all along the way (v. 19).

Unfortunately, Christians have not always been known for doing good. Simone Weil, the luminary and mystic, observed this omission in our behavior and called for a renewed flow of good works when she wrote:

> Never since the dawn of history, except for a certain period of the Roman Empire, has Christ been so absent as today. The separation of religion

from the rest of social life, which seems natural even to the majority of Christians nowadays, would have been judged monstrous by antiquity. The sap of Christianity should be made to flow everywhere in the life of society.[7]

Christianity must flow to the ends of the earth, and our good works ought to provide strength for its movement. May God help us connect the dots of his glory, our suffering, and his judgment that is already making its way into the earth.

Our Heavenly Father, through this brief letter of Peter's you have reminded us to embrace our calling in Christ. You have given us examples of what this looks like before a watching world. Your encouragements have been placed before us. And now may we entrust our souls to you while doing good. In Jesus' name, amen.

So I exhort the elders among you, as a fellow elder and a witness of the sufferings of Christ, as well as a partaker in the glory that is going to be revealed: shepherd the flock of God that is among you, exercising oversight, not under compulsion, but willingly, as God would have you; not for shameful gain, but eagerly; not domineering over those in your charge, but being examples to the flock. And when the chief Shepherd appears, you will receive the unfading crown of glory. Likewise, you who are younger, be subject to the elders. Clothe yourselves, all of you, with humility toward one another, for "God opposes the proud but gives grace to the humble."

5:1–5

17

An Exhortation to Elders

1 PETER 5:1–5

EARLY IN PETER'S LETTER he used the intriguing metaphor of taste. At the time, he was likening the Christian's need for spiritual growth to the physical realm: "Like newborn infants, long for the pure spiritual milk, that by it you may grow up to salvation—if indeed you have tasted that the Lord is good" (2:2, 3). Peter is not the only one to express belief in the gospel in terms of taste. Flannery O'Connor did that as well. In her short story "The Lame Shall Enter First," O'Connor presents a riveting picture of a young man, recently converted, and now forced to defend his newfound hope to an unbelieving skeptic. The result is a poignant look at Christian belief through the symbol of taste.

> "What's that you're reading?" Sheppard asked, sitting down.
>
> "The Holy Bible," Johnson said. . . .
>
> Sheppard shook his head. "You don't believe it. You're too intelligent."
>
> "I ain't too intelligent," the boy muttered. "You don't know nothing about me. Even if I didn't believe it, it would still be true."
>
> "You don't believe it!" Sheppard said. His face was taut.
>
> "I believe it!" Johnson said breathlessly. "I'll show you I believe it!" He opened the book in his lap and tore out a page of it and thrust it into his mouth. His jaws worked furiously and the paper crackled as he chewed it.
>
> "Stop this," Sheppard said in a dry, burnt-out voice. "Stop it."
>
> The boy raised the Bible and tore out a page with his teeth and began grinding it in his mouth, his eyes burning. . . . Johnson swallowed what was in his mouth. His eyes widened as if a vision of splendor were opening up before him. "I've eaten it!" he breathed. "I've eaten it like Ezekiel and it was honey to my mouth!"[1]

O'Connor's affecting literary exchange came to my mind after coming to terms with our text. You see, for the longest time 1 Peter 5:1–5 puzzled me. I couldn't understand why Peter's letter continued on after chapter 4. *After all,* I thought, *with 4:19 acting as an elevated summary for the entire letter, what more needs to be said?*

The verses immediately following—those addressed to elders—appeared disjointed and unnecessary. They looked disconnected to the previous passage. So in my study I kept asking, how is 5:1–5 the logical extension of "judgment . . . begin[ning] at the household of God" (4:17)?

Then at last the fog lifted. To my surprise the answer rests with the metaphor of *taste.* Let me explain. It appears that Peter had been chewing long and hard on God's Word as he wrote the closing verses of chapter 4. In fact, he had been eating the pages of Ezekiel, and they tasted like honey to his mouth. After all, it was Ezekiel, long before Peter, who first connected instructions to elders with judgment that begins at the household of God.

In the ninth chapter of Ezekiel, a season of God's judgment is pronounced upon God's people. To be precise, the claim is made that God's judgment will begin at his own house. In the middle of Ezekiel 9:6 we read, "And begin at my sanctuary." The fascinating bit, and that which helps 1 Peter 5 fall into place, is what Ezekiel says next. The last part of 9:6 reads: "So they began with the elders who were before the house." For Ezekiel, elders bear the initial implications of God's judgment. In all likelihood, then, Peter was chewing on Ezekiel as he finished chapter 4. It is because of this that more needed to be said. Thus he opens chapter 5 by putting some of the same language and ideas into play. First Peter 4:17 and 5:1 even use the same sequence:

For it is time for judgment to begin at the household of God. . . .

So I exhort the elders among you.

Can't you envision Peter feasting on all that the prophet Ezekiel had to say on judgment? Tasting, in full, this prophetic truth, he now goes on to consider the impact it has upon first-century church elders. In fact, it is with the strength of grammar that Peter grounds the connection between 4:17 and what is to follow. Chapter 5 opens with the word "So"—or literally "therefore." This shows us beyond a shadow of a doubt that Peter fully intends for us to connect 5:1–5 with what came before. To put it as clearly as possible, his exhortation to elders is made in light of what he has just said on judgment. Peter was savoring Ezekiel's food and was pondering, "What will elders today need to know if they are going to exercise faithful leadership during this end-time of refining judgment? After all, they are the ones who need immediate direction concerning all that I have just written."

What he ended up writing came in the form of an exhortation. Verse 1 of chapter 5 begins, "So I *exhort* the elders among you." In one sense, Peter's instructions to them were made with a great sense of collegiality. Certainly he is about to preach to them, but he preaches to himself as well, for he writes "as a fellow elder." In identifying with them, he extends himself into the weighty work that needs to be done in light of God's judgment.

Beyond this, the text tells us that Peter wrote with all the solemnity of one who was "a witness of the sufferings of Christ, as well as a partaker in the glory that is going to be revealed." Thus, his directions are not to be taken lightly. Here is a man who has meditated long and hard on the relationship between shepherding God's people and suffering, between the glory yet to be revealed and the judgment under which we live now. His exhortation can be outlined like this:

- Verses 1, 2a: the elders' role
- Verses 2b, 3: the elders' readiness
- Verse 4: the elders' reward
- Verse 5: everybody else's responsibility

The Elders' Role (vv. 1, 2a)

Peter calls upon the elders of these varied congregations to "shepherd the flock of God that is among you." From his vantage point, as long as the church remains far from home, and as long as she continues to exist in the fragility of refining exile, she will need faithful shepherds. And the role of the elders is that of a shepherd.

To Shepherd the Flock of God

And so we ask, what does it mean to "shepherd the flock of God"? This is a beneficial question for all of us. Those who are elders need to know. Those who aspire to be elders must know. And just as importantly, congregants who over the course of their lifetime nominate and elect elders need to understand what kind of leaders they should choose. Sometimes it is helpful to learn by way of contrast. And interestingly it is through Ezekiel, whom Peter has evidently been meditating upon, that we are given the contrasting picture of what elders *shouldn't* look like.

Elders Must Not Lack Character

Ezekiel described the elders of his day as abysmal shepherds. In a vision he bored a hole into the house of God and saw men committing "vile abominations" (8:9). While there, the angelic guide said to him:

Son of man, have you seen what the elders of the house of Israel are doing in the dark, each in his room of pictures? For they say, "The LORD does not see us, the LORD has forsaken the land." (8:12)

Elders Must Not Misunderstand Their Calling

Later God said to Ezekiel:

Son of man, prophesy against the shepherds of Israel. . . . Ah, shepherds of Israel who have been feeding yourselves! Should not shepherds feed the sheep? You eat the fat, you clothe yourselves with the wool, you slaughter the fat ones, but you do not feed the sheep. The weak you have not strengthened, the sick you have not healed, the injured you have not bound up, the strayed you have not brought back, the lost you have not sought, and with force and harshness you have ruled them. (Ezekiel 34:1–4)

Elders who faithfully shepherd God's people will be different from the elders of Ezekiel's day. They will be men of godly character. They will be in the dark what they profess to be in the light. They will not be selfish. They will seek out the weak. They will visit the sick and bind up the spiritually injured. They will be concerned to bring back any who stray from the faith. They will seek out the lost. They will rule with gentleness and grace.

Elders Must Emulate the Chief Shepherd

And yet the list, even to the one who is faithful, appears overwhelming. Who can be all these things for God's people? For this reason God told Ezekiel:

I myself will search for my sheep and will seek them out. As a shepherd seeks out his flock when he is among his sheep that have been scattered, so will I seek out my sheep. . . . And I will feed them on the mountains. . . . And I will set up over them one shepherd, my servant David, and he shall feed them: he shall feed them and be their shepherd. (Ezekiel 34:11–13, 23)

Jesus is God's shepherd. By verse 4 in our text Peter will say as much by referring to him as "the chief Shepherd." Let us all remember this great fact: Jesus alone fulfills the Word of God, given through Ezekiel's charge, to gather God's flock on the mountains and feed them. It was this one, Jesus of Nazareth, who not only fed 5,000 people on the mountainside but fed them God's Word.

We can only imagine the richness that this term *shepherd* had for Peter. Do you remember Peter's early confidence? He felt qualified to lead, he was gifted to lead, but when it counted most, he denied Christ three times.

After the resurrection, Jesus asked him three times if he loved him, and Peter responded, "Yes, Lord, you know that I love you" (John 21:15–17). Interestingly, each time Jesus spoke, he wooed Peter with the imagery of a shepherd and his flock. He said to him, "Feed my lambs. . . . Tend my sheep. . . . Feed my sheep."

Take great encouragement from this—on the day Peter didn't feel able to lead, God restored him, called him, and made him fit for the office. And he will equip men for the same office today. God will continue to raise up qualified men to shepherd his flock. And like Peter, these men will express their love for Christ by extending themselves in love to God's people.

We have been exploring the elders' role and what it means to shepherd the flock of God. This much we can say: an elder must be a model of Christian maturity through godly character. He must protect the flock through selfless service. He must feed the flock by expounding God's Word. He must express his love for Christ by his love for God's people. In short, Peter summarizes his directive with two words in the middle of verse 2: elders fulfill their role as shepherds of God's flock by "exercising oversight."[2]

The Elders' Readiness (vv. 2b, 3)

Given the exalted nature of the work, is it any wonder that Peter goes on to talk of the elders' readiness? Just as we looked at the role of elders by way of contrast, so when it comes to the elders' *readiness*, Peter explains what that means by the same method. He employs three negatives ("not") followed by three affirmations ("but") in the space of two verses.

- Shepherd the flock of God that is among you, exercising oversight
- *not* under compulsion, *but* willingly, as God would have you;
- *not* for shameful gain, *but* eagerly;
- *not* domineering over those in your charge, *but* being examples to the flock.

Three pitfalls impair elders' readiness—duty, greed, and a misuse of power.

Not under Compulsion, but Willingly

The church is not helped when her leaders' readiness falls into the pit of begrudging service. Men who serve only from a sense of duty will not have the requisite love necessary for God's people to flourish. C. S. Lewis put the distinction between love and duty this way:

> A perfect man would never act from a sense of duty; he'd always want the right thing more than the wrong one. Duty is only a substitute for love (of God and other people) like a crutch which is a substitute for a leg. Most

of us need the crutch at times; but of course it is idiotic to use the crutch when our own legs (our own loves, tastes, habits, etc) can do the journey on their own.[3]

Biblical elders need to do the right thing, even when they don't feel like it, but elders who are governed merely by duty and not love are falling short of serving God as he would have them. In this regard, we need to throw away the crutches and walk willingly on our own two feet. We must grow in a genuine love for God's people, especially those whom we find unlovely.

Not for Shameful Gain, but Eagerly

Today, as in Peter's day, far too many teachers and preachers of God's Word are in it for the money. In the end those who exercise leadership in the church for financial gain pervert the truth and peddle God's free gift of true grace. There is not a more fitting example of this than the contrast between the trustworthiness of Elisha and the greed of his servant Gehazi (Numbers 5).

The New Testament also warns us of the ungodly link between one's teaching and one's love for money.

• In 1 Timothy, Paul writes that an elder must not be "a lover of money" (3:3).

• In 2 Timothy we learn that false teachers are "lovers of money" (3:2).

• In Titus we see that an overseer must not be "greedy for gain" (1:7).

• From the ministry example of Paul we learn that true gospel service "covet[s] no one's silver or gold or apparel" (Acts 20:33).

Elders must be eager to teach but not eager for cash. In fact, they ought to readily store up provisions for kingdom use. There is a great moment in Josephus's *Antiquities* when the Jews are joining with Antiochus. In doing so they were said to be "making abundant provision for his entire army and they readily joined his forces."[4] Peter is concerned that elders not join gospel work to make abundant provision for themselves. After all, even in the days of Josephus, the virtuous ones were those who *readily* (the word "readily" in the works of Josephus is the same one Peter uses, which is translated "eagerly") joined the work *and* made all the necessary provisions for its success.

Not Domineering, but as Examples

The third pitfall of leadership is the misuse of power. The axiom that "absolute power corrupts absolutely" (Lord Acton) has long stood the test of time. We see it in politics. We see it in business. But according to Peter, we should never see it in church.

Those men who exercise the office of elder must always remember that the misuse of their power only impairs the church. Instead elders ought to go beyond the call of duty in proving themselves as examples to the flock. We are to emulate Jesus, who came to serve and not to be served (see Mark 10:45). Humility and sacrificial service are the hallmarks of godly leadership.

The Elders' Reward (v. 4)

To say that elders are not to be motivated by duty, avarice, and power does not mean that a proper incentive does not exist. Peter writes in verse 4:

> And when the chief Shepherd appears, you will receive the unfading crown of glory.

Elders do labor for a reward—one that will be given to them on the day of Christ's return. The prize of "the unfading crown of glory" comes in the next life, not this one.

One of the hallmarks of the apostles' teaching on eschatology (the end times) is how they utilize it to motivate present behavior. At times they speak of Christ's appearing to motivate the daily attitudes and actions of God's people. Second Peter 3:11–16 is a great example of this. Note particularly verse 11:

> Since all these things are thus to be dissolved, what sort of people ought you to be in lives of holiness and godliness.

At other times, as in the text before us, they make use of the appearance of Christ as incentive for the present-day action of God's pastors and shepherds.

The reward will certainly be worth the labor—a crown of glory. Therefore, elders everywhere, stay at the work of guarding and guiding God's family. At times this will mean continuing to work under great duress and hardship. As the hymn-writer Samuel Stone wrote:

> Though with a scornful wonder
> Men see her [the church] sore oppressed,
> By schisms rent asunder,
> By heresies distressed:
> Yet saints their watch are keeping,
> Their cry goes up, "How long?"
> And soon the night of weeping
> Shall be the morn of song.[5]

Run the race with patience. The day is fast approaching when you shall dwell on high with the Chief Shepherd. And when he comes, he will bring his reward with him.

Everyone Else's Responsibility (v. 5)

Having directed his comments to the elders, having spoken of their role, their readiness, and their reward, Peter now turns his attention to everyone else. In light of God's present-day discipline, all his children are to know how to conduct themselves. Peter writes in verse 5:

> Likewise, you who are younger, be subject to the elders. Clothe yourselves, all of you, with humility toward one another, for "God opposes the proud but gives grace to the humble."

Humility and submission were the consistent marks of Jesus' character. If any young man had the right to put himself above his elders, it was Jesus of Nazareth. Yet the Bible is clear—he resisted taking the reins of leadership before God's appointed time came. Rather, he was quite content to simply "increase in wisdom and in stature and in favor with God and man" (Luke 2:52). As it was for the Son of God, so it is for every one of us. We are to be known for submission and humility.

In an effort to ground his teaching on the Bible, Peter appeals to the voice of Solomon in Proverbs 3:34. The significance of this particular citation would not have been lost on Peter's first readers. On the whole, Solomon's book of Proverbs, while coming from the hand of David's son, was in fact a reiteration of his elderly father's teaching. Only three verses separate the quotation Peter chooses here from the moment when Solomon made this very point in his own book:

> When I was a son with my father, tender, the only one in the sight of my mother, he taught me and said to me, "Let your heart hold fast my words." (Proverbs 4:3, 4a)

As it was in David's family, so it is to be in the family of God. The younger are responsible to clothe themselves in the garments of humility— eager to listen to those who are laboring for their salvation in Christ.

Peter has set before us a feast. In this day when God's judgment is beginning, let us drink deeply and eat well. Like Flannery O'Connor's character, may we say, "I've eaten it like Ezekiel and it was honey to my mouth!" Elders have an important role to fill until Christ returns. They must make themselves ready. To remain in the work they must look for their reward in the right place and at the right time. And all of us must walk together through this wilderness world in humility and with grace.

Our Heavenly Father, we close out our reading on these verses by praying for those in your church who hold office as elders. Protect them in their labors. Encourage them in their struggles. Help them lead your church well and willingly. Grant humility to us all in order that your family on earth might reflect in greater glory the ways that you are already at work in Heaven. We pray this for your glory and our own good. Amen.

Humble yourselves, therefore, under the mighty hand of God so that at the proper time he may exalt you, casting all your anxieties on him, because he cares for you. Be sober-minded; be watchful. Your adversary the devil prowls around like a roaring lion, seeking someone to devour. Resist him, firm in your faith, knowing that the same kinds of suffering are being experienced by your brotherhood throughout the world. And after you have suffered a little while, the God of all grace, who has called you to his eternal glory in Christ, will himself restore, confirm, strengthen, and establish you. To him be the dominion forever and ever. Amen. By Silvanus, a faithful brother as I regard him, I have written briefly to you, exhorting and declaring that this is the true grace of God. Stand firm in it. She who is at Babylon, who is likewise chosen, sends you greetings, and so does Mark, my son. Greet one another with the kiss of love. Peace to all of you who are in Christ.

5:6-14

18

True Grace and
Eternal Glory

1 PETER 5:6–14

THE EARLY APOCRYPHAL MANUSCRIPT known as The Acts of Peter was the first to purport that the apostle's death came by inverted crucifixion. By the close of the second century Tertullian held the same view, and, in agreement, Origen is recorded as saying, "Peter was crucified at Rome with his head downwards, as he had desired to suffer."1 Later Saint Jerome set his own seal of approval on this view, and eventually Michelangelo painted it into stone in a chapel at the Vatican. Tradition is fixed—Peter was martyred by inverted crucifixion. If this is true, than we can say that Peter's long hoped for exaltation—his entrance into eternal glory—came after one brief and final season of human humiliation. In the end, for the Apostle Peter, Heaven's inheritance (1:4) was gained only after being crucified head downward upon the earth.

The Divine Logic of True Grace

Ironically, according to Christian faith, the way up always comes by going down (5:10). It is this inversion in attaining glory and honor that has been Peter's theme throughout. The Christian's future inheritance and exaltation—our eternal share in the glory of Christ—will be awarded to us on the day of his appearing (1:13; 2:12; 4:13; 5:1, 4, 10). But that promised day only comes *after* this brief season of present-day sufferings. Suffering always precedes subsequent glories. It was so for God's Son (1:11). It will be so for us as well.

Peter's Letter from Beginning to End

Clearly, this bringing together of two seemingly incompatible truths—our status in Christ *and* our sufferings on earth—was how Peter's letter began. He opened with these two ideas standing side by side: "To those who are *elect exiles . . .*" (1:1). And in the body of the letter these incompatible ideas were continually joined to one another. In 1:3–6 we saw that an eternal "inheritance" is linked to "various trials." In 2:11, 12 we found that we can be both God's chosen people and "sojourners" at the same time. And just in case Peter's early readers had trouble grasping this truth, he went so far as to argue that Jesus Christ was the supreme example of this teaching (2:21–25). Later he put forward King David, the anointed one who suffered, as an encouragement for his readers to press on (3:9–17). And finally, in 3:18–22 he grounded the irony of his divine logic in the demonstration of Christ's ultimate vindication as proof for our future hope and present calling (cf. 4:19).

Is it any wonder, then, that this union of present-day sufferings and subsequent glories is how Peter should choose to end his letter? The divine principle of true grace is this: our future inheritance arrives by way of present sufferings. Exaltation follows humiliation. Eternal glory comes after earthly sufferings. The bookends of this last paragraph (before the benediction and final greetings) in Peter's letter press home the point with indelible clarity. Take a look:

• 5:6: "Humble yourselves therefore . . . so that at the proper time he may exalt you."

• 5:10: "And after you have suffered a little while, the God of all grace, who has called you to his eternal glory in Christ, will himself restore, confirm, strengthen, and establish you."

This is the apostolic principle of *true grace* at work. This life is anything but "your best life now." Glory comes by way of the ground. The attainment of Heaven will be by way of an excruciating journey. We will receive Heaven's gains by carrying our cross in the here and now. In Peter's case, he chose to model the Christian's *true grace* for us in the manner of his own death.

This counterintuitive gospel logic is desperately needed in the church today, and nowhere more especially than in the church in the West. It is a lesson that every affluent generation must come to grips with early on in life. We must get this lesson straight, no matter how old we are. For only then will we be able to get on with the task Peter calls us to—living hopeful, productive, and submissive lives for Christ.

Divine Commands and Encouragement (vv. 6–9)

What will it take to carry out the difficult directives of true grace? Peter knows. Take a look at the symmetry with which he closes his letter. He gives the church two couplets, both stated in the form of a command; and taken together, they appear daunting. Fulfilling each one will demand discipline, hardship, and suffering, but, and here is where Peter shines, each difficult command is followed by and finishes with a divine word of encouragement.

Humble Yourselves/God Cares for You (vv. 6, 7)

The first couplet is found in verses 6, 7.

> Humble yourselves, therefore, under the mighty hand of God so that at the proper time he may exalt you, casting all your anxieties on him, because he cares for you.

Christians are commanded to humble themselves "under the mighty hand of God." This is tough stuff. Everything within us seems to rise up and resist such a thought. We are taught that glory comes to those who aggressively make their way in the world. In fact, we are taught at an early age that if we don't get tough with people, we won't learn how to navigate relationships in this world. Vance Havner, a preacher of the twentieth century, put our fears this way: "When I started out, the devil said, 'You mean well, but if you try to stay humble and childlike these days you'll be run over by the steamroller.'"[2]

Believe me, Peter knows that steamrollers *will* come, figuratively speaking. He is aware that meeting the demands of true grace will not be easy. So he follows on the heels of the command with words meant to encourage us to keep from running in the opposite direction. Verse 7b reads:

> . . . casting all your anxieties on him, because he cares for you.

In seasons of self-conscious humiliation it is good to know that God cares for us. Yes, anxiety and grief are present. But remember, God is near too. Peter encourages us to pour out our hearts before God in the light of the knowledge of his concern. George MacDonald, the great nineteenth-century writer, had a mother who put this very idea into practice. Her written prayer, dated May 29, 1820, reads:

> We come dear Jesus to thy Throne
> To open all our grief;
> Now send thy promised mercy down,
> And grant us quick relief.
>
> Though Satan rage and flesh rebel,
> And unbelief arise,

> We'll wait around his footstool still,
> For Jesus hears our cries.[3]

We cast our anxieties upon one who hears our cries. That is Peter's word of encouragement for a people called to a life marked by humility.

Be Sober-Minded and Watchful and Resist (vv. 8, 9)

The second set of commands comes in triplet form. Take a look at the opening words of verses 8, 9:

> Be sober-minded; be watchful. . . . Resist him.

These commands are embedded in Peter's rich personal history. On the night that Jesus was betrayed and arrested, Peter had gone with him into the Garden of Gethsemane to pray. On that fateful night, with all the world hanging in the balance, Peter slept. His mind wasn't ready for battle. His body wasn't prepared to be watchful. And as a result, he was ill-equipped to resist temptation when it came to him.

In the words of Jesus' tender rebuke, Peter first heard the commands he now passes along to us: "Simon, are you asleep? Could you not watch one hour? Watch and pray that you may not enter into temptation. The spirit indeed is willing, but the flesh is weak" (Mark 14:37, 38). Desiring better for us than he was able to achieve for himself, Peter calls upon the night of his failure to commend sober-mindedness, watchfulness, and spiritual resistance.

Why are these three things so hard for us to fulfill? Peter tells us:

> Your adversary the devil prowls around like a roaring lion, seeking someone to devour. (v. 8)

The enemy is at work. Strikingly, Peter likens the devil to a lion on the prowl. He chooses the image that the Bible regularly uses to refer to the Anointed One.[4] Satan is the great, powerful, but cheap imitation of Jesus, the true Lion of the tribe of Judah. The counterfeit is put forward in all his strength.

In C. S. Lewis's *The Last Battle,* an Ape named Shift begins to take all earthly glory for himself. He enlists the assistance of a tired old donkey named Puzzle. Having come across an old lion's skin, the Ape sews it into a cumbersome costume and parades the donkey around in it.

> "Come and try on your beautiful new lion skin coat," said Shift. "Oh, bother that old skin," said Puzzle. "I'll try it on in the morning. I'm too

tired tonight." "You *are* unkind, Puzzle," said Shift. . . . "My dear Shift," said Puzzle getting up at once. "I'm so sorry. I've been horrid. Of course. I'd love to try it on, and look, it looks simply splendid. Do try it on me at once. Please do." "Well stand still then," said the Ape. The skin was very heavy for him to lift, but in the end, with a lot of pulling and pushing and puffing and blowing he got it onto the donkey. He tied it underneath Puzzle's body and he tied the legs to Puzzle's legs and the tail to Puzzle's tail. A good deal of Puzzle's grey nose and face could be seen through the open mouth of the lion's head.

No one who had ever seen a real lion would have been taken in for a moment. But if someone who had never seen a lion looked at Puzzle in his lion's skin, he just might mistake him for a lion—if he didn't come too close and if the light was not so good and if Puzzle did not let out a bray and did not make any noise with his hoofs.

"You look wonderful, wonderful," said the Ape. "If anyone saw you now they'd think you were Aslan, the great lion himself."[5]

Later Tirian, the king, under the night sky, saw the pretend lion for who he really was. "Then the yellow thing turned clumsily round, and walked, you might almost say waddled, back into the stable. And the Ape shut the door behind it."[6]

Puzzle and Shift tried to pull off the impossible. And so it is with Satan. He is a cheap imitation of the Great Lion. So don't be overcome by the fact that he "prowls around like a roaring lion." Remember his true self. He is nothing more than a stubborn and rebellious donkey living out his rebellion against God. Therefore, take heart. "Resist him." Stand "firm in your faith." Do not be overcome by this imitation ruler. The Great Lion, Jesus, demands all your allegiance. And in this, know that you are not alone in the world.

> . . . knowing that the same kinds of suffering are being experienced by your brotherhood throughout the world. (v. 9b)

You are to cast all your cares upon God because he cares for you. And now you are encouraged to resist, knowing that others are sharing in this with you. What a buoyant word for those early outpost churches of Peter's day. What an uplifting word for us as well. Around the globe Christian brothers and sisters are sharing in this battle with you.

Preacher Martyn Lloyd-Jones once said, "I would have been dead long ago if I depended on men for encouragement."[7] Well, thank God, we don't need to depend on people. God has seen fit to encourage us with the text of Scripture.

The Divine Principle Repeated (v. 10a)

Having put forward divine commands accompanied by encouragement for us to follow through, Peter now repeats the general principle of true grace at work. He writes:

> And after you have suffered a little while, the God of all grace, who has called you to his eternal glory in Christ, will himself restore, confirm, strengthen, and establish you. (v. 10)

True grace looks like this: present sufferings are intimately connected to eternal glory. And the one always precedes the other. Peter repeats this here in summary fashion to fix it forever in our mind and heart—and to encourage us with the promise that God will see us through. God will one day bring us home. We will suffer for a little while—that is, this whole life through—but then we will gain eternal reward and glory. Therefore, Peter has chosen to end his letter not with suffering and submission but with our salvation. We are to go forward each day in the light of his promise. Our prayers should mimic those of St. Patrick, who prayed:

> I arise today through God's strength to pilot me: God's might to uphold me, God's wisdom to guide me, God's eye to look before me, God's ear to hear me, God's hand to guard me, God's way to lie before me, God's shield to protect me, God's host to save me from snares of devils, from temptations of vices, from everyone who will wish me ill, afar and anear, alone and in multitude.[8]

Divine Actions Followed by Our Adoration (vv. 10b, 11)

Restore, Confirm, Strengthen, Establish

Peter finishes his letter with a forceful flurry of verbs—all actions that are taken by God to ensure our safe arrival on Heaven's shore. He writes:

> The God of all grace . . . will himself restore, confirm, strengthen, and establish you.

Four marvelous verbs. We will be completely restored, confirmed, strengthened, and established. The word translated "restore" is in other places translated "mend." In fact, it is used when Jesus approaches his disciples and finds them *mending* their nets. Peter the fisherman, more than most, knew what this term meant. And now he uses it to speak of what God will do for each one of us. He will *mend* us. He will attend to us. He will make us whole. He will *stand us up* on our own two feet, for that is what "confirm" means. He will "*strengthen*" and "*establish*" us. Those final verbs, architectural by nature, are terms that echo Peter's earlier teaching that we are being built up into the spiritual house of God (2:3–8). When we arrive at Heaven's gate, we will be his dwelling.

Our Adoration

Is it any wonder that the words that tumble forth from Peter's pen next are those of singular and eternal adoration? Verse 11 says:

> To him be the dominion forever and ever. Amen.

What else could possibly come from the lips of those who have received so much? In all our sufferings, in all our trials, his eternal glory is manifest, his grace is truly known, and his dominion will carry on forever. The dominion of God will never be extinguished. It will never be snuffed out. Throughout the centuries Christians have understood their sufferings in light of what is being accomplished for his eternal dominion.

The Reformer Hugh Latimer and Nicolas Ridley were burned at the stake in Oxford for their faith in October 1555. As the flames of this final trial rose around them, Latimer cried out:

> Play the man, Master Ridley; we shall this day light such a candle, by God's grace, in England, as I trust shall never be put out.[9]

These were the final words of a suffering man who wanted nothing more than to die in adoration. It was enough for him to know that what happened to him on that day would accomplish the purposes of God's unextinguishable and everlasting dominion. As it was for Latimer, so it also was for Peter, and so it must be for each one of us.

Finishing in True Grace (vv. 12–14)

And so we arrive at the final stanza of Peter's letter. We have followed him as he wrote to us of our eternal inheritance and destination. We were built up as he unfolded our exalted identity. We looked on as he exhorted us to engage in gracious living. We were encouraged to continue on in light of Christ's ultimate vindication. And we have been reminded to embrace our calling to submission and suffering until he comes again or takes us home. As he finishes, his pen lands on one final exhortation.

By Silvanus, a faithful brother as I regard him, I have written briefly to you, exhorting and declaring that this is the true grace of God. Stand firm in it. She who is at Babylon, who is likewise chosen, sends you greetings, and so does Mark, my son. Greet one another with the kiss of love. Peace to all of you who are in Christ. (vv. 12–14)

We are told that Peter has exhorted and declared to us the meaning of "the true grace of God." Indeed he has. "True grace" is that mysterious union that joins suffering to glory—this present day with being born again to a living hope.

Susannah Wesley, mother of John and Charles (and seventeen others!), died on July 23, 1742 at the age of seventy-three. Her father had been one of the ministers of England who was ejected by the Act of Uniformity of 1662. So she knew a thing or two about suffering and seeking rest in the coming kingdom of God. She is buried in London's Bunhill Cemetery, and her epitaph provides a fitting close to Peter's letter:

In sure and certain hope to rise,
And claim her mansion in the skies
A Christian here her flesh laid down,
The cross exchanging for a crown.[10]

Our Heavenly Father, thank you for this picture of true grace. Give us the grace to finish well. In our trials, grant us patience. In our suffering, grant us your joy. May we know what it is to share Christ's suffering. To God be the glory, amen.

2 PETER

19

Reading 2 Peter

The Theme of Second Peter

There is a significant need in the world today for direction, for clear truth according to real knowledge. This need even applies to life's most ordinary situations. For example, if someone stopped you on the street and asked for directions to a particular place, your answer had better be clear, accurate, and in accordance with real knowledge! Without possessing a knowledge that conforms to reality, the travelers would have no chance of arriving at their destination safely. More importantly, what holds true in the mundane things of life is magnified beyond measure when the questions asked pertain to matters of life and death. If we are to travel through life and gain entrance into God's eternal kingdom (1:11), we need straightforward instructions. We need clear direction, teaching rooted in truth and according to real knowledge.

Peter's second letter takes as its theme "the knowledge of God" (1:2, 3, 8; 2:20; 3:18; see also 1:5–6, 16, 20; 2:9, 21; 3:3, 17). It is written to provide direction to all who come after the apostolic age. The apostles knew that after their death the gospel message they preached would be challenged by many and discarded by some. In essence, they were aware that the church would need answers on great gospel questions, especially those relating to final judgment, Christ's future coming, and life in light of these realities. And these answers must conform to real knowledge. Put simply, as the apostolic age drew to a close, the future of the Christian faith could not rest merely on the strength of stories told about those who walked and talked with Jesus Christ.

This letter, then, is meant to remind readers across the ages that the content of the apostles' message, as put forward in the preaching of Peter (1:1), reveals what it truly means to "know God."

The letter opens with this knowledge in 1:2: "May grace and peace be multiplied to you in the knowledge of God and of Jesus our Lord." This simple phrase is one to which Peter returns again and again. He goes on in verse 3 to state that through God's "divine power," all things concerning life and godliness are available to us through this knowledge. And by way of contrast, chapter 2 speaks of the certain destruction that awaits anyone who follows in the knowledge of another way.

It is no accident, then, that on either side of chapter 2, Peter uses the forceful phrase "Knowing this first of all . . ." (1:20; 3:3). In the first instance, he is shoring up the belief that Jesus, as God's Son, will come again to judge the living and the dead. This knowledge, he will argue, rests not on the strength of "cleverly devised myths" (1:16) but upon the clear truth of the Scriptures, teachings that were given to us by the Holy Spirit. Again in 3:3 Peter utilizes the phrase, "Knowing this first of all." There Peter is separating the apostles' belief in the return of Christ in judgment with the scoffers' purported "knowledge." Not surprisingly, apostolic knowledge is shown to be rooted in the holy prophets and the commands of Jesus (3:2). In contrast, the scoffers' teaching stems from their own sinful desires (3:3).

In these and numerous other contrasts, Peter describes the differences between a true knowledge of God and the ideas being offered up by false teachers. Peter will return to his theme on two occasions. In verse 17 of chapter 3 he says with emphasis, "knowing this beforehand." With this phrase, it is as if we hear the aged preacher's thundering voice: "Don't ever say that I didn't tell you how to arrive safely." And coupled with that is his thematic conclusion, "But grow in the grace and knowledge of our Lord and Savior Jesus Christ" (3:18).

The Theme's Present-Day Relevance

This letter's theme—a proper knowledge of God—is incredibly relevant in our age. As stated earlier, there is a desperate need in the world today for direction, for clear truth according to real knowledge. After all, the church today is wrestling with significant questions, and Christians need answers that enable them to know God in accordance with truth. At least three such contemporary questions are taken up in Second Peter.

First, *can someone come to know God without knowledge of Jesus as God's Son?* In our twenty-first-century context there is an overabundance of religious choices. And choice after choice dilutes, softens, or outright abandons the absolute necessity of belief in Jesus. For many, knowledge of God is something available from doing good works or being socially active or participating in any number of religious ceremonies or belief systems; Jesus is secondary. To put the question bluntly: can someone come to know God without Jesus Christ being at the center? Second Peter provides the answer. A true knowledge of God includes knowledge of Jesus Christ as God's Son.

Verse 17 of chapter 1 spells this out. This entire section, starting in verse 16 and going through verse 21, is a vindication of the apostles' teaching that Jesus is God's Son and as such is not only our Savior but our King. For the apostles, Jesus has been given the nations as his inheritance. As God's Son, Jesus sits enthroned above all the world's rulers and religious ways. Peter concludes unabashedly that a true knowledge of God must include a belief in Jesus as his Son.

Second, *can one know God and yet abandon the rigorous life that the apostles required of those who profess Christ?* The false prophets of Peter's day were quick to suggest that alternative viewpoints were permissible. Many were willing to advocate sexual and material freedoms that ran contrary to the apostles' message (2:2, 3, 14–16, 19). Amazingly, the great gospel issues of our day remain the same: can one truly know God and yet separate himself or herself from the historic, orthodox understanding of sexual ethics? Can one possess knowledge of God and yet pursue a life of personal gain? Second Peter confronts those who would teach that sensuality and greed are acceptable parts of a Christian lifestyle. In verses 1, 2 of chapter 2 he equates the sexual ethics of these false teachers with that of blaspheming the truth and "denying the Master who bought them." Later in the same chapter (2:14–16) Peter likens those given to avarice to Balaam, that ancient preacher who ended up "forsaking the right way."

Third, *can you know God and reject the notion that Jesus will return?* Put differently, and more precisely, can you possess a knowledge of God that leaves out that bit at the end of the Apostle's Creed about him coming back "to judge the living and the dead"? Peter's letter confronts those who deny that Jesus Christ will return as Judge. In 3:4 he begs the question. The remainder of the chapter is dedicated to showing not just how logical such a belief in judgment is, but how important it is as well. First, it was prophesied as truth (3:2). Further, the idea of God coming in judgment has historical precedent (3:5–7). In addition, the letter will go on to provide reasons for his delay (3:8–10) and put forward motivations to live lives of holiness and watchful care until he comes again (3:11–15).

The Aim of Second Peter

In an insecure world where contradictory views on the gospel and its demands persist, we need reliable footing, a sure foundation to keep us from stumbling. Peter's aim in writing this second letter is simply to provide that foundation, to establish the feet of the church on higher, solid ground. The letter has at least three distinct aims.

First, this letter is written to *establish, strengthen, and stabilize* Christians in the true knowledge of God. The words *establish, strengthen,* and *stabilize* are intentionally chosen. Not only does each of these words appear in the text of 2 Peter in some form, but they all originate from the same word in Greek. The identical word appears in 1:12 as "established," in 3:17 as "stability," and in 2:14 and 3:16 as "unsteady" and "unstable" respectively. Peter's letter is written so that we will not lose our own stability but will find strength and sure footing in a true knowledge of God.

Second, the letter intends to rebuke, warn, and correct those among us who teach and revel in any other knowledge of God. This aim is especially directed at Bible teachers. The structure of the letter reveals this aim as central. Chapter 2 is this letter's gravitational center. As such, it includes some of the strongest language in the entire Bible. And it is directed against pastors and teachers who advocate a different gospel, a more accommodating way—knowledge of a different sort. In essence, it is impossible to preach from this letter without seriously engaging one's own life and practice.

Finally, this letter aims to rescue and reclaim the faithful who have tripped and fallen along the way. Put simply, it not only proves to the stumbling church throughout all ages what it means to know God—it intends to pick us up and put us back on the way. It is *in* such knowledge (1:2) and *through* such knowledge (1:3) that we are said to be effective and fruitful (1:8) and thereby kept from falling (1:9) and are ensured of an entrance into the eternal kingdom of our Lord and Savior Jesus Christ (1:11). In summary, this letter provides us with the works that grow faith (1:3–11), the words that are worthy of following (1:16–21), the warnings that keep us from losing our way (2:1–22), the reminders that hold us fast (3:1–10), and the reasons to be engaged in productive work while we await Christ's return (3:11–18).

A Word on Tone

Before we begin, it is important to recognize the tone of the letter. It is more polemical than pastoral. Notice the strength of the words. In essence, it is a fighting letter more than it is a friendly one. In this respect, the letter is surprisingly belligerent. For instance, much of chapter 2 dramatically underscores this point. Peter holds nothing back in his use of controversial argument, insult, and hyperbole in his battle with those who disagree. Make no mistake, the letter wars over what constitutes a true knowledge of God. That said, it is not written directly to Peter's enemies but to those who are spoken of as having "a faith of equal standing" with the apostles (1:1) and as such is addressed to the beloved (3:1, 8, 14). In summary, 2 Peter is written to the church throughout the ages in an effort to confront the inevitable confusion that persists on great gospel questions. It is written with the hope not only of guarding God's own people but of unmasking all who stand condemned for compromising on what it means to really know God.

Simeon Peter, a servant and apostle of Jesus Christ, To those who have obtained a faith of equal standing with ours by the righteousness of our God and Savior Jesus Christ: May grace and peace be multiplied to you in the knowledge of God and of Jesus our Lord.

1:1, 2

20

This Letter and the Life Experience of Peter

2 PETER 1:1, 2

Aspirations for a Hero

Everybody likes the idea behind Superman—that out there somewhere is someone who can really fly. An individual who rises above it all—one who never falls. We all want a hero to rescue us from failure. Someone who says what he means, does what he says, and finishes whatever he sets his mind to starting.

In his provocative little book *Life After God*, Douglas Coupland explores this longing. He introduces us to a boy watching a television report about a publisher's plan to release a comic book about Superman dying in an air battle over the city with a supremely evil force. As Coupland's character watches this release, he is said to think:

> I have always liked the idea of Superman because I have always liked the idea that there is one person in the world who doesn't do bad things. That there is one person in the world who is able to fly. I myself often have dreams in which I am flying, but it's not flying the way Superman does. I simply put my arms behind my shoulders and float and move. Needless to say, it is my favorite dream.[1]

By the end of Coupland's narrative, the boy has fallen asleep on the sofa, the television is still on, and he dreams. In his dream he is running frantically around the top floor of a skyscraper looking through the big sheets of glass, trying to protect Superman. Coupland's story reminds us of the longings of the human heart. We all want Superman.

Truth be told, however, we all fall. Every one of us fails. We all have faults. Perhaps it is this universal sense of frailty that accounts, in some measure, for the respect and admiration we feel toward the men and women who remain visibly and verbally determined. We still appreciate the sort of person who staunchly says, "I will not fall. I will get it all done." Like heroes in a tragedy, these tarnished men and women of valor are forever among us. We find them in movies and in comics. They are written into the pages of good literature. And they even emerge on the pages of Scripture.

Our Appreciation for Peter

This explains the soft spot we have in our hearts for Simon Peter. Peter was a man who made big claims, yet knew how to fall—and fall hard. One writer pictured Peter this way: "When I think of Peter, I imagine a broad-shouldered, loud, extroverted, assertive man who is always sweating. . . . He was a headstrong, unbridled hulk who was always getting into trouble and causing his Master plenty of the same."[2] What a great description.

Of him another has written, "His impulsive deeds, his frequent questions, his eager exclamations and confessions . . . his sometimes manly and sometimes cowardly acts, his oaths, his bitter tears—all this makes Peter the great companion and the great instructor of his fellow men."[3]

My own eagerness to study this letter stems from the very claim that this fallen yet finishing man stands behind its authorship.[4] Peter is to be our "great companion and . . . instructor," so we'd better get started by taking a closer look at how he is described.

Servant and Apostle (v. 1a)

The text begins, "Simeon Peter, a servant and apostle of Jesus Christ."

Two Names and Two Titles

The letter introduces the author in a unique way, with two names and two titles. He is called "Simeon Peter." *Simeon* is merely "the Greek transliteration of the Hebrew name."[5] It was the name given to Jacob's second son. It was also the name that Jesus' great disciple was given at birth. *Peter,* however, is not Hebrew in origin but Greek. It means "rock." As such, it is the name the Lord gave to his valiant and determined follower years later.

Using both names is a change from what we find in 1 Peter. There Simeon, the birth name, is not used. We simply meet one called Peter. The alteration in the letter before us is not without subtle intention. When our writer is introduced as "Simeon Peter," he wants us to know that we are meeting the whole man. We are listening to instructions from a complete and complex person. Here is a man with a real track record and a real history. Here is one well acquainted with who he was at birth and who he is now in Christ. Using both names conveys the life experience of one who isn't afraid to wed together "The man as I was born" and "I am the man I am today because of the gracious influence of Jesus."

Let's get this straight at the outset. The weight of these two names will settle in as we read on. But for now this is enough. We are studying a letter that claims a "before and after" kind of person as its author. He is not trying to hide his beginnings. Here is a real man, flesh and all.

The two titles used to describe him are "servant" and "apostle of Jesus Christ." By this he wants the readers to know that in the end, he both served *and* led the church for Christ. By putting the names and titles together in the opening line of our text, we have a man who knows the fullness of guilt and grace. We are going to learn from one who was called to bear weight as well as witness for Christ.

One Experience

There is an incident in Peter's life, one dramatic life experience that I have come to believe stands behind the writing of this letter. It is an event that we will return to when we come to 1:10–12. Yet it is a moment of such significance that I want to introduce it to you now. My reason for doing so is simple: there is a dynamic connection between this particular experience in Peter's life and the language and aim of this letter. In particular, I am thinking of the language of *falling* and *strengthening*.

I am referring to the time of Jesus' arrest—the dark night of his betrayal. Earlier that evening, in the presence of all the disciples, Jesus had said, "You will all *fall away* because of me this night. For it is written, 'I will strike the shepherd, and the sheep of the flock will be scattered'" (Matthew 26:31). Note the phrase, "You will all *fall away*." This very word will show up again in 2 Peter 1. Upon hearing these words from Jesus, Peter, our beloved and self-proclaimed superman, shot back, "Though they all fall away . . . I will never fall away . . . Even if I must die with you, I will not deny you" (vv. 33, 35). In essence, on that fateful night Peter dramatically interrupted Jesus and, pointing his finger at each man, said, "Time out. Let's get one thing straight. Even though all these other guys around this table will fall away, *I will not fall*." To the naked eye, Peter was one who both visibly and verbally had the makings of one who can really fly.[6]

Jesus returned the fire. "Oh, Peter, before the rooster gets going in the morning, you will deny me three times." And what happened? Peter did fall. He fell once, he fell twice, and in humiliating fashion he would fall for the third time before the intimidating presence of a young servant girl in the high priest's courtyard.

Intriguingly, it takes a mere ten verses for this theme of *falling* to emerge within the fabric of the letter's aim. "Therefore, brothers, be all the more diligent to make your calling and election sure, for if you practice these qualities *you will never fall*" (1:10).

On that same fateful night, Jesus used other vocabulary that appears early in this letter. And interestingly, it is connected to the author's intention in writing. Jesus said to Peter, "Simon, Simon, behold, Satan demanded to have you, that he might sift you like wheat, but I have prayed for you that your faith may not fail. And when you have turned again, *strengthen* your brothers" (Luke 22:31, 32).

The word translated *strengthen* is the same word used repeatedly in this letter to convey the author's intention in writing, sometimes negatively as "unsteady."

• In 1:12 we read, "Therefore I intend always to remind you of these qualities, though you know them and are *established* in the truth that you have." The words *established* and *strengthened* are one and the same. Thus we can fairly say that Peter wants his readers to attain spiritual *stability*—that is, he wants them to be *established* in the faith.

• This same word appears in chapter 2—but this time to contrast Peter's aim with that of the false teachers. "They have eyes full of adultery, insatiable for sin. They entice *unsteady* souls" (2:14). The word translated *unsteady* is the word used negatively that Jesus gave Peter on the night he was commanded to *strengthen* his brothers. It is used here to speak of those who lead Christians astray and cause them to fall.

• Finally, this brief letter will also close under the weight and intention of this same term. "You therefore, beloved, knowing this beforehand, take care that you are not carried away with the error of lawless people and lose your own *stability*" (3:17).

Stability, unsteady, and *established.* Three times we are given the very word Jesus gave Peter those many years ago as the command "to strengthen" in Luke 22:32. In this little letter, the term is leveraged afresh, along with the word fall, to capture Peter's intention in writing.

Why mention this now? For two reasons. First, to show that 2 Peter is intended to function as the final declaration of a man at the end of his life who is intent on fulfilling the command Christ gave him on that fateful night years ago. There can be no question that Peter fulfilled this call to *strengthen* the brothers when he led that little upper-room band in the early days after the resurrection. Further, he fulfilled it from his strategic role in Jerusalem for the first-century church at large. Yet now, with this letter, his charge to the church throughout all of history is fulfilled as well. With his own death imminent, Peter is set to *strengthen* those of us who follow in his train centuries later. It is as if by this letter he lives today and can still be found preaching on how to move from falling to finishing well. Second Peter is his road map to Heaven. It confirms that we can also possess a faith that will not fail. On that fateful night long ago, Jesus told Peter that he had been praying for him—especially that his faith would not fail.[7] That same Jesus stands today at the right hand of God interceding in like manner for you and for me.

This is good news for every one of us. You can fall and yet still finish. You can wipe out and yet be restored. You can have regrets and yet know what it is to be rescued by Christ. You might have equivocated on your commitment to Christ in the past, but that doesn't mean you can't live to see the day when you are established and in some way strengthen others to do the same. Welcome to Peter's book of lessons that will put you on secure and solid ground. For by grace you were meant to stand and not fall.

Our Faith—God's Righteousness (v. 1b)

Encouragingly, the text goes on to include us in the audience. According to the latter part of verse 1, this letter is written "to those who have obtained a faith of equal standing with ours." By using such a general term—"to those"—we are all included. All who possess abiding faith in Christ should study and apply this letter to their life.

By the term "ours," I think the apostles are meant.[8] In this exalted way, then, we are told that our faith is equal to that of our Lord's earliest and closest followers. While we may be living thousands of years later, our faith is no way deficient or inferior. We have apostolic faith—nothing less. Our faith is given equal standing. And though we have fallen, we too can know what it is to stand with them.

This glorious and exalted standing is said to be ours "by the righteousness of our God and Savior Jesus Christ." How true this must be. Surely, it could not come to us in any other way. We are not Superman. We have faults and frailties and have experienced the awful reality of falling into sin. But the gospel of Christ's righteousness is our comfort. Our ability to stand before God someday as rescued and reclaimed persons depends entirely on the righteousness of Jesus Christ. He alone has flown through this world without falling. He alone can and did make atonement for sin. Thus he alone can bring us home. Ensuring that we remain in the faith is one of the main ideas this letter will pass on to us.

Multiplied Grace and Peace in the Knowledge of God (v. 2)

While verse 2 ("May grace and peace be multiplied to you in the knowledge of God and of Jesus our Lord") has all the trappings of an ordinary greeting, the depth of meaning should not be lost on us. To an audience in need of standing, Peter expresses his desire that we would know God's grace and mercy. And not merely that, but that those benedictions of God would be ours in multiples. Indeed, may it be so.

He goes on to tell us how these great gifts are. We are to receive them "in the knowledge of God and of Jesus our Lord." With divine foreshadowing, we read for the first time what it is that must govern our journey to our heavenly home. The text opens by claiming that we need "knowledge." And the letter will close on the same word. So from beginning to end we stand in need of a certain kind of knowledge, a knowledge of God (1:2, 8; 3:18 and shown by way of contrast in 2:20). For this "knowledge" is the actual basis for strengthening, the sure foundation that Peter means to convey in his letter. It is the central theme, and, as we shall see in the next chapter, this knowledge is not merely intellectual or academic. It involves a firsthand experience of relational intimacy with God through abiding faith in Christ.

Our Desire for a Faith That Finishes Well

For now, that is enough. Let us gather our gains. We have been given a letter that is meant to rescue us from falling. Indeed, it is meant to reclaim those who still might be away from full obedience to Christ. It is written under the hand of one who knew what it was to fall and yet finish well. We are given a teacher whose faith did not fail. May we be eager to learn how to emulate his progress. After all, none of us can fly. None of us is Superman. None of us wants our faith to fail. So then, take heed and learn how to finish well.

Our Heavenly Father, we are not Superman. Thank you for this letter from one whom we know fell hard. Take his life and teaching, and under the guidance of your Holy Spirit enable us to get up and stand on our feet again. Show us what it means to follow in the right way. Help us with what is required. And one day, when our life is nearly done, may we, like Peter, be prepared to stand in your presence firmly fixed in abiding faith. In Jesus' name, amen.

*His divine power has granted to us all things that per-
tain to life and godliness, through the knowledge of
him who called us to his own glory and excellence, by
which he has granted to us his precious and very great
promises, so that through them you may become partakers of the divine nature, having escaped from the
corruption that is in the world because of sinful desire.
For this very reason, make every effort to supplement
your faith with virtue, and virtue with knowledge,
and knowledge with self-control, and self-control
with steadfastness, and steadfastness with godliness,
and godliness with brotherly affection, and brotherly
affection with love. For if these qualities are yours and
are increasing, they keep you from being ineffective or
unfruitful in the knowledge of our Lord Jesus Christ.
For whoever lacks these qualities is so nearsighted
that he is blind, having forgotten that he was cleansed
from his former sins. Therefore, brothers, be all the
more diligent to make your calling and election sure,
for if you practice these qualities you will never fall.
For in this way there will be richly provided for you
an entrance into the eternal kingdom of our Lord and
Savior Jesus Christ.*

1:3–11

21

Our Faith Must Grow

2 PETER 1:3–11

Peter's Fall

Guilt and shame are unwanted companions that dog our lives from behind. I have noticed two things about guilt and shame. First, they bark at our heels most often right after spiritual failure. Second, it's tough to outrun them. Like us, Simon Peter knew the destructive power and debilitating force of guilt and shame. On the back side of his threefold denial, the Bible says that Peter "went out and wept bitterly" (Luke 22:62).

We can almost hear the yelps as guilt and shame doggedly chased him across the night. Not in his wildest dreams did Peter think that he would reconnect with Jesus in a personal way. His mind, so recently filled with failure, thought that Jesus would never welcome him back into the fold. Regret set in, and then remorse, but thankfully, also repentance. But with it came the lingering notion that all the running in the world would not be enough to catch Jesus again.

Recently I finished the book *The Life and Times of Michael K.* by J. M. Coetzee, who won a Nobel Prize for literature in 2003. In it he writes of our attempt to overcome guilt and shame. One of his characters is running hard to catch up to a man named Michaels, a man whom he had recently injured and betrayed. Coetzee writes:

> I would have dodged from shadow to shadow in his tracks, and climbed the wall in the darkest corner, and followed him down the avenue of oaks under the stars. . . . I would have dogged him all night through side streets till at daybreak we would have found ourselves on the fringes of the wastes of the Cape Flats, plodding fifty paces apart through sand and bush. . . .

And I would have come before you and spoken. I would have said: "Michaels, forgive me for the way I treated you, I did not appreciate who you were till the last days. Forgive me too for following you like this. I promise not to be a burden." . . .

At this stage I think you might already have turned your back on me and begun to walk off. . . . So now I would have had to hurry after you, keeping close at your heels so as not to have to shout. "Forgive me, Michaels . . . there is not much more, please be patient. I only want to tell you what you mean to me, then I will be through."

At that moment, I suspect . . . you would break into a run. So I would have run after you, plowing as if through water through the thick grey sand. . . .

Would it be true that at this point you would begin to throw your most urgent energies into running, so that it would be clear to the meanest observer that you were running to escape the man shouting at your back . . . as you plunged far ahead into the deepest wattle thickets, running more strongly now than one would ever expect.[1]

Coetzee perfectly describes the guilt and shame Peter felt on the night of his denial. He was sure that all the running in the world wouldn't restore him to Jesus. For underneath spiritual failure and the subsequent dogs of guilt and shame is a belief that God, whom we have injured so deeply, won't possibly take us back.

Peter Is Forgiven

Yet, within a few days of Peter's colossal failure, God sent an angel with orders to notify Mary Magdalene and the other women that Jesus wanted to see the disciples, *including Peter*, in Galilee. Who would have guessed that God was planning all along to write a gospel script in which Peter is welcomed back with open arms?

Returning to Galilee, Peter was on his fishing boat when Jesus called out to him. Shortly thereafter Peter dove into the water and swam, not ran, after Jesus. In that intimate exchange between them at the end of John's Gospel, Jesus not only forgave Peter but charged him to feed and tend the new people of God.

Peter's Intention for Us to Finish Well

Those are the intimate and human circumstances that lie beneath this letter. Don't soon forget them. Peter, now at the close of his life—having once fallen, yet now knowing that he will finish—writes to help people like us, regardless of how much noise the barking sounds of guilt and shame make.

In our text we find Peter encouraging us with the idea that God has already given us everything it takes to finish in relationship with him. We have what it takes to get where we want to go, where God wants us to go. We have been given the road map to direct us along the way. Peter's road map to Heaven is revealed, and it is open to anyone willing to renounce this world and run with abiding faith in Christ. For our own purposes, it looks like this:

   • *Assertion:* God has given us everything we need for the journey (1:3, 4).
   • *Application:* Here is the golden chain that leads us to Heaven (1:5–9).
   • *Appeal:* We need to take care to ensure our entrance into the kingdom (1:10, 11).

Assertion: God Has Given Us Everything We Need (vv. 3, 4)

In verses 3, 4 we are told that God has already given us everything we need to finish well. Peter writes:

> His divine power has granted to us all things that pertain to life and godliness, through the knowledge of him who called us to his own glory and excellence, by which he has granted to us his precious and very great promises, so that through them you may become partakers of the divine nature, having escaped from the corruption that is in the world because of sinful desire.

Two great truths stand at the forefront of all that we have been given to finish well in life and godliness. The first is mentioned in verse 3, *the knowledge of God.* The second is hidden in verse 4, *the promises of God.* These are the fountainhead gifts that all followers of Jesus have in their possession—the knowledge and promises of God. Therefore, if you want to grow in godliness and gain eternal life, you need to grasp hold of what God has for us in Christ. You will need to cultivate your experiential knowledge of God and a willingness to hold on to his promises in this world that tempts you to grasp other things.

Knowledge of God

Theologian J. I. Packer has written a classic book entitled *Knowing God.* In it he sets out to lead us into the kind of discovery that Peter is writing about. In essence, Packer calls us to the kind of knowledge we already possess in the gospel.

What were we made for? To know God. What aim should we set ourselves in life? To know God. What is the eternal life that Jesus gives? Knowledge of God. "This is life eternal, that they may know thee, the only true God, and Jesus Christ, whom thou hast sent" (John 17:3). What is the best thing in life, bringing more joy, delight, and contentment than anything else? Knowledge of God. "Thus saith the LORD, Let not the wise man glory in his wisdom, neither let not the mighty man glory in his might, let not the rich man glory in his riches; but let him that glorieth glory in this, that he understandeth and knoweth me" (Jeremiah 9:23). What, of all the states God ever sees man in, gives him most pleasure? Knowledge of himself. "I desire . . . the knowledge of God more than burnt offerings," says God (Hosea 6:6). . . . Once you have become aware that the main business that you are here for is to know God, most of life's problems fall into place of their own accord.[2]

Is knowing God your priority in life? Packer, like the Apostle Peter, is not merely interested in what you and I might know about God. The supreme issue is this: are we in relationship with God? Are we being conformed into the likeness of his Son by the power of his Spirit? Or have we strayed from him? Have we turned from him and gone our own way? If we need restoration with God, that will require one thing—giving more and more of our life over to the gracious rule of Jesus.

The Promises of God

The other thing we have already been given are the "very great promises" of God (v. 4). Peter tells us that through them we "become partakers of the divine nature." True knowledge of God is always attended by a fixed belief in God's promises. So often today people want to claim relationship with God while at the same time they abandon the words of the Bible. It is as if we want a God in our own making—one who exists under the authority of our own word.

This verse challenges such a notion. In fact, by the time we reach chapter 2 we will see that the entire letter is at odds with such a belief. Those who finish well in faith do so by holding fast to God's promises. According to Peter's gospel, there is simply nothing else strong enough to pull us home. Indeed, according to verse 4 it is by them that we escape the tug of "the corruption that is in the world." One can almost envision men, women, and children being pulled loose from the muck of this world and ascending to Heaven's skies solely by holding fast to the strong cord of God's Word. If we need rescuing from this world, that will require holding ever more tightly to the "very great promises" of God.

Application: The Golden Chain That Leads You to Heaven (vv. 5–9)

The Golden Chain

Gaining entrance into Heaven ought to be our goal. There we shall know and be fully known. There we shall live under the fullness of "very great promises." The way forward is the way of faith. Interestingly, if making a commitment to faith in Christ is what establishes our relationship to God, Peter moves on in verses 5–9 to remind us that continuing in faith, or growing in faith, is what provides "entrance into the eternal kingdom of our Lord and Savior Jesus Christ" (v. 11).

Let's take a look at how "supplementing your faith," to use Peter's exact language, is the road map we must take if we are to keep from falling. Verses 5–9 read:

> For this very reason, make every effort to supplement your faith with virtue, and virtue with knowledge, and knowledge with self-control, and self-control with steadfastness, and steadfastness with godliness, and godliness with brotherly affection, and brotherly affection with love. For if these qualities are yours and are increasing, they keep you from being ineffective or unfruitful in the knowledge of our Lord Jesus Christ. For whoever lacks these qualities is so nearsighted that he is blind, having forgotten that he was cleansed from his former sins.

The first three verses are commonly referred to as a list of virtues.[3] In reality they are much more, for when things are merely placed in a list, each item stands independently, each has an identity on its own. Here, however, each characteristic is connected to what follows. In fact, the repetition of each word demonstrates that Peter intends us to view them as inseparably linked to one another. In light of this, even the sequence in which they appear matters.

To put an image on it, we could liken verses 5–8 to a golden chain or to stairs that lead one to the stars. Each stair or characteristic is built upon the strength of the previous one. And each subsequent one rises to a higher plane. Put differently, they form a ladder that leads us from our earthly faith in Christ to everlasting life. (See John 1:51 as fulfillment of Genesis 28:10–17).

True Faith Must Grow

Bob Dylan once sang, "May you build a ladder to the stars and climb on every rung. May you stay forever young."[4] Peter here echoes such lyrics. It's a mistake to think that salvation by "faith" alone means that one's faith never needs to work. True faith sweats. It grows. Using the metaphor of Dylan, the stars are attained by first building a ladder. Peter articulates his call for growing faith with these words: "For this very reason make every effort to *supplement your faith* . . ." (v. 5). The kind of faith that takes fallen and frail men and women home to Heaven is one that operates by way of addition.

Virtue

To our faith we are to add "virtue." The Greek word translated "virtue" has a rich and storied history. Plato and Aristotle both made use of it. In *Virtues and Vices* Aristotle writes:

> Fine things are the objects of praise, base things of blame; and at the head of the fine stand the virtues, at the head of the base the vices; consequently the virtues are objects of praise, and also the causes of the virtues are objects of praise, and the things that accompany the virtues and that result from them, and their works, while the opposite are the objects of blame.[5]

Assuming that Peter is using the word in the classical sense, living a virtuous life means living a life that is worthy of praise. In essence, virtue is closely linked to that which is honorable. It means doing the right thing regardless of the outcome. The virtuous person is brave and generous and acts appropriately to all.[6]

For an example of the kind of person Peter is asking us to become, one could turn to Homer's Odysseus or to King Arthur's knights of the Round Table when chivalry still reigned. For Peter, this much is essential: to keep from falling, our faith in Christ must lead us to live honorably. Enough then of behavior that is unbecoming of our profession. To our faith, let us add virtue.

Knowledge

To virtue we are to add "knowledge." Interestingly, these two characteristics are often linked together. The motto of the University of Chicago is *crescat scientia; vita excolatur*—"let knowledge grow from more to more; and so be human life enriched." In shorthand, the University is virtually saying, "Knowledge is virtue." The premise beneath this kind of thinking is clear: if a man or a woman *knows* the right thing, he or she will *do* the right thing. Of course, this might be true. But as our experience proves, it is not always the case. Knowledge does not always lead to virtue. Thus Peter's order is preferred. Knowledge must be added to virtue, and a fully orbed virtue rests on faith in Christ.

Peter is after, as we have already noticed from this text, knowledge of a particular sort. He wants us to know God, not merely about God or his universe. The story is told of a religious gathering where a famous actor and an elderly minister were both present. The actor, while not on the program, was nevertheless asked by the emcee to come forward and give a word. At a loss as to what to say, he turned to the elderly minister and whispered, "I don't really know what to do." The seasoned pastor shoved his Bible into the hands of the actor and replied, "Just read Psalm 23." The actor stood and with his eloquent voice read the psalm. When finished, he wasn't quite sure what to do, so he turned to the minister and announced, "Well, I'd like the minister to come up and say a few words on this." The minister surprised everyone by merely reciting the psalm again and then sitting down. The actor leaned over to him and said, "You did much better than I, and now I understand why. I knew the psalm, but you knew the Shepherd." That's the kind of knowledge we should be after. Peter isn't interested in anything less.[7] Knowing God personally, intimately, is the most important kind of knowledge we should strive to possess.

Is it any wonder, then, that *knowledge* continues to be the repeated refrain in Peter's letter? Back in verse 2 we read, "May grace and peace be multiplied to you in the *knowledge* of God. . . ." He trumpeted it again in verse 3: "through the *knowledge* of him who called us to his own glory." Further on he will allude to it by way of contrast: "For if, after they have escaped the defilements of the world through the *knowledge* of our Lord . . ." (2:20). And Peter will choose to close the letter on this same note: "But grow in the grace and *knowledge* of our Lord and Savior Jesus Christ" (3:18). Peter couldn't make himself any clearer. If we are going to finish this life well, we must know God. To faith in Christ, let us add a praiseworthy life. To that let us add knowledge. We must get to work on knowing God. This is the pathway that leads us home.

Self-Control

To knowledge Peter adds the term "self-control." I recall once or twice turning to one of my children and saying, "Listen to me. If you don't learn to control yourself, who will? If you can't control yourself, what hope is there of someone else doing it for you?" On the rare occasion when this kind of reasoning has been required, they have stared at me quietly in an attempt to process my parental logic. But truly, how can a parent, or an employer or whoever, control others if they stubbornly determine not to control themselves?

Peter is saying to those learning to follow Christ, "Begin to control yourself. Say no to ungodly passions. Grow up. Get on your feet; pick up your faith; do what is right; increase in your knowledge of God; for your own salvation's sake, begin to control yourself." Make no mistake about it—our entrance into an eternal inheritance will be won through self-control. And remember, God has already given us everything it takes to get the job done.

Steadfastness

To self-control we must add "steadfastness." The word is almost synonymous with strength and longevity. It means that as we begin to control our passions, we take the next step by walking in that way for a long way. Having set out for Heaven through faith in Christ, we must now continue on in that same direction. Be loyal to that which you have taken up. When sin overtakes you, don't let it derail you for long. Get back on the track of steadfastness. Peter learned this experientially, and he now passes it on to us. He can see the finish line before him (1:14), and he would have us follow in his steps.

Godliness

To steadfastness we must add "godliness." The Apostle Paul picks up on this word in Titus 1:1. There he writes about possessing "knowledge of the truth" in such a way that it "accords with godliness." Later on in that pastoral letter Paul equates godliness with "good works."[8]

For Peter, the term *godliness* was explicitly defined in his first letter. There he wrote, "Keep your conduct among the Gentiles honorable, so that when they speak against you as evildoers, they may see your good deeds and glorify God on the day of visitation" (2:12). Following this, he went on to describe what this looks like using three words. Godliness was *submission* to authority (2:13, 18; 3:1), a willingness to embrace *suffering* (2:20; 3:14; 4:1, 19), and *service* (4:1–11). Therefore, when Peter joins godliness to steadfastness, he is calling us to the exalted plane of a Christlike life. Like Jesus, may we be known for submissive lives, the ability to suffer for the gospel in joy, and service to the church and world.

Brotherly Affection

To godliness we must add "brotherly affection." Peter was the recipient of Jesus' brotherly affection that morning on the beach after the resurrection. After being wounded by Peter's three denials, Jesus shared a meal with him. They remained brothers, family. We are now called to do the same thing. When a brother or sister in Christ fails us, will we run in the opposite direction when they seek restoration? Will we determine to hold on to the hurt in case we need it later as leverage over them? Or will we exhibit the mark of brotherly affection? Our affections for others must be warmed by our own experience of Christ's love for us.

Love

It comes as no surprise to anyone that the golden chain finishes on the landing of "love." Here we stand upon the threshold of Heaven. We have arrived at the gate. For God is love. In poetic form Peter has given us the golden chain. The way forward for fallen people—the ascending journey home for any who desire to finish well—has been written down.

In these short verses Peter has summarized his ideas on Christian discipleship. This is how to keep from falling. And this is how to remain effective for Christ in this world as well as in the next. We know this because he goes on to write:

> For if these qualities are yours and are increasing, they keep you from being ineffective or unfruitful in the knowledge of our Lord Jesus Christ. For whoever lacks these qualities is so nearsighted that he is blind, having forgotten that he was cleansed from his former sins. (1:8, 9)

Our faith must be a growing faith if we are going to be useful to God on earth. To think otherwise is foolish, unwise, and blind toward the activity of God in our life and his plans for our growth. May we all apply these words to our heart and life! This is the road map. Live out verses 3–8 and find your way home.

Appeal: Take Care to Ensure Your Entrance into the Kingdom (vv. 10, 11)

Peter closes this portion of his teaching by making an appeal. He writes:

> Therefore, brothers, be all the more diligent to make your calling and election sure, for if you practice these qualities you will never fall. For in this way there will be richly provided for you an entrance into the eternal kingdom of our Lord and Savior Jesus Christ. (1:10, 11)

Imagine gaining entrance into the eternal home of the One we failed so miserably. It doesn't get any better than that. Getting there, though, demands diligence, repentance, and walking in the way that Peter is showing us.

Satan would have every Christian think that there is no way back to a vibrant relationship with God once he or she has fallen and failed him. What Peter has told us though is, "That's not true. Don't believe it. I fell, and I am going to finish well. You can do so too. For God has already given you what you need (1:3, 4). Begin walking the road back (1:5–9). Take care to arrive safely (1:10, 11)."

If Peter could preach to us, I think he would say something like, "I know you've fallen. I know you've failed Jesus. So did I. I have also experienced those unwanted companions of guilt and shame. They were once at my heels. But in God there is hope and grace. So, on your feet, ascend the path to Heaven."

Our Heavenly Father, give us the true knowledge of God. And help us to hold tight to your promises in Christ. Encourage and strengthen each person to supplement his or her faith with godly qualities. And may you provide an entrance for us into the eternal kingdom of our Lord Jesus Christ. In Jesus' name, we pray, amen.

Therefore I intend always to remind you of these qualities, though you know them and are established in the truth that you have. I think it right, as long as I am in this body, to stir you up by way of reminder, since I know that the putting off of my body will be soon, as our Lord Jesus Christ made clear to me. And I will make every effort so that after my departure you may be able at any time to recall these things.

1:12–15

22

Final Words on Matters of First Importance

2 PETER 1:12–15

Final Words

Final words are often meant to communicate things of first importance. Parents remind children of something important just before walking out the door—"Now, remember what I told you. Don't forget!" Bosses give their employees final instructions before leaving for an extended vacation. And every spring, educational institutions gather their graduating seniors for one final speech before sending them out into the world. Final words communicate things of first importance.

I suppose this explains why the church has always placed special significance on the last words of her leaders. When Samuel Rutherford was on his deathbed, someone was close by with a pen to record his dying testament: "Dear brethren, do all for Him. Pray for Christ. Preach for Christ. Do all for Christ; beware of men-pleasing. The chief shepherd will shortly appear."[1] John Wesley's final declaration was captured as well: "The best of all is, God is with us." He would say those words three times in succession, as if for emphasis, and then he expired with, "Farewell."[2] Lyle Dorsett, able historian and lover of Jesus, retells some of the closing declarations of the great evangelist D. L. Moody. "The ailing preacher roused from sleep and in slow, measured words announced: 'Earth recedes; Heaven opens for me.'" Dorsett goes on to speak of various family members coming to Moody's bedside to receive final instructions about their role in the work after his departure.[3]

The Literary Style of 2 Peter

The letter before us gives some indication that we are reading Peter's farewell address—his final declaration and testament.[4] Verses 13, 14 read, "I think it right, as long as I am in this body, to stir you up by way of reminder, since I know that the putting off of my body will be soon, as our Lord Jesus Christ made clear to me." Concerning the literary style of this letter, New Testament scholar Douglas Moo has commented:

> Many scholars classify it as a "testament" or at least think that it has many of the characteristics of a testament . . . a book or part of a book, in which a person makes a final speech from his or her deathbed. . . . Typical features of these testaments are:
>
> 1. The speaker knows (sometimes by prophecy) that he is about to die.
> 2. The speaker gathers around him his children or a similar audience.
> 3. The speaker often impresses on his audience the need for his hearers to remember his teaching as an example.
> 4. The speaker makes predictions about the future.
> 5. The speaker gives moral exhortations.[5]

While the parallels between 2 Peter and other first-century final testaments are not exact, there are enough similarities to allow us to think of the letter in this way. Like Moody of old, Peter has come to terms with the idea that his days on earth are receding. Heaven will soon be opened to him. Knowing that the church couldn't possibly make it to his bedside, Peter, ever the productive one, picks up his pen in an effort to put his final testament down on paper.[6] These final words, no doubt, were meant to convey that which is most important.

Matters of First Importance

The Lessons Peter Has for Us to Learn: Faith and Following

We would do well to pay attention. In the previous passage (1:5–9) we have been reminded that *our faith must grow*. If we want to finish well, our faith must be supplemented with qualities that will keep us from falling. In the passage we will study next (1:16–21), the reminder on growing faith will give way to our need to *follow in the apostolic way*. We will see that finishing well demands abiding in the fullness of the teaching and the final authority of all the Scriptures.

The verses we consider here, however, stand in between these two great lessons. As such they provide us a transition in the text. In them we are introduced to the heart of Peter and the aim of this letter. For him, the night of his falling must have seemed like ancient history. Decades now separate him from his threefold denial of Jesus. Years of faithful service stand in between, years in which he lived vigorously for Christ. Jesus had been right all along—his faith had not failed. Peter would have those words be true for us too.

The Method Peter Uses to Teach Us: A Threefold Reminder

In disclosing the nearness of his death, Peter not only underlines the urgency of the hour and, therefore, the importance of his words but he reveals the method by which he would have us learn. He teaches by way of *reminder*. In fact, in these four brief verses he puts his favorite pedagogical term into play no fewer than three times.

- 1:12: "Therefore I intend always to *remind* you."
- 1:13: "I think it is right . . . to stir you up by way of *reminder*."
- 1:15: "I will make every effort so that . . . you may be able at any time to *recall* these things."

"I am writing to *remind* you . . . by way of *reminder* . . . so that . . . you may be able . . . to *recall* these things." Peter's commitment to this method of teaching is so thoroughgoing that he extends it to the entire letter. In the closing chapter he will say again, "This is now the second letter that I am writing to you, beloved. In both of them I am stirring up your sincere mind by way of *reminder*, that you should *remember* . . ." (3:1, 2).

What are we to make of this if not that finishing well requires returning to things we have already learned. What a comfort this truth should be in this day and age. Spiritual teachers abound who seem to always be chasing something new. Like salesmen, they are restless with the apostolic gospel. They claim to be able to give us more. In essence, they would have us think that the gospel that we were saved by is not strong enough to be the gospel by which we should continue standing.

Evidently our day has many things in common with the early church. Those early followers of Christ were accosted by new teachings, doctrine cut loose from the moral and ethical standards of the One whom Peter preached. Knowing this, Peter decides to close out his life as a preacher by way of reminder. We should mark this insight well. We can never outgrow the good news that Jesus came to make substitution for sin and that this teaching—received by faith—makes demands upon us to live upright, changed, and holy lives. So remember that, according to Peter, nothing new will have the power to establish us in the faith.

The Intentions Peter Has for Us: Established in Truth

Peter intends for us to be established in the faith.

> Therefore I intend always to remind you of these qualities, though you
> know them and are established in the truth that you have.

This is an interesting sentence. On the one hand, he claims that his readers already "know . . . and are established." Yet, on the other hand, if their
knowledge and footing in the truth was firmly fixed, there would be no need
to remind them of anything.

By embedding his intention within a threefold call to remember, we
can be assured that he desires us to be more firmly rooted. The word
translated "established" here can also mean to *stabilize* or *strengthen*. In
this way, Peter wants his readers to progress in the gospel from strength
to strength. Indeed, as we said in the opening chapter, the word *strengthen*
was the very word Jesus gave to Peter on the fateful night in which he not
only predicted about his impending threefold denial but also prophesied
what would be his role in the church after he had come to repentance (Luke
22:31, 32).

Some of what I want to say now was already said in an earlier chapter.
However, given the emphasis in this text on preaching by way of *reminder*,
it is worth repeating here. One dramatic life experience stands behind the
writing of this letter—the dark night of Jesus' betrayal. Earlier that evening,
in the presence of all the disciples, Jesus had said, "You will all *fall* away
because of me this night, for it is written, 'I will strike the shepherd, and the
sheep will be scattered'" (Matthew 26:31). Upon hearing these words from
Jesus, Peter, our beloved and self-proclaimed superman, shot back, "Though
they all fall away . . . I will never fall away. . . . Even if I must die with you,
I will not deny you!" (vv. 33, 35). Jesus returned the fire: "Oh, Peter, before
the rooster gets going in the morning, you will deny me three times." And
what happened? Peter did fall.

Interestingly, in 2 Peter it only takes ten verses for Peter's desire to keep
us from *falling* to emerge as one of this letter's aims. "Therefore, brothers,
be all the more diligent to make your calling and election sure, for if you
practice these qualities *you will never fall*" (1:10). In addition to this linguistic connection, on that same fateful night Jesus also said, "Simon, Simon,
behold, Satan demanded to have you, that he might sift you like wheat, but I
have prayed for you that your faith may not fail. And when you have turned
again, *strengthen* your brothers" (Luke 22:31, 32). Intriguingly, the word
translated *strengthen* is the same word we are exploring in the text before us.

In 1:12 we read, "Therefore I intend always to remind you of these
qualities, though you know them and are *established* in the truth that you
have." This same word appears in chapter 2, but there in contrast with false
teachers. Verse 14 reads, "They have eyes full of adultery, insatiable for sin.
They entice *unsteady* souls."

Finally, this brief letter closes under the weight and intention of this same language. Second Peter 3:17 reads, "You therefore, beloved, knowing this beforehand, take care that you are not carried away with the error of lawless people and lose your own *stability*."

To state this clearly, the term "established" in 1:12 is being leveraged here, along with the word "fall" in 1:10, to capture afresh the dying preacher's aim and intention in writing. With his own death imminent, Peter is determined to fulfill his calling before God by *strengthening* those of us who would follow in his train centuries later. In this sense, then, and by this letter most especially, Peter lives on. He can still be found preaching his "how-to" manual on the manner in which our faith is to be nurtured from the point of personal failure to finishing well. Therefore, let us sit together under the preaching ministry of Peter and apply these lessons to our heart and life, for they are born out of nothing less than the perfect and authoritative voice of Christ.

A Faith That Flourishes

The term translated at different times in the New Testament as "steady," "established," and "strengthen" is an architectural one at its core. Thus, as we set out to apply it to our lives we can turn for insight to the role of today's structural engineer. After all, like Peter who is building the church, the primary role of the structural engineer is that of ensuring *stability*. One structural engineer has written:

> Most people readily think of vertical stability and can quickly relate that to the need for securing solid foundations. . . . Heavier loads require deeper, more solid foundations lest they become unstable. Also important is the horizontal stability of a structure. This is what ensures that a building doesn't blow over in a hurricane, or shake loose during a seismic (earthquake) event.[7]

For everyone coming to grips with the aim of Peter the application can't be missed. Christians who keep themselves from falling—Christians who have a faith that flourishes—Christians who will finish well—will be those who dig a little deeper as well as those who find ways to resist the winds in their spiritual efforts to go a little higher.

Take the apostolic reminder to heart. Walk in such a way that the qualities of mature faith become your own. Add virtue and then knowledge. Add to knowledge by exercising self-control. Be steadfast and grow in godliness. Start demonstrating by your actions that you have a godly and familial affection for others. End in love. And remember, Peter's last words were meant to remind you that Heaven is gained by way of these important and grace-filled qualities.

Our Heavenly Father, help us to mark well these final words of first importance. May we give ourselves to the joyful task of remembering all that we have learned about the gospel, especially those matters that demonstrate what it demands of us. In Jesus' name, amen.

For we did not follow cleverly devised myths when we made known to you the power and coming of our Lord Jesus Christ, but we were eyewitnesses of his majesty. For when he received honor and glory from God the Father, and the voice was borne to him by the Majestic Glory, "This is my beloved Son, with whom I am well pleased," we ourselves heard this very voice borne from heaven, for we were with him on the holy mountain. And we have something more sure, the prophetic word, to which you will do well to pay attention as to a lamp shining in a dark place, until the day dawns and the morning star rises in your hearts, knowing this first of all, that no prophecy of Scripture comes from someone's own interpretation. For no prophecy was ever produced by the will of man, but men spoke from God as they were carried along by the Holy Spirit.

1:16–21

23

Following in the Apostolic Way

2 PETER 1:16–21

THE *CATECHISM OF THE CATHOLIC CHURCH* reserves a unique, powerful, and exalted place for Peter among all the apostles. It states:

> The Lord made Simon alone, whom he named Peter, the "rock" of his Church. He gave him the keys of his Church and instituted him shepherd of the whole flock. . . . This pastoral office of Peter and the other apostles belongs to the Church's very foundation and is continued by the bishops under the primacy of the Pope. The *Pope*, Bishop of Rome and Peter's successor, "is the perpetual and visible source and foundation of the unity both of the bishops and of the whole company of the faithful. For the Roman Pontiff, by reason of his office as Vicar of Christ, and as pastor of the entire Church has full, supreme, and universal power over the whole Church, a power which he can always exercise unhindered."[1]

The statement is striking, not only for the elevated position it bestows upon Peter over and above the others, but perhaps more so for the unparalleled power it bequeaths to every bishop of Rome who follows him in succession.

The Issue of Authority in the Post-Apostolic Era

I suppose, if ever there was a time for Peter to put down in writing this plan of apostolic succession, the text before us would be it. After all, in the preceding verses he stated that "the putting off of my body will be soon, as our Lord Jesus Christ made clear to me. And I will make every effort so that after my departure you may be able at any time to recall these things" (vv. 14, 15). Thus, with dominical knowledge that the apostolic era was drawing to a close, and an awareness that he was writing this letter to establish the church after his impending death, we might rightly expect Peter to interact with the succession plan during this time when he asks the faithful to contemplate the implications of his departure. Put simply, in 1:16–21 we expect to learn what it will look like to follow in the apostolic way long after the great apostle has died.

In light of this, verses 16–21 are fascinating, both for what they tell us as well as what they leave unsaid. There is not a word here that even hints that Peter intends for us to follow in the way of apostolic succession. No other person or plan is put forward. Rather, in response to an *accusation*, Peter advances an intricate *argument* elevating the Scriptures above everything else. A person's willingness to submit himself or herself to the authority and teaching of the Bible alone is held up by Peter as the unique, powerful, and exalted way for all those following in the apostolic faith.

Arriving at your own conclusion on the role and primacy of the Scriptures will require a working knowledge of the *accusation* made against Peter as well as the *argument* he puts forward to combat it.

The Insidious Accusation against Peter

Faith, Fairy Tales, and Final Judgment

The text opens with Peter defending his gospel against the accusation that his teaching, along with that of the other apostles, followed the stuff of fairy tales. The opening line states:

> For we did not follow cleverly devised myths when we made known to you
> the power and coming of our Lord Jesus Christ. (v. 16a)

A careful reading of this verse discloses that some people in the early church were willing to dismiss *certain aspects* of the apostles' teaching as outdated and antiquated. The challenged teaching, that which was being called fable, or myth to be more exact, pertained to "the power and coming of our Lord Jesus Christ."

The word translated "coming" is an important one. It must refer here to Jesus' Second Coming and not to his first—for words have meaning in context, and the context of 2 Peter is eschatological throughout.[2] To confirm this, simply look ahead to 3:4, where Peter writes, "They will say, 'Where is the promise of his *coming*? For ever since the fathers fell asleep, all things are continuing as they were from the beginning of creation.'" In addition to this, a few verses later Peter uses *coming* for a third time in relation to the end of the age. In 3:11, 12 we read:

> Since all these things are thus to be dissolved, what sort of people ought you to be in lives of holiness and godliness, waiting for and hastening the coming of the day of God, because of which the heavens will be set on fire and dissolved, and the heavenly bodies will melt as they burn!

In view of this, the accusation against Peter's teaching at the close of his life is as clear as a light shining in a dark place. Other more enlightened teachers have arrived on the church scene, and they have begun to question, "What is all this dark talk about Jesus coming again to judge the living and the dead? Certainly this must be false. After all, the apostles themselves are all passing away before our very eyes, and there is no sign of his return."

This charge against Peter was truly insidious, the fullness of which we will take up in future chapters. At this point, however, know this: their rejection of the Second Coming had more to do with their desire to dismiss the notion that everyone will be held personally accountable for moral and ethical infidelity than anything else. This should not come as any surprise. Within the history of the church there have always been teachers willing to tell you that you are free to do whatever you want, whenever you want, with whomever you want, without fear of divine punishment. This insidious teaching rests upon the false premise that insists that because God is love, God will forgive all vices that were once thought of as incompatible with godly virtue. In essence, the doctrine of the Second Coming was jettisoned because people want to secure the ability to live as they please. Our studies in chapters 2 and 3 will help make this point more clear. But for now it is enough to summarize the accusation against Peter and the apostles this way:

> The apostles' belief in the final judgment, a day when Jesus will hold each of us accountable for moral and ethical infidelity, is simply the stuff of fairy tales that stems largely from the fertility of Peter's imagination. Therefore, following the strict ethical and moral force of his faith is unnecessary.

To this charge, Peter would have his readers know that everything he taught, including his views on the Second Coming of Christ in judgment, rested not on fable or fairy tale but on the strength of the Hebrew Scriptures, particularly the prophetic discourses that confirmed the veracity of his personal experience. To see this for ourselves we turn to the intricate argument that he advanced in defense of his view.

Peter's Intricate Argument

Attacking Negative Reviews by Use of the Negative
(vv. 16a with v. 20b and v. 21a)

For starters, the intricacy of Peter's argument involves even the manner in which he chooses to begin and finish his defense. Notice, the text begins and ends with two negatively stated truths. The first is found at the outset (v. 16), while the other appears at the close (vv. 20, 21). The negatively stated truths that Peter advances are:

- 1:16: "For we did *not* follow . . ."
- 1:20: "*No* prophecy of Scripture comes from someone's own interpretation. . . ."
- 1:21: "For *no* prophecy was ever produced by the will of man. . . ."

On each occasion Peter positions authority in the post-apostolic era away from people and persons. And in their place he puts the very words of God. Ironically, Peter attacks the glaring negativity of his personal rivals by use of the grammatical negative! In fact, as we will soon see, the only person left with "a power which he can always exercise unhindered" (*Catechism of the Catholic Church* on Peter) will be Jesus Christ, the living Word of God, who is spoken of here as God's "beloved Son" (1:17).

Thus, with two negatively charged lines serving as bookends for his thought, Peter canonizes the living and written Word of God as our sole authority in the post-apostolic age. It will be the *words* of the biblical apostles and prophets, as given to them by the Holy Spirit, that provide the lone voice for the faithful after Peter's death.

In essence, following in the apostolic way will not involve submitting your faith to fairy tales or fanciful teachers. The apostles and the prophets were men whose personal experience and teaching was the result of hearing God's voice—which came to them in the form of words—and that in the power of the Holy Spirit. And God confirmed their experiences, visions, and revelations by the light afforded to them in the rest of the Scriptures.[3]

The Limits of Fairy Tales, Fables, and Faith (vv. 16b–18)

A second aspect of the intricacy of Peter's argument is seen in verses 16b–18. Now remember, he is still waging verbal war against the accusation that certain aspects of his teaching were nothing more than the stuff of myths, fables, or old wives' tales. By following the logical flow of the text we will see that while Peter links his teaching on Christ's coming judgment to what he *sees* and *hears*, he will go on, and this is most important, to submit the entire fairy-tale-like existential experience to that which he *reads* in the prophets. For Peter, that word alone is most sure. Thus the prophetic voice written down in the Scriptures and independent of his own experience will be enough to support his teaching on the final judgment.

At first blush, though, it does appear that Peter attempts to support himself against his accusers strictly on the basis of what he sees and hears.

> But we were eyewitnesses of his majesty. For when he received honor and glory from God the Father, and the voice was borne to him by the Majestic Glory, "This is my beloved Son, with whom I am well pleased," we ourselves heard this very voice borne from heaven, for we were with him on the holy mountain. (vv. 16b–18)

Four times in these brief verses Peter writes about what he saw and heard. The personal experience he recounts is the Transfiguration event (see Matthew 17, Mark 9, and Luke 9). On that day long ago, Jesus had taken Peter, James, and John to "the holy mountain." There, before their very eyes (v. 16), Jesus was transfigured in brilliant and translucent light. On either side of Jesus stood the great Hebrew prophets Moses and Elijah. Then, as if seeing this fable-like experience wasn't enough, Peter and the others with him later claimed that they also *heard* the voice of the Majestic Glory coming from Heaven declaring that Jesus was greater than both Moses and Elijah—"This is my beloved Son, with whom I am well pleased" (2 Peter 1:17).

We can only imagine what Peter's accusers would do with this story. "Well, that's nice for you, Peter, but we didn't see it and we didn't hear it. But if you can produce a god-like figure before our very eyes, and a voice that calls to us from Heaven, one that we hear with our own ears, then we might be willing to believe the implications you are drawing from such an event about the supremacy and final reign of Jesus. But if you can't, well, we don't think the world is obligated to hold certain aspects of your view. For all the supposed light present in your experience, it simply leaves us in the dark."

During World War II six Allied fighter pilots were on a mission when their aircraft carrier received orders for a blackout because enemy submarines were in the area. The fighter pilots completed their mission but were surprised to find no landing lights where the ship ought to have been. One of the pilots radioed the ship, "Give us some light so we can land." The response came back, "Negative. We can't give you any light at this time. A full blackout has been ordered." A bit later a second pilot requested, "Give us some light so we can land." "Negative. Blackout still in effect." A third pilot, dangerously low on fuel, said, "Can't you at least give us *one* light so we can land?" The radio operator was told to discontinue all contact. As a result, six fighters reportedly went down in the dark waters of the Atlantic.

Like the accusers in Peter's day, many people today refuse to submit their life and behavior to Jesus on the charge they have not been given enough light to land. Until they see something or hear something or feel something, they simply will not believe they are ultimately going to be accountable to Someone for anything. To them, Peter's God-man, standing in transfigured light, is nothing more than a hardened and callous being— one who has turned off the switch and left them completely in the dark. In contrast to the experience of those fighter pilots, these persons are refusing the light that is available to them; like those pilots, they are headed for certain death.

Submitting Personal Experience to the Prophetic Word of Psalm 2 (v. 19)

Peter is well aware that his detractors will argue along these lines. So he quickly moves beyond that which he saw with his eyes and heard with his ears to speak of a light more sure and reliable than both—the prophetic word that God so graciously gave us to read.

> And we have something more sure, the prophetic word, to which you will do well to pay attention as to a lamp shining in a dark place, until the day dawns and the morning star rises in your hearts. (1:19)

It is as if Peter, on the verge of departing from this world, desires to lift up his voice one final time in an effort to declare to the church throughout all time, "Listen to me—I was an eyewitness to the saving acts of God in history. And I know that after Christ's death and resurrection God will have no need to ever again perform these things in the presence of another generation. But remember, this in no way means that your faith is inferior to mine [1:1]. We have both been given the prophetic promises of God. We can all read the words written down long ago. They are a more sure light than anything I ever saw or heard. Beloved, my seeing these things is important. Witnesses are essential. But God does not need to appear in the flesh every forty or fifty years to enlighten us and confirm his love to us. Seeing isn't essential for believing—reading God's Word is!"

The particular prophetic word that helped Peter make sense of the Transfiguration event, as well as the text that confirmed his belief in Christ's coming judgment, was probably Psalm 2. The connection between the two undoubtedly arose from the voice he heard from Heaven, a voice that thundered, "This is my beloved *Son*, with whom I am well pleased."

Like the Transfiguration event, this Psalm also has a voice calling out from Heaven: "I will tell of the decree: The LORD said to me, 'You are my *Son*, today I have begotten you. Ask of me, and I will make the nations your heritage, and the ends of the earth your possession'" (vv. 7, 8). Further, this messianic Psalm proclaims beyond a shadow of a doubt that the one whom God calls "my Son" is the same one who will come in power and glory to judge all the peoples of the earth. "You shall break them with a rod of iron and dash them in pieces like a potter's vessel" (v. 9). The Psalm ends by ordering all who are on the earth to "Serve the Lord with fear, and rejoice with trembling. Kiss the *Son*, lest he be angry, and you perish in the way, for his wrath is quickly kindled. Blessed are all who take refuge in him" (vv. 11, 12).

Notice: this Psalm on the Son makes the irrefutable argument for a coming return in judgment. Peter's teaching that *this* Jesus is God's anointed Son may have its origins in what he saw and heard, but the notion that this same One will one day hold each of us accountable for our moral and ethical infidelity is rooted in God's prophetic Word. According to 2 Peter 1:19, that truth is fixed—it is surer than anything the mind of man could dream up. A coming final judgment is not the stuff of fairy tales. It is no myth. This view rests upon the foundation of God's unalterable revelation put into words.[4]

I don't know what you have been taught about a fixed day when Jesus will come to judge the living and the dead. Perhaps you still have questions about the words written down long ago. Perhaps, like Peter's readers, you find it hard to place your trust in ideas that you can't see with your own eyes or touch with your own hands or hear with your own ears. If so, listen for a moment to the voice of Charles Spurgeon, a prominent nineteenth-century London preacher who responded to the enlightened and urbane doubters of his own age:

> If I heard a voice speaking from the sky I would obey it, but the form in which your call has come has been better than that, for Peter in his second epistle tells us that he himself heard a voice out of the excellent glory when he was with our Lord in the holy mount, but he adds, "we have also a more sure word of prophecy"; as if the testimony which is in the word of God, the light that shineth in a dark place, which beams forth from the word of God, was more sure than even the voice which he heard from heaven. . . . Do not say that you would accept that call if it were spoken with a voice rather than written; you know that is not so in daily life. If a man receives a written letter from his father or a friend, does he attach less importance to it than he would have done to his spoken communication? I reckon that many of you in business are quite content to get written orders for goods, and when you get them you do not require a purchaser to ask you in person, you would just as soon that he should not; in fact you commonly say that you would like to have it in black and white. Is it not so? Well then you have your wish, here is the call in black and white: and I do but speak according to common sense when I say that if the Lord's call to you be

written in the Bible, and it certainly is, you do not speak truth when you say, "I would listen to it if it were spoken, but I cannot listen to it because it is written." The call as given by the book of inspiration ought to have over your minds a masterly power, and if your hearts were right before God that word spoken in the Scriptures by the Holy Ghost would be at once obeyed.[5]

What Spurgeon said to the people of his own day is true for us who live in this present age. The surprise is in recognizing the similarity between us and those who wrestled with the issue of impending final judgment in the first century. Indeed, all humanity is cut from the same cloth. On this issue of faith the centuries converge and collapse into one.

So, don't think that your doubts are unique or anything new. Don't think that God has left you in the dark with no place to land. The Scriptures proclaim that this Jesus of Nazareth is God's Son. And he will come to judge the living and the dead. Believe what you read. As Peter says:

> You will do well to pay attention as to a lamp shining in a dark place, until
> the day dawns and the morning star rises in your hearts. (v. 19)

Perhaps you awoke this morning under the darkened illusion that you need a gleaming vision of the living God to appear in your cubicle at work before coming to faith. That is a myth, a fairy tale indeed. Simply take God at his Word, and the fog will lift, the light of his Word will illumine your path, and the day will dawn with the warmth of God's morning star taking up residence in your heart.

The All-Inclusive Authority of Scripture (vv. 20, 21)

No Prophecy Came Forth from the Mind or Will of Man

Before Peter closed out his intricate argument, he had one more important point to make. He wanted his readers to know that what was true for him was true for every prophet. Just as his teaching on final judgment found its roots in the authority of Scripture rather than coming from the fertility of his imagination, the same could be said for every ancient spokesman for God. He writes:

> . . . knowing this first of all, that no prophecy of Scripture comes from
> someone's own interpretation. For no prophecy was ever produced by the
> will of man, but men spoke from God as they were carried along by the
> Holy Spirit. (vv. 20, 21)

In essence, he is arguing that the Bible, in particular the fullness of its message from first to last, isn't myth. It isn't the stuff of fables and fairy tales. Nothing written down here came forth from the mind or will of man. As such, the Scriptures are not a human record of the history of God; rather, they contain the true and authoritative story of God as he enters into human history.

Carried Along by the Holy Spirit

Peter uses an interesting word to capture this reality. He writes that the authors of Scripture were *"carried* along by the Holy Spirit." "Carried" is the Greek word *pharoe*, from which we get our word *ferry*. In essence, Peter argues that all the writers of Scripture were ferried along by the Holy Spirit and arrived at the same destination. One has to imagine these writers as cars aboard a ferry. Each one got on the ferry—each one appeared to be doing his own thing—each one delivered his own distinctive word. But at the same time the owner of the ferry—in this case, God—made sure they all landed together at his port of call because he carried them to their destination on the ballast and strength of his Spirit.[6]

The aging apostle, the one who sits at the close of life writing his last will and testament, is leaving in a blaze of glory. Under Peter's hand and with truly enlightened logic this letter gives the rights, privilege, and power of "unhindered authority" only to the living and written Word of God. Submitting yourself, therefore, to the full teaching of the Bible is what it means to follow in the apostolic way.

I never tire of reading Tolkien's The Lord of the Rings. Like Peter, Bilbo Baggins, the aging voice of an era, is aware that the time of his departure has come. So he invites the good folks of Hobbiton to gather around him one last time. His final declaration and testament is given on the night that he throws a party to celebrate his one hundred and eleventh birthday, which he calls his eleventy-first birthday. Just before slipping on his magic ring and disappearing forever from their sight he concludes with these words:

> I wish to make an ANNOUNCEMENT. . . . I regret to announce that—
> though, as I said, eleventy-one years is far too short a time to spend among
> you—this is the END. I am going, I am leaving. NOW. GOODBYE!

Tolkien then writes, "He stepped down and vanished. There was a blinding flash of light, and the guests all blinked. When they opened their eyes Bilbo was nowhere to be seen. One hundred and forty-four flabbergasted hobbits sat back speechless."[7]

What a way to go—in a blinding flash of light! As it was for Bilbo, so it was for Peter. But by way of contrast, after Peter's departure, the light still shines bright. The way home remains illuminating and clear. May we all get home before dark.

Our Heavenly Father, we thank you for each day and for your Word. And we thank you that aged Peter put down on paper what we need to know to keep from falling. Help us believe all that we read in the Bible. And, by your Holy Spirit, bring our lives into conformity to its truth. In Christ's name, amen.

But false prophets also arose among the people, just as there will be false teachers among you, who will secretly bring in destructive heresies, even denying the Master who bought them, bringing upon themselves swift destruction. And many will follow their sensuality, and because of them the way of truth will be blasphemed. And in their greed they will exploit you with false words. Their condemnation from long ago is not idle, and their destruction is not asleep. For if God did not spare angels when they sinned, but cast them into hell and committed them to chains of gloomy darkness to be kept until the judgment; if he did not spare the ancient world, but preserved Noah, a herald of righteousness, with seven others, when he brought a flood upon the world of the ungodly; if by turning the cities of Sodom and Gomorrah to ashes he condemned them to extinction, making them an example of what is going to happen to the ungodly; and if he rescued righteous Lot, greatly distressed by the sensual conduct of the wicked (for as that righteous man lived among them day after day, he was tormenting his righteous soul over their lawless deeds that he saw and heard); then the Lord knows how to rescue the godly from trials, and to keep the unrighteous under punishment until the day of judgment, and especially those who indulge in the lust of defiling passion and despise authority.

2:1–10a

24

Portraits of Failing Faith

2 PETER 2:1–10a

IN OCTOBER 1855, at a time when society's views on the nature of biblical authority and human freedom were evolving and subject to change, Vincent van Gogh, the wildly talented yet tortured artist, completed an oil on canvas and titled it *Still Life with Bible*. Looking at it, one observes a table, and upon the table an open Bible. To the right of God's Word is a candle, burned out, standing in its holder. In the foreground the artist has painted a small yellow book. The print on the binding is still legible—it is Emile Zola's *The Joy of Life*.

By placing a burned-out candle beside the Bible and by putting both in the background, van Gogh is telling us that the time for walking through this world by the illumination of the Holy Spirit, who shines down upon God's Word, is past. Biblical authority no longer holds sway. People are guided by different, if not lesser lights. That is what he is saying. Even the flaming color of yellow is now reserved for the cover of another book. Humanity's new pursuit is governed by whatever brings us *the joy of life*.

Interestingly, that which van Gogh painted in oils in 1855, Peter had already pictured and commented on centuries ago. Like us, the aging apostle lived in a day when the light of God's Word seemed to be in danger of being snuffed out and extinguished altogether. People were following another path, carried along by a candle of a different sort.

Two Contrasting Galleries

Chapter One: The Anteroom

In chapter 1 of 2 Peter we watched the apostle paint his own set of portraits. We looked on as he presented a spellbinding portrait of Christ, vibrant and transfigured, all lit up on the holy mountain. Behind him, Peter splashed the ever-burning colors and superior illumination of God's Spirit and Word (1:16–21).

Earlier we gave attention to another painting in Peter's exhibit. That one drew upon his own spiritual fall many years earlier. It explored the nature of faith, especially the growing-faith qualities needed to finish well (1:3–11). Both of these portraits were done when Peter knew the time of his departure was at hand (1:12–15). Thus we sense that they were painted in a season of urgency—bold strokes all, racing against time, in an effort to establish us in the faith.

Through this artisan's fire, we now know two things: if we intend to make it across the threshold of Heaven with Peter, our *faith must grow* (1:3–11), and we must *follow in the apostolic way* (1:16–21). With that much in place, we take leave of this anteroom and follow the apostle into his second gallery.

Chapter 2: The Room of Conflict

The pictures hanging on the walls of 2 Peter 2 are painted with colors of a different palette. Here the apostle ushers us into his gallery of contrast. Here we come face to face with reminders that not everyone finishes the walk of *faith* well. Here we encounter a vast host who are tragically *following* a different way and encouraging others to do the same. Regarding his desire for us to take note of the intended contrast, Peter could not have been more obvious.

- 1:16: "For we did not *follow* . . ."
- 2:2: "And many will *follow* . . ."
- 2:15: "Forsaking the right way, they have gone astray. They have *followed* . . ."

In the end, Peter reveals, their faith will fail, and they will fall headlong into the dark place forevermore (2:1, 3, 4, 9, 12, 17).

Thus humanity is divided into two masses, each heading in an opposite direction. The first group, led by the Heaven-bound apostles, supplements their faith with good things and follows in the way of God's Word. The second band of travelers, a hideous-looking lot, is comprised of those of whom Peter says:

> But false prophets also arose among the people, just as there will be false teachers among you, who will secretly bring in destructive heresies, even denying the Master who bought them, bringing upon themselves swift destruction. And many will follow their sensuality, and because of them the way of truth will be blasphemed. And in their greed they will exploit

you with false words. Their condemnation from long ago is not idle, and their destruction is not asleep. (2:1–3)

The immense conflict represented by the two galleries jars the senses. The paintings here are constructed on entirely different lines. Gone are true prophets and teachers, and the faithful followers are nearly lost from view. Godly qualities are swept away. In their place stand sensuality and greed. The comforts and destination of Heaven are traded for condemnation and destruction. If it weren't for our presence and that of Peter's faithful onlookers, the entire lot in this gallery would seem headed toward one unwanted end, the final judgment of God.

Three Portraits of Those Who Fail to Finish Well

Three portraits hang starkly on the walls of the first ten verses.[1] In each, God's judgment is seen in the foreground. In fact, verses 4–9 are one long sentence in Greek, which allows us to think of the trio of paintings as a set. They were meant to hang together. If nothing else, the three "if" clauses that separate the pictures in verse 4, 5, and 6 prove it.

Importantly, as we will soon see, on three occasions Peter also elects to paint in the hues of those who finish well. Almost hidden from view, tucked into the background, are images of God rescuing the faithful who dwell in this world of God's ongoing wrath. When we arrive at the "but" of verse 5, the "if" clause in verse 7, and the "then" clause in verse 9, this aspect will become clear. In essence, then, even in this horrific gallery Peter will show us that God knows how to rescue his own while punishing the rebellious. It was that way in the ancient days of Israel's history. It was true for those dwelling in Peter's day. It will be true for those living at the end of time.

Collectively, the paintings make a powerful impression, especially coming on the heels, as they do, of what Peter has shown us in 1:16–21. There Peter was defending that central aspect of his teaching that declared that Jesus, God's Son, would come again in power and judgment. He was combating the notion, picked up and advanced by others, that coming judgment was a clever myth. Here he follows up with compelling portraits meant to communicate, "Where in the world did you ever come up with the idea that God would never judge anyone? Biblical history is filled with historical events that confirm the opposite. God has always judged those who follow the ways of the world rather than the ways of his Word." Thus it comes as no surprise to learn that all three paintings take biblical events as their theme. The subject matter for the collection includes the *angels*, the *ancient world*, and the *indecent cities*.[2]

The Angels: A Portrait of Autonomy (2:4)

With verse 4, we find a frightening painting of angelic autonomy. And as we gaze at it, we see God's fixed and final judgment falling, not on earth's congregation, but upon those who once were part of the worshiping host of Heaven:

> For if God did not spare angels when they sinned, but cast them into hell and committed them to chains of gloomy darkness to be kept until the judgment . . .

How incredible to be reminded that the road to Hell is paved by some who knew what it was, firsthand, to have *life* in the presence of God.[3] John Milton, in *Paradise Lost*, depicts Satan addressing his vanquished legions in their first astonished moments of defeat and despair after casting off God's authority and being thrown out of Heaven. The sense of autonomy Milton puts in the voice of the devil cannot be missed. Looking around at his faith-failing host, the fallen foe declares:

> All is not lost—the unconquerable Will,
> And study of revenge, immortal hate;
> And courage never to submit or yield:
> And what is else not to be overcome? . . .
> We may with more successful hope resolve
> To wage by force or guile eternal war,
> Irreconcilable to our grand Foe,
> Who now triumphs, and in the excess of joy
> Sole reigning holds the Tyranny of Heaven.[4]

Interestingly, if the portrait here is painted from the same charcoal drawings found in the book of Jude, Peter may not be referring to the Milton-like description of the angels' early fall from Heaven, but the later act of demonic activity found in the opening verses of Genesis 6. There the sons of God (at times a biblical term for angels) transgressed their proper domain and began to take up demonic residence in some men for the purpose of pleasing their own insatiable, lustful appetite for ravishing women.

In either case, the message for us is clear. By way of contrast, we have seen just how far autonomy will take us. God's righteous judgment will descend to earth. Make no mistake. Do not be misled. Are you in danger of forgetting that God did not even spare the angels? When tempted to follow today's cadre of teachers, those who have abandoned belief in a fixed and final judgment because of sensuality and greed, come and stand before this portrait in Peter's gallery—be reminded to stay the course by following in the apostolic way. Put away all thoughts and behavior leading to, and caught in, the death grip of avarice and adultery. God's judgment came as a result of these things, and surely it will come again.

The Ancient World: A Portrait of Apostasy (v. 5)

The second frame affixed to the wall holds a picture of the ancient world. Verse 5 reads:

> If he did not spare the ancient world, but preserved Noah, a herald of righteousness, with seven others, when he brought about a flood upon the world of the ungodly . . .

Peter floods the canvas, in depth and pathos, with brushstrokes that capture the watery grave of Noah's day. Lest his repentant readers forget and slide back into the drowning lie that God never punishes sin, Peter portrays God's judgment as it occurred in ancient times. In that day people and teachers alike lived and ate and drank. They married and gave themselves to the joys of life. Until, that is, it was too late. The ground underneath them was saturated with water, ever rising water, until it swept them all away.

This portrait is rightly thought of as one of *apostasy* since Noah, who lived among them, continued preaching the word of God to them about the coming day of wrath. Peter will draw upon this painting again when he argues that what took place then, with water, will come again, but this time in fire (3:1–7).

The one ray of hope in the painting is the background colors given to Noah and seven others who were rescued. This is Peter the painter at his best. All those who make their way through this gallery of conflict are afforded some grace and hope. Therefore take heed, onlookers, and begin in earnest to live lives worthy of the fullness of the apostolic gospel.

Indecent Cities: A Portrait of Ease and Immorality (v. 6)

Peter continues on, fast and furious with his paints. Before the oils even dry, he squeezes more colors from his tubes and splashes out yet a third picture, this one a portrait of ease and immorality. Look at verse 6:

> . . . if by turning the cities of Sodom and Gomorrah to ashes he condemned them to extinction, making them an example of what is going to happen to the ungodly.

On the night that angelic visitors came to the home of Lot, they told him that God was coming to judge the city. The true account in Genesis 18, 19 of the destruction of Sodom and Gomorrah retells one of the most horrific events that ever occurred.

There's no indication that Lot thought these angelic destroyers to be anything but human visitors—travelers on their way though town. Yet, in righteousness he tried to keep them from being molested by the men of the city. He brought them into his home. Evidently Sodom and Gomorrah were places of self-indulgence. The appetites of their citizens were without restraint. People were never sated; they were always famished and wanting more.

Through another ancient prophet of that day God would later say of these two cities:

> . . . she and her daughters had pride, excess of food, and prosperous ease, but did not aid the poor and needy. They were haughty and did an abomination before me. (Ezekiel 16:49b, 50a; see 16:44–52 for full context)

Peter would say to the city-dwellers among us, "When you see the indecent city, filled with materialistic ease, comfort, and self-gratification, remember that indecency and ease, those constant companions of affluence, brought about God's judgment long ago." Those who gorge themselves without respect for God's created order or concern for the poor will one day be incapable of restraining God's anger on the day that he visits them.

What a powerful reminder for those of us who are trying to keep from falling. When we return to the appetites of this world, we are only demonstrating that we have no power over it. And when we begin to think that there are no consequences for our private behavior, that God is love and only love, that nothing bad will ever happen to us, we are in danger not only of self-deception but of becoming the recipients of God's righteous wrath. Men, to you I speak most especially: when you live in unrestrained material ease and indulge every sexual freedom, you reduce your dignity to that of a moth drawn to the flame. And beneath the bright lights of the immoral city, God's fiery judgment will come once again.

Three Insets of God's Righteous Grace

The Rescued and Reclaimed

Thankfully, hidden in these three portraits is one astounding surprise. Quietly placed in the background of Peter's paintings are small insets of men and women who are rescued and reclaimed. So there is hope for us to finish well. Within two of the portraits we see that God had the ability to call some in history *righteous*. In verse 5 we find *righteous* Noah and seven others *rescued* on the day of wrath. And later, in verse 7, we find Lot, three times called "*righteous*," *rescued* from disaster.

Could Peter have painted anything more hopeful than these insets? Indeed, they convey the core of his purpose. Before he dies he wants everyone, throughout all time, to remember that God knows how to rescue and reclaim the righteous as well as to punish the wicked. The high point in this gallery is when Peter acts as docent, not painter, to declare that this rescuing and reclaiming truth applies not only to the past but to all the godly throughout all time: "the Lord knows how to rescue the godly from trials" (v. 9). Imagine—you and I have been painted into the portraits by Peter! Peter—the one who fell, the one who denied his Lord three times, the one who walked away from him in shame—this one who had found God's forgiveness and finished well now proclaims that this can be true for us too. He says as much to his contemporary readers.

> Then the Lord knows how to rescue the godly from trials, and to keep the unrighteous under punishment until the day of judgment, and especially those who indulge in the lust of defiling passion and despise authority. (vv. 9, 10a)

Notice who does the rescuing—Peter calls him "the Lord." This is not the ancient term for Yahweh; it is the Greek term that is used in reference to Jesus of Nazareth. This is the One who not only comes to judge but to save as well. By his grace and in his strength may we continually find ways for our faith to grow, and may we always follow in the apostolic way. Therefore, we must curb our worldly appetites and back away from the bounty of this world's table. After all, a better feast awaits us in Heaven.

Our Heavenly Father, the time we spend in this gallery of conflict is well worth it, for we want to finish well. Emblazon these portraits into the memory of our minds, that we might remember the warnings they convey. Thank you for painting us into the portraits by grace. May the script of human history function as an instrument of peace. Rescue us; reclaim us, for your own glory, and for our eternal good. In Jesus' name, amen.

Bold and willful, they do not tremble as they blaspheme the glorious ones, whereas angels, though greater in might and power, do not pronounce a blasphemous judgment against them before the Lord. But these, like irrational animals, creatures of instinct, born to be caught and destroyed, blaspheming about matters of which they are ignorant, will also be destroyed in their destruction, suffering wrong as the wage for their wrongdoing. They count it pleasure to revel in the daytime. They are blots and blemishes, reveling in their deceptions, while they feast with you. They have eyes full of adultery, insatiable for sin. They entice unsteady souls. They have hearts trained in greed. Accursed children! Forsaking the right way, they have gone astray. They have followed the way of Balaam, the son of Beor, who loved gain from wrongdoing, but was rebuked for his own transgression; a speechless donkey spoke with human voice and restrained the prophet's madness. These are waterless springs and mists driven by a storm. For them the gloom of utter darkness has been reserved. For, speaking loud boasts of folly, they entice by sensual passions of the flesh those who are barely escaping from those who live in error. They promise them freedom, but they themselves are slaves of corruption. For whatever overcomes a person, to that he is enslaved. For if, after they have escaped the defilements of the world through the knowledge of our Lord and Savior Jesus Christ, they are again entangled in them and overcome, the last state has become worse for them than the first. For it would have been better for them never to have known the way of righteousness than after knowing it to turn back from the holy commandment delivered to them. What the true proverb says has happened to them: "The dog returns to its own vomit, and the sow, after washing herself, returns to wallow in the mire."

2:10b–22

25

Preachers Who Forsake
the Faith

2 PETER 2:10b–22

MARVIN GARDINER WROTE the twentieth-century novel *The Flight of Peter Fromm*. Set on the streets of Hyde Park, within the shadow of the University of Chicago, the book traces the disheartening journey of one young man, Peter Fromm, from his belief in the gospel to something else, a faith more suitable for his enlightened age. At one point in the narrative, the young man's mentor schools his student on the makeup of a good preacher.

> To be a minister today in the typical church of a prosperous suburb, one must be as skilled as a politician in the rhetoric of ambiguity, circumlocution, and doubletalk. He must talk plain language though in such a way that no listener can take offense. He may attack race prejudice, but it must be done obliquely so that no one in the congregation imagines that it refers to him. He may attack business ethics, but it must be done in such a manner that no businessman who listens will think that he is implicated. Today's preacher can indeed use all doctrinal phrases but always so cunningly that conservative listeners will take them one way, liberal listeners another. In brief he must learn to preach without saying anything.[1]

Not to be outdone by a novelist, the poet Steven Crane presents us with the makeup of the kind of parishioner whom our newly made preacher would most likely attract.

> The wayfarer perceiving the pathway to truth was struck with astonishment. It was thickly grown with weeds. "Ahh," he said, "I see that none has passed here in a long time." Later he saw that each weed was a singular knife. "Well," he mumbled "at least, doubtless there are other roads." So he went another way.[2]

Gardiner's *preacher* and Crane's *people* appear to be made for each other. Both are palatable and pathetic. The pulpit follows the crowd; and the crowd, not wanting to grasp the nettles for fear of getting cut, wanders away from tough biblical injunctions in search of an easier, less difficult way. As things are, so it appears they always will be. Preachers are ever going astray, and people continue wandering off into their own futile ways.

The Apostle Peter waged war on this very issue during the waning years of the apostolic age. In fact, in the text before us he encourages us to take a good, long, hard look at false preachers and failing people. By calling the preachers out, he hopes his readers might learn how to spot them before they do irreversible harm.

While Peter's aim is to equip us to stand on the Day of Judgment, he is well aware that others seek only to "entice unsteady souls" (v. 14). This little phrase stands at the center of our text and provides a summary for the whole. In fact, *unsteady* is one word that functions for Peter as the antithesis of his aim. Whereas he would strengthen us in faith (1:12; 3:17), these men would love nothing more than to see us stumble into spiritual failure.

The word translated "entice" is particularly alluring—it's a fishing term. Perhaps the irony was intended. Peter was fulfilling his divine calling as a fisher of men as others, uncalled by God, were trolling for the same souls but with evil intent. Of necessity, then, Peter throws his line into the waters of our age. He would have us know how to distinguish true preachers from those who are merely luring us to follow after false ways. We could outline Peter's invective this way:

- Verses 10b–16: Forsaken preachers: aspects of their person
- Verses 17–22: Forsaken preachers: aspects of their performance

Forsaken Preachers: Aspects of Their Person (vv. 10b–16)

In one sense, preachers all look the same. We stand about the same height, we generally dress along the same lines, and we eat, very nearly, the same foods. If left to these characteristics alone, distinguishing false preachers from faithful ones would be nearly impossible. Thankfully, Peter gives us a better way—one that involves other aspects of our person. In particular, the preacher who is true is set apart from the one who is false by what he says with his *mouth*, sees with his *eyes*, and desires in his *heart*.

What a Preacher Says with His Mouth (vv. 10b–13a)

False and forsaken preachers can be measured by what they say with their mouths. Peter distinguishes them this way:

Bold and willful, they do not tremble as they blaspheme the glorious ones, whereas angels, though greater in might and power, do not pronounce a blasphemous judgment against them before the Lord. But these, like irrational animals, creatures of instinct, born to be caught and destroyed, blaspheming about matters of which they are ignorant, will also be destroyed in their destruction, suffering wrong as the wage for their wrongdoing. (vv. 10b–13a)

Three times in these short verses, Peter uses the word *blasphemy* to describe what these preachers say with their mouths. The word *blaspheme* means to speak with a sense of irreverence, especially about God or other holy things. From the text it appears, then, that false preachers were raising their voices flippantly and irreverently against "the glorious ones." It is difficult to understand, from this text alone, exactly whom these false teachers were blaspheming.[3] We do know, however, that "the glorious ones" were not God. Peter writes that "angels, though greater in might and power, do not pronounce a *blasphemous judgment against them before the Lord.*"

Perhaps these forsaken preachers are speaking irreverently against heavenly angels. The upright host would never think of rejecting authority or stepping out of God's ordained ways. It is also possible, though, that they are blaspheming against faithful preachers like Peter. This is certainly a possibility given the fact that the word for *angels* can simply mean God's faithful *messengers*.

In either case, the point Peter makes is clear. You can learn a lot about preachers simply by paying attention to what they say with their mouths. False preachers evidence a certain disdain for those who obediently carry out God's Word. They repudiate anything glorious and good. And in doing so, their voices become nothing more than the grunts of an animal merely caught to be destroyed. Irrational creatures of instinct, these preachers are difficult, if not impossible, to reason with.

What a Preacher Sees with His Eyes (vv. 13b, 14a)

A second characteristic of false preachers can be deduced by what they look at with their *eyes*. Peter writes:

They count it pleasure to revel in the daytime. They are blots and blemishes, reveling in their deceptions, while they feast with you. They have *eyes* full of adultery, insatiable for sin. (vv. 13b, 14a)

In the days of Alexander's ancient republic, the human *eye* was often the metaphor of choice to speak of the inner desires or pursuits of a person. Follow a man's eyes, and they will lead you to the hidden desires of his heart. In this case, Peter claims that false preachers have eyes "full of adultery and insatiable for sin." False preachers are known for sexual licentiousness and an unrequited hunger for pleasure.

These are probing words for those of us who preach. After all, an adulterous eye and a sinful appetite are easily hidden for a time. Pastors are adept at wearing just the right pair of sunglasses. We are fully capable of navigating this world in ways that keep the true terrain of our souls from being seen. For far too many pastors, sensuality rules, and women are reduced to the form of objects to be ravished. Thankfully, God has ways of bringing these eyes out into the open. For the glory of his name, the purity of the church, and the welfare of every believing Christian man, woman, and child, God will disclose the pastor's heart in the presence of the assembly.

The text goes so far as to prove this very point. Peter tells us that self-deceived preachers will, in the end, remove their glasses and cast their naked eye before a watching world. In broad daylight and by their dinner-table discussions we will know them. Again, he has written, "They count it pleasure to revel *in the daytime*. They are blots and blemishes, reveling in their deceptions, *while they feast with you*."

Finally, did you notice, twice in verse 13 alone, that Peter puts their behavior in the language of *reveling*. A preacher's eyes are disclosed by observing what he *revels* in. Ask yourself: What do my eyes focus on? Do I revel in unpleasant pleasures? Am I putting to death my appetite for sin?

What a Preacher Seeks with His Heart (vv. 14b–16)

The third twisted feature of forsaken preachers moves beyond what they *say* with their mouths and *see* with their eyes. You will know them by what they seek with their *hearts*. Peter writes:

> They entice unsteady souls. They have *hearts* trained in greed. Accursed children! (v. 14b)

Avarice is the accursed vice of forsaken preachers.[4] One could use a number of questions to discern the heart of a preacher in this respect. What are his views on money? What does he do with the money God has entrusted to him? Does this preacher reduce the gospel to the gaining of wealth? Each of these questions is important to ask—for people and pastor alike.

Balaam: A Case in Point

After describing the contorted appearance of forsaken preachers by showing the various aspects of their person, Peter goes on to give his readers a biblical case in point—Balaam, who embodied all three.

> Forsaking the right way, they have gone astray. They have followed the
> way of Balaam, the son of Beor, who loved gain from wrongdoing, but
> was rebuked for his own transgression; a speechless donkey spoke with
> human voice and restrained the prophet's madness. (vv. 15, 16)

One gets the feeling that Peter wanted to do more than help the reader
discern false preachers through studying personal characteristics. At the end
of the day, giving the example of a particular person packs just as much
punch.

Balaam, perhaps more than any other preacher in Israel's history, set
his voice, his eyes, and his heart on God-forsaken ways. When a foreign
king came to Balaam and offered him great wealth to preach against
God's people, Balaam eventually caved in. In addition, he was the leading religious voice that led the sexual revolution forward during the days
when Moses shepherded the people upon the plains (Numbers 31:16).
Defying God's law, this forsaken preacher promoted sexual union with
outside neighboring nations—and in doing so, he lined his pockets with
money.

Balaam was a bold, willful, daytime reveler if ever there was one. He
rejected God's authoritative ways and was restrained from preaching more
words by a created being not made for speech. In the end, Balaam was killed
by messengers from God while living in the midst of a godless and sensual
city (Numbers 31:8).

Such is the ironic judgment of God. Stray from the path, and it could
well cost you your life—and soul.

Forsaken Preachers: Aspects of Their Performance (vv. 17–22)

False preachers can be detected not only by certain aspects of their person,
but by their performance as well. In business, the phrase *the performance
gap* seeks to describe the difference that separates what a business claims
to be capable of doing from that which it actually performs. The greater the
gap, the greater the loss of credibility.

During a review meeting at work, an employee may say something
like, "You know, team, our company promised our clients that this prod-
uct would be online a month ago. And unless we begin finding ways to
narrow the performance gap we are going to be in trouble." As it is in
business, so it is in the church. Preachers are known not only by what
they promise but by what they deliver. Peter uses three images to convey
this point.

Waterless Springs and Mists Driven by a Storm (v. 17)

Peter knows with visceral conviction that the health of the church depends on preachers possessing *living water*. The spiritual stakes are that high. In the words of Thomas Mann:

> If the rains do not come,
> if instead of the moisture-bearing west wind
> it blows regularly from the south and east, from off the desert,
> then there is no hope of a harvest;
> aridity, crop failure, and famine follow
> and not only here.[5]

Perhaps this explains why Peter's depiction of these forsaken preachers now comes with an unparalleled oratorical fury: "These are waterless springs." I have wrestled to articulate the relationship between preachers and preaching, water and mist:

> According to Genesis, the book of beginnings, God's Spirit hovered over the face of the waters. Only then did God speak. Shortly thereafter, we are told that a mist went up from the land and watered the whole face of the ground. Indeed, throughout history, whenever God is gracious to his people, it is attended by Word and Spirit going forth together in great power—and often expressed in the language of water.[6]

Every Christian ought to long for the Spirit and Word to water the world with gospel glory. And that is what makes Peter's tirade against false preachers so searching. These preachers were promising water, the refreshment of the Holy Spirit with all his good gifts and assurance. What they delivered instead was a deposit from an empty well. They lowered their buckets into the wellspring of their own self-delusion and pulled it back up in the presence of the people. And when they poured it out before God's thirsty flock, nothing except dry, gritty sand fell uselessly to the ground—no true refreshment and no soul satisfaction or invigorating relationship with God.

Further, these men are "mists driven by a storm" (v. 17). A mist promises rain. Farmers need rain; the ground needs soaking. But these false preachers deliver nothing more than a passing haze. T. S. Eliot, in *The Wasteland*, captures this perfectly.

> There is not even silence in the mountains
> But dry sterile thunder without rain
> There is not even solitude in the mountains
> But red sullen faces sneer and snarl

From doors of mudcracked houses
If there were water

And no rock
If there were rock
And also water
And water
A spring

A pool among the rock
If there were the sound of water only
Not the cicada
And dry grass singing
But the sound of water over a rock
Where the hermit-thrush sings in the pine trees

Drip drop drip drop drop drop drop
But there is no water.[7]

The warning for preachers, me included, is immense. Any of us who abandon the apostolic way, promote sensuality, and seek our own gain are springs that can't produce water; we are vapors that drift past the spiritually indigent like a haze. The end for any of us who conduct our ministry in such a lifeless way is haunting—"For them the gloom of utter darkness has been reserved."

The same horrific end need not be your destination. Peter would have you know which preachers to follow and which to avoid. So, if you walk away from church week after week without the watery teaching of God's grace *and* judgment, of mercy *and* apostolic moral imperatives, then begin looking elsewhere. Find a preacher who will tell you the gospel according to Peter. Press on. Leave the platitudes behind; funny stories and gripping illustrations are of no help if they are not accompanied by life-giving water and rain.

The Image of Enslavement in Chains (vv. 18, 19)

Before he is done, Peter brings forth one more image, that of a man in the streets crying, "I give you freedom," but who is known by all to be enslaved in chains.

For, speaking loud boasts of folly, they entice by sensual passions of the flesh those who are barely escaping from those who live in error. They

> promise them freedom, but they themselves are slaves of corruption. For
> whatever overcomes a person, to that he is enslaved. (vv. 18, 19)

This is the sad but true state of many in pastoral ministry today. They
stand on platforms that allow for loud boasts, yet in the end are culpable for
enticing wayward sinners who don't know God's intended design for sexuality. In 1989 Rowan Williams, the Archbishop of Canterbury, gave a lec-
ture to the Lesbian and Gay Christian Movement in London. It was entitled
"The Body's Grace." In it he argued for the inconsequential difference of
same-sex unions. It is true that Biblical Christians have not displayed God's
love in a manner consistent with the gospel. In many respects we have failed
through compassionless condemnation. Yet, it must also be said that when
preaching argues for the "inconsequentialness" of human sexuality, it won't
be long before Christianity is stripped of any ethical implication at all.

If you want to be free from any ethical imperative, preachers abound
to satiate your desire. But in the depth of your heart, don't you find Peter's
words true? Without the waters of God's Spirit dwelling within, none of us
possesses the internal strength to walk away from that which corrupts us.
The alluring pull of sin is too strong. Perhaps it is nowhere as strong as the
Internet. With all of its pornographic pull, the illicit use of the home and
office computer is turning men into brute animals who act on instinct alone.
The elephant under the carpet of the church is enslaving and corrupting a
generation. Men's souls, which ought by now to be strong, are languish-
ing; men's minds are filled with frustration; and all around the world their
relationships with spouses and with God are fracturing. The last thing we
need, then, are preachers unwilling to call men to holiness because they
themselves are enslaved in chains.

Dogs and Pigs: Two Cases in Point (vv. 20–22)

Just as in the first half of this chapter when Peter followed the three defining
characteristics of the forsaken preacher's person with an illustration, so here
too he follows the three images of their performance with a case in point.
But here the preachers are compared to the degrading likeness of the animal
world. They are like dogs who return continually to that which made them
sick in the first place. Peter goes on to call them brute dogs and pigs who are
no better off for having washed yesterday.

> For if, after they have escaped the defilements of the world through the
> knowledge of our Lord and Savior Jesus Christ, they are again entangled
> in them and overcome, the last state has become worse for them than the
> first. For it would have been better for them never to have known the way
> of righteousness than after knowing it to turn back from the holy com-

mandment delivered to them. What the true proverb says has happened to them: "The dog returns to its own vomit, and the sow, after washing herself, returns to wallow in the mire." (vv. 20–22)

You can spot forsaken preachers by their performance. A great gap exists between what they promise and what they deliver. Peter closes by decrying their condition and baseness. In essence, these verses proclaim that such preachers are worse off now than they were before. Further, they would have been better off then for never having known what they know now. And all of this is so tragic given that without repentance they are headed toward a worse state in the future than either their past or present would indicate.

Notice also the return of the word "knowledge." In this case, it is not only the knowledge of God, but the knowledge of "our Lord and Savior Jesus Christ," and then is almost immediately equated with "the way of righteousness." Here Peter brings back the thematic phrase to demonstrate the contrast of knowing God with the baseness of the false and forsaken preachers. A true knowledge of God is lived out in righteousness. And abandoning this knowledge is demonstrated in the self-induced defilement of the false teachers.

A Frightening Reminder for Us All

In Pearl S. Buck's great novel *The Good Earth* we are introduced to Wang Lung, a man who rose from poverty to great riches and wealth. Yet, in him we see one who was destroyed by the very things he sought. Carried away by lust and greed, he plodded like a brute beast into the brothel of gloom and utter darkness.

> Then it was that he looked at O-lan, his wife, as a man looks at the woman whose body he knows thoroughly and to satiation and who has lived beside him so closely that there is nothing he does not know of her and nothing new which he may expect or hope from her.
>
> And it seemed to Wang Lung that he looked at O-lan for the first time in his life, and he saw for the first time that she was a woman whom no man could call other than she was, a dull and common creature, who plodded in silence without thought of how she appeared to others. He saw for the first time that her hair was rough and brown and unoiled and that her face was large and flat and coarse-skinned, and her features too large altogether and without any sort of beauty of light. Her eyebrows were scattered and the hairs too few, and her lips were too wide, and her hands and feet were large and spreading. Looking at her thus with strange eyes, he cried out at her, "Now anyone looking at you would say you were the wife of a common fellow and never of one who has land which he hires men to plow."

It was the first time he had ever spoken of how she seemed to him, and she answered with a slow painful gaze. . . . "I have labored and have grown rich and I would have my wife look less like a hind. And those feet of yours—" He stopped. . . . He was ashamed that he was angry at her and angry because she would not be angry in return but only frightened. And he drew his new black robe on him saying fretfully, "Well, and now I will go . . . and see if I can hear anything new. There is nothing in my house except fools and dotard and two children. . . ."

Now there was in the town a great tea shop but newly opened and by a man from the south, who understood such business, and Wang Lung had before this passed the place by, filled with horror at the thought of how money was spent there in gambling and in play and in evil women. But now, driven by his unrest from idleness and wishing to escape from the reproach of his own heart when he remembered that he had been unjust to his wife, he went toward the place. He was compelled by his restlessness to see or to hear something new. Thus he stepped across the threshold . . . he went in, bold enough in his bearing. . . .

At first he did not speak at all in the great tea house but he bought his tea quietly and drank it and looked about him with wonder. This shop was a great hall and the ceiling was set about with gilt and upon the walls there were scrolls hung made of white silk and painted with the figures of women. Now these women Wang Lung looked at secretly and closely. . . .[8]

With narrative force, Buck has captured the sudden descent of an "unsteady" soul. Sad irony abounds in preachers and people alike. Any preacher or parishioner who imagines his faithful wife as an unsightly animal is himself dumber than a mule. He has become like a dog or a pig; he is an irrational animal, a creature of instinct, which is destroyed by his own destructive ways.

Our Heavenly Father, in your strength, we ask that we would think our way clear. We want to finish well. So, for those preachers and parishioners who find themselves entrapped and continually falling, bring the waters of repentance and faith. Help each one of us to be on our feet, growing up into the likeness of our Lord. In Jesus' name, amen.

This is now the second letter that I am writing to you, beloved. In both of them I am stirring up your sincere mind by way of reminder, that you should remember the predictions of the holy prophets and the commandment of the Lord and Savior through your apostles, knowing this first of all, that scoffers will come in the last days with scoffing, following their own sinful desires. They will say, "Where is the promise of his coming? For ever since the fathers fell asleep, all things are continuing as they were from the beginning of creation." For they deliberately overlook this fact, that the heavens existed long ago, and the earth was formed out of water and through water by the word of God, and that by means of these the world that then existed was deluged with water and perished. But by the same word the heavens and earth that now exist are stored up for fire, being kept until the day of judgment and destruction of the ungodly.

3:1–7

26

A Reminder on the Return of Christ

2 PETER 3:1–7

His Measured Reminder (vv. 1, 2a)

"Beloved." What a refreshing word. It expresses the heartfelt affection one has for another. Parents use it of children. Bereaved ones choose it to reflect the keen attachment for those preceding them in death. Men and women employ it to state the undivided partiality they have for their spouse. It was Solomon's choice term to convey the intimate relationship of the courting couple in the Song of Songs. And it appears that Simon Peter was an admirer of the tender term as well. "This is now the second letter that I am writing to you, beloved."

I must confess, finding "beloved" in the opening verse of chapter 3 brings a measure of comfort. At long last Peter has come back to the "beloved." Gone, for the moment at least, are the belligerent preachers of the last chapter. Harsh words recede, and we appear to be planted on more pleasant ground.

Not only have we arrived back to the "beloved," but notice, Peter has brought us back to the beginning. Concerning this second letter he writes, "In both of them I am stirring up your sincere mind by way of *reminder*, that you should *remember . . .*" (3:1, 2a). We have seen the word translated *reminder* before—way back in the opening chapter. There Peter used it three times in the space of four short verses (vv. 12–15). So Peter accomplishes two things in his opening lines of chapter 3. He returns to God's "*beloved*" and in doing so returns our attention to the *beginning*.

Peter's Dying Concern

Evidently, after his vehement denunciation of forsaken preachers, Peter felt compelled to remind his readers of important truths. The reason Peter gives for this deliberate, fivefold use of *remembering* is his fear that Christians will be swayed by vocal opposition from others on the street.

> . . . knowing this first of all, that scoffers will come in the last days with scoffing, following their own sinful desires. They will say, "Where is the promise of his coming? For ever since the fathers fell asleep, all things are continuing as they were from the beginning of creation." (vv. 3, 4)

By naming those who discount the Second Coming "scoffers" who are "following their own sinful desires," Peter discloses in no uncertain terms that their rejection of Christ's return is rooted in their determination to fashion a god in their own image. Simply put, they want a silent god when it comes to rendering a final accounting for deeds done in the flesh.

Earlier they opposed Peter's gospel teaching as a fabrication of his fertile imagination (1:16–21). They said he follows the stuff of myths and fairy tales. Now with "Where is the promise of his coming?" they reiterate their contempt for the old man. Peter has become for them an aged and outdated windbag blowing smoke.

Illustrating Their Contempt: Wolves

One of Aesop's fables is titled "The Shepherd's Boy." The story goes like this:

> A Shepherd-boy, who watched a flock of sheep near a village, brought out the villagers three or four times by crying out, "Wolf, Wolf!" and when his neighbors came to help him, laughed at them for their pains. The Wolf, however, did truly come at last. The Shepherd-boy, now really alarmed, shouted in agony of terror: "Pray do come and help me; the Wolf is killing the sheep"; but no one paid any heed to his cries, nor rendered any assistance. The Wolf, having no cause of fear, at his leisure lacerated or destroyed the whole flock. There is no believing a liar, even when he speaks the truth.[1]

In cunning and twisted fashion, the wolves of Peter's day were planning to attack God's sheep in the wake of Peter's death. And he knew it! Once he was gone, they fully intended to cut the apostolic gospel free from any notion of a final judgment.

Peter's Calmness and Care in Addressing the Concern

Keenly attuned to the inevitability of this attack, Peter, with a clear mind, and illumined by the Holy Spirit, set out to vindicate his message. Before delving into the text, though, two quick observations deserve mention.

First, in reading Peter on the return of Christ I am struck by how straight-forward he is about it all. Unlike many preachers today, Peter doesn't wield the Second Coming of Christ like a club in the hands of a lunatic. He is not out to get us all worked up. He is not asking us to keep looking to the sky in fright and fear. That is simply not the way he teaches on the coming end. Rather, he promotes a realistic view of life. He claims that God created the world, and as Creator he will pull the curtain down on this world when he has had enough of its rebellion. In light of this, we should give ourselves to careful, quiet preparation for that inevitable fact.[2]

Second, a fair critique against preachers throughout the ages has been their tendency toward being 1) overly imaginative in shaping the substance of their message and 2) overly emotional in the style of their delivery. In essence, they depend too much upon experiential giftedness and on per-sonal charisma. Certainly this is the critique leveled against the Apostle Peter. There were strong hints that some felt that the content of his message, especially the Second Coming of Christ in power and glory, was the result of an overly fertile imagination (1:16ff). In addition, by the end of chapter 2 a charge of being overly emotional in delivery could be leveled against Peter as well. After all, chapter 2 contains, perhaps, the most highly charged words in the whole of the Bible.

So as we come to chapter 3, Peter steps back, gathers his thoughts, and defends himself against this twofold critique. And as we will now see, Peter will first defend the foundation of his message (3:2b–4) and then the neces-sity of his manner (3:5–7).

The Foundation of His Message (vv. 2b–4)

Peter knows, far better than most, that the Word of God alone is strong enough to hold the church in an ongoing belief in the final, victorious return of Christ. And here is where the forsaken preachers vastly underestimated the aging fisherman's abilities. He was quite capable of defending his mes-sage. Once again (as he did in 1:16–21) Peter vindicates the gospel by resting the foundation of his message upon God's good words. In verse 2 he writes:

> Remember the predictions of the holy prophets and the commandment of
> the Lord and Savior through your apostles.

With these words, Peter makes a triple-braided cord that unites his understanding of the Second Coming in God's objective words rather than merely in his subjective experience. By taking on his accusers in this way, Peter weaves a rope of immense power and strength. In short, his personal belief in the final judgment is the result of three factors:

- the holy prophets' predictions
- Jesus Christ's commands
- the apostles' public preaching

To beat Peter at this game they would have to defend their own disbelief with Biblical arguments. And that would be an impossible assignment indeed.

The Prophetic Word

Many places in the Prophets and the Psalms predict a final day of punishment for the deeds we have done in the flesh.[3] Here we will only glance at one such passage, from the holy prophet Isaiah, who spoke God's holy words:

> Behold, the LORD will empty the earth and make it desolate, and he will twist its surface and scatter its inhabitants. And it shall be, as with the people, so with the priest . . . the earth shall be utterly empty and utterly plundered; for the LORD has spoken this word. The earth mourns and withers; the world languishes and withers; the highest people of the earth languish. The earth lies defiled under its inhabitants; for they have transgressed the laws, violated the statutes, broken the everlasting covenant. Therefore a curse devours the earth. . . . The earth is utterly broken, the earth is split apart, the earth is violently shaken. The earth staggers like a drunken man; it sways like a hut; its transgression lies heavy upon it, and it falls, and will not rise again. (Isaiah 24:1–20)

This world will come to an end. But, importantly, it won't come to an end because of temporal physical properties. Many nonbelieving scientists also hold that the world will come to an end—for instance, when the physical properties that fuel the sun are completely used up. In one sense, then, a simple belief that the world will end is nothing special. It is shared by Christians and non-Christians alike. What is unique to the apostolic gospel is that the end will come by the intentional command and word of God—in the very hour he so decides—to give final supremacy to his Son and draw the curtain down in judgment on that which he began.

The Incarnate Word

Peter appeals to more than the prophetic word to defend himself. He also bases his belief in the return of Christ "on the commandment of the Lord and Savior" (3:2). And indeed, the Gospel accounts concur. Jesus did give commandments about his return.

In Matthew 25 Jesus speaks of himself as God's Son. He commands us to prepare for his return and the final judgment with three explicit parables—the ten virgins, the ten talents, and the final separation of the sheep and the goats. At the close of the parable of the ten virgins Jesus *commanded*, "Watch therefore, for you know neither the day nor the hour" (v. 13).

In finishing his teaching on the servants who were each given ten talents, Jesus declares that on that day God will "cast the worthless servant into the outer darkness" (v. 30). But the most direct statement Jesus makes about the certainty of a day of judgment in Matthew 25 comes at the outset of his teaching on the division of the sheep and the goats: "When the Son of Man comes in his glory, and all the angels with him, then he will sit on his glorious throne" (v. 31). What he accomplishes while on the throne, the parable makes expressly clear. He judges the living and the dead. He divides the sheep from the goats. He separates those entering into Heaven from those cast into the eternal, conscious state of punishment in Hell.

The Apostolic Word

Interestingly, the phrase "outer darkness" used by Jesus in Matthew 25 bears strong resemblance to what Peter spoke of in 2:17 when referring to the final resting-place for the worthless servants of his own day: "For them the gloom of *utter darkness* has been reserved." This connection is only one of many that we could put forward to demonstrate that the apostles' own preaching consisted simply of passing on the commandments of the Lord and Savior.

In addition, we should remember that the disciples stood watching on the day Jesus ascended into Heaven in a cloud. It was the apostles who stood staring until an angel came and said in essence, "Why do you look into Heaven? He will return just as he came" (Acts 1:11). Indeed, Christ will return. The prophets foretold it; Jesus gave commandments in light of it; and the apostles knew it. Therefore Peter was unashamed to proclaim it.

The Necessity of His Manner (vv. 5, 6)

Facing Ignorance

If Peter's argument is as strong as this, then what was the real reason for their rejection of it? Peter goes on to tell us (vv. 5, 6):

> For they deliberately overlook this fact, that the heavens existed long ago,
> and the earth was formed out of water and through water by the word of

God, and that by means of these the world that then existed was deluged with water and perished.

Did you see the emphasis in Peter's opening phrase? "They deliberately overlook . . ." In essence, he accuses them of intentionally blinding themselves from the activity of God in history.

He appeals to the great flood at the time of Noah for proof that this world, once created by the power of God's word, was deluged by the authority of that same word. But they would forget this. Like carriage horses wearing blinders, these men cultivate eyes of ignorance. They intentionally *ignore* the facts of God's Word and the data from history. They don't desire a true *knowledge* of God—the very thing Peter is trying hard to cultivate in his final years (1:2, 3, 8; 2:20; 3:17, 18).

When writing on the sad crisis of real *knowledge* in education, the French writer Jean-Francois Revel described the underlying issue brilliantly:

> After five or six years of elementary "instruction" a good third of the children ready to enter secondary school were practically illiterate, and almost half of the students entering universities could read but hardly understand what they were deciphering. This devastating decadence was due only in part to the increase in the numbers of students and to a scarcity of qualified teachers. *It has been primarily the result of an official doctrine, of a deliberate option, according to which the school should not have the function of transmitting knowledge. Let no one think I am joking. Ignorance today is—or at any rate was until very recently—the object of a deliberate cult* whose theoretical, pedagogical, political, and sociological justifications have been explicitly expounded in many texts and become a kind of "convivial" phalanstery of "place of like" in which boys and girls practice an "opening to others and to the world." The aim is to abolish the "reactionary criterion of competence." The student is not expected to learn anything, and the teacher does not need to know what he or she is teaching.[4]

What is true in some parts of the educational world is evidently at work in spiritual domains as well. A deliberate setting aside of knowledge, an intended ignorance, is advanced by scoffers in their effort to create a culture that is "opening to others and to the world"—even if the openness fails to conform to words revealed to the holy prophets, Jesus Christ, and his apostles.

Intentionally Following Their Own Desires

The pursuit of the mind often submits itself to the desires of the body. Peter says as much in this text: "Scoffers will come in the last days with scoffing, following their own sinful desires." He has made similar charges before.

- 2:2: "Many will follow their sensuality."
- 2:3: "In their greed they will exploit you."
- 2:10: ". . . those who indulge in the lust of defiling passion and despise authority."
- 2:14: "They have eyes full of adultery, insatiable for sin. . . . They have hearts trained in greed."
- 2:18: "They entice by sensual passion of the flesh."

The mounting evidence for the scoffers' rejection of the return of Christ conveys one overriding truth: preachers and people alike reject the doctrine of the Second Coming because they desire to live in a universe without moral accountability.

Who leads the charge for this in our own day? Generally speaking, they are the same ones who took up this banner at the end of the apostolic age—preachers and teachers. In the vernacular of Peter, they are "false prophets" and "false teachers" (2:1). The parallel in our day are the institutions of the church and the academy.

In their dreamlike world, many religious preachers today assert that you can enjoy the pleasures of free sex and fast money without moral consequences. Perhaps this stems from a fatal flaw in the temperament of those who pursue ministry. Far too many preachers are people-pleasers. They try to keep everyone happy. They never want to offend a soul. In demeanor, these ministers resemble the bumbling clerics portrayed in so many Jane Austen novels.

As far as teachers are concerned, who would argue that the central cry among today's academics is, "Freedom. We must have unrestricted academic freedom." And indeed, with freedom comes many advantages. But all too often this mantra is used to permit one to tear apart any notion of divine revelation. Living in the shadow of one of the world's great universities, I hear from students about this abuse of freedom all the time. In actual fact, at times some professors are simply working out their own rebellion against God and his Word in their classroom.

The eminent New York University philosopher Thomas Nagel, in his book ironically titled *The Last Word*, provides us with one such example:

> I want atheism to be true and am made uneasy by the fact that some of the most intelligent and well-informed people I know are religious believers. It isn't just that I don't believe in God . . . it's that I hope there is no God! I don't want there to be a God; I don't want a universe to be like that.[5]

Aldous Huxley, the well-known agnostic, once confessed:

> Is the universe possessed of value and meaning?
> I took for granted that there was no meaning.

I had motives
for not wanting the world to
have a meaning.[6]

We can at least credit such men for their honesty. They are quite straight-forward in stating the reasons that lie behind their rejection of God—they prefer to live and think as they please.

Unfortunately, wherever this kind of deliberate forgetting takes hold, religious institutions, churches and classrooms are emptied of clear-thinking, hard-hitting realists within a generation. Men and women who understand how the world really works go elsewhere; only sentimentalists remain.

Peter Finishes by Way of Reiteration (v. 7)

From my own experience, people in business are much less likely than preachers or teachers to reject the Bible's repeated words on coming judgment. Perhaps this is because they live in a world where bills must be paid. Often preachers and teachers are too far removed from what it really takes to keep something afloat. Thus it doesn't surprise the businessman to learn that one day God will oversee a day of accounting. One day a line will be drawn at the bottom of the page, and on that day no one will be able to fib. Owe no man a dime, and you would still owe God your soul. For the men and women who get up each day and go to work, Peter makes sense.

Over the course of these verses Peter has made a persistent appeal to the power of God's words. He finishes (v. 7) true to form: "But by the same word the heavens and earth that now exist are stored up for fire, being kept until the day of judgment and destruction of the ungodly." The Apostle Peter was a hard-hitting, straight-talking man. He would have appreciated the lyrics to one of Johnny Cash's most powerful songs, titled "The Man Comes Around." The first two verses go like this:

There's a man going round taking names
And he decides who to free and who to blame
Everybody won't be treated all the same
There will be a golden ladder reaching down
When the man comes around.

The hairs on your arm will stand up
At the terror of each sip and each step
Will you partake of that last offered cup
Or disappear into the potter's ground
When the man comes around.[7]

Our Heavenly Father, I pray that just as our lives will inevitably come to an end, we would understand that this earth is not long for this world. Help us to prepare to give a true accounting for all that we have said and done. In Christ's name, amen.

But do not overlook this one fact, beloved, that with the Lord one day is as a thousand years, and a thousand years as one day. The Lord is not slow to fulfill his promise as some count slowness, but is patient toward you, not wishing that any should perish, but that all should reach repentance. But the day of the Lord will come like a thief, and then the heavens will pass away with a roar, and the heavenly bodies will be burned up and dissolved, and the earth and the works that are done on it will be exposed.

3:8–10

27

Reasons for a Delay
in Christ's Return

2 PETER 3:8–10

IT IS ONE THING to staunchly hold your ground when your convictions come under attack. It is quite another thing to take charges head-on—to provide an answer for why your convictions seem to be at odds with the way things really are. Throughout this letter we have seen the aged apostle staunchly holding his ground on his conviction that the Lord will come again in power and glory. He has reiterated this conviction in each chapter. He has supported it with personal experience (1:16–19), prophetic discourse (1:20, 21), and historical evidence (2:1–10), as well as with God's word at creation (3:4–7). What he has not done to this point is to take the charges leveled against him head-on. He has not answered the question, Why? Why the delay in Christ's return? Why are his convictions at odds with the way things are? Put simply, the question of 3:4—"Where is the promise of his coming?"—needs a direct answer.

Many people today are still looking for an answer to these questions. For some, their disbelief in the Lord's return is simply the result of having given up on a belief in God altogether. Now suppose that one of these doubt-filled and disbelieving friends of mine stood before us:

"Hi. Thanks for seeing me today. I'm a bit embarrassed to be talking to you, and I want to say right up front that I'm not really here to upset your faith. I only mean to be honest with you. You see, lately I've been wrestling with my belief in the Christian faith. Quite honestly, I think I am more of a skeptic at the present time. If there is a God and that God is good, then certainly he would have returned by now. You know, to put everything in order and all. There is so much hatred in the world, so much unkindness. There are too many acts of violence and war. Don't you think he would have come back by now? I mean, we could sure use him around here. My friends tell me to grab as much enjoyment and pleasure out of life as I can. Well, thanks for listening to me anyway."

As my imaginary friend departs, we must confess that many of us resonate with the logic that has led this person to doubt. After all, why hasn't God pulled down the curtain on history? Where is the promise of his coming? What can a good God possibly be waiting for—especially in light of the clear teachings found in the prophetic writings, the commands of Jesus, and the preaching of the apostolic age?

Contemporary Christian artist David Wilcox wrote a song that describes the tension between God's purposes and the world's evil:

> Look, if someone wrote a play just to glorify what is stronger than hate
> Would they not arrange the stage to look as if the hero came too late.
> He's almost in defeat, it's looking like the evil side will win
> So on the edge of every seat from the moment that the whole thing begins.
> It is love who mixed the mortar. It is love that stacked these stones,
> It is love who made the stage here—though it looks like we're alone.
> In this scene set in the shadows like the night is here to stay,
> there's evil cast around us . . . but it's love who wrote the play.
> And in this darkness love will show the way.

The Apostle Peter has encouraging words not only for my doubting friend but for anyone in Christ who is struggling for reasons to believe. Peter puts forward two arguments—better yet, two reasons—in addition to the Biblical arguments of 3:1–7 to explain the delay in Christ's return. Then he follows them both up with one urgent warning. The headings look like this:

- Verse 8: The Lord is not like us.
- Verse 9: The Lord is patient toward us.
- Verse 10: The Lord's return will surprise us.

The Lord Is Not Like Us (v. 8)

Peter addresses those needing reasons for a continuing belief in the Second Coming with these words:

> But do not overlook this one fact, beloved, that with the Lord one day is as
> a thousand years, and a thousand years as one day. (v. 8)

Peter is arguing here that God's perception of time is vastly different from our own. For us, this present age of waiting seems interminably long—

so long, in fact, that we find ourselves tempted to doubt that Jesus will ever return at all. Peter helps us by showing the contrast between our temporal existence and God's eternal nature. In essence, he reminds us that our perspective on time is different than God's.

As a parent of five, I recall the days when the children were little and my folks were coming for a visit. My dad and mom, driving all the way from their mountain home in northern Georgia, had told us, "We think we will get there sometime around three o'clock in the afternoon." In anticipation, Mariah, our youngest, dashed to the window by 2:40. By 2:43 she wondered aloud, "Where are they? When are they coming? Why aren't they here yet?" When they hadn't arrived by 3:05 (highly unlikely given my dad's relentless attention to being on time), Mariah, now exasperated, said, "Dad, are Grandma and Grandpa really coming?"

As parents, Lisa and I never worried about the arrival time the way our little ones did. The reason, of course, was simple—our perspective on time was very different than that of our small children. Our perspective was more mature. In the same way, Peter writes to stabilize the faith of his readers by putting forward a mature perspective on time.

Interestingly, Peter's argument is not his own—he pulls it from God's Word in an effort to reclaim readers who have grown discontent with Christ's delay. The words of verse 8 came first from the lips of Moses, the great prophet. Psalm 90 opens with the words:

Lord, you have been our dwelling place in all generations. Before the mountains were brought forth, or ever you had formed the earth and the world, from everlasting to everlasting you are God. You return man to dust and say, "Return, O children of man!" For a thousand years in your sight are but as yesterday when it is past, or as a watch in the night. (vv. 1–4)

The Psalm begins by contrasting our temporal existence with God's eternal nature. "From everlasting to everlasting you are God. You return man to dust and say, 'Return, O children of man.'" Then, to illustrate the difference between God's perspective on time and our own, Moses says, "For a thousand years in your sight are but as yesterday when it is past, or as a watch in the night."

Peter draws upon this ancient understanding of time. He submits his own sense of Christ's delay to God's trustworthy Word. For there we are reminded that God is so unlike us. What we hold to be a long time—two millennia in this case—is for God a mere "watch in the night." We are like the five-year-old standing at the window.

The early church father Augustine, a man converted during adulthood, helped us understand just how different God's view is from ours in relationship to time. In his *Confessions* he wrote:

Thy years neither come nor go; whereas ours both come and go. . . .
Thy years stand together, because they do stand;
nor are departing thrust out by coming years, for they pass not away;
but ours shall all be, when they shall be no more.
Thy years are one day; and Thy day is not daily, but To-day. . . .
[for] Thou hast made all things;
and before all times Thou art.[1]

Therefore, whenever you begin doubting the truth of God's Word regarding the Lord's return, come back to this mature perspective on time. Satan would have you think that Christ is never coming back.

In one sense there are two great lies at work in the world today, two ideas the evil one uses to discourage us from a fixed faith in God. First, Satan tries to cut us off from our Creator as he did in the beginning, and, second, to cut us off from our King by dismantling our belief in how the world will end. These two lies are always at work in the world. And in this letter Peter is intent on overcoming the second.

So when you are tempted to doubt whether or not you will give a moral accounting for your life, remember the words of Moses and Peter. Get a mature perspective on time. God is so unlike us. This is one reason Peter gives to account for the delay in Christ's return.

The Lord Is Patient toward Us (v. 9)

Patient

The second reason Peter puts forward to explain why the Lord has not yet returned is found in verse 9:

> The Lord is not slow to fulfill his promise as some count slowness, but is patient toward you, not wishing that any should perish, but that all should reach repentance.

God is not only so unlike us, he is incredibly patient toward us. The fact that Christ has not returned is evidence of God's abundant mercy toward us. Now, I am aware that some would call Peter's idea into question: "You know, if I was God for a day, my first decision would be to get rid of all evil—and I would do it immediately!" Such is their outrage over the purported "patience" God seems to have toward all the injustice and wickedness in the world.

We might reply, "That sounds great. Let's suppose you were God for a day. However, if, as your first act you decide to get rid of all the evil in the world, wouldn't you also have to rid the universe of potential evil as well?

After all, what's the point of limiting evil if you leave the door open for it to return and plague us later?"

Our friend might reply, "Well, certainly I must rid the earth of the potentiality for evil as well."

Then we might respond, "Let's suppose you did this on the count of three. One. Two. Three. Now tell me, what and who is left? Are you and I still here? Is anyone? Don't all of us possess the capacity for mean-spirited actions that are selfish and harm others? Are you ready to give an accounting for all the things you have done?"

"Well," our friend says, "perhaps we can do with a little delay."

What Peter says in verse 9 makes sense: "The Lord is not slow to fulfill his promise as some count slowness, but is patient toward you, not wishing that any should perish, but that all should reach repentance."

Salvation

Why hasn't Christ come? According to Peter, he wants us to dwell with him forever. His apparent slowness is our salvation. Entering into that relationship with God demands time—and for most of us, it takes a little bit more than one might at first think.

Martyn Lloyd-Jones, a preacher of the mid-twentieth century, had a businessman in his congregation named William Thomas. Thomas was a salesman—a Welshman—who sold fish door to door. One day several men at the local watering hole were drinking and talking. Suddenly Thomas, who was also having a pint, found himself listening to their conversation at the table next to him. "Yes," said one man to the other, "I was there last Sunday night, and that preacher said nobody was hopeless. He said there was hope for everybody."

Of the rest of the conversation, Thomas heard nothing, but arrested and completely sobered, he said to himself, "If there's hope for everybody, there's hope for me. I'm going to that chapel myself to see what that man says." That first Sunday he walked to the opened gate of the railings that fenced the church, stood for some minutes, and then, his nerve failing him, turned and went home.

Throughout the wretched week he waited for the next Sunday evening to arrive, and somehow he reached the chapel only to hear singing. Faced with the realization that he was late, he once more turned away and went home. The third Sunday evening came, and William Thomas was once again at the gate, wondering nervously what he should do next when one of the members of the congregation welcomed him with the words, "Are you coming in? Come and sit with me."

That night William Thomas passed from condemnation to life. He found, as Mrs. Lloyd-Jones tells us, that "he could understand the things that were being said, and he believed the gospel and his heart was flooded with a great peace. Old things had passed away; old things had become new."[2]

Imagine what the end would have been like for William Thomas if the Lord had said after that first week, "Well, I think I'm done now. I'll return in judgment today." What would it be like for you? How many times have you come under the hearing of God's Word? How many years have you silently wondered whether or not you should make a fresh start with God? Do you not see, do you not yet understand? The delay in Christ's coming is not only because he is so unlike us, but because he is so patient toward us.

Repentance

Today is the day of salvation. Repent and believe in the gospel. But I must tell you, repenting is not an easy thing to do. It doesn't come naturally to any of us. But repentance is what is required to enter into a true relationship with God. Peter writes that God is "not wishing that any should perish, but that all should reach repentance." The late-in-life repentance of world-renowned teacher and philosopher Mortimer Adler demonstrates this point. When asked why he had been so reluctant to become a Christian, Adler said:

> That's a great gulf between the mind and the heart. I was on the edge of becoming a Christian several times, but didn't do it. I said that if one is born a Christian, one can be light-hearted about living up to Christianity. But if one converts by a clear conscious act of will, one had better be prepared to live a truly Christian life. So you ask yourself, are you prepared to give up all your vices and the weaknesses of the flesh?[3]

The Bible presents a gracious portrayal of God. While he is just and will one day judge the world in righteousness, he is for a time merciful to sinners. Christ has not come yet because God is gracious toward us. In patience he seeks our salvation and waits for our repentance. Do not neglect so kind a gift. Do not despise the mercy of God.

The Lord's Coming Will Surprise Us (v. 10)

It Will Be Sudden

Having given his reasons for the delay of Christ's return, Peter warns us not to make light of his grace. The Lord may have refrained from coming because he is not like us. And he may have kept back the Day of Judgment until now because he is patient toward us. But make no mistake, the day *is* coming. It is fast approaching. And according to verse 10, the Lord's coming will be a surprise to us. That verse begins, "But the day of the Lord will come like a thief."

Borrowing from the words of Jesus, Peter likens the return of Christ to a thief coming in the night. A thief, you see, comes suddenly, unexpectedly, when you are unaware. Living in a big city, as I do, one comes to accept that robberies on the street are common. They are simply bound to occur. Yet, whenever I speak with someone recently violated in this way, the response is nearly always the same. "I never saw him coming. I was walking along, and suddenly he was upon me." By way of analogy, so it will be when Christ returns. The world has been told that he is coming back. But when it actually occurs, he will catch us unawares.

How did it come about that Pearl Harbor was attacked by Japanese planes on December 7, 1941? The American forces there were caught unawares. When an Army radar operator saw blips on the screen and reported them, an officer said, "It's probably just a pigeon with a metal band around its leg." At that time the attacking planes were fifty minutes away. At 7:55 the first wave of the attack began, and eight of our battleships and three light cruisers were sunk or damaged, 220 planes destroyed or severely damaged, 2,300 men killed. We were caught entirely unawares. So it will be when Jesus returns. We will be surprised. Better that, however, than unprepared!

It Is Certain

No one should be caught unprepared, given the *certainty* of the coming event. Peter continues:

> And then the heavens will pass away with a roar and the heavenly bodies will be burned up and dissolved, and the earth and the works that are done on it will be exposed. (v. 10)

Did you catch all the certainties in this verse on the Lord's return? They come in the language of what *will be*:
- "The heavens *will* pass away with a roar."
- "The heavenly bodies *will* be burned up and dissolved."
- "The earth and the works that are done on it *will* be exposed."

Notice the phrases here. The first is, "the heavens will pass away with a roar." "The heavens" are the canopy above us. In Greek, "roar" is equivalent to the swish of an arrow through the air or the rumbling of thunder. It can also be the crackling of flames, the screams of a lash as it descends, the rushing of mighty waters, or the hissing of a serpent.[4] In essence, the canopy, with an immense roar, will roll up like a rattling window blind when one loses a grip on it.

Peter goes on, "The heavenly bodies will be burned up and dissolved."

It will be as if everything in the universe, every aspect of the galaxies, every component of the universe—stars and planets, people, trees, oceans—will catch fire and dissolve.

Finally, "the earth and the works that are done on it will be exposed." Simply put, there will be no place to hide on that great and terrible day. Everything and everyone will be exposed. The game will be up for all those who desire to live without God's Son as their mediator and savior from sin.

Peter Has Done All He Can to Prepare Us

We began this chapter by listening to the voice of people who have doubts about Jesus' returning to judge the world. Indeed, we can empathize with their concerns. Yet, we must also be prepared to present a view of the world as Peter has given it to us. For more often than not, our own struggles on this important and essential teaching rest in an immature notion of true justice. J. I. Packer put it well when he wrote:

> Do you believe in divine judgment? By which I mean, do you believe in a God who acts as our Judge? Many, it seems, do not. Speak to them of God as Father, a friend, a helper, one who loves us despite all our weaknesses and folly and sin, and their faces light up; you are on their wavelength at once. But speak to them of God as Judge, and they frown and shake their heads. Their minds recoil from such an idea. They find it repellent and unworthy.[5]

Peter's words should make us consider again the need for the return of Christ. We would do well to remember the reasons he gave for the delay. God is very much unlike us. God is very patient toward us. But remember, his word *will* be fulfilled fully and surprisingly. In the meantime, we need instruction on what to do while we wait.

Our Heavenly Father, we thank you for this day and for this world. Some of us have doubts and questions as to the validity of your return. Shore up our faith. Help us to rest in what Moses has said. Help us not to measure your return on our timetable. And thank you for giving us a glimpse into the reasons for your delay. May many yet come to repentance. We pray this in Christ's name, amen.

Since all these things are thus to be dissolved, what sort of people ought you to be in lives of holiness and godliness, waiting for and hastening the coming of the day of God, because of which the heavens will be set on fire and dissolved, and the heavenly bodies will melt as they burn! But according to his promise we are waiting for new heavens and a new earth in which righteousness dwells. Therefore, beloved, since you are waiting for these, be diligent to be found by him without spot or blemish, and at peace. And count the patience of our Lord as salvation, just as our beloved brother Paul also wrote to you according to the wisdom given him, as he does in all his letters when he speaks in them of these matters. There are some things in them that are hard to understand, which the ignorant and unstable twist to their own destruction, as they do the other Scriptures.

3:11–16

28

What to Do
While Waiting

2 PETER 3:11–16

A Lost World in Waiting

On the streets of Paris in 1953, Samuel Beckett premiered what was to become his most powerful play. Concerning *Waiting for Godot (En Attendant Godot)*,[1] one reviewer wrote:

> The play is not about Godot, who he is or whether he will ever arrive, but about waiting; or to be more precise what people do while they wait.

The two central characters are Vladimir and Estragon. They are of indeterminate age, dressed as homeless bums and sitting alongside a road where there stands a solitary tree. That's it. The rest of the stage is empty. As the curtain ascends, the audience sees these two characters waiting for a figure named Godot. He will remain a figure who never comes.

The very name *Godot* might give us a small hint as to his identity. It is simply the word *God* with an *ot* suffix. In French, or so I am told, the *ot* gives the noun a smallish, endearing quality. If that is indeed the case, then the characters have perhaps already given up on a belief in God, with a capital *G*. The one they are waiting for, then, is one who might encompass some diminutive god-like qualities or give some direction or purpose to life.

Act 1 opens with Vladimir saying, "Nothing to be done." In other words, "All we're doing here is killing time." Aimless conversations ensue, often mixed with humorous dialogue. However, midway through the first scene, two other characters come onto the stage. One is named Pozzo, the

other Lucky. Like Vladimir before him, Pozzo's first word is also symbolic.
"On." This set of characters fills the stage with relentless activity. They are
not just killing time—they are filling time.

And therein Beckett makes his powerful point. As night falls and Godot
hasn't come, the actors are on the verge of despair. Beckett had earlier written about the sense of angst when "the boredom of living is replaced by the
suffering of being."[2] That statement seems to prefigure *Waiting for Godot.*

I don't pretend to know if something like this has happened to you. I
don't know what you think about God, or even Godot. But who among us
isn't aware of those moments in life when we ask ourselves, "Has it happened to me? Has the boredom of living been replaced by the suffering of
being?"

In Act 2 the characters are both filling and killing time. Only one thing
is certain—Godot never enters time. Imagine a world without God. Not even
a Godot. Imagine living without any hope of ever finding meaning, purpose,
or direction. The concluding dialogue in Beckett's play is:

Estragon: What's wrong with you?
Vladimir: Nothing.
Estragon: I'm going.
Vladimir: So am I.
Estragon: Was I long asleep?
Vladimir: I don't know.
Estragon: Well where should we go?
Vladimir: Not far.
Estragon: Oh yes, let's get far away from here.
Vladimir: We can't.
Estragon: Why not?
Vladimir: Well, we have to come back tomorrow.
Estragon: For what?
Vladimir: To wait for Godot.
Estragon: Ahh, he didn't come, did he.
Vladimir: No.
Estragon: And now it's too late.
Vladimir: Yes, now it's night. . . .
Estragon: Why don't we hang ourselves?
Vladimir: With what?
Estragon: You haven't got a bit of rope?
Vladimir: No.
Estragon: Ahh, then we can't.
Silence.
Vladimir: Let's go. . . .
Estragon: You say we have to come back tomorrow?

Vladimir: Yes. . . .

Estragon: I can't go on like this.

Vladimir: Well, that's what you think.

Estragon: If we parted? That might be better for us.

Vladimir: We'll hang ourselves tomorrow. *Pause.* Unless Godot comes.

Estragon: And if he comes?

Vladimir: We'll be saved.

Estragon: Well, shall we go? . . .

Vladimir: Well, shall we go?

Estragon: Yes, let's go.

They do not move.

Curtain.[3]

In Beckett's play one can nearly hear the voices of 2 Peter 3:4 asking, "Where is the promise of his coming?" And tragically, in such a world as Beckett conceives, nothing is put forward in answer.

In contrast, the Apostle Peter has been treating his audience to a different play—one with a fixed belief in God and the victorious return of his Son to earth. There are a host of important things to be done while we *wait*. In fact, on three separate occasions we are given the word *waiting* in this text (3:12, 13, 14), and each time the word is pregnant with deliberate, purposive intention for our lives.

God's Purposes for Us while Waiting (vv. 11, 12a, 14)

Evidently God has good things for us to do while we wait, and none of them appear to be passive.

Holiness and Godliness (v. 11)

Peter begins his productive charge to the saints in verse 11:

> Since all these things are thus to be dissolved, what sort of people ought you to be in lives of holiness and godliness.

We are to wait in "holiness and godliness." In the original Greek, Peter chose to display a bit of grammatical humor at this juncture in his letter. The words *holiness* and *godliness* are both plural. Literally this reads, "It is necessary for you to live in holy conducts and in godlinesses." In English that sounds humorously absurd. But when you consider it, it is as if he is telling us, "Look, beloved, there are a lot of things for you to do while you wait. There are manifold opportunities to be productive. A waiting life is filled with varied splendor and activity. So get about all your holinesses and godlinesses."

It was in 1 Peter that we initially came across this word *holiness* from the aged apostle's pen. There it encompassed the fullness of life in the presence of an ungodly world. Generally, it simply means to be "set apart." But on the street, Peter told us, holiness takes on many forms. It means:

• Getting about your own *sanctification* (1 Peter 1:14–21).

• Expressing a *sincere love* for brothers and sisters in Christ (1 Peter 1:22—2:3).

• Being *subject* to every human institution (1 Peter 2:11–13, 18; 3:1).

• Being willing to embrace *suffering* for the gospel (1 Peter 4:1–6, 19).

• Loving *service* to the family of God (1 Peter 4:7–11).

Not only are Christians to be known for this plethora of holinesses but godlinesses as well. This is the third time that we have seen Peter use the idea of godliness in this letter. In fact, he opened this letter with this very term. In chapter 1 he wrote, "His divine power has granted to us all things that pertain to life and godliness" (v. 3). Then it appeared again in that great golden chain of qualities that leads us to Heaven (1:6, 7).

What does it mean to be godly? It simply means to reflect the character of your Creator. In essence, when God looks upon Christians and the whole body of Christ, he expects to see in our lives a reflection of who he is. That's what godliness looks like while we wait. We represent God in the world. We are to possess a Godot-like diminutive and endearing quality to our lives. Therefore, we wait by being pure and righteous and just. Remember, we represent him to a lost world in waiting. In his own time Charles Spurgeon, that great London preacher, put it best: "As you walk the streets of London, remember you've got the reputation of God in your hands."[4]

Persistent Purity and Peace (v. 14)

Skipping ahead in the text for a moment, Peter gives us further instruction on how we are to wait for the Lord's return. He writes:

> Therefore, beloved, since you are waiting for these, be diligent to be found
> by him without spot or blemish, and at peace. (v. 14)

To paraphrase, we are to be persistently pure and at peace. Persistence is one way to define diligence. We are to be persistently pure.

Many people are putting water filters on their sinks or water purifiers in their homes. The reason for this is clear: that which is coming into their home contains some sediment from the earth. In the same way, Christians in waiting purify themselves from taking in the sins of the world. We filter our lives with diligent obedience to God's Word. Since the Lord is coming at a time we do not know, we desire to meet him in purity and peace.

The phrase Peter uses to convey this is "without spot or blemish." What a contrast to those who were "blots and blemishes" (2:13). In telling us that we are to be "without spot or blemish," Peter calls upon the language of the Old Testament concept of sacrifice. The lamb was to be pure and spotless. This alone would bring peace with God. Therefore, our marching orders are clear. In this letter Peter has contrasted two kinds of people on the street— those who have no regard for the state of their purity and those who are looking to keep it intact for Christ.

Waiting for and Hastening the Coming Day of God (v. 12a)

God has good purposes for us to fulfill while we wait. We are to walk in the ways of holiness and godliness. We are to be persistently pure and at peace. And next we learn that by doing so, we are "waiting for and hastening the coming day of God" (v. 12).

This is an incredibly striking phrase. I don't think I understand it fully. But this much can be said: while no one knows when Jesus is going to return in power and glory, we nevertheless have a part to play in speeding it along. What a different perspective on life from the one Samuel Beckett left us! We are not here just to fill time; we are no longer here to kill our time. Our life is filled with end-time significance! Therefore, we ought to put off sin. We ought to disdain doing anything that we would be ashamed of at his coming. Living a life of sin is simply no longer an option for us. Juliana of Norwich said:

> If afore us were laid together all the pains in Hell . . . and by itself, sin, we would rather choose all that pain than sin. For sin is so vile and so greatly to be hated that it may be likened to no pain that is not sin.[5]

Therefore, let us wait productively. Be holy and godly. Be persistently pure and at peace. Hate sin. For by these things you hasten the coming of the Lord.

God's Promises to Us while Waiting (vv. 12b, 13)

As is often the case in life, there is an intimate connection between waiting and receiving, between promise and fulfillment. More often than not, it is the coming promises that encourage us in the season of waiting. Recognizing this, Peter connects our active waiting with God's promise.

. . . because of which the heavens will be set on fire and dissolved, and
the heavenly bodies will melt as they burn! But according to his promise
we are waiting for new heavens and a new earth in which righteousness
dwells. (vv. 12b, 13)

We are waiting for "new heavens and a new earth in which righteousness dwells." What an encouragement to stay faithful. Christians are not
merely waiting for the world to end. That would be a secular view. Peter
does not motivate us with fear. He is not saying, "Get your act together
before the curtain falls." Rather, he is saying, "Live in light of the fact that
the veil on the next world is about to be pulled back. Before you know it,
in the blink of an eye, you are going to be walking onto a stage more grand
and more glorious than anyplace you've ever set foot on upon earth. We are
heading to a promised land where righteousness dwells!"

The sacred truth is this: when the Lord returns, we will have reached
the very beginning days of human history, before sin entered the world.
That vital reality ought to motivate us to possess a growing faith as well
as a faith that follows in the apostolic way. Knowing this, how can we be
content with anything less than a full commitment to holiness, godliness,
purity, and peace?

God's Patience toward Us in Waiting (vv. 15, 16)

If the promise of "new heavens and a new earth in which righteousness
dwells" isn't enough to get our blood pumping, Peter finishes his thoughts
with one more encouraging word. We press on, knowing that the patience
of our Lord is for our salvation. God not only has purposes for us while we
wait or promises for us while we wait—our waiting is one of God's great
means of accomplishing our salvation. Peter writes:

> And count the patience of our Lord as salvation, just as our beloved
> brother Paul also wrote to you according to the wisdom given him, as he
> does in all his letters when he speaks in them of these matters. There are
> some things in them that are hard to understand, which the ignorant and
> unstable twist to their own destruction, as they do the other Scriptures.
> (vv. 15, 16)

Notice the implication of counting God's patience as our salvation: our
waiting must be productive; after all it is producing our salvation. George
Matheson wrote insightfully about this when he said:

> We commonly associate patience with lying down. . . . Yet there is a
> patience that I believe is harder—the patience that can run. . . . It is the

power to work under stress, to continue under hardship, to have anguish in your spirit and still perform daily talks. This is a Christian thing. The hardest thing is that most of us are called to exercise patience, not in the sickbed but in the street.

One final thought from verses 15–16 before we are through—isn't it nice to know that you are not alone when you read Paul at certain points. As you read the difficult text of Romans 9—11, for example, Peter joins you in your Bible study and says, "My goodness, I understand our need for salvation and how God accomplished it in Christ's death on the cross, but the implications of it in these chapters are about as difficult as it gets. Does anyone have a handle on this?"

But notice what Peter does with Paul—something that most people today won't do. He doesn't say, "Well, since Paul is difficult to understand and he says some things that are difficult for me to swallow, I think I will dismiss his teachings when I am confused or find myself disagreeing." No. What he does is confirm for the church that everything Paul has written are the very words of Scripture.

In this light, passages like Romans 9—11 open up to us! It is as if Peter is arguing here, "What I have told you about God's patience being the means of your salvation is the same thing Paul wrote to you about. The delay in Christ's return will bring about the salvation of the full number of Jews and Gentiles."

Since that is the case, let's get on with productive waiting. We know what is asked of us. We know what awaits us. And we know that God has more people to be introduced to him through us. Therefore, in the words of the sixteenth-century preacher Richard Baxter, words that would infuse Beckett's play with divine perspective,

Up, and be doing.
Run, and strive.
And fight and hold on
For thou has a certain glorious prize before thee.[6]

Our Heavenly Father, as so many days seem aimless, and the wait sometimes seems eternal, I pray that you would energize us to live holy, godly lives that please you. And may those who are yet looking for ultimate meaning find comfort in all we do and say. In Jesus' name, we pray, amen.

You therefore, beloved, knowing this beforehand, take care that you are not carried away with the error of lawless people and lose your own stability. But grow in the grace and knowledge of our Lord and Savior Jesus Christ. To him be the glory both now and to the day of eternity. Amen.

3:17, 18

29

A Faith That
Finishes

2 PETER 3:17, 18

The Phoenix and a Faith That Finishes

From ancient Egyptian mythology we learn of a sacred firebird known as the phoenix. Supposedly, the bird possessed "beautiful gold and red plumage."[1] We are told that when a phoenix grew old and sensed that it was not long for this earth—that the putting off of its body was soon—it would build a nest out of cinnamon twigs. After being ignited by flame, the nest and the bird would burn fiercely until each was reduced to ashes. At that moment all appeared lost. The majestic bird had fallen from the sky forever, never to fly again. But then, according to the myth, suddenly a young phoenix would rise from the ashes and return by wing to the skies where it would live to fly high overhead once more.

For ten chapters we have been saying that this second letter functions as the Apostle Peter's phoenix-like rise from the ashes. It comes from a man who knew what it was to fall—and fall hard. On the night of Jesus' own death, the Savior had said to his disciples, "You will all fall away because of me this night" (Matthew 26:31), and Peter was the one who replied, "Though they all fall away . . . I will never fall away. . . . I will not deny you!" (vv. 33, 35).

Our beloved and self-proclaimed superman! "I will never fall away!" And what happened next? Peter fell once. He fell twice. He fell for the third time before the all-intimidating presence of a young servant girl in the high priest's courtyard.

But two other important events also took place that night. First, in Luke

22:32 we learn that Jesus had prayed that Peter's "faith may not fail." And second, and this is most significant for our understanding of 2 Peter, in that same event Jesus prophetically charged Peter to "*strengthen* his brothers" upon his rising and taking to the air again.

For me, that command to *strengthen* or *establish* his brothers is one of the keys to unlocking the aim of this letter. Could this letter be Peter's conscious attempt to finish fulfilling his Savior's command, given him that fateful night those many years ago? Certainly he had *strengthened* the disciples in those early days after Jesus' ascension. And clearly he went on to *strengthen* the early church during the apostolic age. Yet here we find him, at the close of life—in a time when he knew that the putting off of his body was soon—*strengthening* the church that would follow him down through the ages. By his own admission, his aim has been to remind us of all that is necessary to *establish* us in the faith (1:12). That very word, *strengthen*, the one Jesus gave him as a young man, is the same word he takes off from in 1:12, and it is the same word he lands upon in 3:17 ("stability").

> Take care that you are not carried away with the error of lawless people
> and lose your own *stability*.

So as we come to the close of the letter, be encouraged. It was written under the authority of one who knew what it was like to fall. Yet it comes to you by the hand of one whose faith did not fail. And as such it contains the words of his final apostolic charge to *strengthen* the brothers in the faith. In these final verses, Peter has two last things to say and one final song to sing:
- 3:17: The importance of staying on guard
- 3:18a: The command to keep seeking to grow
- 3:18b: The privilege of singing, "all glory"

The Importance of Staying on Guard (v. 17)

As Peter prepares to utter his last words to the church, we find him picking up the term *beloved* one last time. His heart was full of love for God's people. Over the years he had learned to love the sheep. And now they were his "beloved"—just as they had always been for God. Knowing that after his death, other, unloving teachers would come along to distort the truth, Peter reminds the beloved to take care.

> You therefore, beloved, knowing this beforehand, take care that you are
> not carried away with the error of lawless people and lose your own sta-
> bility. (v. 17)

Not Wanting Us to Be Swept Away by Lawless People

He actually lists two reasons for this important reminder to *"take care."* The first is so "that you are not carried away with the error of lawless people." The image of being carried away is a frightening one. Throughout this letter, the idea that people are being carried along one path of life or another has been present. In 2:2 we saw the dangerous reality that some "will follow their sensuality." In 2:15 we watched others who "forsaking the right way . . . have gone astray. They have followed the way of Balaam." In 2:21 Peter comments that "it would have been better for them never to have known the way of righteousness than after knowing it to turn back from the holy commandment delivered to them." Aware that we are all on a dangerous journey, Peter plants one last warning sign along the road—"take care that you are not carried away." In crowds it is easy to be swept along. The high school I attended had a strong Christian man as the head football coach. He was forever warning the athletes, "Be careful—you will become like those you hang around with." Wise words.

The "lawless people" whom Peter refers to were those who claimed that we will never have to give a final accounting for the way we live our lives because Jesus is not coming back. So here we learn that an intimate relationship exists between what we believe about the return of Christ and the kind of people we run with through life. In essence, tell me what you believe about Christ's return and I will tell you the sort of people with whom you run. Run with sensuality, and you join the slaves of sensuality. Chase down avarice, and you become greedy. No wonder Peter wants to warn us one last time to stay on our guard. For he knows that if we make the "error" of running with lawless people, we will be disqualified in the race for Heaven. Apostasy is always a real danger.

Not Wanting Us to Lose Our Stability

The second reason Peter reminds us to take care is found in the latter part of verse 17: "You therefore, beloved, knowing this beforehand, take care that you are not carried away with the error of lawless people *and lose your own stability.*" With the word "stability," Peter comes full circle—not only in this letter, but in his life. From the outset of this letter our stability has been his utmost concern (cf. 1:12). His aim in writing has been that we would be "established" in the faith. He has been laboring for firmness of faith—sure footing—people planted squarely on solid ground.

The image of stability and sure footing has marked this brief letter. In 1:1 we saw that Peter was writing "to those who have obtained a faith of equal standing with ours." In 1:10 we learned that "if you practice these qualities you will never fall." He wants us to be established in the faith

(1:12). In 1:19 we heard echoes from the Psalms speaking of God's Word as a light for our path. Peter said that in God's Word "we have something more sure, the prophetic word, to which you will do well to pay attention as to a lamp shining in a dark place." Stay the course. Don't lose your stability. Like Bunyan's Christian in *Pilgrim's Progress*, stay on the path until it leads you to the rich entrance of the eternal kingdom (cf. 1:11).

The Command to Keep Seeking to Grow (v. 18a)

Peter now writes:

> *But grow* in the grace and knowledge of our Lord and Savior Jesus Christ. (v. 18a)

Just as we are to stay on our guard against spiritual adversaries, we must also keep seeking to grow spiritually strong. This, too, is nothing new for Peter. From the outset of the letter he has enjoined us to grow in our faith (1:5–11). We are commended to "supplement our faith" with the qualities that will lead us to our heavenly home. To put Peter's understanding of faith as simply as possible, while we are saved by faith alone, our faith must grow if we are to keep from falling while traveling home. The Christian life is a long journey, and we are not there yet.

H. C. Morrison gave his best years to Christian missionary service in China at the turn of the twentieth century. Returning to the States, he happened to be traveling on the same ship that carried President Teddy Roosevelt. The adventuring Commander-in-Chief was coming back from a safari on the continent of Africa. Arriving in the harbor of New York City, Morrison was leaning on the deck rail just taking in the sights. Signs of welcome were everywhere for the President. Bands were playing. Flags were flying. Banners were displaying kind words of reception. Firefighting boats were spraying their greetings to the sky. Looking at it all, Morrison began to feel a rush of self-pity, for no one was there to meet him. Sulking on the deck, he suddenly sensed the words that God would have spoken to him at that moment, "H. C., you're not home yet!" Yes, we all have a lot of "growing" to do!

Grow in Grace and Knowledge

In this concluding verse Peter summarizes it all with two key words.

> But grow in the *grace* and *knowledge* of our Lord and Savior Jesus Christ. (v. 18a)

Peter uses his thematic word, "knowledge," one last time in this verse. Much like in his comparison in the second chapter (2:20), Peter writes of a knowledge of "our Lord and Savior Jesus Christ." This knowledge is fundamental to the foundation, to what he is so adamantly trying to establish in his readers. Strength and stability in the faith comes from *this knowledge*. A clear warning to those who would live by another knowledge comes from *this knowledge*. And those who have fallen away will be picked up with *this knowledge*. But "knowledge" is not the only thing at work in this last statement. Peter also writes of "grace."

Grace is given, but it is to be grown too. Too many grow weary and quit along the way. They end up stopping altogether and take up with presumptuous sin. May it not be so for you and me. May we be known for *knowing* God. Recently I was sitting with a group of men who have been following Jesus for many years. One of them turned to us and said, "I'm at a point in my life where I need a fresh recollection of time spent with him." How true for us all. You have to keep growing. You have to keep knowing. You have to remain connected to the grace that comes from our Lord and Savior Jesus Christ.

The Privilege of Singing, "All Glory" (v. 18b)

Peter leaves the pages of Scripture singing. His final refrain reads:

To him be the glory both now and to the day of eternity. Amen. (v. 18b)

This song of praise contains the final words we hear from Peter on this earth. In writing them, it is as if he has already arrived. Imagine the joy of singing your way into Heaven.

My mother was living as a young girl in the West Dutch Indies (now Indonesia) at the time of the attacks on Pearl Harbor. As a daughter of missionaries, she was right in the heart of the Sumatran jungles. When news came of the attack on American soil, it was attended by the news that the Japanese were invading Indonesia as well. So my grandfather and grandmother took my mom and the other kids and fled the country. Under a fog they let loose the ropes of the last boat to depart without being sunk.

My mom tells me that as they left, their dad began singing one of his favorite refrains, one he would sing along the jungle trails of Sumatra after a long trip was drawing to a close. It went like this:

We're on the homeward trail,
We're on the homeward trail,
Singing as we go,
Going home.

In early March 2003, my grandfather's funeral took place in the mountains of Colorado. With the snow coming down and a herd of buffalo running in the distance, his sons and daughters, his grandchildren and great-grandchildren walked behind the hearse singing that same song until we arrived at the burial plot.

On that day we felt as if we were singing him into the presence of his gracious King. I will never forget that day—never. The baton song of praise has been passed. In like manner, Peter passed along the privileged song of "all glory" long before. He sang it in the presence of the early church. And they learned it well and sang it to others. Generations of faithful people passed it along, and now it comes to us. Walk the road. Sing the song. For a never-ending day of glory waits all who do.

Our Heavenly Father, strengthen us in Christ, that like Peter, we too might finish well. In Jesus' name, amen.

JUDE

30

Reading Jude

THE THEME OF JUDE'S LETTER comes out of verse 3, "contend for the faith." But this contending for the faith is not put forward in a vacuum. Verse 4 supports the theme by contributing the occasion for the letter with the little word "for." Thus, the call to contend is rooted in Jude's conviction that *the faith is being challenged* by opponents he only will call "certain people" (vv. 4, 8, 10, 12, 16, 19).

The structure of the entire letter flows from these ideas. The conclusions Jude makes about the challenges facing Christianity in verse 4 will be defended by him in verses 5–16. Further, the appeal to contend for the faith in verse 3 will find its explanation in verses 17–23. Thus, the Bible does not leave us to our own imagination in determining how to "contend for the faith." Rather, it actually shows us how. Here is the structure of the letter:

- Jude 3: contending for the faith—Jude 17–23: showing us how
- Jude 4: challenges to the faith—Jude 5–16: supporting his case

Seeing this built-in construction should prove helpful. The theme, then, is an urgent appeal to "contend." And it should come as no wonder to find that the Greek word translated "contend," when verbalized, sounds like our word *agonizing*. It carries the idea of athletes who, in an effort to win, find themselves intensely struggling, competing, even fighting with all their might. Interestingly, elsewhere the word often is attached to things that are intrinsically worthy of full effort. As one lexicon puts it: ". . . effort expended . . . in a noble cause."[1] This is what Jude means. And with it, he aims at enlivening the church of his day to an immediate and intense struggle, a very real fight requiring all of their available energy.

When it comes time in his letter to articulate precisely what this contending looks like, Jude will put forward a trenchant manual on discipleship. First, in verses 17–23 we will see that contending for the faith is linked to the *calling* that Christians are to keep. In particular, we must "*remember*" the words of the apostles (vv. 17–19) and "*keep* ourselves in the love of God" (vv. 20, 21). Beyond this calling, we have *commitments* to make. Christians are to *build one another up in their most holy faith* (v. 20), "*pray in the Holy Spirit*" (v. 20), and "*wait for the mercy of Jesus Christ that leads to eternal life*" (v. 21). In addition to both this high calling and these elevated commitments, we are to contend by our *conduct*. Christians are to be known for having "*mercy on those who doubt*" (v. 22), *saving others from the fires of Hell* (v. 23), and *showing mercy, even upon the unrepentant* (v. 23).

Before this prescription, however, Jude will provide the reader with a rationale for his belief that we live in a day that demands contending for the faith. Simply put, we are called to "contend" because certain people are challenging the faith (v. 4). In one sense, verses 5–16 can be thought of as two sermons, complete with biblical texts and preaching outlines to support his case. In verses 5–10 he selects three historical *events* (the apostasy of the wilderness rebels, the autonomy of some angelic creatures, and the immorality of some ancient cities) to help his readers understand that challenges to the faith have always been present and that God has always met them with divine judgment. In verses 11–16 he will follow those three events with three Old Testament *examples* of people who challenged the faith and brought judgment upon themselves (Cain, Balaam, and Korah).

In both sections, verses 5–10 and verses 11–16, Jude will powerfully exegete God's revealed Word and provide illustrations from well-known contemporary literature (vv. 9, 14). In doing so, Jude intends to shore up those in the early church who with martyrdom at hand are fearful and wondering if God is strong enough to protect them in the hour of their contending—strong enough to protect them in death (as he did the body of Moses, v. 9) as well as to bring them safely through to the final resurrection (as he did with Enoch of old, v. 14).

Jude's urgent appeal to "contend for the faith" should quicken our minds for action as well. He asks us to read his letter, standing as it were, in readiness—a readiness to engage extraordinary challenges. Jude is finished with pleasantries; something *required* is at hand. Urgency and immediacy move him. In other words, Jude wants contenders, and he wants them now. And with this letter he means to raise them up. In this sense Jude's letter reads as though it were written for the church today. All over the world, challenges are on the rise, and persecution of the faith is growing. In fact, if he were alive in our day, I doubt Jude would change a thing. He would tell us that we live in an hour requiring us to "contend for the faith," for the ancient challenges are still being brought against the faith.

Jude also finds time in verses 24, 25 (and I love this about him) to state the theme he had desired to close with if the circumstances were different. At the outset of his letter he had told his readers that he was "very eager to write to you about our common salvation" (v. 3). Well, it appears that Jude was the kind of preacher who couldn't resist accomplishing what was fully in his heart to do. For the last two verses of Jude provide us with the most elevated and concise summary of all that we have in *common* in Christ. They unfold, in benediction and praise, all that God has accomplished for us in Christ as well as all that God will receive from us in eternity.

*Jude, a servant of Jesus Christ and brother of James,
to those who are called, beloved in God the Father and
kept for Jesus Christ: May mercy, peace, and love be
multiplied to you.*

vv. 1, 2

31

Letter from the Ancient Jewish World

JUDE 1, 2

IN THE ANCIENT JEWISH WORLD, the manner of sending and receiving mail differed greatly from today. Back then, sending a letter from one family member to another, or from a small business owner in Ephesus to a company man in Corinth, required a fair bit of work.

While there certainly existed an imperial postal service, the *cursus publicus*, it was generally restricted for those with privileged access on matters of public importance. For the rest of society, the mail got through in other ways. The wealthy tended to send and receive mail through the aegis of a slave or hired hand. But the common person, more often than not, sent his letters by way of someone who *just happened* to be traveling in the right direction.

For example, a particular document from ancient times has somehow survived the centuries. The note contains a letter as well as a set of directions to a house. With a bit of imagination we can envision it being scratched out hurriedly by a letter writer and given to an agreeable traveler—now turned letter carrier—who promises to deliver the mail. Tucking the letter into his garment, the traveler set out. We can envision the honest traveler arriving at his destination perhaps days or weeks later. In keeping with his promise he pulls the note of directions from its secure place of hiding, looks at it hard, and perhaps now reads it for the first time:

From the Moon gate walk as if towards the granaries and when you come to the first street turn left behind the thermae, where there is a shrine, and go westwards. Go down the steps and up the others and turn right and after the precinct of the temple on the right side there is a seven-story house and on top of the gatehouse a statue of Fortune opposite a basket-weaving shop. Inquire there or from the concierge and you will be informed. And shout yourself; Lusius will answer you.[1]

He presses on, both eyes fixed on passing landmarks, until at last with a shout of "Lusius!" his duty is all but done. In the near distance one emerges, rather excitedly, into the light from beneath an archway or from behind a door. His feet make quick work across the stone toward the sound of his name. He arrives with interest, for the unknown voice means that mail has come, and with it the likelihood of a letter and news from far away.

For a time the two speak. They exchange questions on what is happening abroad. They talk of distant places. The traveler gives the man an update on the welfare of his friend who was kind enough to write. And after all the news that is news at all has been imparted, the recipient of the letter, now wordlessly eager to be alone in a place where he can read, puts a coin or two into the hand of the carrier, thanks him many times over for his efforts, and after making sure he knows how to get back to Moon Gate from here, releases the principled traveler from his commitment.

And what of Lusius? Here is where I expect the ancient world and our own are the same. He finds a pleasant place to sit, a quiet corner where he can read without interruption.

Today we are Lusius—the happy ones eagerly emerging from the shadows in anticipation of receiving mail. A letter has come to us, and it brings news from far away. And it will be ours without distraction.

Taking it now in hand, the name appears straightforward enough; it is simply called The Letter of Jude. Glancing at its length we quickly notice its brevity, a short twenty-five verses. If we had lived then instead of now and were familiar with the way in which ancient letters were formed, a cursory look at the opening lines might lead us—mistakenly—to believe that this letter is ordinary, one among a multitude of mundane letters to survive the ancient world.[2]

After all, it was commonplace for the *author* to begin by identifying himself by name, just as Jude does in the opening of verse 1. Further, ancient letters expressed the intended *audience* next, just as Jude does in closing out verse 1. And finally, with both author and audience now identified, a brief *acknowledgment* was made—a greeting of sorts or best wishes or a prayer for the readers' welfare—just as Jude does in verse 2. Nearly all the correspondence we have from that ancient and agrarian time conforms to this. At first glance Jude is nothing more. Old, short, and common. Standard mail.

In the coming chapters of this book, I hope this simplistic view will change, for the sweeping importance of Jude's words will mount and crash like waves. In Jude's waters we will be mysteriously refreshed, yet also laid low. We will be enveloped in the letter's potency and its consolation. Like sojourners caught between ecstasy and abyss, we will traverse the literary terrain of Jude's rugged truths. If we read alertly and listen well, we will find ourselves more arduously committed to the noble fight of daily *keeping ourselves* in the faith by living under Jude's furious array of admonitions and commands. And when we are finished and spent, when all our reading is done, when each of us will have chewed on Jude time and time again, in the quiet of our home at night as well as by early morning's light, then we will know Jude for what it is—a letter to us from God, a far cry from standard mail.

The Author

Verse 1 simply begins: "Jude, a servant of Jesus Christ and brother of James." The author of our letter goes by the name of Jude, or Judas as it stands in the original. That name is followed by two descriptive phrases meant to identify him further:
  • "a servant of Jesus Christ"
  • "brother of James"

Brother of James

Who was this obscure one called Jude? And can we know for sure? A case can be made for many, yet the traditional thought remains as good as any and better than most. During these ancient times the James with the strongest affiliation with the decidedly Christian material in Jude was James the Just, leader of the church in Jerusalem. One can read about him in the book of Acts as he oversees the first church council (Acts 15). But in the letter to the churches in Galatia the Apostle Paul refers to this James as "James the Lord's brother" (1:19).

Interestingly, when we canvass the Gospels for Jesus' family we find James listed, and not only him but one by the name of Jude as well.

> . . . is not this the carpenter, the son of Mary and brother of James and Joses and Judas and Simon. And are not his sisters here with us? (Mark 6:3)

It is certainly possible, and many think probable, that Jude, the writer of this letter, is the younger brother of James and blood relation to Jesus Christ. If so, he comes from the family of first rank in the early Christian church. Describing himself as the brother of James is an effort to distinguish him from others by the same name and thereby make his own identity readily known.

Servant of Jesus Christ

He also describes himself as "a servant of Jesus Christ." "Servant." As it is for all of Jesus' followers, so it was for Jude. Here is a great and comforting truth, one worth stopping to observe: *The people closest to Jesus are happy to call themselves servants.*

Don't forget it. Jesus is God's King, and as such he is our rightful ruler. At times when each of us is tempted and even taught to take offense or act affronted at the notion of yielding to the authority of another, remember Jude. He will have more to teach us about the importance of living under authority in this short letter. And in the coming chapters we will see that this subject is very close to his heart.

In preparing this book I have come to believe that our persistent desire to get out from under the Biblical notion of authority, be it ecclesiastical, civil, vocational, or marital, is often problematic and in most cases self-destructive—in the case of Jude's opponents eternally so.

Our propensity to play the rebel, to answer to no one, to throw off any and all vestiges of authority is perhaps why—right out of the gate—Jude identifies himself as Jesus' servant. He is modeling Christian maturity for every reader—strikingly by the third word in the English text. That he does so with such matter-of-fact joy ought to be encouraging. Never think it wrong or demeaning to identify yourself as one under authority. There is great sweetness in living by God's design.

The Audience

Jude writes his letter, according to the final words of verse 1, "To those who are called, beloved in God the Father and kept for Jesus Christ." Verse 1 followed up the author's name with two descriptive phrases, and Jude does the same with the audience to whom he writes. The recipients of the letter are "those who are called," and the two phrases that describe them are:
  • "beloved in God the Father"
  • "kept for Jesus Christ"

To Those Who Are . . .

With the phrase "to those" we are wonderfully joined to the invigorating realization that Jude's letter was intended for many people. No single person is listed, nor is the letter limited to a particular church.[3] Jude wrote for masses of men and women and perhaps even a multitude of churches.

Do you remember our opening illustration in which the letter carrier shouted out, "Lusius!" Well, delivering the letter of Jude to the right address would have been a bit more complicated. When the mailman raised his voice to announce its arrival, Lusius would not be the only one smiling from behind the shadows. Gobs of people would have appeared! Can you see them? Moving in close with anticipation and excitement—running in from the market and the fields—along back alleys and big boulevards. All those people, God's people, running in anticipation. And with a spontaneous church meeting now under way, the letter of Jude would be read aloud, the first time, for all.

Called

Asserting his audience as those who are "called" discloses another exalted yet staggering certainty of the Bible. God's people are so because of God's choice. God is the initiator, first pursuer, lover. His will beckons us, and we come; we come because he called.

Charles Spurgeon was once trying to fathom the depths of the wonderful reality of being sought out by God. He was overwhelmed by the truth that God, the Lord of the universe, decided, even *delighted*, to be in relationship with him. In reaching for words to express his fortune he said:

> I believe the doctrine of election, because I am quite sure that if God had not chosen me I should never have chosen him; and I am sure He chose me before I was born, or else He never would have chosen me afterwards. And He must have elected me for reasons unknown to me, for I never could find any reason in myself why He should have looked upon me with special love.[4]

To be looked upon with the special love of God—isn't that great? The experiential effect of knowing that God has called us to himself is unconditional love flowing like strong, slow, rich, hot molasses into the inner chambers of our being. That God would have me—how rich a thought. I am sure that Jude's first readers felt something of that comfort too. Who knows, perhaps his letter arrived just when they needed that comforting reminder the most. Maybe it is that way for you too.

The balancing biblical notion of effort is seen in the little word "kept" (v. 1). Mark it well. We will run across this word again. It will come many times and in many ways, but especially take note of it in verse 21. Being "called" or "kept" for Jesus doesn't mean we don't keep ourselves. God is not a God of presumption. But the emphasis in verse 1 is this: those who are called by the Spirit are kept for Jesus Christ. And nothing can shake these noble fruits loose from the tree.

Called, Beloved, and Kept

The fullness in the phrases "called, beloved in God the Father and kept for Jesus Christ" only deepen our sense of good fortune. Incredible—loved by the Father, kept for the Son, and called by the Spirit. *Called, beloved*, and *kept*. Like a river, the words when put together flow effortlessly, soothing weary listeners in need of shoring up their faith.

Think of these three words—*called, beloved*, and *kept*—as one. After all, the text of Jude gives us good reason to do so. In the original language the audience ("those who are called") is described in bookend fashion. The Greek verse opens with "to those" and adds the matching subject only after both descriptive words ("beloved" and "kept") have been scripted in. Thus, it isn't until he closes out verse 1 (in the Greek) that Jude pens "who are called." So it literally reads, *"To those . . . beloved . . . kept . . . who are called."*

Jude wanted his readers to sense something of the overwhelming power and glory of being "called" *and* "beloved" *and* "kept." He doesn't want today's preacher to be overly concerned about breaking the verse into its constitute parts. There are times when a mechanic needs to take an engine apart—pieces all around, separate, lying on the floor. But engines were really made for running. And Jude's language here was built to soar.

It looks to me like he got his ideas on this from the prophet Isaiah.[5] Isaiah, the towering prophet, had proclaimed God's word many years earlier. He loved to use these three words together as a description of God's people. We see this, for example, in Isaiah 42: "Behold my servant, whom I uphold [*love*]" (v. 1), and continuing in verse 6, "I have *called* you in righteousness; I will take you by the hand and *keep* you." Jude expresses himself like Isaiah. To be God's people is to be the "called" *and* "beloved" *and* "kept."

A major work of literature capable of sustaining the elevated heights and vast depths of what these three words convey is John Milton's *Paradise Lost*. Milton writes first of the Great War before the world, when Heaven was a bloody battlefield and Satan flew with his iniquitous minions in full-blown insurrection. After being thrown down from Heaven, the defeated despot waited for revenge. Then Milton shows our world made in beauty. But Satan now sights man, and our own great fall draws near.

It is precisely here in Milton's text, with God on the throne in Heaven, man and woman in the garden unsuspecting, and Satan in hurried flight, that Milton writes of the Godhead speaking and in mutual love deciding to *call* and *love* and *keep*:

> On his right the radiant image of his glory sat.
> His only son. On Earth he first beheld
> Our two first parents, yet the only two

Of mankind, in the Happy Garden placed. . . .
He then surveyed Hell and the gulf between, and Satan there. . . .
Ready now to stoop, with wearied wings and willing feet. . . .
Him God beholding from his prospect high,
Wherein past, present, future, he behold,
Thus to His only son foreseeing spoke: —
"Only-begotten son, seest thou what rage
Transports our Adversary . . . he wings his way . . .
Directly towards the new-created World,
And Man here placed, with purpose to assay
If him by force he can destroy, or, worse,
By some false guile pervert: and shall pervert;
For Man will hearken to his glozing lies,
And easily transgress the sole command. . . .

And then, contrasting the destiny of Satan and his demons with that of our
own, Milton has the Father say:

The first sort by their own suggestion fell,
Self-tempted, self-depraved; Man falls, deceived
By the other first: Man, therefore, shall find grace.

To which the Son resounds:

O Father, gracious was that word which closed
Thy Sovereign sentence, that Man should find grace. . . .
Happy for Man, so coming! He her aid
Can never seek, once dead in sins and lost —
Atonement for himself, or offering meet,
Indebted and undone, hath none to bring.
Behold me, then: me for him, life for life,
I offer; on me let thine anger fall;
Account me Man: . . . on me let Death wreak all his rage.
Under his gloomy power I shall not long lie vanquished. . . .
Then, with the multitude of my redeemed,
Shall enter Heaven, long absent, and return.
Father, to see Thy face, wherein no cloud
Of anger shall remain, but peace assured
And reconcilement: wrath shall be no more
Thenceforth, but in thy presence joy entire.[6]

So ends the reading of Milton. A literary window into the measureless
glory of the gospel. This is what Jude is after with these words "called,"

"beloved," and "kept." They are names from Heaven. And in selecting them Jude exalts his audience to the place of greatest grace. Like jewels they signify limitless grace and life. Think of it—before the beginning of time, God delighted in a decided love. Are there words to compare to these three? Jude knows of none higher.

And so we come in our little letter, by the end of verse 1, to holy ground. And we stop. And we worship, praise, sing songs to God. How can we not? We are stronger for this fresh understanding of God's goodness toward all who believe.

The Prayer of Acknowledgment

Jude closes out his introduction with verse 2—a prayer for his readers. "May mercy, peace, and love be multiplied to you." I especially enjoy the word "multiplied." May our time spent in Jude help us see these things in abundance. May we know God's mercy more intimately, his peace more completely, and his love more firmly—all of this and more.

One last observation, something to think on, and it stems from what we have read thus far. Jude begins with power in his pen, with strong words and deep phrases. "Servant," "called," "beloved," "kept," good things in abundance. This is all so nourishing and perhaps foreshadowing. I get the idea that Jude's first readers needed structural support—some undergirding early on—a clear sense of identity and place. And these are the things soldiers need when compelled into the fray.

Thus we begin our consideration of the letter of Jude. Aren't you glad it is in your possession at last? Find a pleasant and quiet place to read it in the coming days. It will prove to be nothing less than manna from Heaven, food given to those contending in a wilderness world.

Our Heavenly Father, what a joy it is to know that this letter of Jude comes to us from you. We thank you for it and we commit our study of it to you. Our hearts rise in gratitude when we consider that we are your "beloved" who are "called" and "kept" for you. Please teach us all that you want us to learn from this epistle, and use it to help us contend for the gospel in our own day. We commit our time in it to you. In Jesus' name, amen.

Beloved, although I was very eager to write to you about our common salvation, I found it necessary to write appealing to you to contend for the faith that was once for all delivered to the saints. For certain people have crept in unnoticed who long ago were designated for this condemnation, ungodly people, who pervert the grace of our God into sensuality and deny our only Master and Lord, Jesus Christ.

vv. 3, 4

32

Contending for This Noble Faith

JUDE 3, 4

THE ARTHURIAN LEGENDS are rich with tales of brave knights who freely expend themselves for noble causes. The story of *Sir Gawain and the Green Knight* is no exception. It was Christmastime in Camelot, and Arthur's knights were celebrating the season with relaxed conversation at the king's Round Table. Everyone was at ease—characters without a care in the world.

Until, arriving on horseback, unannounced and without warning, a Green Knight enters. And when his sporting challenge to Arthur's men is met by silence, the intruder shames them as unworthy combatants, undeserving of Arthur's name:

> "What! Is this King Arthur's house . . .
> the rumor of which runs through realms unnumbered?
> Where now is your haughtiness, and your high conquests,
> your fierceness and fell mood, and your fine boasting?
> Now are the revels and royalty of the Round Table
> Overwhelmed by a word by one man spoken . . . !"
> With that he laughed so loud that their lord [Arthur] was angered.

At last the unlikely and obscure Gawain the Good accepts the Green Knight's game:

> "Would you my worthy lord," said Gawain to the king,
> "bid me abandon this bench and stand by you there;

so that I without discourtesy might be excused from the table . . .
and since this affair is so foolish that it nowise befits you,
and I have requested it first, accord it then to me!"[1]

Something awakened Gawain on that day. For him, the honorable name of Arthur was worth competing for—even if he should lose. He became a man fully committed to contend with a menace whose rude challenge interrupted their season of relaxed celebration. And it is due to this solitary action that we even know of Sir Gawain today.

In Gawain I am reminded of Jude. Jude the Obscure he would have remained, an unheralded figure in history, if not for the single action of writing this letter. Yet by it he is known. And with it he proves himself valiant, one willing to forgo the camaraderie of fellowship in order to take a stand against those who have crept into the church in mockery of Christ's name. A quick glance at verses 3, 4, and the connections become apparent.

By the way verse 3 begins, Jude, like Gawain, had a desire to be at a table of celebration, something a bit more relaxed:

Beloved, although I was very eager to write to you about our common salvation . . .

Yet, by the second half of verse 3 we see Jude pushing his chair back from the table, now on his feet and compelled to enlist in some noble cause:

I found it necessary to write appealing to you to contend for the faith that was once for all delivered to the saints.

And beginning with verse 4 we read of the menacing presence, the unannounced and unwelcome intruders who would change everything and challenge the name of the king:

For certain people have crept in unnoticed who long ago were designated for this condemnation, ungodly people, who pervert the grace of our God into sensuality and deny our only Master and Lord, Jesus Christ.

Jude and Gawain—the two are like brothers. Yet, one great thing separates Jude from Gawain—the matter of importance. Gawain's story is the stuff of legends. It's fun to read while relaxing on a beach. In contrast, Jude's letter contains nothing less than the voice of God for his people. The book of Jude, therefore, is literature unlike any other: it is essential reading for anyone who wants to live and die in Christ.

The Letter's Structure

So, with Jude's letter in our hands, we explore these verses earnestly. And by the looks of them, verse 3 gives us the *theme*, while verse 4 reveals the letter's occasion. The theme is an appeal to "contend for the faith." After that we are clued in that verse 4 supports the theme by the little word "for," and reading on it becomes obvious that the occasion for the letter rests in Jude's knowledge that *the faith is being challenged* by opponents he only will call "certain people."

The structure of the entire letter flows out of these two verses. The conclusions Jude makes about the challenges facing Christianity in verse 4 will be defended by him in verses 5–16. Further, the appeal to contend for the faith in verse 3 will find its "how to" in verses 17–23. The Bible doesn't leave us to our own imagination in determining how to contend for the faith. The Bible answers this for us. It is its own interpreter. And so, with all that in mind, here is the structure of the letter:

- Jude 3: Contending for the Faith—Jude 17–23   Showing Us How
- Jude 4: Challenges to the Faith—Jude 5–16   Supporting His Case

This built-in construction[2] should prove helpful as we unpack Jude's theme and occasion.

The Letter's Theme (v. 3)

An Appeal to Contend

The word translated "contend," when verbalized, sounds like our word *agonizing*. It possesses the idea of athletes who, in an effort to win, find themselves intensely struggling, competing, even fighting with all their might. Interestingly, the word also seems to attach itself to things that are intrinsically worthy of full-orbed and all-engaging effort. Or, as a Greek-English Lexicon puts it, "effort expended . . . in a noble cause."[3]

"Effort expended . . . in a noble cause." This is what Jude is after. He aims at enlivening the church of his day to an immediate and intense struggle, a very real fight requiring all of their available energy. So, what does this early observation mean for us?

Well, for starters, understanding this to be Jude's theme changes everything for us as readers. In the last chapter we envisioned settling down with Jude in some quiet corner for uninterrupted reading. We soaked in his opening words, and they buoyed our spirits—how good it was to be reminded so unhurriedly by him of God's decided love for us.

But now, with Jude's urgent appeal in verse 3 to "contend," our mind is forced to go on red alert. We are being asked to read standing in readiness. Jude is finished with pleasantries; some required action is at hand. Urgency and immediacy move him. He wants contenders, and he wants them now.

And with this letter he means to raise them up. If Jude were to write a letter to the church in our day, he wouldn't change a thing. We need this generation of Christians to contend. It is the hour for Gawain.

For the Faith . . .

. . . Once for All Delivered to the Saints

Jude is smart. He doesn't ask for effort without making known the noble cause that lies behind his appeal. They are to "contend for the faith." Note two key words—a bare minimum—simply "the faith." The Christian faith is noble and honorable and worth every bit of the readers' agonizing efforts. Two things stand out about this noble faith—its fullness and its completeness.

Faith's Fullness

What does Jude mean by "the faith"? He means faith in all its *fullness*. Many people today can still recall some rudiments of the Christian faith. God's creation. Our fall. Separation. Judgment. A big promise. The coming of Jesus. His death. His resurrection and ascension. His grace and coming again. Hopefully, others would add to its fullness with expressions like the Scriptures, Jesus, David's Son, God's King, Savior, faith, repentance, the Holy Spirit, baptism, church.

I wonder, though, how many of us readily speak of *the faith* with apostolic depth and fullness? Would we include faith's demands? A life lived in faith? They all did.

• Paul understood it to mean "the obedience of faith" (Romans 1:5). And to Titus he wrote that he labored for "the sake of the faith of God's elect and their knowledge of the truth, which accords with godliness" (Titus 1:1)

• James put the fullness of faith this way: "faith apart from works is dead" (James 2:26).

• Peter wrote about "the tested genuineness of your faith" (1 Peter 1:7).

• John said, "I have no greater joy than to hear that my children are walking in the truth. Beloved, it is a faithful thing you do . . ." (3 John 4, 5)

And we could go on. For Jude, "the faith" is not merely a list of propositions. When defined fully, it includes the life-changing activity of God, conformity to its moral imperatives, and complete obedience to Jesus. Jude means all of this and then some! There is fullness to the apostolic faith.

A seminary professor might express it this way: "Moral imperatives are the natural derivatives of all gospel indicatives." I prefer the simplicity of the ancient preacher who likened faith's fullness to putting "the life of God in the soul of man."[4] That says it well.

Faith's Completeness

The second thing we see about the faith is its *completeness*. Again note verse 3: ". . . that was once for all delivered to the saints." Aren't you struck by that little phrase "once for all"? London's Rev. Dick Lucas, a faithful contender for the gospel, put the stunning reality behind these words this way: "[I]n Jude, the Christian faith is already in existence as a settled and final body of saving truths."[5] Imagine! We are not free to change it, as if the faith were somehow still evolving and making its way in the world. According to Jude, "the faith" is not only full, but it already exists in final form. It is not subject to change!

And so we come to the end of verse 3. Our first look at the letter's theme is finished. And Jude's word to the church is this: "On your feet. The time for leisure is past. Contend. Agonize. Exert maximum effort. The Christian faith, in all its fullness and completeness, is worthy of your struggle." May Jude's noble theme shake us from any complacency and bring us into apostolic conformity. With verse 4 Jude's first readers soon discover the reason for the urgency in his voice.

The Letter's Occasion (v. 4)

Certain People

Verse 4 opens, "For certain people have crept in unnoticed . . ." The disdain in Jude's voice is palpable—"certain people." Throughout the letter Jude speaks in this derisive way when mentioning his opponents. It becomes his angry mantra. The *certain creeping people* of verse 4 become simply "these people" by verses 8 and 10. And "these people" are disgustingly relegated to "these" by the time he reaches verses 12, 16, and 19. What we will see in coming studies is that Jude's call to contend for the faith stems from his assessment of "these people," about whom he has absolutely nothing good to say. Look at the descriptive phrases with which he describes them in verse 4. The first two show *who* they are:

- "who long ago were designated for this condemnation"
- "ungodly people"

When we look at verses 5–10, I will explain what it means that they "long ago were designated for condemnation."

For now we want to center in on the next two descriptive phrases. These tell us *what* these "certain people" were doing, and it's the *what* of verse 4 that provides us with the reasons why the letter was written.

What were these people doing? The answer is straightforward and clear. Certain people were challenging the faith in two ways: First, they were "pervert[ing] the grace of our God into sensuality," and second, they were "deny[ing] our only Master and Lord, Jesus Christ." To put it in the form of headings, they were taking advantage of God's grace and setting aside God's authority. These were the two challenges Jude faced.

Challenging the Faith: Taking Advantage of God's Grace

The word translated "pervert" means "to change or alter."[6] Evidently some Christian leaders were changing the intended effect of God's grace. Rather than modeling a life dedicated to increasing in conformity to the image of Christ, these people exercised their freedom by living however they pleased—in this case, continued sensuality. The word translated "sensuality" is a general word meant to convey loose living marked by sexual pleasure and greed.

In other words, they were gutting the faith of its moral imperatives. They altered Christian liberty—they changed and transformed it into carnal license. You want a woman who is not your wife? Take her. Take her in bed. Take her on the screen. Take hundreds of them in an hour if you please. A man? Why not? He's yours. Money? Grab it. Grace covers it all, they claimed.

Is there a verse in the Bible more appropriate for our day than this one? When we talk about "certain people" taking advantage of God's grace, we need to listen. It is too easy and convenient to assume that when Jude speaks to "certain people," he speaks to others and not to us. But this verse reveals *our* underbelly. Isn't Jude's trouble with *insiders*? Didn't they "creep in unnoticed"? And in verse 12 aren't they seated at the Lord's Table?

The truth is, this verse unmasks *our* propensity. Who among us, if left alone by the Holy Spirit for a single second, might not risk all Heaven holds for a moment of earthly satisfaction. Daily, the temptation is to presume upon grace. Presumption is our greatest sin. This verse belongs to the church. According to Jude, many are heading ever so unwittingly toward condemnation, never having been saved at all.

Centuries later this teaching was given a name. When Martin Luther's friend and fellow-worker Johannes Agricola (1494–1566) declared to his hearers, "Art thou steeped in sin, an adulterer or a thief? If thou believest thou art in salvation," Luther promptly denounced him as "antinomian"— the first use of the word in history.

According to Jude, a personal encounter with God's grace does not permit us to play fast and loose with the moral imperatives of God's Word.[7] To be a Christian means being saved *from* sensuality and *to* sanctification. There are things in life to which God says no. Calvin defends God's wisdom this way: "It is bad to live under a prince who permits nothing, but much worse to live under one who permits everything."[8] We live in a permissive time. You might call it the days of Jude. Knowing this should give us occasion to contend. And remembering verses 20, 21 should give us the blueprint for how.

Challenging the Faith: Casting off God's Authority

The second challenge that occasioned Jude's letter comes in the closing words of verse 4. He writes of those who "deny our only Master and Lord, Jesus Christ." Not only were Jude's opponents antinomian—they were anti-authority. They rejected the notion, either by their teaching or de facto by their loose living, that Jesus was their King.

Again, we are confronted with the contemporary call of Jude. Denying Jesus the place of ultimate rule is common fare *in the church* today. "He was a great figure, to be sure, but only one among many." Do you see the difference between how we use the word *only* and the way Jude uses it? In our day, Jesus is "only one among many." According to what we read in Jude 4, Jesus is our *only* Master. We saw the importance of this idea foreshadowed in the previous study when Jude early acknowledged himself to be Jesus' servant. Christians willingly identify themselves as under authority. For others, though, coming under any notion of authority is viewed with disdain.

And Jude simply will not let this issue go. We will see it reappear in coming studies when we arrive at verse 6 and again in verse 11. Casting aside the authority of Jesus is what calls for a generation that will contend for the faith.

The Letter's Call upon Our Life

We must ask ourselves, so what? What does this mean for me? Living under the shadow of one of the world's great universities (the University of Chicago) compels me to set these two challenges to the faith side by side. I gave these challenges the headings of *Taking Advantage of God's Grace* and *Casting off God's Authority*. In the place of *Taking Advantage of God's Grace*, substitute the word *interpretation*. And in the place of *Casting Off Christ's Authority*, substitute the word *inspiration*. The parallels are precise.

Christian students and scholars must engage the discipline of Biblical *interpretation*. Why? Because those who would cut the faith loose from her moorings of moral imperatives do so on the grounds of interpretation. In every generation we have a new hermeneutic—faulty but fresh principles meant to guide our search for meaning. We need people who give themselves to contending for the apostolic interpretation of the Scriptures. Given this, some of you have a particular calling. "Contend."

Others must get engaged in contending for Biblical *inspiration*. Why? Because those who would undermine the faith from Christ's authority do so on the grounds of inspiration—or the lack of it. Do away with the notion that the Bible's words are God's words, and all semblance of authority is overturned.

The contemporary nature of this ancient letter is astounding. The issues confronting the church in our day are identical to the ones Jude faced. The same challenges flow down through the centuries, like meandering rivers, cut with deep beds and proven to wind great distances.

Jude would have us "contend." He wants us on our feet exerting great energy for the faith. Ours is a noble cause. The faith needs our action. Do nothing, and the gospel will be entirely gutted of her transforming strength. Do nothing, and the glory of Jesus will be utterly dismissed. And how are we to contend? We must "keep ourselves in the love of God" (v. 21). We must build ourselves up in our most holy faith (v. 20). We must keep watch in prayer lest we fall into temptation (v. 20).

To put a concluding and contrasting picture on this, we must reject the life of the fictional character who centuries later would go by Jude's name. Thomas Hardy came out with his completed novel *Jude the Obscure* in 1895. In it he creates another Jude, one who strived to belong at Christminster, a place of noble pursuits and elevated company. Eventually he crept in unnoticed, but only after he had run himself aground on the sandbars of sensuality. Hardy's Jude changed the grace of God into an opportunity for the flesh. He rejected authority. And at the close of his life he was still defiant, saying, "The time was not ripe for us! Our ides were fifty years too soon."[9]

His descent into condemnation, though, began years earlier on a day when he sat in his home, at table, with the relaxed prospects of an afternoon spent in reading the Greek New Testament. However, having promised previously to meet a girl that same afternoon, he had a choice to make—the Biblical text before him in all its fullness and completeness or the woman who so attracted him. Hardy imagines Jude's reasonings:

> In short, as if materially, a compelling arm of extraordinary muscular power seized hold of him—something which had nothing in common with the spirits and influences that had moved him hitherto. This seemed to care little for his reason and his will, nothing for his so called elevated intentions, and moved him along, as a violent schoolmaster a schoolboy he has seized by the collar, in a direction which tended towards the embrace of a woman for whom he had no respect, *and whose life had nothing in common with his own except locality.* H KAINH ΔIAΘHKH was no more heeded, and the predestinate Jude sprang up and across the room. Foreseeing such an event he had already arrayed himself in his best clothes. In three minutes time he was out of the house and descending by the path across the wide vacant hollow of corn-ground which lay between the village and the isolated house of Arabella in the dip beyond the upland.[10]

Two Judes. Two destinies. One faith. One choice to make. Push back from the table toward condemnation, or stand to contend for this most noble faith.

Dear Lord Jesus Christ, as our only Master and Savior, we long for your name to be honored among all. Enable us therefore, in the power of your Spirit, to arise and contend for the faith. And protect us as we do. For your glory and our own good we pray. In Jesus' name, amen.

Now I want to remind you, although you once fully knew it, that Jesus, who saved a people out of the land of Egypt, afterward destroyed those who did not believe. And the angels who did not stay within their own position of authority, but left their proper dwelling, he has kept in eternal chains under gloomy darkness until the judgment of the great day—just as Sodom and Gomorrah and the surrounding cities, which likewise indulged in sexual immorality and pursued unnatural desire, serve as an example by undergoing a punishment of eternal fire. Yet in like manner these people also, relying on their dreams, defile the flesh, reject authority, and blaspheme the glorious ones. But when the archangel Michael, contending with the devil, was disputing about the body of Moses, he did not presume to pronounce a blasphemous judgment, but said, "The Lord rebuke you." But these people blaspheme all that they do not understand, and they are destroyed by all that they, like unreasoning animals, understand instinctively.

vv. 5–10

33

The Past Becomes
the Present

JUDE 5–10

THOMAS MANN, in his masterwork *Joseph and His Brothers,* pauses occasionally to consider history and time. Especially enchanting is Mann's way of expressing the connections between the past and the present. He shows how the great distance separating the ancient world from our own is at times transparent. He writes:

> History is that which has happened and that which goes on happening in time. But also it is the stratified record upon which we set our feet, the ground beneath us; and the deeper [we] go down into the layers that lie below and beyond . . . in our moments of less precision we may speak of them in the first person and as though they were part of our flesh-and-blood experience.[1]

Did you catch Mann's sense? People from long ago can be said to rise up again in the present. Each of us can imaginatively step back in time and find a connection with someone whose situation not only mirrors our own but permits us to call it our own. We pull the past into the present; we push the present into the past. We can read history and at moments find ourselves present. On this enchanted ground all centuries become one.

The mesmerizing inference from Mann's creative genius is this: ancient archetypes, men and women who lived long ago, are today walking around in our world. They have come to life again, as it were, only under a different name.

It is no surprise, then, that we commonly call a deceptive man who is nevertheless blessed by God Jacob, just as Jacob in his own day saw himself as the blessed embodiment of Isaac and of Abraham. In like manner, the impatient and unchosen in our world we sometimes call Esau, just as Esau in his own day typified Ishmael and Edom before him. Mann put it this way:

> Deep-sunk in musing, yet mightily uplifted, was the soul of Jacob in these days when he with his brother Esau buried their father; for all past events stood up in him and became present again in his flesh according to the archetype; and to him it was as though the ground beneath his feet were transparent, consisting of crystal layers going down and down without any bottom and lighted up by lamps which burned between the layers. But he walked above them among the experiences of his proper flesh, Jacob, present in time, and gazed at Esau, who likewise walked again with him according to his archetype and was Edom, the Red.[2]

Why am I beginning this study on Jude 5–10 with musings from Thomas Mann? Well, Jude does something very Mann-like in this letter. And if you don't see it now, the next portion of his letter won't make much sense.

Proving His Claim

Do you remember the important but puzzling little phrase that went largely unexplored in the last chapter? It was hidden in verse 4: "For certain people . . . long ago were designated for this condemnation." Well, with those seven words—"long ago were designated for this condemnation"—Jude is doing something very Mann-like.

With "long ago" Jude, like Mann, is making use of history. He asserts a connection between the *present* danger facing the church and a *past* event; he links the appalling presence of "certain people" in the church to some prediction that envisioned their ultimate downfall. The puzzling part is this: What record is Jude referring to when he speaks of "condemnation" from "long ago"? Was it an ancient prophetic word in Scripture? Or perhaps some lost oral tradition? At first it seems difficult to know.

What we do know, though, is that Jude follows up his claim of fixed condemnation with verses 5–10. And interestingly, as we will soon see, in them we not only stumble upon the answer to our question, but we find ourselves running into Thomas Mann at the same time.

Three Events

First, notice that in verses 5–7 Jude follows his belief in a fixed "condemnation" for "certain people" with three events from the Old Testament (verse 7 even uses the word "example").

• In verse 5 he reminds us that unbelieving Jews were *"destroyed"* because of unbelief.

• In verse 6 he recounts that fallen angels were *judged* for their rebellion.

• In verse 7 Jude relates that *"punishment"* fell on Sodom and Gomorrah.

The three events all support a claim that God judges certain people. Look next at how Jude pulls the condemnation of the three events into the present day by attaching them to the troublemakers of verse 4.

• In verse 8 he says, "Yet in like manner *these people* also . . ."

• In verse 10 he connects the three events to *"these people* . . . [who] are destroyed."[3]

In verse 11 and following, Jude will continue this same use of history. But instead of reminding us of historical events to prove his claim, Jude there summons three personal examples. And with that the entire letter opens up to us like a puzzle now solved.

So, in the body of this letter we find Jude stepping through layers of time, grabbing hold of historical events and examples in groups of three, and pulling them into the present day and applying them in the first person—and all of this under divine authority. Once we make that connection we are inside the mind of Jude: "Hey, beloved, be careful. Haven't you read Thomas Mann? You have in-house religious teachers who are heading toward judgment. You want proof? I'll give you proof. Long-ago events and long-ago examples are at work in them. These guys are those guys! Ancient archetypes are walking in our world. They have come to life again—only they go by different names."

Providing God's Meaning

Here we should pause for a moment. For if what we have said is true, then we have stumbled upon much more than Jude's method or Mann's ingenuity. We are face to face with what God means for us to take away from our reading. Christians must "contend for the faith" because the past proves that impostors will always be present. While we can all be encouraged in knowing that their eventual downfall is sure, nevertheless we need Jude, and especially this middle part of his letter if we are going to equip ourselves in learning how to spot them and, even more importantly, ensure that we don't become one of them.

Chaplain Harry Roundtree works with the Good News Jail and Prison Ministry in Chicago's Cook County Jail. One day we were talking, and the book of Jude came up. His eyes lit up, and he said, "Jude! That's my jailhouse book!" "Your jailhouse book?" I said. "Yeah," he replied. "That's the book that I give the guys to help them get straight on all the different preachers who come through here." Jude shows us where false teachers are headed and how we can spot them. We must take in Jude's three pictures to keep us straight.

A Picture of Apostasy

The first picture is one of apostasy. In verse 5 the large throng that God delivered from Egypt silently emerges from the ancient ground like mist; for our sake, Jude disturbs them and raises them from their sleep. And for a brief moment this "long ago" people stand before us as a vast congregation. Their shadowy presence is meant to remind us (verse 5 opens with, "Now I want to remind you") that God's judgment will come—even on those who once lived within the bounds of the church as recipients of grace. And Jude makes the stunning claim that what they rejected was the very ministry of Jesus!

Their sin? The text says that they were "destroyed" because they "did not believe." In the Hebrew Scriptures we find a generation that rejected God. God saved, God spoke, God settled in their midst, but they did not believe God's word. They were faithless again and again. They did not trust God for daily provisions; they turned from solitary worship. The example Jude may have in mind here is their decision to not enter the Promised Land. Psalm 95 and Numbers 14 recount that fateful event when God said:

> But as for you, your dead bodies shall fall in this wilderness. And your children shall be shepherds in the wilderness forty years and shall suffer for your faithlessness, until the last of your dead bodies lies in the wilderness. According to the number of the days in which you spied out the land, forty days, a year for each day, you shall bear your iniquity forty years, and you shall know my displeasure. I the Lord, have spoken. Surely this will I do to all this wicked generation who are gathered against me: in this wilderness they shall come to a full end, and there they shall die. (Numbers 14:32–35)

The frightening thing about this picture of apostasy is in what it reveals. That which happened then can also occur today, to us. No one is immune. Not you and certainly not me. So we are reminded of the importance of belief, faith, and our need to daily take God at his word.

A Picture of Autonomy

In verse 6 the earth's congregation fades from view, and in its place we find a picture of something equally frightening—autonomy. God's fixed and final judgment will fall not only on some from among earth's congregation, but upon those who once were part of the worshiping host of Heaven:

And the angels who did not stay within their own position of authority, but left their proper dwelling, he has kept in eternal chains under gloomy darkness until the judgment of the great day. (v. 6)

How incredible to be reminded that a road to Hell is paved for some who knew life in the presence of God firsthand. John Milton in *Paradise Lost* has Satan addressing his vanquished legions in their first astonished moments of defeat and despair. The sense of autonomy cannot be missed:

All is not lost—the unconquerable will,
And study of revenge, immortal hate,
And courage never to submit or yield;
And what is else not to be overcome? . . .
We may with more successful hope resolve
To wage by force or guile eternal war,
Irreconcilable to our grand Foe,
Who now triumphs, and in the excess of joy
Sole reigning holds the tyranny of Heaven.[4]

Some from among the angelic host failed to show proper respect for God's created boundaries. They rejected the authority of God and embraced autonomy from God. With intended irony, going back to verse 1, the text says that they "did not stay [NIV, *keep*] within their own position of authority," and as a result they are now "*kept* in eternal chains under gloomy darkness" until the great day of God's judgment.

Interestingly, the Old Testament incident that Jude may have in mind may not be, as in Milton's description, their early fall from Heaven but a later act of demonic force found in the opening verses of Genesis 6. There we read that the sons of God (the Biblical term for angels) transgressed their proper domain and took up residence in certain men for the purpose of pleasing their insatiable appetite for lust by the ravishing of women.

Jude's message for us is clear. Whenever we find ourselves succumbing to the temptations to live autonomously, to do as we please, to reject authority, to remove any notion of proper place or position, we are waging war against Heaven and are in danger of becoming subjects of judgment.

A Picture of Immorality

Jude continues with his fast and furious paintings, and before the oils on the canvas of verse 6 are dry he splashes on the hues of another picture, a picture of immorality. Look at verse 7:

> . . . just as Sodom and Gomorrah and the surrounding cities, which like-
> wise indulged in sexual immorality and pursued unnatural desire, serve as
> an example by undergoing a punishment of eternal fire.

Taken from Genesis 18, 19, this picture recalls the night that Lot, Abraham's nephew, took in angelic visitors who had been sent by God to destroy those cities. There is no indication that Lot thought they were anything other than human travelers. Later that night the men of the place congregated at Lot's door and desired to take these visitors for themselves. Sodom and Gomorrah was a place of self-indulgence, appetite without restraint, people never sated, always famished, and wanting more. Much later God would say of Sodom:

> She and her daughters had pride, excess of food, and prosperous ease, but
> did not aid the poor and needy. They were haughty and did an abomination
> before me. (Ezekiel 16:49, 50)

Sexual immorality is the eager companion of the affluent society. And according to Jude, those who gorge themselves without restraint are heading toward God's punishment.

While the men in Genesis intended to engage in homosexual relations with these visitors, there is no indication that they knew they were angels. And that makes the later part of our verse especially instructive. It reads that they pursued "unnatural desire." The word there is literally "other flesh," flesh different than their own. If that is the case, then the connection between verses 6 and 7 is even more extraordinary. The angels of verse 6 reject God's authority and desire relations with humans, and in verse 7 it is the humans who find themselves on the verge of desiring bodily union with the angelic host.

As strange as all this sounds, it is not that far-fetched when you turn on the TV or sit in the movie theater. The unrestrained violent and sexual crossover in play today is commonplace. Humans are often portrayed sexually in union with a demonic host, and when you see this, you realize just how contemporary Jude's warning is. Are we attracted to this kind of thing? Will we indulge every appetite? If so, we are heading toward an end that Jude describes in verse 7 as "eternal fire."

After preaching his three pictures of apostasy, autonomy, and immorality, Jude says in verse 8, "These people also, relying on their dreams" rather than on God's word—these who defile the flesh and reject authority—these people are those people—and God will not tolerate it on the last day.

A Preacher's Illustration on Presumption

Jude's exegesis of those Old Testament texts is now complete. He is ready to apply his sermon. And he does so with verse 9:

> But when the archangel Michael, contending with the devil, was disputing about the body of Moses, he did not presume to pronounce a blasphemous judgment, but said, "The Lord rebuke you."

With verse 9 Jude complements his three-point sermon from the Old Testament by doing what any good preacher does: he illustrates and applies his point from the contemporary literature of his own day. Drawing upon a well-known piece of apocryphal literature, *The Assumption of Moses*, Jude presses home his point. Did you see how this illustration contrasts "these people" (v. 8) with the archangel Michael? Michael was unlike them in every respect. He did not dare to presume or step outside of his rightful appointed place.

Now, we shouldn't think of this angelic confrontation over the body of Moses as merely fanciful or beyond the realm of factual possibility. After all, we have our own incredible history of battles over the bodies of the deceased. In 1418 a church council ended deliberations that had been going for over four years. It condemned Wycliffe, the great Bible translator, "as a heretic; and ordered his bones to be exhumed and removed from consecrated ground." Why? They were incensed that his body had received an honorable burial. "This decree was finally (and reluctantly) carried out in the spring of 1428. . . . Wycliffe's remains were disinterred and burned on a little arched bridge that spanned the river Swift (a tributary of the Avon), and his calcined ashes cast into the stream. From thence the prophecy arose:

> The Avon to the Severn runs,
> The Severn to the sea,
> And Wycliffe's dust shall spread abroad,
> Wide as the waters be.[5]

Yes, an angelic encounter over the body of Moses is possible. But whether Jude chose it because it is factual or merely illustrative, the point of his intended use cannot be missed. With the angelic tug of war, Jude has given us an example of whom to emulate. We are to be like Michael. Follow his example, and you will keep yourself straight. You will steer clear of apostasy. You will live under authority. You will guard yourself against all temptations toward immorality. Follow the way of Michael, and in doing so you will not only be equipped to spot the present-day embodiment of ancient archetypes who were designated for condemnation but will ensure that you don't become one of them yourself.

Our Heavenly Father, we thank you for recording the events of history. And we thank you for all that we can learn from the past. Help us in this day to remain faithful to you. Keep us from apostasy, autonomy, immorality, and sins of presumption. Have mercy. Amen.

Woe to them! For they walked in the way of Cain and abandoned themselves for the sake of gain to Balaam's error and perished in Korah's rebellion. These are hidden reefs [margin, blemishes] at your love feasts, as they feast with you without fear, shepherds feeding themselves; waterless clouds, swept along by winds; fruitless trees in late autumn, twice dead, uprooted; wild waves of the sea, casting up the foam of their own shame; wandering stars, for whom the gloom of utter darkness has been reserved forever. It was also about these that Enoch, the seventh from Adam, prophesied, saying, "Behold, the Lord came with ten thousands of his holy ones, to execute judgment on all and to convict all the ungodly of all their deeds of ungodliness that they have committed in such an ungodly way, and of all the harsh things that ungodly sinners have spoken against him." These are grumblers, malcontents, following their own sinful desires; they are loud-mouthed boasters, showing favoritism to gain advantage.

vv. 11–16

34

The Making of Midrash

JUDE 11–16

IN 1947 A TEL AVIV PUBLISHER brought out a book entitled *The Novella in Hebrew Literature, from its Origins to the End of the Haskalah*. It would not be until years later that Amos Oz, a man whose present-day writings greatly enrich us, would recount the day *The Novella,* written by his father, arrived home for the first time:

> The parcel contained five copies of *The Novella in Hebrew Literature*, hot from the press, virginal, wrapped in several layers of good-quality white paper . . . and tied with a string. . . . I remember how my father mastered his trembling enthusiasm, and did not forcibly snap the string holding the parcel together or even cut it with scissors but—I shall never forget this—undid the strong knots, one after another, with infinite patience, making alternate use of his strong fingernails, the tip of his paper knife, and the point of a bent paper clip.
>
> When he had finished, he did not pounce on his new book but slowly wound up the string, removed the wrapping of glossy paper, touched the jacket of the uppermost copy lightly with his fingertips, like a shy lover, raised it gently to his face, ruffled the pages a little, closed his eyes and sniffed them, inhaling deeply the fresh printing smells, the pleasure of new paper, the delightful, intoxicating odor of glue. Only then did he start to leaf through his book, peering first at the index, scrutinizing the list of addenda and corrigenda, reading and rereading [the] foreword and his own preface, lingering on the title page, caressing the cover again, then, alarmed that my mother might be secretly making fun of him, he said apologetically:
>
> "A new book fresh from the press, a first book, it's as though I've just had another baby."

"When it's time to change its nappy," my mother replied, "I expect you'll call me."[1]

Later we are told:

> Father's happiness lasted for three or four days, and then his face fell ... he now rushed every day to Achiasaph's bookshop in King George Avenue, where three copies of the *Novella* were displayed for sale. The next day the same three copies were there, not one of them had been purchased. And the same the next day, and the day after that.
>
> "You," Father said with a sad smile to his friend Israel Zarchi, "write a new novel every six months, and instantly all the pretty girls snatch you off the shelves . . . while we scholars, we wear ourselves out for years on end checking every detail, verifying every quotation, spending a week on a single footnote, and who bothers to read us? If we're lucky, two or three fellow prisoners in our own discipline read our books before they tear us to shreds. Sometimes not even that. We are simply ignored."[2]

I love that retelling for what it reveals about authors—a soul's satisfaction in holding their book for the first time coupled with the unquenchable thirst for an audience.[3] For a writer, nothing is as sad as being ignored. And that has me thinking of Jude. We have considered four studies since we undid the strings on this parcel and first held it in our hands. But now we begin to clearly see Jude's subtle but definite aspirations for an audience.[4]

Let me explain. In Jude's day, a writer whose mouth was watering for readers would never have employed the genre of novella. Instead, an aspiring writer would more than likely adopt the form of *midrash*. Midrash was the stuff that moved instantly off the bookshelves in Jude's ancient era. The word *midrash* refers to a genre of literature committed to unfolding the Hebrew Scriptures with immediate application to a contemporary situation.[5] To put it as simply as I can, in general, *midrash* was a sermon in written form. A writer would select a text, explain the text, and apply the text for his contemporary world. And in Jude's day, the buying public had a voracious appetite for midrash.

Jude the Preacher

Jude 5–16 is vintage midrash. These middle verses are two sermons in written form. The first sermon extends from verses 5–10. We looked at it in the last chapter. The three Scripture readings consisted of texts highlighting the wilderness years of apostasy, the autonomous angelic insurrection, and the punishment exacted on immoral Sodom and Gomorrah. Together we listened as Jude expounded upon those texts in verses 5–7. And then Jude did what any good preacher does—he illustrated his preaching by citing a contemporary source, in this case the story of the assumption of Moses in verse 9. Jude then concluded his sermon or midrash by applying it forcefully to his contemporary situation (v. 10).

Now we get a second sermon from Jude; verses 11–16 are classic midrash. And fortunately for us, Jude has left behind his sermon outline for all of us to see. In this sermon, rather than selecting three large-scale events from Scripture to confirm God's judgment, Jude selects three individual *examples*. We see them in verse 11—Cain, Balaam, and Korah. Behind each of these people, and well-known to his first readers, stood the biblical texts of Genesis 4, Numbers 22—31, and Numbers 16.

So, with a bit of imagination we can see Jude rising to the pulpit on a particular Sunday and reading aloud his sermon texts. By verses 12, 13 Jude is busy applying those texts to his own day. And with verses 14, 15 he does some cutting-edge stuff by illustrating his point from what was a well-known piece of literature, in this case a book about the man named Enoch. In his conclusion the takeaway becomes obvious: God still judges the ungodly; so be like Enoch and not like these. Now I want you to know that as a preacher, this is about as exciting as it gets! It's helpful to find sermon outlines this simple and this clear. And it's especially nice to find them from a preacher in the Bible.

So taken together, Jude 5–16 give us two three-point sermons. Each is grounded in the living text of God's Word, both come complete with contemporary illustrations, and each finishes with direct, hard-hitting application.

We watch Jude the preacher step into his pulpit. We await his opening words. And when he looks up and begins, it becomes obvious that he knows a thing or two about the importance of a compelling introduction.

Jude Introduces

Jude opens his sermon in eye-catching fashion: "Woe to them!"

The words are meant to remind us of Jesus when he was lambasting the scribes and Pharisees for their unbelief. Or of John who in his Apocalypse warns of impending judgment. Jude wanted our attention, and now he has it. We are ready to hear from God's Word; so Jude quickly moves from introduction to exposition. Look again at verse 11:

> For they walked in the way of Cain and abandoned themselves for the sake of gain to Balaam's error and perished in Korah's rebellion.

Jude Expounds

Cain the Faithless

The way of Cain is about more than violence. It is true that he is the Bible's first murderer. But Jude selects him for a different reason. He is an example of a teacher who rejects God's Word. To see this you will need to take a look at Genesis 4:3–7:

> In the course of time Cain brought to the LORD an offering of the fruit of the ground, and Abel also brought of the firstborn of his flock and of their fat portions. And the LORD had regard for Abel and his offering, but for Cain and his offering he had no regard. So Cain was very angry, and his face fell. The LORD said to Cain, "Why are you angry, and why has your face fallen? If you do well, will you not be accepted? And if you do not do well, sin is crouching at the door. Its desire is for you, but you must rule over it."

Before Cain became a murderer, God gave him a message. God spoke to him. God instructed him. God preached to him. God taught him what was and wasn't acceptable behavior. The fact that Cain committed a violent act of murder tells us that in the end, Cain rejected God's word. One Jewish commentary, the *Targum of Jonathan*, put what was going on in the mind of Cain this way:

> There is no judgment, no judge, no reward to come; no reward will be given to the righteous, and no destruction for the wicked.[6]

I appreciate that *Targum*'s insight. It reveals that Cain was a teacher and that he had his own message to proclaim. By his words and his deeds Cain preached that God doesn't mean what he says. He killed Abel because he believed that God's word wasn't true. There would be no destruction for the wicked, he thought.

What judgment came on Cain? Genesis tells us that just like his disbelieving, wandering counterparts (Jude 5), Cain was to be a fugitive and a wanderer on the earth.

Jude preaches from the story of Cain because the problem facing his own day was teachers who did whatever they wanted with God's word. Like Cain, they disbelieved it. They felt free to change it. They preached something else. They left Jude no choice but to preach. And with this letter we see Jude standing in his pulpit and making midrash with his *woes* and *warnings*.

Balaam the Self Indulgent

Next Jude calls upon Balaam:

. . . and abandoned themselves for the sake of gain to Balaam's error.

Balaam is found in the fourth book of Moses, Numbers. Like Cain, Balaam was a teacher. His downfall though came through a love of money and openness to sensuality. In the book of Numbers we see Balaam, a teacher of God's people, turning against Israel and cursing them, all because a foreign king promised to pay him handsomely for it. At first Balaam fought off the temptation and refused. But later he reversed his position, advising God's people to engage in orgies and sensuality with the foreign women of Midian (cf. Numbers 31:16). In essence, he laid aside God's word and taught something else. And he did it so that his own pockets would be lined with cash.

What judgment came on Balaam? Numbers tells us that just like his sensual counterparts in Jude 7, Balaam was killed by the Lord's army while living in the midst of a godless and sensual city (Numbers 31:7).

Korah the Rebellious

Jude now preaches on his third example from Scripture, Korah. Korah was the one who led a mutinous mob against Moses. And like Cain and Balaam before him, he was a teacher. His distinguishing mark of instruction was his disdain for the Biblical notion of authority. He hated the fact that Levites could hold a place of authority over God's people, but he could not. We read about this in Numbers 16:1–4:

> Now Korah . . . [and others] took men. And they rose up before Moses, with a number of the people of Israel, 250 chiefs of the congregation. . . . They assembled themselves together against Moses and against Aaron and said to them, "You have gone too far! For all in the congregation are holy, every one of them, and the LORD is among them. Why then do you exalt yourselves above the assembly of the LORD?"

Do you see Korah's teaching? He takes God's words at Sinai about the priesthood of all believers (Exodus 19:6) and interprets them in a way that levels any notion of authority. Like the angels of verse 6, Korah is unhappy living under the authority of another.

And the judgment that came on Korah? Numbers tells us that just like his autonomous counterparts in Jude 6, Korah was swallowed alive into the earth's grip of "gloomy darkness." In light of what we said in the last chapter about archetypes, Robert Alter's comments, from his newly completed translation *The Five Books of Moses*, proves confirming: "Korah . . . becomes the archetype of the presumptuous rebel against just authority."[7]

Even today, we have our Korahs in type, those who espouse a democratic leveling of any divinely intended order.

Jude Applies

At this point in the sermon, Jude pauses. His exegesis is done. He has opened God's Word and from three separate texts expounded one great truth: judgment will fall on any pastor or teacher who loves freedom or money or sex or power more than fidelity to God's Word. Let's hear him! A horrific ground-opening punishment awaits every pastor, teacher, and seminary leader who succumbs to personal temptation by capitulating to culture in an effort to accommodate compromised faith. Nothing less is at stake for those of us who call ourselves teachers.

So incensed is Jude with this reality in his own day that at this point in his midrash he can't help but apply his message, even before he is finished expounding it! In the last phrase of verse 11, "perished" is in the aorist tense. Do you see the implication? It isn't merely that God's judgment *will fall* or that God's punishment is *waiting to come*. What Jude is preaching is, "Beloved, hear me on this: these people today who pervert the gospel, these church leaders who reject God's Word, these preachers who are out for your money, these pastors who permit you to have both Jesus and sensuality, these upstarts who level any notion of ecclesial authority, have *already* perished long ago. They died with Korah. *These* guys who are eating and drinking with you were *those* guys. Watch out. Be careful. Their ways are deadly."

Jude's depiction of these church leaders comes with an unparalleled oratorical fury that somehow manages to remain under the strict control of poetic beauty. In this respect I believe verses 12, 13 surpass anything else in all of literature:

> Waterless clouds, swept along by winds; fruitless trees in late autumn, twice dead, uprooted; wild waves of the sea, casting up the foam of their own shame; wandering stars, for whom the gloom of utter darkness has been reserved forever.

Can you imagine what this means in our day? All Bible teachers, myself included, who abandon the faith, promote sensuality, seek out their own gain, or work to undo the true nature of authority are clouds that can't bring rain, trees that won't bear fruit, and wild waves whose shame is relishing in the exposure and public display of what is better left hidden under modest dress. *These* among us are *those* for whom "the gloom of utter darkness" has been kept forever.

T. S. Eliot's *The Waste Land* is considered by many to be the most important poem of the twentieth century. He wrote it with the inspiration of Weston's book *From Ritual to Romance*. In that work "there exists the legend of a King rendered impotent, and his country sterile, both awaiting deliverance by a knight on his way to seek the Grail."[8] And in *The Waste Land* it seems that the valiant knight will never come:

> There is not even solitude in the mountains
> But dry sterile thunder without rain
> There is not even solitude in the mountains
> But red sullen faces sneer and snarl
> From doors of mudcracked houses
>   If there were water
> And no rock
> If there were rock
> And also water
> And water
> A spring
> A pool among the rock
> If there were the sound of water only
> Not the cicada
> And dry grass singing
> But the sound of water over a rock
> Where the hermit-thrush sings in the pine trees
> Drip drop drip drop drop drop drop
> But there is no water.[9]

As a midrash man—a preacher—Jude is thirsty for readers precisely because he possesses the deep and satisfying waters of God. Jude has a voracious appetite for fidelity. He preaches to protect God's flock from leaders who are nothing more than waterless wells and dry riverbeds. He knows with visceral conviction that the health of the church depends on pastors who possess living water. The stakes are that high.

> If the rains do not come, if instead of the moisture-bearing west wind it blows regularly from the south and east, from off the desert, then there is no hope of a harvest; aridity, crop failure, and famine follow and not only here.[10]

In writing this chapter I have caught myself listening for how the voice of Jude might sound in our own day: "Beloved, the church is filled with men and women who are speaking and preaching their way toward a black hole of judgment from which there will be no return. Up! On your feet! Contend for the faith lest you follow them or, worse yet, become one of them."

Jude Illustrates

To quicken us, Jude provides an illustration.

> It was also about these that Enoch, the seventh from Adam, prophesied, saying, "Behold, the Lord came with ten thousands of his holy ones, to execute judgment on all and to convict all the ungodly of all their deeds of ungodliness that they have committed in such an ungodly way, and of all the harsh things that ungodly sinners have spoken against him. (vv. 14, 15)

Three quick observations about Enoch. First, while Enoch is a biblical character, the quotation here is not a biblical reference. It comes from a text called 1 Enoch. What Jude is doing here is exactly what we saw him do with the Assumption of Moses (v. 9). He is pulling from the literature of his own day when it lends support, by way of illustration, to his claim. In this case 1 Enoch, and especially the portion he grabs hold of, supports his teaching that God will execute judgment against everyone who perverts his ways. It's as if he is saying, "The Bible isn't the only book that teaches what I am saying. Read your own stuff, and you will see that the same thing holds true there."

Second, Enoch clues us into the idea that these false teachers were circulating in their own church sermons—that God is a God of love and not wrath; that God would never condemn anyone; that no person or behavior can really be called ungodly; that unconditional love must mean that God places no demands on his children; that entering into a relationship with Christ doesn't require any meaningful life change.

So, using 1 Enoch, Jude wants his listeners to see that even in the literature of their own day, the ungodly exist. Did you notice that he used that word four times? According to 1 Enoch people are said to be ungodly, some behaviors are said to be ungodly, and, most striking one of all, such ungodliness done by the ungodly can be carried out in ungodly ways! It is as if Jude is bellowing from the pulpit, "Enough about this silly notion that God won't judge anyone. The ungodly who are everywhere and in every generation will be judged!" Jones Very's poem "Enoch" describes the sheer universality of ungodliness:

> I looked to find a man who walked with God,
> Like the translated patriarch of old;
> Though gladdened millions on His footstool trod,
> Yet none with him did such sweet converse hold;
> . . . God walked alone unhonored through the earth.[11]

Finally, by using this well-known piece of literature Jude not only supports his conviction that the Lord will execute judgment, but he provides, by way of example, a positive model for God's people to emulate. Be like Enoch, not like Cain or Balaam or Korah. Like us, Enoch lived in an ungodly day; yet he had such character that people described him as walking with God. And remember, although Enoch lived in an ungodly hour, there came a time when he was delivered from it, and he no longer was found on earth. Where did this righteous man go? He went into the presence of the living God where he now dwells happily forevermore. Here is encouragement for us to remain faithful.

Jude Concludes

And with that Jude brings his midrash to a conclusion. In one short verse he tells us how to see the difference between godly teachers like Enoch and these others in the church who are destined for destruction.

> These are grumblers, malcontents, following their own sinful desires;
> they are loud-mouthed boasters, showing favoritism to gain advantage.
> (v. 16)

You can almost see Jude as he stops preaching. What more needs to be said? He stands now in silence. The preaching is done. His midrash is complete. Stepping out from behind the pulpit, he pronounces the benediction and heads toward home. And as he puts himself to bed on this exacting Sunday, we can imagine his Evensong prayer, softly spoken:

> Dear Lord, I have worn myself out.
> I have checked every detail; I have verified every quotation.
> I have spent a week on a single footnote, but who will bother to read it?
> Oh, God, please, may these words not simply be ignored.

Almighty God, your Son shall come again in power and glory to judge the living and the dead. May we receive this warning from Jude with humility. Help us to stay clear of the love of money. Enable us to finish well. And fill the land with faithful preachers. In Jesus' name, amen

But you must remember, beloved, the predictions of the apostles of our Lord Jesus Christ. They said to you, "In the last time there will be scoffers, following their own ungodly passions." It is these who cause divisions, worldly people, devoid of the Spirit. But you, beloved, building yourselves up in your most holy faith and praying in the Holy Spirit, keep yourselves in the love of God, waiting for the mercy of our Lord Jesus Christ that leads to eternal life.

vv. 17–21

35

Contending for the Faith:
The Calling We Keep

JUDE 17–21

Contend: Remembering the Words
of the Apostles

At the Dachau Concentration Camp near Munich, Germany, is a museum containing some relics as well as grim photos depicting conditions during the horrific years of World War II. As visitors leave, they pass by a sign next to the door that reads:

> Those who do not learn from history are condemned to repeat its mistakes.

Jude would agree. For him the importance of studying history is nothing new. In fact, in the last two studies we have listened to him instruct us from history. He began back in verse 5 with a line that every teacher seems to make use of—"Now I want to remind you, although you once fully knew it." From there, Jude took us back in time. He traced out for us the topography of Israel's past; he reminded us of ancient *events* and *examples* from "long ago" (v. 4). As Jude's students, our appreciation for his grasp over his chosen terrain grew; and under his tutelage, a better understanding of the importance of history began to emerge.

As we arrive at his next paragraph Jude is still hammering away at the same idea. In verse 17 it takes all of four words before the historian in him surfaces again: "But you must remember." With those words Jude calls us, as readers, to the work of remembering. He fixes our attention on the past.

In this case, the recent past. Jude reminds us of an era that resounded with the authoritative voice of apostles. And with the quote in verse 18 the very language and intonation of those voices ring out one more time: "In the last time there will be scoffers, following their own ungodly passions."

As we prepare to leave these middle verses behind, we should by now recognize them for what they are, Jude's own posting—his own sign— warning every regular attendee and teacher who passes by. Over the lintel of verses 5–19 hang the words of Jude:

> Those who fail to learn from Israel's history and those who dare to forge beyond the apostles' ministry—these are the ones who stand condemned by God.

And then, with the suddenness of verse 19 Jude's lessons in history come to a close. He tells us one final time how to recognize these enemies of the gospel: "It is these who cause divisions, worldly people, devoid of the Spirit."

This is vintage stuff—the professor at work behind the lectern. It appears that Jude should be remembered as more than being a letter writer, or even a preacher—he should be known as a historian. For fifteen verses he has been Jude the historian: "Now I want to remind you" and "But you must remember." May Jude's emphasis on studying history fly like arrows destined for their mark. Remembering history is one of God's best remedies in awakening his church to the task of contending for the faith.

Jude is not the only one to recognize the present-day value of making a good study of history. Martyn Lloyd-Jones, a pastor who served Westminster Chapel, London, during the last century understood this importance in much the same way. After watching countless people in his own day drift from biblical orthodoxy, he committed himself, in his preaching, to engage Christians in the study of history. His biographer tells us:

> From 1927 onwards, the guidance of the past was absolutely basic to his understanding of the purpose of preaching. Indeed, one of his favorite quotations, adapted for another purpose, was the words of the French novelist Anatole France who, when tired and discouraged used to say, "I never go into the country for a change of air and a holiday. I always go instead into the eighteenth century."[1]

Had he lived long enough, I think Jude would have liked Lloyd-Jones and Anatole France. As Jude places his period at the end of verse 19 and stops to let the ink dry, he is convinced that his lessons from history are sufficiently hung and adequately fixed in the hearts and minds of his readers.

Jude's Letter Turns

Starting with verse 20 we find Jude firmly planted in the present. In fact, everything he has to say from this point on requires present-day action. Take a look: in verses 20–23 the three participles and the one all-encompassing command are written with the vigor of present-tense ongoing reality. Jude's gaze has shifted, and as a result Jude's letter is turning. He is now fixed on *today*. And with the literary force that every good writer possesses, he plants us right there with him; verse 20 is that jarring. It feels almost as if Jude has grabbed us by the collar, pulled us out of the ancient past (vv. 5–16) straight through the recent past (vv. 17–19), and set us down firmly in the present with great force and decided intention. From this point on he has one thing on his mind. He is looking us squarely in the eye and is speaking with a renewed sense of urgency regarding his great theme. "Listen to me," says Jude. "I'm going to tell you with staccato-like urgency just what it means to contend for the faith, and especially how you are to go about doing it."

The Biblical scholar Richard Bauckham, in his commentary on Jude, connected verses 20–23 back to the theme of contending in verse 3.

> These verses contain Jude's appeal to his readers to fight for the faith as announced in v. 3, and are therefore not an appendix to the letter, but its climax. . . . In this section Jude comes to the main purpose of his letter, which is to give his readers positive instructions about how, in the situation in which they find themselves, they are to "carry on the fight for the faith" (v. 3).[2]

Do you see the implications of this insight for us? Let me put it as clearly as I can: Beginning at verse 20 we are reading Jude's "how-to manual" on contending for the faith. Once that penny drops, the entire letter warms and begins to open up like flowers under the sun of spring. There are good reasons for us to draw a dotted line connecting verses 20–23 to verse 3.

Connections

Do you see the repeated refrain "But you, beloved" in verse 20? This appears not only here but in verse 17 as well:

- Verse 17: "But you must remember, beloved . . ."
- Verse 20: "But you, beloved . . ."

Interestingly, "beloved" can be taken all the way back to the beginning of the letter. It appeared in the opening verse when Jude referred to his audience as "those who are . . . *beloved* in God the Father." And then, more importantly, the term showed up again in verse 3 with direct ties to the theme of contending for the faith:

Beloved, although I was very eager to write to you about our common salvation, I found it necessary to write appealing to you to *contend* for the faith that was once for all delivered to the saints.

Jude wrote this letter in hopes of stirring the *beloved* to *contend*. It shouldn't surprise us, then, that having secured his claim that certain people were designated long ago for condemnation by the end of verse 19, he is now free to pick up with clarity and unction about what it means for the *beloved* to *contend* for the faith. Bauckham is right. We have arrived at the heart of his letter. And the comforting term *beloved* is again here to greet us.

Quiet Allusions

One more thing should be mentioned about "beloved" before moving on. Jude's first readers might have needed this particular word more than we realize. *Beloved*, more than any other word Jude could have chosen, possesses quiet allusions to the sufferings borne by early-century Christians. Let me explain. In the Greek-speaking world, *beloved* was intimately tied to those undergoing suffering and death. The same is true for us as well. If we were to open today's newspaper to the obituary section, it would immediately confirm for us that even in our own day *beloved* is the word we choose to refer to those who encountered suffering and death. We read of the *beloved* husband or mother, sister or brother.

Beloved's association to suffering and death has a long history. In Genesis 22 in the Septuagint (the Greek translation of the Hebrew Scriptures), we find that Abraham has been told to sacrifice his son, his only son—in that translation, his "beloved" son. The word in Genesis is the same as the one in Jude. And in the New Testament the word is used in reference to Jesus just before he undergoes his great sufferings and death. At the Transfiguration the heavens open, and God's voice rings out: "This one—the one who stands on the threshold of death—is my *beloved* Son." Interestingly, the word in the Gospels is identical to the one in Jude.

Why mention these quiet allusions? Because Jude's readers are more than likely suffering and perhaps facing death for their faith. In fact, it appears that the only way to get out of their suffering was to curse Christ and deny Jesus as their only Lord and Savior—the very thing the false teachers of verse 4 were encouraging Christians to do. Could it be that by selecting *beloved* Jude wants them to associate with Isaac and Jesus? Could he be steeling their hearts? Could it be that he chooses this word because he wants his generation to contend for the faith, even unto death?[3]

An important historical document from the close of the Common Era's first century supports this thought. At that time a governor by the name of Pliny served in a distant province under Trajan. Trajan ruled the world from the center, Rome. Pliny needed help. And he wrote Trajan a letter asking for guidance on handling Christians who follow Jesus as their king. Fortunately for us, Pliny's letter survived the centuries. His letter is important because it contains the fullest answer *by someone outside the faith* as to why the Romans persecuted Christians. And in it you can hear the call for God's beloved to curse Christ and renounce him as their only Lord. Pliny writes:

> I interrogated these as to whether they were Christians; those who con-fessed I interrogated a second and a third time, threatening them with a punishment; those who persisted I ordered executed . . . when they invoked the gods . . . offered prayer to your image . . . and moreover cursed Christ—none of which those who are really Christians, it is said, can be forced to do—these I thought should be discharged. . . .[4]

Beloved was used four times by Jude, who lived in a day when God's beloved stood in real need of comfort—men and women who were in the heat of battle. By holding on to the word *beloved*, they would gain strength to persevere through the dark night of suffering. The word would quietly roll off their lips as their minds remembered that Isaac was spared and that Jesus, while killed, yet arose and entered into the presence of God.[5] These early-maligned Christians needed resolute conviction in God's salvation and the promise of an eternal morning yet to come, and the word *beloved* gave it to them.

When the morning comes
I gaze on you with desire
When the morning comes
My look will be perfectly plain
When the morning comes
My beloved one
When the morning comes
You'll know that we both feel the same.[6]

So Jude's first readers stand in readiness, awaiting his next word. They have been warned of God's judgment. They have been reminded of the apostles' truthfulness. And now, in the strength of being God's "beloved," they are prepared to finish well by contending for the faith.

Contend: Keeping Yourselves in the Love of God

The great question of Jude is now before us. Other than the importance of remembering, what does it mean to "contend for the faith"? And how are we to go about doing it? For starters, the answer is found in a single phrase in verse 21:

> Keep yourselves in the love of God.

The Greek Grammar

At first glance you might think it is a bit reductionistic of me to say that "keep[ing] yourselves in the love of God" adequately answers Jude's how-to on contending for the faith. I can almost hear you saying, "Don't verses 20, 21 present us with a host of things, including building, praying, keeping, and waiting? Why limit your focus on the single phrase about keeping ourselves?"

It is a matter of Greek grammar. In the list of things Jude calls us to do in verses 20, 21, the word "keep" is the only one that appears as an imperative. In other words, it is Jude's only command. The other items in Jude's how-to list are what are called participles, which means that grammatically speaking they are dependent on the phrase "keep yourselves." In essence, Jude's call in verse 21 to keep ourselves is the center of gravity for everything else being said.

So, from the grammar we can say with confidence that if we want to contend for the faith we will need to learn how to "keep ourselves in the love of God." And to know what that means, we can do no better than recall the words of Jesus:

> If you love me, you will keep my commandments. . . . Whoever has my commandments and keeps them, he it is who loves me. . . . If anyone loves me, he will keep my word, and my Father will love him, and we will come to him and make our home with him. Whoever does not love me does not keep my words. (John 14:15, 21, 23, 24)

Here is our answer. We contend for the faith by keeping Jesus' commandments. We contend by living under his good word, by submitting our lives to him in every respect.

The Greater Context

Now, most of us want to know just what it means to *keep* his word. And in this respect Jude has already shown himself more than willing to help. On two previous occasions Jude used the term *keep* when referring to those who failed to contend. In other words, by the time he gets to verse 20 he has already shown his readers—twice—how to keep themselves in the love of

God by giving them examples of behavior that Christians must keep away from. The first time he did this was back in verse 6:

> And the angels who did not stay *within [literally, keep]* their own position of authority, but left their proper dwelling, he has *kept* in eternal chains under gloomy darkness until the judgment of the great day.

Humble submission to God is a mark of keeping. Conversely, when we find ourselves succumbing to self-willed, self-ruling, self-exalting autonomy, we are in danger of being numbered among those being kept for condemnation. Jude uses this term again at the close of verse 13:

> . . . for whom the gloom of utter darkness has been reserved [lit. kept] forever.

To whom is Jude referring here? To people like Cain and Balaam and Korah. To teachers and those like them who reject God's word, who imbibe in and encourage sensuality and greed, and who despise any ecclesial authority. These are the ones for whom the darkness has been kept. Two examples from Jude's greater context inform our keeping. And with them we have seen Jude at his pedagogical best: "Beloved, you will know that you are keeping yourselves in the love of God by that from which you keep yourselves."

The Christian's Calling

There is a third way for us to get a handle on what it means to contend by *keeping*. We have made use of Greek grammar and the greater context, but understanding our term in light of the Christian's calling will stimulate us to action as well. To see the Christian's calling take a look at verse 1:

> Jude, a servant of Jesus Christ and brother of James, To those who are called, beloved in God the Father and *kept* for Jesus Christ.

Part of the Christian's calling is that we are being "kept for Jesus Christ." And when we come to understand the significance of that knowledge, we are truly liberated! Let me explain by using the analogy of marriage. In previous generations the solemn vows of a bride included the words, "Do you promise to *keep thyself* only unto him as long as you both shall live?" And the bride-to-be would respond with, "I do." She united herself to the groom with undivided loyalty because she knew that he loved her with a decided and determined love of his own. She had no problem keeping herself for him. Indeed, she knew that all along she had been kept for him.

In the same way, the beloved, the church, is being "kept for Jesus Christ." He is our bridegroom. The astounding truth is that he has already placed his decided and eternal love upon us, on people like you and me! Well, then, we must submit ourselves to being loved in this way by keeping ourselves only unto him. What I want to impress upon us is the treasured privilege that is ours in keeping ourselves in the love of God. This isn't something we do to attain God's love or merit our salvation. We don't save ourselves by keeping ourselves. Rather, as his promised bride we work hard at keeping ourselves because we are being kept for the day when we will become the bride of Christ and will celebrate with him at the great wedding feast. Do we need any more motivation than that?

So what does it mean to "*keep ourselves* in the love of God"? According to the grammar, we keep the commandments of Christ. We live in total obedience to him. According to the greater context, we keep ourselves away from presumptuous rebellion and sin. And as Christians with a holy calling, we carry ourselves unto death in light of the treasured privilege that is ours—the eternal union that awaits us on that day.

Picturing Yourself Contending

I have been wrestling to provide you with a picture of what "keep[ing] yourselves in the love of God" looks like. After all, it's one thing to tell you what it is in relationship to grammar or context or calling. But having a mental picture of it will help as well. So here are two pictures.

Bunyan's Christian

Back in the seventeenth century John Bunyan wrote a book titled *The Pilgrim's Progress*. It tells the story of a man named Christian. In other words, it is the story of every man or woman who follows Christ. The book is not about whether or not this pilgrim will get into Heaven, but rather what it is like to keep oneself in the love of God while heading to Heaven.

Bunyan's pilgrim becomes a Christian as early as page thirty-seven (in my volume), which means that the body of the book is about his journey. Therefore, its value is in showing us what it looks like to keep in step with Christ. We see him struggle, and we read of his misguided failings. We watch him progress and at times lose his way. Yet all the while we see Christian intent on one thing—keeping himself in the love of God and arriving safely at the Celestial City. He obeys Christ. He steers clear of danger as best he can. And he is carried along by the power of the Holy Spirit, hidden as a scroll in his cloak. Along the way we see him taking it out to look at, for it reminds him of his calling and gives him assurance of his end. Buy and read this wonderful tale. Discover through literature what it looks like to "keep yourselves in the love of God."

George Whitefield

The second picture is of the great preacher of the First Great Awakening, George Whitefield. His final day on earth exemplifies what it looks like to keep yourself in the love of God. He was only fifty-four years old, he had suffered much for the gospel, and he was near death. And yet he was intent on finishing well. His biographer writes:

> After preaching for a week in the Portland [Maine] area, Whitefield was again forced to recognize that he was too unwell to proceed. . . . Accordingly, he once more turned southward, to begin, as he thought, the long journey back to Georgia. The date was Saturday, September 29, 1770.
>
> By noon of that day he reached the town of Exeter. He had not planned to preach there but on arriving found he could not refrain from doing so. That is, an outdoor platform had been erected and a large company of people had gathered and were waiting to hear him. . . . Whitefield's sermon . . . was two hours in length. . . .
>
> Following this tremendous effort Whitefield continued his journey and late that afternoon arrived at . . . Newburyport, Massachusetts . . . the street in front of the house had filled with people, and as he began to make his way up the stairs, several of them were at the door, begging him to preach.
>
> Unwilling, despite his weariness . . . he stood on the landing, halfway up the stairs, candle in hand, preaching Christ. He was soon greatly alive to his subject and becoming heedless of time he continued to speak, till finally, the candle flickered, burned itself out and died away. That dying flame and that burned out candle were representative that evening of the man himself and of his life.[7]

Whitefield went up to his room and died that very night. He had kept himself in the love of God—which meant keeping himself all the way to death. His message never changed. He *kept* the faith. He never perverted it by accommodating it to the age. He never denied Christ. He disciplined his life. He fled from the presence of sin. And he did it all until the candle of his life was extinguished. And on that night, as a result, he entered into the presence of God.

May it be so for you and for me. May our lives burn brightly in our keeping. And may we not live one day beyond their flame. Do you want to contend for the faith? Then remember the apostolic testimony and "keep yourselves in the love of God" until death. As the hymn-writer sang:

When we have run with patience the race,
we shall know the joy of Jesus.[8]

*Our Lord Jesus Christ, we come to God through you. We thank you that
we are your "beloved." Build us up in your Holy Spirit. Keep us from divisions and worldliness. And help us keep ourselves in the love of God, for we
desire eternal life. In Jesus' name, amen.*

But you, beloved, building yourselves up in your most holy faith and praying in the Holy Spirit, keep yourselves in the love of God, waiting for the mercy of our Lord Jesus Christ that leads to eternal life.

vv. 20, 21

36

Contending for the Faith: The Commitments We Make

JUDE 20, 21

IN SHAKESPEARE'S FAMOUS TELLING of *Henry V*, King Harry (Henry) disguises himself for a pre-dawn walk among his men, who are just hours away from battle with the French. Vastly outnumbered, Henry's troops are in need of courage—the courage to contend. Shakespeare prepares us for the king's late-night mission with a chorus:

> The clocks do toll,
> And the third hour of drowsy morning came. . . .
> The poor condemned English,
> Like sacrifices, by their watchful fires
> Sit patiently and inly ruminate
> The morning's danger. . . .
> O now, who will behold
> The royal captain of this ruin'd band
> Walking from watch to watch, from tent to tent,
> Let him cry "Praise and glory on his head!"
> For forth he goes and visits all his host.
> Bids them good morrow with a modest smile
> And calls them brothers, friends and countrymen. . . .
> . . . every wretch, pining and pale before,

Beholding him, plucks comfort from his looks:
A largess universal like the sun
His liberal eye doth give to every one,
Thawing cold fear, that mean and gentle all,
Behold, as may unworthiness define,
A little touch of Harry in the night.[1]

Few things steel a soldier's heart for battle like the confident presence of a man among men. We have watched Jude walking among the embattled early church with "a little touch of Harry in the night." During our time in his letter we have seen his frame in the distance and have heard his voice. From watch to watch and tent to tent, Jude has been instilling in us courage to "contend for the faith." In the last study he steadied us with two demands:

- *Remember* the words of the apostles (vv. 17–19)
- "*Keep* yourselves in the love of God" (v. 21)

Jude also calls us to contend with a challenge to:

- *Commit* ourselves to Christian growth (vv. 20, 21)
- *Conduct* ourselves with Christian grace (vv. 22, 23)

Do you see the three commitments to Christian growth that Jude asks his readers to make? Verses 20, 21 spell them out. Tucked on either side of the great command to "keep yourselves in the love of God" are three commitments Christians must make if they are to "contend for the faith": "building yourselves up in your most holy faith," "praying in the Holy Spirit," and "waiting for the mercy of our Lord Jesus Christ." These are striking commitments, but Jude is only half done.

After calling for commitment, Jude will walk among us in our subsequent studies to continue pressing us to maintain Christian conduct. Take a look at verses 22, 23: Christians who contend for the faith conduct themselves with three Christian graces: "hav[ing] mercy on those who doubt," "sav[ing] others by snatching them out of the fire," and "show[ing] mercy with fear." Could anything be clearer than that? We can summarize this with two headings with three points each. To contend for the faith in our day we must:

- commit ourselves to *building, praying, and waiting*
- conduct ourselves with *mercy, salvation, and purity*

Committing Ourselves to Christian Growth

Building Ourselves Up in Our Most Holy Faith

We have seen Jude as letter-writer, preacher, and historian. And now, with this first commitment, we see him as architect as well. Verse 20 begins,

"But you, beloved, *building* yourselves up in your most holy faith . . ." The term Jude chooses to rally the troops—"building"—is borrowed from the realm of architecture. Like Paul, Jude views the Christian community as an edifice, a structure meant to rise to the glory of God. He calls the Christian community to *build*. It is as if he walks in our midst and says, "It's time to *build people*! You've been dwelling too close to the ground. Rise! The apostles poured a godly foundation—they have given you Jesus. Now build yourselves up in him. Know the faith. Study God's Word. The challenges facing the church are grave, and they require all the structural support the Bible can give."

The architect Daniel H. Burnham was a towering figure on the landscape of Chicago's history. He once famously said, "Make no small plans. They have not the magic to stir men's blood." Chicago owes its ascendant claim of being the architectural capital of the world to him. He was the one who pulled the city skyward at the close of the nineteenth century. He was largely responsible for the Chicago School of architecture as well as the design of the 1893 World's Fair. Yet above all, Daniel Burnham should be remembered as the leading figure of The Chicago Plan, also known as the Burnham Plan—the most significant document in modern times concerning the growth of a city:

> Part of the influence of the Burnham Plan stemmed from the breadth of its approach. It was not designed to reconstruct just one part of the city . . . rather, in the words of the authors, " the purpose [is] to take up the pressing needs of today, and to find the best methods of meeting [them] . . . as a component of a great entity—[a] well-ordered . . . and unified city.[2]

As an architect of the Christian's soul, Jude seems to have similar convictions. He has taken up the pressing needs of his day, and in this word "building" he claims to have found the best method to meet them. Jude's heart burned with a desire for the church to rise in glorious splendor. He envisioned spiritually strong and healthy Christian men and women. He planned to take the young people of his generation and reconstruct the church as a great, well-ordered, and unified city.

Dear brothers and sisters in Christ, if we are to become strong, if we are to meet the need of the hour in which we live, we must *build ourselves up in the faith*. And I know of no better way to do this than to spend more time in the study of God's Word. Concerning this matter, the faithful expositor Kent Hughes has said, "You cannot be profoundly influenced by that which you do not know." And yet, if the polls are correct, most of the people attending our churches today are incapable of reciting the books of the Bible in order. We must commit ourselves to building.

Pray in the Holy Spirit

Jude presses on, moving now from tent to tent calling his band to the commitment of prayer. The second part of verse 20 reads, ". . . *praying* in the Holy Spirit." I don't know about you, but I find it fascinating that the call to "contend" back in verse 3—with all its hurried importance and sense of urgency—does, at the end of the day, plant us on the well-known ground of a more rigorous reading of God's Word and a greater devotion to Spirit-filled prayer. The main things are the plain things. And evidently it is that way regardless of the century in which you live.

I once had the privilege of meeting J. Sidlow Baxter. He was a godly man, an influential Christian, a preacher, and a writer. He was already elderly when my grandfather introduced me to him at the close of a church service in Colorado in 1983. I had just finished my undergraduate work and was making plans for seminary. My grandfather, himself a preacher, was pleased, and his eyes twinkled as he told the elderly statesman, "This is my grandson, and he is going into the ministry!" At that J. Sidlow Baxter took my hand in both of his wrinkled ones and—I will never forget this—said, "Young man, I have a word for you while I have you in my clutches. Give yourself to personal Bible study and to private prayer. Then you will not only be ready to be a minister but God's messenger."

Aged Jude reaches out through time and grabs us by the hand, and his message is the same. I find regular, sustained prayer in the Holy Spirit challenging. And if you are like me we are not alone. The hardest part of a missionary career, Hudson Taylor found, is to maintain regular, prayerful Bible study. "Satan will always find you something to do," he would say, "when you ought to be occupied about that, if it is only arranging a window blind."[3]

In the book *Hudson Taylor's Spiritual Secret* we find out that as difficult as this was, the great missionary found time to contend! Why?

> He knew that it was vital. Well do those traveling with him month after month in northern China remember his practice. Often, with only one large room for [sleeping], they would screen off a corner for [him] and another for themselves, with curtains of some sort; and then, after sleep at last had brought a measure of quiet, they would hear a match struck and see the flicker of candlelight which told that Mr. Taylor, however weary, was poring over the little Bible in the two volumes always at hand. From two to four A.M. was the time he usually gave to prayer; the time when he could be most sure of being undisturbed to wait upon God. That flicker of candlelight has meant more to them than all they have read or heard on secret prayer; it meant reality, not preaching but practice.[4]

Contending for the faith is not easy. Yet, the life of Hudson Taylor teaches us the secret—good old-fashioned discipline. The need of the hour is great. It is time for us to compete, to fight, to take up with the Spirit in prayer.

Waiting for the Mercy of Our Lord Jesus Christ

Having looked in the last chapter at the great command to keep ourselves in the love of God, we pass by it here to see what is on the other side, and when we look there we find a third participle in the Greek language, a third commitment to spiritual growth. The last part of verse 21 reads, "*waiting* for the mercy of our Lord Jesus Christ that leads to eternal life." Jude fixes the eyes of those embattled early Christians on their future hope.

Do you see what Jude is doing here? He understands the power of a future hope. Hope is a potent motivator for present action. Knowing the end encourages vigorous action now. So as we read God's Word, as we pray in the Spirit, as we keep ourselves in the love of God, we do it all in eagerness and *waiting*. The future looks bright! Eternal life is the prize for everyone who contends. There is to be no dichotomy between the vigorous activity of contending and the, at first glance, seeming passivity of waiting. In reality, the hope of a future eternal life with Christ fuels our vigorous fight for the faith in the present. Richard Baxter had it right when he said:

> Up and be doing,
> run, and strive and fight,
> and hold on;
> for thou hast a certain,
> glorious prize before thee.[5]

Yet too often we get it turned around. In our shallowness we would rather remain here. And to the degree that happens, our ability to contend suffers.

The true story of Harry Wood exemplifies what it means to contend by *waiting*. Mr. Woods was an elderly member of Dr. Martyn Lloyd-Jones's congregation in Sansfields. Lloyd-Jones's biographer tells us:

> After one especially memorable prayer meeting on the morning of Good Friday, Dr Lloyd-Jones was surprised when Wood expressed his disappointment as he left. In response to his pastor's enquiry . . . the older man replied that it had been his prayer that he should be allowed to go 'straight Home' from just such a prayer meeting . . . at a prayer meeting early in 1931 Harry Wood was called upon to open the meeting. He did so by reading Christ's High-Priestly prayer recorded in John 17, and then he prayed

with such 'glorious unction' that Dr Lloyd-Jones felt that he had heard nothing like it. The man seemed to be more in heaven than upon earth. When he stopped, and went to take a seat in the front row, Dr Lloyd-Jones heard heavy breathing and, opening his eyes, had only just time to catch the beloved Harry Wood as he fell to the floor, dead. . . .The departure of Harry Wood was one of the events which marked the beginning of an extraordinary spiritual stirring. In the winter of 1930–31 the whole church seemed moved as by a consciousness of the presence of God and Dr Lloyd-Jones traced a quickening of his own spirit to this same period.[6]

Harry Wood was a man who knew how to contend. He lived in a state of readiness and waiting. He *waited* on "the mercy of our Lord Jesus Christ that leads to eternal life."

Carrying On in Our Commitments

Let's stop for a minute to gather our gains. From what we already know, we can say that Jude's call to contend is full-orbed! In one sense, verses 17–23 are as complete a core curriculum for Christian discipleship as one could ever write. You could title it, *Jude's How-to for Contending Christians*.
   • Part I: The Calling We Keep
   • Part II: The Commitments We Make
   • Part III (which we will consider in the next chapter): The Conduct We Embrace
   As curricula go, this one is loaded. He has packed an enormous amount of material in the space of a few short verses on how to contend.
   One final word on the three commitments Jude is asking us to make. We don't have the strength in ourselves to carry them out. Our spiritual tendency is to over-promise and under-deliver. Building, praying, and waiting are impossible for us to maintain over a long stretch of time. Jude knows this. He is aware of our weakness. Did you happen to see that he subtly embedded two means that energize our commitments?

Carried Forward in the Strength of the Trinity

We fulfill our commitments by remaining in the Godhead. The Trinity is our source of strength. Take a look: the Holy Spirit is mentioned in verse 20, and the Father and Son in verse 21. Jude knows that we cannot possibly carry out our intentions to contend under our own strength of will. But thankfully, we only need to remain in God. "Keep yourselves *in* the love of God." "Pray *in* the Holy Spirit." We make these commitments in confidence because our confidence is in the triune God. He possesses everything we need to accomplish them.

Carried Forward in the Strength of the Triune Virtues

Hidden within these same verses are the triune virtues of Christianity—faith, hope, and love. Take a look: faith and love are overtly mentioned in verses 20, 21, while the attending virtuous gem of hope lives quietly in verse 21. What else is meant by the words "waiting for the mercy of our Lord Jesus Christ that leads to eternal life"? Take comfort in this: because God dwells within you, these virtues will flow from you.

So we find in these verses everything we need to contend. Jude's curriculum is established in the Father, Son, and Holy Spirit. It is centered in the command to "remember" and "keep"; it is attended by commitments to "build," "pray," and "wait"; and it is carried along by the virtues of "faith," hope, and "love." Could anything be more pristine or truly awesome? Make it a point to make Jude's manual your own. Read it. Learn it. Meditate on it. And put it into practice. In this way our lives will prove worthy of battle and useful to him come morning light.

Like Harry in the night, Jude has faded from sight. Yet we have once again heard his voice: "Contend. Do so with care. Remember the words of the apostles. Keep yourself in the love of God. Build yourselves up in your most holy faith. Pray in the Spirit. Wait for the mercy of our Lord Jesus Christ that leads to eternal life."

Heavenly Father, help us make healthy commitments. For we want nothing less than to grow in the grace and knowledge of our Lord Jesus Christ. May our lives display the graces of faith, hope, and love. Amen.

*And have mercy on those who doubt; save others by
snatching them out of the fire; to others show mercy
with fear, hating even the garment stained by the flesh.*

vv. 22, 23

37

Contending for the Faith: The Conduct We Embrace

JUDE 22, 23

WRITING IS NOT EASY. Especially difficult is the task of crafting words in such a way as to instill in the reader an underlying affection for the subject. After all, words are the only tools an author is given; therefore words must do all the heavy lifting. They must be strong enough to communicate an idea as well as implant a feeling. And more often than not, a single word must be capable of doing both. That is why the best writers pay very close attention to the words they select. C. S. Lewis, one of the best, gave a child in America some commonsense advice on this very subject in a letter dated June 26, 1956:

> What really matters is:
> 1. Always try to use the language so as to make quite clear what you mean, and make sure your sentence couldn't mean anything else.
> 2. Always prefer the plain direct word to the long vague one. Don't "implement" promises, but "keep" them.
> 3. Never use abstract nouns when concrete ones will do. If you mean "more people died," don't say "mortality rose."
> 4. Don't use adjectives which merely tell us how you want us to feel about the thing you are describing. I mean, instead of telling us a thing was "terrible," describe it so that we'll be terrified. Don't say it was "delightful," make us say "delightful" when we've read the description. You see, all those words (horrifying, wonderful, hideous, exquisite) are only saying to your readers "please will you do my job for me."

5. Don't use words too big for the subject. Don't say "infinitely" when you
mean "very"; otherwise you'll have no word left when you want to talk
about something really infinite.[1]

If anyone understood Lewis before Lewis, it was Jude. Jude knew that
finding the precise word was critical in helping his readers feel a particular
way about his ideas. And nowhere is his care over the choice of words more
evident than in his section on how to contend for the faith (vv. 17–23). Here
he often selects the only word or phrase that will with precision instill in his
readers an underlying affection for his subject. Listen to his choices: "build
. . . mercy . . . snatching them out of the fire . . . mercy . . . garment stained
by the flesh."

With these words and phrases, the call for the church to "contend for
the faith" has a rich heritage. In fact, the relationship between Jude's words
here and similar words in the Hebrew Scriptures are so strong that most
of Jude's early readers would have made his intended connection without
much effort. For us, though, it will take some exploring before we can
begin expounding.

Centuries earlier, the prophet Zechariah had received a series of visions
that contained similar words and lines. In his first vision (Zechariah 1) we
find two of Jude's contending words, yet with one significant difference—
God is the one who will *build*, and God is the one coming with *mercy*. In a
vision Zechariah was told:

> Thus says the LORD, I have returned to Jerusalem with *mercy*; my house
> shall be *built* in it, declares the LORD of hosts. (v. 16)

Zechariah lived long after the Babylonians under Nebuchadnezzar had
destroyed Jerusalem's walls. In his day Israel finally arrived at the backside
of seventy years of captivity. Decades had passed since God's people had
been in a position to contend for the faith by building anything with mercy.
But in this vision Zechariah is told the most encouraging news he could
have possibly imagined. God was coming with mercy; God was coming to
build. In another vision, God confirmed his decision to rebuild. Zechariah
records:

> And I lifted my eyes and saw, and behold, a man with a measuring line
> in his hand! Then I said, "Where are you going?" And he said to me, "To
> measure Jerusalem, to see what is its width and what is its length." . . .
> "Run, say to that young man, 'Jerusalem shall be inhabited as villages
> without walls, because of the multitude of people and livestock in it.' . . .
> Sing and rejoice, O daughter of Zion, for behold, I come and I will dwell
> in your midst, declares the LORD." (Zechariah 2:1–4, 10)

Notice: when God comes mercifully to build his people, it results in God's people erupting in song! What a great prophecy. Imagine being the first to hear that God was coming with *mercy*, that he had roused himself and renewed his promise to *build* up his people again. Then Zechariah received still another vision, and it filled him with awe. He learned that not only was God committed to build and to show mercy—he was committed to doing it through his people! This is the vision with close connections to our text.

> Then he showed me Joshua the high priest standing before the angel of the LORD, and Satan standing at his right hand to accuse him. And the LORD said to Satan, "The LORD rebuke you, O Satan! The LORD who has chosen Jerusalem rebuke you! Is not this a brand plucked from the fire?" Now Joshua was standing before the angel, clothed with filthy garments. And the angel said to those who were standing before him, "Remove the filthy garments from him." And to him he said, "Behold, I have taken your iniquity away from you, and I will clothe you with pure vestments. . . . Hear now, O Joshua the high priest, you and your friends who sit before you, for they are men who are a sign: behold, I will bring my servant the Branch . . . and I will remove the iniquity of this land in a single day. In that day," declares the LORD of hosts, "every one of you will invite his neighbor to come under his vine and under his fig tree." (3:1–10)

Now put it all together. Can you hear the underlying affection of Jude in Zechariah? Not only does God come with mercy to build God's people—his work fills his people with joy and singing. In mercy, God saves his children as "brands plucked from the fire." In mercy, "filthy garments" are changed into "pure vestments." But then strikingly, and here is the underlying affection Jude is after, it is *with mercy* that those who follow the high priest (*Joshua* is Hebrew for Jesus) contend by inviting neighbors to come under the protection of God's vine and the fruit-laden branches of his fig tree.

With the words of Zechariah, Jude intentionally stirs the affections of his readers regarding the exalted privilege that is theirs to "contend for the faith": "Hey, beloved, are you aware of the awesome and immense privilege that is yours? God's work of salvation has been given to you. Jesus, the high priest, came to build and show mercy. Don't merely endure sinners; you are here in God's place to save them. Don't merely put up with the world; snatch some from the fires of Hell. Don't think that contending for the faith means telling unrepentant sinners that God hates them, have mercy, even on them. Contend for the faith by conducting yourselves with grace! Become the mercy of God."

Can you think of a gospel truth more compelling or energizing? Jude wants us to feel that we have found our calling in the world. When it comes to bearing gospel witness, he wants us to feel the pleasure a child has who sits excitedly on his father's shoulders while he dances along. We should be as excited about the idea that our mercy builds up spiritual Israel as a young Jewish boy and his father felt on that historic night in November 1947 when United Nations Resolution 181 paved the way for Israel to become a nation:

> I jumped into my trousers but didn't bother with a shirt or sweater and shot out our door, and some neighbor or stranger picked me up so I wouldn't be trampled underfoot, and I was passed from hand to hand until I landed on my father's shoulders near our front gate . . . my very cultured, polite father was standing there shouting at the top of his voice, not a word . . . not even cries of joy . . . but one long naked shout like before words were invented . . . there was dancing and weeping on Amos Street, in the whole of Kerem Avraham and in all the Jewish neighborhoods. . . . But my father said to me as we wandered there, on the night of November 29, 1947, me riding on his shoulders, among the rings of dancers and merrymakers . . . Just you look, my boy, take a very good look, son, take it all in, because you won't forget this night to your dying day and you'll tell your children, your grandchildren and your great grandchildren about this night when we're long gone.[2]

Jude has nothing less in mind. These verses, connected as they are to Zechariah, were written to thrill us. They were meant to carry us aloft. They were meant to instill the feeling of "At last we have found our place in the world. To us goes the honor of having mercy on those who doubt. To us goes the joy of saving others from the fires of Hell. To us goes the responsibility of showing mercy, even to those who don't appear to repent."

Jude knew what these words would do for the church. They elevated believers' spirits and instilled a sense of privileged resolve. And they should do the same for us. How amazing—we are co-laborers with God in his work of grace.

Conducting Yourselves with Christian Grace

Have Mercy

The first of the three groups of people Jude wants us to contend for is found in verse 22. "Have mercy on those who doubt." Churches are filled with people who doubt. Young Christians especially have doubts. They have doubts about the Bible. They have doubts about the Christian faith and the exclusivity of our message. After all, stimulating professors and newfound friends from a variety of backgrounds can challenge a faith that was merely assumed to be true until now.

"Pastor, how can I be sure that the Bible is true? And are you really sure that I can't love Jesus and still do what I want with my body? You know, others teach differently than you do on this. And they seem kind and sincere."

On such as these, Jude says, "have mercy." Interestingly, the word here translated "doubt" is the same as the word translated "disputing" in verse 9. Every word has a range of meaning, and while doubt is probably the better choice here, I can say from pastoral experience that sometimes a young Christian with questions falls into disputation.

How are we to handle this when it happens? Perhaps some words Paul gave Timothy can be broadly applied to all of us, and not merely those of us who are shepherds. "The Lord's servant must not be quarrelsome but kind to everyone . . . correcting . . . with gentleness" (2 Timothy 2:24, 25). Don't be harsh. Don't think that behind every question a budding heretic is getting ready to emerge. Be helpful. Invest in relationships. Be known for your patience and your love. "Have mercy." That is how to contend for the faith.

Save Others

The second group of people Jude wants us to contend for with gospel grace is found in verse 23: "save others by snatching them out of the fire." Most often we think of contending in terms of warfare and fighting. Well, what a strange battlefield Jude places us on with these words. In this war we awake in the morning to the task of saving people, not killing them.

I love these words. In the past they have been the only words in the Bible strong enough to comfort me during difficult pastoral situations. Years ago a dear friend walked away from the Christian faith. Somehow he had come to believe the lie of verse 4; he had come to think he could change the grace of God into sensuality and get away with it. To put it bluntly, he thought that he could have Jesus, his wife, and other women too.

I found that after being in conversation with him I was so drained that I needed time alone. It was then, with tears running down my face, that I would open up my Greek text in order to stare at these words in the original tongue. It was as if I needed to see them put down exactly as God gave them. Somehow these words reassured me that God does still save wayward sinners and that my counsel might bear fruit in my friend's life. I held on to them for *his* dear life. And I would run my fingers over them praying that he might be counted among the "others." Restorative evangelism is the work of contending. We must give ourselves to the immense privilege of saving people for God.

C. T. Studd lived from 1860–1931. He was educated at Cambridge and was one of the top cricket players of his time. In fact, he was so good that others in the sporting world compared him to America's Babe Ruth or Ty Cobb. Well, it so happened that C. T. became a Christian. As a result he decided to contend for men and women who seemed headed for the fires of Hell. He gave away a fortune and became part of the famous Cambridge Seven, bright university students who left comfortable England and went instead to the mission field. Eventually Studd died an old man in distant Africa, but not before saying:

> Some want to live within the sound
> Of church or chapel bell,
> I want to run a rescue shop
> Within a yard of hell.[3]

C. T. was a Jude-like Christian. He knew what it meant to contend. And I can tell you that the times haven't changed. We need some from this generation to conduct themselves with the contending grace of seeing to the work of getting others saved.

Perhaps you have seen the movie *Schindler's List*. After the war is over, Oskar Schindler is on-screen preparing to leave in his car. For a brief moment he stops to talk to a Jewish foreman at the plant. The foreman wants somehow to thank Schindler for all that he did during the war.

> Foreman: One who saves one life saves the world in time.
> Oskar: I could have got more. I could have got more. I made more money, threw away so much money, didn't do enough. Why did I buy this car? Ten more people (sobs), and this gold pin, two more people, at least one more person, one more person who is dead. I didn't—I didn't . . . [4]

Beloved, what are you investing in? Where are you going? What do you intend to do with your life? Jude is walking among us today, and he is calling us to the honorable work of contending.

Show Mercy with Fear

Jude finishes this section on conducting ourselves with Christian grace with a third group of people in need of our mercy. The last half of verse 23 reads, "to others show mercy with fear, hating even the garment stained by the flesh."

This is a difficult verse because it's not all that easy to identify exactly who Jude has in mind. Let me take a run at it in two ways. If we put our interpretive emphasis on the phrase "with fear," the verse becomes less concerned with the group and more of a warning of sorts to those of us engaged in the work of mercy. This makes good sense, especially in light of Jude's call for us to hate even the garment that is stained by the flesh. None of us is immune to falling into temptation. In the blink of an eye an act of mercy or a reach to save puts us not only in touch with evil but also in the presence and fullness of fallen desires.

In a city such as the one I live in, temptations of the flesh are all around us. And how sad to think that while we live here for gospel reasons, we could, for lack of care, find ourselves succumbing to the very evil that we hate and in the end keep ourselves from Heaven altogether. In light of that, Jude is warning us that contending for the faith requires great care. Stay pure.

The distinguished Christian gentleman William E. Gladstone can help us on this point. Gladstone served twenty-seven years in the House of Commons and was Prime Minister four times. He committed himself to Christian growth, and he conducted himself with Christian grace. Yet he knew first-hand the battle of compassionate conduct. In his diary he revealed his struggle with the secret sin of pornographic reading. It was a sin that caught him at first unawares. After all, it opened up to him while he was in the process of doing something else altogether—and with good intentions! He writes:

> I bought this book . . . and I began to read it, and found in some parts of it impure passages . . . so I drank the poison, sinfully. . . . I have stained my memory and my soul—which may it please God to cleanse for me, as I have need.

Five days later, after another go at the book, Gladstone confided again to his diary:

> But it seems to me necessary to shut up these last two volumes for good, having fallen yet again among impurities: how strong and subtle are the evils of this age, I read sinfully, although with disgust, under the pretext of hunting soberly for what was innocent; but—criminal that I am—with a prurient curiosity against all the rules of pious prudence, and inflaming the war between the better qualities of man and the worse.[5]

If Gladstone can fall, so can we. Only a fool would think otherwise. So be careful. Show mercy, but do so in the fear of God. Don't grow to secretly love for yourself what mercy is trying to put away in the life of another.

There is another lesson for us from his life. Gladstone started a mercy ministry to prostitutes on the streets of London. And in showing mercy he walked straight into the path of mixed motives and temptations that needed resisting. His biographer writes:

> Gladstone . . . directed the charitable efforts of the Margaret Street brother-hood towards the redemption of "fallen women" . . . throughout the 1850's (and for decades beyond) he continued with sporadic rescue work. . . . Did Gladstone believe that he was doing much good with his rescue efforts?

Probably not. . . . In 1854 he recorded that in differing circumstances, he had over five years or so engaged with between eighty and ninety prostitutes of whom "there is but one of whom I know that the miserable life has been abandoned and that I can fairly join that fact with influence of mine." He was perfectly aware that his motives were mixed and that his obsession must be explained by temptation and could not be justified by results.[6]

May Gladstone's life instruct us to heed the words of Jude. So much for looking at this verse in terms of its emphasis on us. It could be that Jude is referring here to a group of people who need our mercy, even though they remain unrepentant. The last phrase, "the flesh," is the term for human waste. This means that the problem isn't the garments but the sin that comes from inside the sinner. In light of this, perhaps this third group of people are men and women who after repeated warnings and acts of mercy still remain unrepentant and defiled on the inside.

If this is the case, then we are dealing here with hardened, unbelieving people for whom there is no hope. Recalcitrant sinners. Condemned and contaminated reprobates who hate everything about our faith. And how does Jude ask us to contend for them? We are to "show mercy"! Stunning. What a rebuke to the church of our day. Large sections of the church in this country seem to have gotten this aspect of contending desperately wrong. From the world's vantage point:

- We are better known for contending with might, not mercy.
- We are bent on condemning the world's faults and failings.
- We leave very little room for God to be their judge.
- We spend astounding amounts of time, money, and energy in causes solely given to pronouncing condemnation.
- We spew forth judgment and then go home to bed looking for some sanctimonious sleep as the just reward for having contended well.

Jude would show us all a better way. We are to "show mercy." The Greek word translated "mercy" is *eleate*. Perhaps the church should consider taking up this name. Perhaps we ought to begin calling ourselves *eleatecals* rather than evangelicals. The merciful ones. I like that. It has the ring of weakness in it.

Concluding Comment on Contending

We have come to the end of Jude's instructions on how to contend. We have a calling to keep. We have commitments to make. And we have a conduct to embrace. In summary:

- "Remember" the words of the apostles (v. 17).
- "Keep yourselves in the love of God" (v. 21).
- "Build" one another up "in your most holy faith" (v. 20).

- "Pray in the Holy Spirit" (v. 20).
- "Wait for the mercy of our Lord Jesus Christ that leads to eternal life" (v. 21).
- "Have mercy on those who doubt" (v. 22).
- "Save others by snatching them" from the "fire" of Hell (v. 23).
- "Show mercy with fear, hating even the garment stained by the flesh" (v. 23).

This is how to contend. And according to Jude, these words and this work ought to thrill us!

Lord, have mercy. Have mercy on us, your children. And move our hearts that we might have mercy on those who reject your name. Bring assurance to all who doubt and conviction to all who yet disbelieve. And in doing so, use us as instruments of humble grace. In Jesus' name we pray, amen.

Now to him who is able to keep you from stumbling and to present you blameless before the presence of his glory with great joy, to the only God, our Savior, through Jesus Christ our Lord, be glory, majesty, dominion, and authority, before all time and now and forever. Amen.

vv. 24, 25

38

An Exalted Ending

JUDE 24, 25

WHEN JUDE BEGAN HIS LETTER, he did so by telling his readers of his desire to write about the salvation they shared in common (v. 3). But the day was urgent. The hour was late. So he wrote a letter that called them to "contend for the faith" (v. 3) instead, and in verses 17–23 Jude let loose with a furious array of admonitions and commands on how to do just that.

- "Remember" the words of the apostles (v. 17).
- "Keep yourselves in the love of God" (v. 21).
- "Build" one another up "in your most holy faith" (v. 20).
- "Pray in the Holy Spirit" (v. 20).
- "Wait for the mercy of our Lord Jesus Christ that leads to eternal life" (v. 21).
- "Have mercy on those who doubt" (v. 22).
- "Save others by snatching them" from the "fire" of Hell (v. 23).
- "Have mercy," even on those who are unrepentant (v. 22).

But in the end it appears that Jude couldn't resist his initial desire. As he closes his letter, he decides to return to his intended aim. His thoughts on *contending for the faith* have concluded; he now writes about their *common salvation*. Verses 24, 25 are Jude's contemplation of the beauty and wonder of all that we commonly share in Christ. His description is doxological, and as such we find Jude finishing his letter in the exalted prose of prayer and praise.

> Now to him who is able to keep you from stumbling and to present you blameless before the presence of his glory with great joy, to the only God, our Savior, through Jesus Christ our Lord, be glory, majesty, dominion, and authority, before all time and now and forever. Amen. (vv. 24, 25)

We now know the heart of Jude in full. He would have us contend and contemplate. He calls us to be fully engaged in this world *and* fully invested in Heaven. We are to be active in battle, yet lost in wonder. In this way Jude was the visionary forerunner of Gregory the Great:

> Gregory the Great's formulation of the doctrine of the vision of God is interesting and important. Gregory delights in describing the joys of the vision of God; but he insists on emphasizing the constant need for works of the active life. . . . For him there is, strictly speaking, no such thing as a purely contemplative life at all. . . . There are at best moments, or periods, of contemplation which are achieved or experienced intermittently in the active life, thereby mingling both action and contemplation in a single "mixed life." . . . "We cannot stay long in contemplation" . . . we have to return to the active life, and occupy ourselves with good works. But good works help us again to rise to contemplation, and to receive nourishment of love from the vision of Truth. . . . Then, once more moving back to the life of service, we feed on the memory of the sweetness of God, strengthened by good deeds without, and by holy desires within.[1]

In the words of Gregory the Great, Jude's final strokes "rise to contemplation," where we receive "nourishment of love from the vision of Truth." "Our common salvation" (v. 3) consists in what God will accomplish for us through Christ, as well as the activities we will engage in together through Christ forevermore. The substance of Jude's common salvation through Christ could be put this way:

- Verse 24: what God accomplishes for us
- Verse 25: what God receives from us

What God Accomplishes for Us (v. 24)

Now to Him Who Is Able to Keep You from Stumbling

We can easily imagine how Jude's first readers felt when they came, at last, to the words "Now to him who is able to keep you from stumbling . . ." These words are a balm for anxious souls. And they must have felt like the well-warmed waters of a shower after getting through a difficult day—the kind of waters that one likes to stand under awhile, without any sense of having to get out. After all, for the better part of the letter Jude has been writing about those who appear to start out in Christ but who stumble and fall along the way.

We too have seen them stumble on the pathway to Heaven. They stumble down the steps of autonomy, apostasy, and the insatiable appetite for sensuality and greed (vv. 5–10). We looked on as men like Cain, Balaam, and Korah fell headlong into eternal darkness (vv. 11–16). We watched them as they tumbled down in rebellion:

... descending incontinently, fecklessly, the stairway which leads to a dark gulf. It is a fine broad stairway at the beginning, but after a bit the carpet ends. A little farther on still there are only flagstones. A little further on still these break beneath your feet. . . .[2]

As readers, the continuing waves of stumbling in Jude's letter are frightening. It seems to happen to so many. And we wonder, could it not happen to us as well? Only a fool thinks he has no chance of falling. A story is told that the once-famous circus acrobat Philippe Petit was rehearsing in Bayfront Auditorium in St. Petersburg, Florida, when he fell about thirty feet to a concrete floor. According to a witness, Petit rolled over on his stomach, began pounding the floor with his fists, and cried, "I can't believe it! I can't believe it! I don't ever fall." Mature Christians think differently. We all know that we are capable of falling. Therefore, hearing the promising words "Now to him who is able to keep you from stumbling," one's heart rises in fresh hope of finishing well. It strengthens us in our resolve to remain in Christ.[3]

These words must have done this much and more for Jude's first readers. They certainly do so for us. For we have a God who is able to *"keep* [us] from stumbling." The word *keep* has been a crucial one for Jude. In the opening verse of his letter he claimed to be writing "To those who are called, beloved in God the Father and *kept* for Jesus Christ." Notice: the active agent in being kept for Christ is God the Father. Yet at the midpoint of his manual on how to contend for the faith, Jude raised the idea of *keeping* again, but this time with the words, *"keep* yourselves in the love of God" (v. 21). Clearly we are to be active in doing our part to remain in faith. In concluding, Jude chooses a word translated *"keep"* ("guard") and attributes it to the One who alone is able to *"keep* [us] from stumbling." Thus, with these three occurrences of the same motif, we enter into the full and mysterious work of salvation. We are being *kept* for Christ and *guarded* by God—and in the midst of it all we rise each day to the righteous work of *keeping* ourselves in his love.

The Scriptures promise elsewhere that the righteous man, though he fall seven times, will rise up still, because God is able to *keep* him from stumbling (Proverbs 24:16). Therefore, never forget—it is the guarding constancy of God that keeps us from utter destruction and eternal ruin. This much we all share in common.

And to Present You Blameless before the Presence of His Glory
with Great Joy

So, concerning those things that are common to our salvation, God is able to keep us all from something. In addition, he is able to present us before the presence of something. Jude writes, "Now to him who is able to keep you from stumbling *and to present you . . . before the presence of his glory.*" If you have ever studied courageous men and women in church history who pursued "the beatific vision," you can immediately resonate with what Jude promises us here.[4] In these words we find the ultimate goal of life and the full longing of every heart. We are told here that one day we will stand in the presence of God's glory. What vision could ever surpass this? This ought to be the longing of every follower of Jesus. It was the longing of every prophet and priest. And as C. S. Lewis writes, it was the longing of every psalm writer too.

> They express a longing for him, for his mere presence, which comes only to the best Christians or to Christians in their best moments. They long to live all their days in the temple so that they may constantly see "the fair beauty of the Lord" (27:4). Their longing to go up to Jerusalem and "appear before the presence of God" is like a physical thirst (42). From Jerusalem his presence flashes out "in perfect beauty" (50:2). Lacking that encounter with him, their souls are parched like a waterless country-side (63:2). They crave to be "satisfied with the pleasures" of his house (65:4). Only then can they be at ease, like a bird in the nest (84:3). One day of those pleasures is better than a lifetime spent elsewhere (10). I have rather—though the expression may seem harsh to some—called this the "appetite for God" than "the love of God."[5]

Every Christian ought to have this "appetite for God"—*to be presented* "before the presence of his glory" (v. 24). Unfortunately, and tragically, this exalted promise that thunders from the mouth of Jude is often met within Christian circles with apathy and indifference. It is as if our appetite for Heaven has been sated by the filling activities of this world. There is a story of a man who walked more than seven hundred miles to see Niagara Falls. When he came within a few miles of his destination, he thought he heard a thundering roar. Seeing a farmer in a nearby field, he called out, "Is that the roar of the Niagara?" The man replied, "I don't know, but it may be." With surprise, the other asked, "Do you live here?" "Born and bred here," came the answer. "And you don't know whether that noise is from the falls?" "No, stranger. I have never been there. I'm too busy looking after my farm."[6] May that not be true of us, for that which we share in common is a destination filled with wonder and unique majesty.

Blameless and with Great Joy

It is one thing to consider that we will stand in the presence of the living God. It is quite another to learn that when we do, we will be presented to him "blameless" and "with great joy." The word translated "blameless" has a rich Biblical history. The book of Exodus ends with Moses standing before the newly built tabernacle—constructed exactly "according to all that the LORD commanded him" (40:16). In building it, God had promised Moses that this tent would be the place where he would come to meet with his people.

However, at the time when Moses first finished it, ironically, "Moses was not able to enter the tent of meeting because the cloud settled on it, and the glory of the LORD filled the tabernacle" (v. 35). Thus, while God saved his people from Egypt (Exodus 1—18) and spoke to his people from Mt. Sinai (Exodus 19—34), Moses could not simply be brought into "the presence of his glory," even though God had come to settle among them in the tabernacle (Exodus 35—40).

Communion with God still required one thing—blood. No wonder the book of Leviticus comes right after the book of Exodus. It is this book of blood that mediates the relationship between God and his people. And it was from this context that God said, "If his offering is a burnt offering from the herd, he shall offer a male without blemish" (Leviticus 1:3). The words "without blemish" in Leviticus contain the substance of Jude's word "blameless." In essence, what Jude is saying is that all those trusting in the sacrifice of Christ will become like the blameless sacrifice that secured access to the Father. We will be presented, through Christ, as acceptable in his sight!

No wonder Jude says that we will all have "joy" in common. And not just joy—we will enter into his presence with "*great* joy"!

> Only to sit and think of God
> Oh what a joy it is!
> To think the thought, to breathe the Name;
> Earth has no higher bliss.
> Father of Jesus, love's reward!
> What rapture will it be,
> Prostrate before thy throne to lie,
> And gaze and gaze on Thee![7]

Through Christ

Thus far we have seen the ascendant glories and joys of our common salvation. God is able to keep us *from* something. He is able to present us *before* something. Before Jude finishes describing what God accomplishes for us, he wants to remind us that this uncommon salvation comes to us *through* someone—"through Jesus Christ our Lord" (v. 25).

In one sense it would be true to say that Jesus has been the gravitational center holding Jude's entire letter together. He is present from beginning to end. All things are done *for* him or *by* him. We are protected *in* him, and now at the close we are reminded that we come to God *through* him.

- Verse 1: "kept *for* Jesus Christ."
- Verse 5: The Israelites were delivered from Egypt *by* Jesus.
- Verses 9, 14: The earthly bodies of the saints are protected in death and resurrection *in* Jesus.[8]
- Verse 25: We come to the only God "*through* Jesus Christ."

Jesus is everything to us, from first to last. And in him we see the Father's great love for us. As the hymn-writer has said:

How deep the Father's love for us,
How vast beyond all measure,
That He should give His only Son
To make a wretch His treasure.

Why should I gain from His reward?
I cannot give an answer.
But this I know with all my heart,
His wounds have paid my ransom.[9]

Jude has given us, incredibly, in the space of half a sentence perhaps the most concise summary ever put down on paper of all that God accomplishes for us. This uncommon salvation consists of what God is able to keep us from, that which he is able to present us to, and the one through whom he accomplishes it all. In considering all this, our hearts swell with thanksgiving and praise.

What God Receives from Us (v. 25)

"Our common salvation" (v. 3) entails not only those things that God accomplishes for us—it includes the things God will receive from us all as well. Jude writes:

> . . . to the only God, our Savior, through Jesus Christ our Lord, be glory, majesty, dominion, and authority, before all time and now and forever. Amen. (v. 25)

To put it as simply and boldly as I can, the corporate worship and everlasting praise of God will be the eternal privilege of all who through Christ have a share in God's good salvation.

On that day, on that day without end, God will finally receive the fullness of all the praise that is due his name. Truly, the everlasting event of worship was not intended to be received by God in isolation. The kind of worship of God that is worthy of his name is worship that demands that others join in. C. S. Lewis, in his *Reflections on the Psalms*, observed:

> Just as men spontaneously praise whatever they value, so they spontaneously urge us to join them in praising it: "Isn't she lovely? Wasn't it glorious? Don't you think that magnificent?"[10]

The praising of God in Heaven will resemble this very kind of occurrence. At the time when God is supremely valued, and certainly he must be so valued in Heaven, we will all possess the spontaneous urge to speak highly of him in the presence of others. Not satisfied however, we will urge them to join us in praising God for what we see in him. When this occurs, the happy ones to whom we have spoken will gladly join us, and a ripple of praise will begin running through the redeemed like rolling, mighty waters, resulting in new songs cascading across the full expanse of Heaven.

George Whitefield, eighteenth-century evangelist, seemed to be able to peer beyond the veil of this present world when he wrote:

> Think, think with what unspeakable glory those happy souls are now encircled, who, when on earth were called to deny themselves, and were not disobedient to the call. Hark! Methinks I hear them chanting their everlasting hallelujahs and spending an eternal day in echoing triumphant songs of joy. And do you not long, my brethren, to join this heavenly choir. . . . Behold then a heavenly ladder reached down to you, by which you may climb to this holy hill. . . . By this we, even we, may be lifted into the same blissful regions . . . and join with them in singing doxologies and songs of praise to the everlasting, blessed, all-glorious, most adorable Trinity, for ever and ever.[11]

Knowing this, may we all make it our life's ambition to praise God from whom all blessings flow. May we make a fresh start with God, through Christ. Begin giving him all the "glory, majesty, dominion, and authority" that is due his name. Jude would say more, but what more could he really say? And besides, it is time for lovers of God to contend.

Dear God, we long to stand in your presence. We long to be with you in glory with great joy. For you alone are God. Through Jesus Christ our Lord, you keep us from stumbling. You alone make us blameless. May our lives be a doxology of praise and adoration to you, even as we continue to contend for the faith. Amen.

Soli Deo Gloria!

Notes

Chapter Two: A Letter to Elect Exiles

1. In this chapter I only deal with the charge leveled against Petrine authorship that is made on the basis of the author's elevated ability with language, style, and rhetoric. There are, of course, other charges made against Peter as the author, the most significant among them being that the content of the letter requires some severe persecution along the lines of official Roman persecution, which from all we know of the history of the time period in which Peter was still alive and able to have written this just did not exist. I do deal with this second objection to Peter's authorship in chapter 4. I purposely waited until then to interact with this particular objection because that chapter addresses the type of persecution facing Peter's early readers.

2. C. S. Lewis as quoted in John Stott, *Between Two Worlds* (Grand Rapids, MI: Eerdmans, 1982), p. 235.

3. See John Calvin's *Institutes of the Christian Religion*, Book III, Chapter II.

4. William Shakespeare, *The First Part of Henry VI* (Act I, Scene 3), as it is quoted in *William Shakespeare: The Complete Works*, ed. Stanley Wells and Gary Taylor (Oxford: Oxford University Press, 1988), p. 158.

5. While some commentators make much of the phrase "exiles of the dispersion" in identifying the original audience as primarily comprised of Jewish Christians, I feel it is primarily used by Peter metaphorically to speak of both Jewish and Gentile believers (see 1:14; 4:3, 4).

6. C. S. Lewis, *The Weight of Glory*, as quoted in James Hewett's *Parables, Etc.*, Vol. 6, No. 1, March 1986, p. 8.

7. Toni Morrison, *Sula* (New York: Penguin, 1973), p. 174.

Chapter Three: Salvation's Future Goal

1. Iain H. Murray, *D. Martyn Lloyd-Jones: The First Forty Years* (Southampton, UK: Camelot Press Ltd., 1983), pp. 23, 24.

2. Robert Louis Stevenson, as quoted in *The Christian Reader*, July-August, 1977, pp. 94, 95.

3. William Shakespeare, *Macbeth*, Act V, Scene 1, ed. K. Muir (London: Methuen, 1985), pp. 143–146.

4. Jean-Paul Sartre, *Dirty Hands*, in *No Exit, and Three Other Plays* (New York: Vintage, 1946), pp. 216–218.

Chapter Four: Salvation's Present Trials

1. These are thoughts that George Richmond is said to have written to Samuel Palmer three days after Blake's death. See http://en.wikipedia.org/wiki/William_Blake; accessed January 31, 2007.

2. William Blake, *Auguries of Innocence*, quoted in R. Kent Hughes, *Acts: The Church Afire*, Preaching the Word series (Wheaton, IL: Crossway Books, 1996), p. 179.

3. See J. Ramsey Michaels, *Word Biblical Commentary: 1 Peter* (Nashville: Thomas Nelson, 1988), p. 30 for an example. Many commentators unite this phrase with the later reference to "fiery trial" in 4:12 to suggest a late date for the book as a result.

4. "How Firm a Foundation," from John Rippon's *Selection of Hymns, 1787*, in *The Hymnal for Worship & Celebration*, #275, ed. Tom Fettke (Waco, TX: Word Music, 1986).

5. Malcolm Muggeridge, *A Twentieth Century Testimony* (Nashville: Thomas Nelson, 1978).

6. Dietrich Bonhoeffer, "New Year 1945," quoted in G. Liebholz, "Memoir," included as introduction, in Dietrich Bonhoeffer, *The Cost of Discipleship* (New York: MacMillan, 1948), pp. 16, 17.

7. Thomas Mann, *Joseph and His Brothers* (London: Vintage of Random House, 1997), pp. 468, 469.

Chapter Five: Salvation's Past Glories

1. T. S. Eliot, *The Complete Poems and Plays* (New York: Harcourt, Brace & World, 1971), p. 56.

2. Marilynne Robinson, *Gilead* (New York: Farrar, Straus and Giroux, 2004), p. 49.

3. Homer, *The Odyssey*, trans. George Herbert Palmer (Cambridge, MA: The Riverside Press, 1884), p. 142ff.

Chapter Six: A Settled Hope

1. Viktor Frankl, *Man's Search for Meaning* (New York: Washington Square Press, 1984), p. 96.

2. In 2 Peter the great apostle is on the verge of death (see 2 Peter 1:13–15). It is one thing for his readers' hopes to fail while the great apostle is yet alive and with them. It will be another to have to go on without him. Peter, sensing all of this and knowing how difficult it will be for Christians the world over to go on hoping for Christ's return after all the apostles have died, will give himself in the second letter to a full-blown treatment of the longed-for day of Christ's return—especially, and more particularly, how his readers are to go on in light of its apparently never coming. Indeed, in 2 Peter the subject of the day of Christ's return dominates the letter. In this first letter, things are not quite so bad. What I find most interesting about the relationship between the two letters is that by the time Peter writes the second one, he will need to shore up the Christians' very belief in Christ's return (2 Peter 1, 3). Thus, the emphasis on the Second Coming in the second letter is that it will indeed occur, while the emphasis in the first letter is living life in light of it.

3. John Owen, as quoted in *The Works of John Owen*, Vol. 1, ed. William H. Goold (Carlisle, PA: Banner of Truth Trust, 1965), p. cxiv.

4. C. S. Lewis, *The Weight of Glory and Other Addresses* (New York: HarperCollins, 1949), pp. 15, 16.

5. Wayne Grudem, *Tyndale New Testament Commentaries on 1 Peter* (Grand Rapids, MI: Eerdmans, 1988), p. 76.

6. Thomas Cahill, *How the Irish Saved Civilization* (New York: Anchor Books, 1995), p. 204.

7. Iain Murray, *D. Martyn Lloyd-Jones: The Fight of Faith 1939–1981* (Carlisle, PA: Banner of Truth Trust, 1990), p. 70.

8. Harry Blamires, *The Christian Mind* (Ventura, CA: Vine Books, 1997), p. 3.

9. J. I. Packer, *Knowing God* (Downers Grove, IL: InterVarsity Press, 1973), p. 182.

10. In light of this point, I cannot help but be continually perplexed about those within the Christian community who would admonish us to do away with the gender particular term "Father" in translations of the Bible. The logic behind this appears wrongheaded and rooted in a misunderstanding of what new Christians actually need.

11. C. S. Lewis, *The Voyage of the Dawn Treader* (New York: HarperCollins, 1952), pp. 263–265.

Chapter Seven: A Sincere Love

1. John Piper, *Desiring God* (Portland: Multnomah, 1986), p. 119.

2. According to Kenneth Kirk in *The Vision of God*, Augustine's true greatness "lies in the doctrine that the essence of grace is *love*, and the essence of man's salvation that he should become *loving*" (Harrisburg, PA: Morehouse), 1991, p. 138.

3. See http://www.albatrus.org/english/potpourri/quotes/john_wesley_quotes.htm; accessed January 26, 2007.

4. H. Richard Niebuhr, *The Purpose of the Church and Its Ministry, Reflections on the Aims of Theological Education* (New York: HarperCollins, 1956), pp. 34–36.

5. Marilynne Robinson, *Gilead* (New York: Farrar, Straus and Giroux, 2004), p. 166.

Chapter Eight: A Spiritual House

1. Kyle Dugdale, "The Hero, The Mercenary, and the Architect: Cures for the Nostalgia of Modernity," M.A. thesis, Harvard University, 2002.

Chapter Nine: Good Deeds

1. Before taking up these headings, it appears that in verse 11 Peter is borrowing words that had a long history in the ancient world. In fact, he is intentionally pulling on language that extends as far back as Plato. In verse 12, however, Peter changes his tact. There Peter undergirds his call for good living—not from the common ground shared with philosophers of ancient Greece but from the very lips of Jesus. Good living is grounded in the dominical words of Jesus (see Matthew 5:14–16). If this is indeed the case, Peter, in these two verses, shows himself to be an able Christian writer and preacher. His feet are planted firmly in this world. Yet, at the end of the day he enlarges upon the world's understanding of the good life by appealing to the authority of Christ who alters all meaning and now reigns over human thought. Put simply, Peter will show us in these two verses that Christians are to "abstain from the passions of the flesh" like any good earthly citizen. Yet, unlike them, Christians are to "keep [their] conduct" in accord with and under the authority of the dominical words of Christ.

2. Plato, *Phaedo*, trans. Benjamin Jowett (New York: Random House, 1892), p. 466 (81e).

3. *Ibid.*, p. 467 (82c), emphasis added.

4. I hope that every preacher reading this will enjoy the sense that this sorry indictment on my inability to think Biblically about the role of good works and thereby collect illustrations accordingly can, at the end of the day, be a means of illustrating the point after all!

5. Some commentators think that the emphasis of this verse applies to some future day of an unbeliever's conversion. For me, however, it is the final day, the day of the Second Coming, that seems to always be in the forefront of Peter's mind in this letter (1:5, 7, 13; 4:5, 13; 5:1). This view doesn't do away with any evangelistic intention, but it doesn't make the verse rise or fall on the notion of underlying evangelistic purpose.

Chapter Ten: Honorable Living

1. I am not quite certain of the origin of this statement. Timothy Dudley-Smith recounts a version of it in his biographical work on John Stott. A different and likely origin of it, however, is from Scottish-born advertising giant David Ogilvy who either said it in reference to "research" or may have attributed it to George Gallup.

2. Recently I have been preaching through the book of Amos. His prophetic voice is clear and distinct and in many respects would be an excellent book to help any church think through its calling in matters pertaining to issues of human dignity and social justice.

3. We often preach by way of qualification when we must explain difficult texts. For instance, when I first preached this text, I desperately wanted to make a real appeal to Augustine's line, "an unjust law is no law at all." One could also draw on Dr. Martin Luther King's eloquent Birmingham jail letter that reads, "I have been arrested on a charge of parading without a permit. Now, there is nothing wrong in having an ordinance which requires a permit for a parade. But such an ordinance becomes unjust when it is used to maintain segregation and to deny citizens the First Amendment privilege of peaceful assembly and protest. . . . I submit that an individual who breaks a law that

conscience tells him is unjust and who willingly accepts the penalty of imprisonment in order to arouse the conscience of the community over its injustice, is in reality expressing the highest respect for law." These are great examples of the proper role of civil disobedience. The only thing I am trying to say here is that as much as possible, the preacher's role is to explain, illustrate, and apply the text before him rather than truths that arise from another place in Scripture.

4. *Haustafel* is simply a German word meant to refer to the biblical texts that treat the household overriding relationships in play in any home. It refers to the fullness of the household code.

5. See John Witherspoon, *Lectures on Moral Philosophy,* 1768, ed. Jack Scott (Cranbury, NJ: Associated University Presses, 1982).

I. It is frequently observed, that in every government there is a supreme irresistible power lodged somewhere, in king, senate, or people. . . . How far does this extend? If the supreme power wherever lodged, come to be exercised in a manifestly tyrannical manner, the subjects may certainly if in their power, resist and overthrow it. But this is only when it becomes manifestly more advantageous to unsettle the government altogether, than to submit to tyranny. (145)

This doctrine of resistance even to the supreme power is essentially connected with what has been said on the social contract, and the consent necessary to political union. If it be asked who must judge when the government may be resisted, I answer the subjects in general, everyone for himself. (145)

We must obey and submit [to authorities] always, till the corruption becomes intolerable; for to say that we might resist legal authority every time we judged it to be wrong, would be inconsistent with a state of society, and to the very first idea of subjection. (145)

II. Dominion, it is plain from all that has been said, can be acquired justly only one way, viz. by consent. (146)

That which is called the right of conquest ought to be exploded altogether. We shall see by and by what is the right of a conqueror in a just war. It was his right before, and he obtains possession of it by conquest. But to found any claim merely on conquest is not a right, but robbery. (146)

6. Personal correspondence on June 4, 2007 with Benjamin Lynerd, a dear friend and doctoral student at the University of Chicago working on some of these issues. His note is worth reading in its entirety: "My two years on the topic have given me considerable peace with the fact that the Bible does not condemn slavery as such. The passages promoting submission serve as a fitting reminder that political/social freedom is neither essential to nor in any way comparable to freedom in Christ. That 18th-century American Christians (including most abolitionists) conflated the two has only confused our understanding of why American slavery was unjust.

"The Biblical injustice of American slavery comes down to two things, working in tandem: its permanence (complete legal barriers to manumission) and its purely racial basis. Even ancient Hebrew slaves enjoyed periodic jubilee. Certainly New Testament slaves had various means to earn their freedom, depending on context. This much can be said: God never permits his people to use slavery as a means of permanent exploitation, the gluttonous feeding off of others and their children, generation after generation.

"The far more insidious aspect of North American slavery, of course, is its racism, but the two work together: Americans saw an opportunity to institute a permanent slave race by virtue of the African's distinctive appearance. It would be nearly impossible to enforce permanent slavery among whites—and all too easy for whites to enforce it among blacks.

"In my view, it would be difficult to find a Biblical justification for the systematic demeaning and exploitation of people on the basis of their race, particularly in light of God's promise to Abraham that "all the families of the earth will be approved" through his line, and the fulfillment of that promise in Christ (Ephesians 2:11–22).

"At the heart of American chattel slavery was a perception, either sincerely felt or cynically deployed, that dark-skinned people bore less of God's image than white-skinned people. Such a sadistic fiction, however, was not exclusive to slave-holding colonies, and it did not end with emancipation (see Du Bois's *Souls of Black Folk,* chapter 1). The central problem here, as you have said and should say again, is racism.

"It is so unhelpful to frame the problem in terms of liberty. American Christians need to get past liberty as a religious norm, and 1 Peter 2:18ff. (and Colossians 3 for that matter) can help. None of us, black or white, is entitled to political freedom as a natural 'right.' Nor are we, by any claim of nature, entitled to deny the advantages of freedom to others.

"On the topic of enslaving war captives, I'll say just a couple of things. First, the practice was common in ancient warfare, and was indeed considered more humane than simply killing them. The practice was not particularly racist (all principalities did it to each other) or permanent (given the frequency of such wars). A slave today could be a master tomorrow. If Paul wanted to take on the ethics of wartime slavery, he may as well have taken on the justice of war itself.

"Incidentally, the war-captive rationale was used in the early days of American slavery (17th century) to convince dubious Christians that Africans had been fairly enslaved. Most claims of this nature, though naively believed by many, were entirely bogus: most African slaves were not soldiers on the losing side of some battle; they were men, women and children who had been kidnapped for the sole purpose of their manual labor."

Chapter Eleven: Internal Adornment

1. Augustine, *Confessions*, quoted in J.N.D. Kelly, *Thornapple Commentaries: A Commentary on the Epistles of Peter and Jude* (Grand Rapids, MI: Baker, 1969), p. 128.
2. The Greek word for knowledge, which is untranslated in most English versions, is *gnosis*. This word and its cognates find a Hebrew linguistic counterpart in *yada*, the word used for intimate knowledge in Genesis 4:1, 19:8, and several other texts. The Septuagint frequently uses a form of *gnosis* in these passages.
3. From a letter by a family member to the author, March 16, 2006.

Chapter Twelve: Encouragement to Continue

1. Bob Dylan, "Ballad of a Thin Man," *Highway 61 Revisited*, Sony, 2003.
2. David Maraniss, *When Pride Still Mattered* (New York: Simon & Schuster, 1999), p. 248.

Chapter Thirteen: Encouragement in Christ's Victory

1. Martin Luther, ed. John Lenker, *Commentary on Peter and Jude* (Grand Rapids, MI: Kregel, 1982), p. 166.
2. Wayne Grudem, *Tyndale New Testament Commentary: 1 Peter* (Grand Rapids, MI: Eerdmans, 1988), p. 157.
3. Edmund P. Clowney, *The Message of 1 Peter*, The Bible Speaks Today (Downers Grove, IL: InterVarsity Press), p. 156.
4. Karen H. Jobes, *1 Peter*, Baker Exegetical Commentary on the New Testament (Grand Rapids, MI: Baker, 2005), pp. 237, 239.
5. Mortimer Adler and Charles Van Doren, *How to Read a Book* (New York: Simon & Schuster, 1972), pp. 35, 36.
6. J. Ramsey Michaels, *1 Peter*, World Biblical Commentary (Nashville: Thomas Nelson, 1988), pp. 197, 198.
7. Adler and Van Doren, *How to Read a Book*, p. 75.
8. R. Kent Hughes, *Acts: The Church Afire*, Preaching the Word (Wheaton, IL: Crossway Books, 1996), p. 253.
9. It contains something of his sufferings for sure (v. 18), but certainly nothing like what we saw in chapters 1, 2.

10. Quoted in Hughes, *Acts*, p. 102.

11. For one compelling answer to these questions, which would have required a sermon in and of itself, see Grudem, *Tyndale New Testament Commentary: 1 Peter*, pp. 155–166.

Chapter Fourteen: Embrace Your Calling to Suffer in the World

1. Albert Schweitzer, *The Quest of the Historical Jesus* (New York: Macmillan, 1968), pp. 370, 371.

2. It is interesting that until this time suffering appears in the letter to be "if necessary." But now he speaks with definitive force, preparing the church for the inevitable.

3. From the hymn "Rise Up, O Men of God," lyrics by William P. Merrill; http://www.cyberhymnal.org/htm/r/i/riseupom.htm; accessed July 31, 2007.

4. C. S. Lewis, *Letters to Malcolm: Chiefly on Prayer*, chapter 13, as quoted in Wayne Martindale and Jerry Root, *The Quotable Lewis* (Wheaton, IL: Tyndale House, 1989), p. 547.

5. Malcolm Muggeridge, *Jesus Rediscovered* (London: Collins, 1969), pp. 101, 102.

6. R. C. Sproul, *The Holiness of God* (Wheaton, IL: Tyndale House, 1985), pp. 91–93.

Chapter Fifteen: Embrace Your Calling in the Church

1. Quoted in James Sire, *The Universe Next Door* (Downers Grove, IL: InterVarsity Press, 1976), p. 58.

2. Iain Murray, *D. Martyn Lloyd-Jones: The Fight of Faith 1939–1981* (Carlisle, PA: Banner of Truth Trust, 1990), p. 756.

3. E. Stanley Jones, *Song of Ascents* (Nashville: Abingdon, 1979), pp. 129, 130; quoted in R. Kent Hughes and Bryan Chapell, *1 and 2 Timothy and Titus: To Guard the Deposit*, Preaching the Word (Wheaton, IL: Crossway Books, 2000), p. 79.

4. Thomas Cahill, *How the Irish Saved Civilization* (New York: Anchor Books, 1995), pp. 173–175.

5. From "A Word to Those Who Preach the Word," in every volume in the Preaching the Word series.

6. Nevil Shute, *On the Beach* (New York: Random House, 1957), inside cover.

Chapter Sixteen: Glory, Suffering, and Judgment

1. Some commentators believe that impending martyrdom may be in view. In Jewish history, fire is often associated with death (e.g., the three faithful ones in the book of Daniel). However, given that all the internal evidence of the letter brings out lesser things, I have adopted a view that the two uses of the term (1:6 and 4:12) refer to the same kinds of things. Further, in the opening chapter I have argued that the lack of a definite period of persecution for the letter validates seeing these things as normal trials that afflict all believers, rather than martyrdom.

2. George Whitefield, as quoted in Arnold Dallimore, *George Whitefield* (Carlisle, PA: Banner of Truth Trust, 1970), p. 72.

3. Ella Wheeler Wilcox, "Gethsemane"; http://www.litscape.com/author/Ella_Wheeler_Wilcox/Gethsemane.html; accessed January 26, 2007.

4. To understand these verses I would suggest that you look ahead to the following chapter, especially the opening paragraphs. I say this because I didn't fully understand this connection until I was forced to wrestle with it in light of the following verses.

5. Charles Haddon Spurgeon, "Chastisement Now and Afterwards," preached on September 6, 1863; *Metropolitan Tabernacle Pulpit* (Carlisle, PA: Banner of Truth Trust, 1988).

6. George Matheson, "O Love That Will Not Let Me Go," *The Worshipping Church Hymnal* (Carol Stream, IL: Hope Publishing Company, 1990), #531.

7. Simone Weil, "The Love of God and Affliction," in *Gateway to God* (Oxford: Oxford University Press, 1962), pp. 87–102.

Chapter Seventeen: An Exhortation to Elders

1. Flannery O'Connor, "The Lame Shall Enter First," in *Flannery O'Connor: Collected Works* (New York: Library of America, 1988), pp. 626–628.
2. As an aside, what Peter did in these verses was highly unusual given the thrust of his letter. Previously Peter has shown himself to be highly reticent to give directions to people who hold positions of *authority*. Generally speaking, he wrote this letter to show Christians how to live gracious lives for Christ *under* authority. But here in chapter 5 he alters his perspective. He decides to give a directive to the elders who are charged with oversight. And by doing so, he wants us to recognize the significance that he attaches to the fullness of the Christian life as it is lived out within the family of God. He must have a word for elders. Overseers, or the *episcopate* as we have it from a transliteration of the Greek, serve as a representative body over each local church, and they are ultimately responsible for that church's practice, purity, and preaching.
3. C. S. Lewis, *Letters of C.S. Lewis*, July 18, 1957, as quoted in Wayne Martindale and Jerry Root, *The Quotable Lewis* (Wheaton, IL: Tyndale House, 1989), p. 171.
4. Flavius Josephus, *Josephus: Jewish Antiquities*, Books XII-XIV, Loeb Classical Library (No. 365), VIIs. trans. Ralph Marcus (Cambridge, MA: Harvard University Press, 1933), pp. 66, 67.
5. Samuel Stone, "The Church's One Foundation," in ed. Tom Fettke, *The Hymnal for Worship & Celebration* (Waco, TX: Word Music, 1986), #277.

Chapter Eighteen: True Grace and Eternal Glory

1. Origen's statement here actually comes from Eusebius's *Ecclesiastical History*, Book II, chapter 1.
2. Vance Havner, *Threescore and Ten* (Old Tappan, NJ: Revell, 1973), p. 62.
3. Helen MacDonald, mother of George MacDonald, as quoted in Greville MacDonald, *George MacDonald and His Wife* (Whitethorn, CA: Johannesen, 1924), p. 33.
4. See Amos 1:2; 3:8; and Revelation 5:5 among others.
5. C. S. Lewis, *The Last Battle* (New York: HarperCollins, 1956), pp. 11, 12.
6. *Ibid.*, p. 50.
7. Iain Murray, *D. Martyn Lloyd-Jones: The Fight of Faith 1939–1981* (Carlisle, PA: Banner of Truth Trust, 1990), p. 765.
8. Thomas Cahill, *How the Irish Saved Civilization* (New York: Anchor Books, 1995), pp. 116–119.
9. See http://en.wikiquote.org/wiki/Hugh_Latimer; accessed January 26, 2007.
10. As stated in *John Wesley's Journal*; http://www.godrules.net/library/wesley/274wesley_a11.htm; accessed August 2, 2007.

Chapter Twenty: This Letter and the Life Experience of Peter

1. Douglas Coupland, *Life After God* (New York: Simon & Schuster, 1994), p. 76.
2. R. Kent Hughes, *Luke: That You May Know the Truth*, Vol. 2, Preaching the Word (Wheaton, IL: Crossway Books, 1998), p. 348.
3. Clarence McCartney, as quoted in *ibid.*
4. Richard Bauckham, *Jude, 2 Peter*, Word Biblical Commentary (Nashville: Thomas Nelson, 1983), pp. 158–162.
5. *Ibid.*, p. 166.
6. We can easily imagine what the other men at the table must have been thinking as Peter bellowed on. "Oh no! Here he goes again." But for all their discontent, I'll tell you what I love about Peter. He had a burning desire to fulfill what he had given himself to—and he wasn't afraid to say it. He was the kind of person who was not always right, but never in doubt.
7. For discussion on this, see G. Campbell Morgan, *The Gospel According to Luke*, ninth edition (New York: Revell, 1954), p. 247.

8. Regarding "ours" = apostles, there is no mention in this letter of Jews or Gentiles. See Bauckham, *Jude, 2 Peter*, on 1:16; 1:12–15.

Chapter Twenty-One: Our Faith Must Grow

1. J. M. Coetzee, *The Life and Times of Michael K.* (New York: Penguin, 1983), pp. 161–167.

2. J. I. Packer, *Knowing God* (Downers Grove, IL: InterVarsity Press, 1973), p. 29.

3. Compiling lists of desirable virtues has a rich and storied history in Western civilization. Benjamin Franklin amassed thirteen, including temperance, silence, order, resolution, frugality, industry, sincerity, justice, moderation, cleanliness, tranquility, chastity, and humility. It is said that he went so far as to write them down in a small book that he carried with him. Such practice made personal evaluation a continuing habit. Long before Franklin, Greek philosophers such as Plato and Socrates gave considerable attention to making lists of virtues. Aristotle entered the arena as well, and in our own day leading universities are trying to instill virtues into the education of students, especially as they relate to ethics. The closest thing the Bible puts forward to a list of virtues might be the fruit of the Spirit as found in Paul's letter to the Galatians (5:22, 23).

4. Bob Dylan, "Forever Young," *Planet Waves*, Asylum Records, 1974.

5. Aristotle, *Virtues and Vices*; http://www.logoslibrary.eu/pls/wordtc/new_wordtheque. w6_start.doc?code=11450&lang=EN; accessed on January 31, 2007. You can also see a table of virtues and vices in Aristotle's *Ethics*.

6. To see further treatment on how far the present-day church has fallen away from even the Greek understanding of virtue, see my chapter on 1 Peter 2:11, 12, under the section "Beloved, Abstain from the Passions of the Flesh."

7. Even Karl Marx got it right when he said, "Discussion on thought isolated from practice is sheer scholasticism." See Jean-Francois Revel, *The Flight From Truth* (New York: Random House, 1991), p. 242.

8. See Titus 1:8; 2; 3:1, 8, 14. For Paul, the theological foundation for doing good is rooted in the mercy of God who has kept his promise to us through the death and resurrection of Jesus, in whom we place our hopes for attaining eternal life. It is little wonder, then, that doing good in Titus is embedded in each chapter with a summary statement concerning the gospel and its relationship to our looking forward to eternal life. For these foundational summaries, out of which doing good arises, see 1:2; 2:13; 3:7.

Chapter Twenty-Two: Final Words on Matters of First Importance

1. Samuel Rutherford, ed. Frank E. Gaebelein, *The Letters of Samuel Rutherford* (Chicago: Moody Press, 1951), p. 32.

2. Herbert Lockyer, *Last Words of Saints and Sinners* (Grand Rapids, MI: Kregel, 1969), p. 64.

3. Lyle Dorsett, *Passion for Souls* (Chicago: Moody Press, 1997).

4. *Testament* is a recognized literary genre with several biblical examples (see Deuteronomy 31—32 and Acts 20:17–38). It is generally a discourse from an important figure whose death is looming. It typically contains expectations for future events and exhortations for present circumstances. See Daniel J. Harrington, *1 Peter, Jude and 2 Peter*, Sacra Pagina (Collegeville, MN: The Liturgical Press, 2003), pp. 252–254 or J.N.D. Kelly, *The Epistles of Peter and of Jude*, Black's New Testament Commentary (Peabody, MA: Hendrickson, 1969), pp. 311–315 for more information.

5. Douglas Moo, *2 Peter, Jude*, The NIV Application Commentary (Grand Rapids, MI: Zondervan, 1996), p. 64.

6. According to legend contained in the apocryphal book The Acts of Peter, Jesus appeared to Peter at a time when he was attempting to flee from Nero and Rome to escape arrest and the death sentence. Jesus is said to have appeared to him, and Peter asked him, "Where are you going?" (Latin, "*Quo vadis?*"). When Jesus replied, "To Rome, to be

crucified," Peter realizes the futility of trying to escape his true calling of martyrdom and returns to the city.

7. This is taken from personal correspondence on November 22, 2006 with Josh Dortzbach, structural engineer by trade during the day, member and elder of Holy Trinity Church by night, and most importantly a Christian and family man throughout.

Chapter Twenty-Three: Following in the Apostolic Way

1. *Catechism of the Catholic Church*, Part One, The Profession of Faith, 881, 882 (San Francisco: Ignatius Press, 1994), pp. 233, 234.
2. See 1:11; 2:9, 17; 3:2–4, 7–10, 12, 13.
3. Peter's understanding of the prophets' view on this was set down in 1 Peter 1:10–12. For his view on what constituted apostolic authority, Peter goes so far as to extend it to include the writings of Paul (see 2 Peter 3:15, 16). By way of structural overview, then, by this point in the text Peter has already imparted two massively important truths before dying: First, he desires that every Christian possess a *faith that is growing* (1:3–11), for nothing else will enable them to finish well and keep from falling. Second, the deposit put forward in the apostolic and prophetic writings is the sufficient and authoritative means for the *faithful to follow in the right way* (1:16–21).
4. Peter alludes to two other Hebrew Scriptures to support his claim when he writes that "you will do well to pay attention as to a lamp shining in a dark place" (see Psalm 119:105), and when he writes that "the day dawns and the morning star rises in your hearts" (see Malachi 4:1–2). This second allusion is all the more important given its context of the day of coming judgment.
5. Charles Spurgeon, "Chastisement Now and Afterwards," preached on September 6, 1863, *The Metropolitan Tabernacle Pulpit*, Vol. XXL (Carlisle, PA: Banner of Truth Trust, 1988), p. 375.
6. For this illustration I am indebted to Rev. David Camera, a colleague in ministry for many years, a friend, and a faithful preacher of the gospel.
7. J.R.R. Tolkien, *The Fellowship of the Ring*, The Lord of the Rings (Boston: Houghton Mifflin, 1954), pp. 38, 39.

Chapter Twenty-Four: Portraits of Failing Faith

1. Likewise, Jude makes use of dramatic historical scenes, be they Biblical or apocryphal. I preached through Jude prior to 2 Peter and therefore have elected to borrow a few paragraphs from that series that I thought might apply here as well. Some important differences between the two books remain though. In regard to the author's intentions for this material, the language and images are largely put forward to validate Peter's teaching on the Second Coming of Jesus in power and glory—with punishment in his hands for all who rebel against him. For Jude's particular use, see the messages covering Jude 5–16 in this same volume.
2. The biblical texts used by Peter for his portraits are all taken from the book of Genesis. The basis for his painting of *the angels* is Genesis 6:1–4. For his work on the *ancient world* he must be referencing Genesis 6:5—9:17. For *indecent cities* see Genesis 18:16—19:29.
3. The word for "hell" here is *tartarus*, a Greek mythological term for the part of Hell reserved for rebellious gods. See R. C. Lucas and Christopher Green, *The Message of 2 Peter and Jude*, The Bible Speaks Today (Downers Grove, IL: InterVarsity Press, 1995), p. 96.
4. John Milton, ed. Charles W. Eliot, *Paradise Lost*, in *The Complete Poems of John Milton* (New York: P.F. Collier & Son, 1937), pp. 90, 91.

Chapter Twenty-Five: Preachers Who Forsake the Faith

1. Marvin Gardiner, *The Flight of Peter Fromm* (Amherst, MA: Prometheus Books, 1994), p. 9.

2. As quoted in *ibid.*, p. 13.

3. See the chapters on the book of Jude in this volume for a possible parallel.

4. For comments on the phrase "They entice unsteady souls," see the introduction to this chapter. I referenced it there as opposed to here in light of its overall description of false preachers, especially as they are to be contrasted with Peter and the apostles who labored to see that the church remains on solid and established soil.

5. Thomas Mann, *Joseph and His Brothers* (London: Vintage of Random House, 1999), p. 1044.

6. David Helm, "A Few Are Not Enough," in *Preach the Word*, eds. Leland Ryken and Todd Wilson (Wheaton, IL: Crossway Books, 2007).

7. T. S. Eliot, *The Wasteland*, from *The Wasteland and Other Poems* (San Diego: Harcourt, 1934), pp. 42, 43.

8. Pearls Buck, *The Good Earth* (New York: Washington Square Press, 1931), pp. 168–171.

Chapter Twenty-Six: A Reminder on the Return of Christ

1. Aesop, "The Shepherd's Boy," in *Folk-Lore and Fable* (New York: P.F. Collier & Son, 1937), p. 28.

2. In a conversation with Dick Lucas once, he said something to the effect that the doctrine of the Second Coming got a bad name in the 1920s–1940s, largely because of too much enthusiastic preaching on it. As a result, the world began to dismiss the idea altogether as fable or fairy tale. The pendulum, however, in the last fifty years may have swung too far the other way. Today there is very little preaching in the West on the Second Coming of Christ. Peter's clearheaded approach might give us the way forward in this present age.

3. See Psalm 1:5 or Jeremiah 25:31 for two such examples.

4. Jean-Francois Revel, *The Flight from Truth* (New York: Random House, 1991), p. 315.

5. Thomas Nagel, *The Last Word* (Oxford: Oxford University Press, 1997), p. 130.

6. Quoted in Iain Murray, *D. Martyn Lloyd-Jones: The Fight of Faith 1939–1981* (Carlisle, PA: Banner of Truth Trust, 1990), p. 57.

7. Johnny Cash, "The Man Comes Around," *American IV: The Man Comes Around*, Lost Highway, 2002. I love the phrase in the song that speaks of "a golden ladder reaching down." It reminds me of Jesus, as well as Peter's golden chain leading to Heaven in 1:5–9.

Chapter Twenty-Seven: Reasons for a Delay in Christ's Return

1. Augustine, *Confessions*, trans. Edward Pusey (New York: Collier Books, 1961), p. 194.

2. Iain Murray, *D. Martyn Lloyd-Jones: The First Forty Years* (Southampton, UK: Camelot Press, 1983), pp. 220, 223.

3. *Pulse*, Vol. 25, No. 14, July 27, 1990.

4. R. C. Lucas and Christopher Green, *The Message of 2 Peter and Jude*, The Bible Speaks Today (Downers Grove, IL: InterVarsity Press, 1995), p. 142.

5. J. I. Packer, *Knowing God* (Downers Grove, IL: InterVarsity Press, 1973), p. 125.

Chapter Twenty-Eight: What to Do While Waiting

1. Samuel Beckett, *Waiting for Godot* (New York: Grove Press, 1954).

2. Samuel Beckett, in the essay and book *Proust*, 1930; see http://en.wikipedia.org/wiki/Proust_%28Beckett_essay%29; accessed September 4, 2007.

3. *Ibid.*

4. Iain Murray, *D. Martyn Lloyd-Jones: The Fight of Faith 1939–1981* (Carlisle, PA: Banner of Truth Trust, 1990), p. 400.

5. See http://www.worldofquotes.com/author/Juliana-Of-Norwich/1/index.html; accessed January 31, 2007.

6. Richard Baxter, *The Saints' Everlasting Rest* (Charlestown, MA: Samuel T. Armstrong, 1811), p. 69.

Chapter Twenty-Nine: A Faith That Finishes

1. See http://en.wikipedia.org/wiki/Phoenix_%28mythology%29.

Chapter Thirty: Reading Jude

1. Walter Bauer, ed. Frederick William Danker, *A Greek-English Lexicon of the New Testament and Other Early Christian Literature* (Chicago: University of Chicago Press, 2000), p. 356.

Chapter Thirty-One: Letter from the Ancient Jewish World

1. P. Oxy 2719 (III), as referenced by Peter Head, "Papyrology: Session 3: Greek Letters," in *New Testament and Papyrology*; http://www.tyndale.cam.ac.uk/Tyndale/staff/Head/NT&Pap3.html; accessed March 2, 2005.

2. From a University of Chicago classics professor, David Martinez, a friend and follower of Jesus as well as an ardent lover of first-century Greek manuscripts, I have learned that "ancient letters, after they were written on a sheet of papyrus, were rolled up and folded. The writer would have torn away one of the fibers of the papyrus and tied the letter together (keeping in mind that the papyrus sheet was made from cutting strips from the triangular stalk of the papyrus plant, and then interposing a horizontal layer of strips on a vertical layer, and then pounding the two together, the juices from the plant itself acted as a kind of adhesive to hold the two layers together. Writing was usually done on the 'recto' side, which is the side with the fibers running horizontally). The body of the letter would thus be hidden. On the outside (that is, the verso side of the papyrus, where the fibers run vertically) would be written the name of the one to whom the letter was addressed. Sometimes just a simple name! In the dative case: Απολλονιοι, 'to Apollonius'; sometimes this formula was used: αποδος Απολλονιοι, 'deliver to Apollonius.' If the recipient was a family member the familial relationship 'my son,' 'my mother' would be brought out. If the person was someone of note, such as an official, you often have that specified: Απολλονιοι αρξηιπηψλακιτει, 'to Apollonius, chief of police.' In the case of more important correspondence, concerning important matters of business or letters between government officials, instead of or in addition to tying up the letter, a seal (σψραγις) would be affixed: a lump of wax which was then stamped with the official imprint of the sender. This seal would be very carefully scrutinized by the recipient before the letter was opened and its contents were read and carried out, to insure that the seal was unbroken and authentic. Some of these have survived. To have a letter delivered one did have to find someone traveling to the destination city. Sometimes the address of the recipient would be written on the verso side in more detail. The Greek word for address is σεμασια, a close cousin of the word σεμειονλ, 'sign,' so often used in the New Testament. For example on one papyrus letter we read σεμειον · εν Τενμενουτει εντοι ρψμειοι αντιτου ψλετρος, 'address: at the Teumenous quarter in the lane opposite the well.'"

3. See *Anchor Bible Dictionary: D-G*, ed. David Noel Freedman (New York: Doubleday Dell, 1992), pp. 569, 570.

4. Charles H. Spurgeon, *Lectures to My Students* (Grand Rapids, MI: Zondervan, 1954), p. 227.

5. Richard J. Bauckham, *Word Biblical Commentary on Jude, 2 Peter* (Nashville: Thomas Nelson, 1983), p. 25.

6. John Milton, *Paradise Lost*, Norton Critical Edition, second edition (New York: W.W. Norton & Company, 1993), pp. 65–71.

Chapter Thirty-Two: Contending for This Noble Faith

1. *Sir Gawain and the Green Knight*, trans. J.R.R. Tolkien (New York: Valentine Books, 1975), p. 28.
2. Richard J. Bauckham, *Word Biblical Commentary on Jude, 2 Peter* (Nashville: Thomas Nelson, 1983), p. 5ff.
3. Walter Bauer, ed. Frederick William Danker, *A Greek-English Lexicon of the New Testament and Other Early Christian Literature* (Chicago: University of Chicago Press, 2000), p. 356.
4. Arnold Dallimore, *George Whitefield* (Carlisle, PA: Banner of Truth Trust, 1989), p. 85.
5. Richard Lucas, *The Message of 2 Peter & Jude* (Downers Grove, IL: InterVarsity Press, 1995), p. 159.
6. Bauer, *A Greek-English Lexicon of the New Testament and Other Early Christian Literature*, p. 642.
7. Kenneth Kirk, *The Vision of God* (Harrisburg, PA: Morehouse, 1991), p. 171.
8. Quoted in Charles Colson, *Kingdoms in Conflict* (Grand Rapids, MI: Zondervan, 1987), p. 205.
9. Thomas Hardy, *Jude the Obscure* (New York: Fine Creative Media, 2003), p. 409.
10. *Ibid.*, p. 45.

Chapter Thirty-Three: The Past Becomes the Present

1. Thomas Mann, *Joseph and His Brothers* (London: Vintage of Random House, 1999), p. 121.
2. *Ibid.*, p. 123.
3. Richard J. Bauckham, *Word Biblical Commentary on Jude, 2 Peter* (Nashville: Thomas Nelson, 1983), p. 5ff.

    Jude 11–19 Three Examples

    Second, in verses 11–19 Jude pulls three Old Testament examples into the present with Mann-like life, calling his opponents by their ancient name. Take a look:

    • In verse eleven he stands up Cain and Balaam and Korah, condemned men all. And what does Jude do with these three figures from history?

    • In verse twelve they become the ancient archetypes who are now *these* blemishes who are present at your love feasts.

    • In verse sixteen, the ancient ones are *these* present day grumblers, malcontents, boasters and opportunists. And,

    • In verse nineteen, they are today's worldly people, *these* who cause divisions and are devoid of the Spirit.
4. John Milton, *The Complete Poems of John Milton*, Vol. IV (New York: P.F. Collier & Son, 1937), pp. 90, 91.
5. Benson Bobrick, *Wide as the Waters* (New York: Simon & Schuster, 2001).

Chapter Thirty-Four: The Making of Midrash

1. Amos Oz, *A Tale of Love and Darkness*, trans. Nicholas de Lange (Orlando: Harcourt Brace & Company, 2004), p. 132.
2. *Ibid.*, p. 133.
3. As an aside, I have come to believe that this best explains why my own neighborhood in Chicago, lying as it does under the shadow of one of the world's great universities, is bewitched by deep relational insecurity.
4. For this insight we are all indebted to E. Ellis as noted by Richard J. Bauckham, *Word Biblical Commentary on Jude, 2 Peter* (Nashville: Thomas Nelson, 1983), p. 4.
5. *Ibid.*, p. 5ff.
6. Richard Lucas, *The Message of 2 Peter & Jude* (Downers Grove, IL: InterVarsity Press, 1995), p. 198.

7. Robert Alter, *The Five Books of Moses* (New York: W. W. Norton & Company, 2004), p. 762.

8. Nick Selby, as quoted in *Columbia Critical Guides: T.S. Eliot, the Waste Land*, ed. Nick Selby (New York: Columbia University Press, 1999), p. 15.

9. T. S. Eliot, *The Waste Land* (Orlando, FL: Harcourt Brace & Company, 1962), pp. 42, 43.

10. Mann, *Joseph and His Brothers*, p. 1044.

11. See http://www.poemhunter.com/poem/enoch/; accessed February 12, 2007.

Chapter Thirty-Five: Contending for the Faith: The Calling We Keep

1. Iain Murray, *D. Martyn Lloyd-Jones, The First Forty Years* (Southampton, UK: The Camelot Press, 1983), pp. 195, 196.

2. Richard J. Bauckham, *Word Biblical Commentary on Jude, 2 Peter* (Nashville: Thomas Nelson, 1983), p. 5ff.

3. The four references to Jude's audience as *agapetoi* or "beloved" (vv. 1, 3, 17, 20) in the course of this short letter may suggest a situation of persecution. In Genesis 22 (LXX) and at Jesus' baptism (Mark 1:11; cf. Mark 9:7) this Greek word (*agapetos*) connotes a human life about to be sacrificed. John P. Meier explains:

   Behind *agapetos* in this text [Mark 1:11] may lie the Hebrew *yahid*. The Hebrew word strictly means "only," "only one." But in a context of family relationships, when applied, e.g., to a son, it may mean "only beloved" or "uniquely beloved." This seems to be the sense when it is applied to Isaac (Genesis 22:2, 12, 16), since Abraham (at least according to the canonical form of Genesis) did have other children by other women, notably Ishmael by Hagar. The sense of love contained in *yahid* is underlined in the first verse that uses it of Isaac: "Take your son, your only one, whom you love, Isaac" (Genesis 22:2). . . . Interestingly, in the LXX, in every instance where *yahid* in the Hebrew text is translated by *agapetos*, it is used of an "only" or "only beloved" son or daughter who has died or who is destined for death: Isaac in Genesis 22:2, 12, 16; Jephthah's daughter in Judges 11:34; mourning as for an only son in Amos 8:10 and Jeremiah 6:26; and the mysterious "pierced one," who is mourned as an only son in Zechariah 12:10. ("A Marginal Jew," 2.188–189, emphasis added)

   The above quote comes from a note to me from Dr. Clare Rothschild on Pliny to the Emperor Trajan.

4. Pliny, *Letters*, 10.96–97; http://ccat.sas.upenn.edu/jod/texts/pliny.html; accessed on January 31, 2007.

5. Jude's audience here, as he writes concerning the likeliness of martyrdom, must be wondering what the eternal implications of their convictions are. One of the most fascinating aspects of Jude's letter is that he turns to the persons of Moses and Enoch in verses 9 and 14 respectively. In the case of Moses, we have one whose earthly body Jesus protects in death. In Enoch, we have one who does not die but was taken up to live with God (via an immediate resurrection).

6. Mary Black, "Summer Sent You," from the album *Looking Back*, Curb Records, 1995.

7. Arnold Dallimore, *George Whitefield* (Carlisle, PA: Banner of Truth Trust, 1989), pp. 503, 504.

8. Kathleen Thomerson, "I Want to Walk as a Child of the Light," Celebration Music, 1970.

Chapter Thirty-Six: Contending for the Faith: The Commitments We Make

1. William Shakespeare, *Henry V* (Act 4).

2. Harold M. Mayer and Richard C. Wade, *Chicago: Growth of a Metropolis* (Chicago: University of Chicago Press, 1969), p. 276.

3. Howard Taylor, *Hudson Taylor's Spiritual Secret* (London: China Inland Mission, 1932), pp. 165–166.

4. *Ibid.*, p. 165.

5. Richard Baxter, *The Saints' Everlasting Rest* (Vancouver: Regent College, 2004).

6. Iain Murray, *D. Martyn Lloyd-Jones, The First Forty Years* (Southampton, UK: The Camelot Press, 1983), pp. 211, 212.

Chapter Thirty-Seven: Contending for the Faith: The Conduct We Embrace

1. C. S. Lewis, quoted in John Stott, *Between Two Worlds: The Challenge of Preaching Today* (Grand Rapids, MI: Eerdmans, 1994), p. 235.
2. Amos Oz, *A Tale of Love and Darkness*, trans. Nicholas de Lange (Orlando, FL: Harcourt Brace & Company, 2004).
3. Norman Grubb, *C. T. Studd: Cricketer & Pioneer* (Fort Washington, PA: Christian Literature Crusade, 1978), p. 166.
4. *Schindler's List* (Universal Studios, 2004).
5. Roy Jenkins, *Gladstone* (New York: Random House, 1995), p. 102.
6. *Ibid.*, pp. 104, 114, 115.

Chapter Thirty-Eight: An Exalted Ending

1. Kenneth Kirk, *The Vision of God*, abridged edition (Harrisburg, PA: Morehouse, 1991), p. 108.
2. Winston Churchill as quoted in William Manchester, *The Last Lion, Winston Spencer Churchill* (Boston: Little, Brown & Company, 1988), p. 299.
3. Remaining in Christ is the central issue for us all. For, as Jude has made abundantly clear, those who possess a faith that fails are those who "pervert the grace of our God into sensuality and deny our only Master and Lord, Jesus Christ" (v. 4).
4. For an excellent treatment of the beatific vision, see Kenneth Kirk's 1929 Brampton Lectures. They would later be published as the book *The Vision of God*.
5. C. S. Lewis, *Reflections on the Psalms* (Orlando, FL: Harcourt, 1958), pp. 50, 51.
6. Attributed to Charles Spurgeon.
7. Frederick Faber, as quoted in A. W. Tozer, *The Pursuit of God* (Camp Hill, PA: Christian Publications, 1982), pp. 38, 39.
8. The significance should not be lost on us. When I claim that Jesus "protects us in death and in resurrection" I mean this very thing. He protects our earthly bodies and will see that we, in perfectly restored heavenly bodies, will dwell on high with him. Thus the earth's soil which comes to rest on our bodies on the day of our funeral will give way and open up to the protecting call of Jesus' voice who will not let the evil one have his way with us. The impact this might have had on Jude's first readers is significant, especially as, I think, many of them were soon to be martyrs. Though hounded, accused, and even maimed and killed by the enemy, God will see them through.

    To illustrate his protecting power, we need only think of Frederick Nolan, fleeing from his enemies during the North African persecution. Hounded by his pursuers over hill and valley with no place to hide, he fell exhausted into a wayside cave, expecting to be found. Awaiting his death, he saw a spider weaving a web. Within minutes the little bug had woven a beautiful web across the mouth of the cave. The pursuers arrived and wondered if Nolan was hiding there, but they thought it impossible for him to have entered the cave without dismantling the web. And so they went on. Having escaped, Nolan emerged from his hiding place and proclaimed, "Where God is, a spider's web is like a wall. Where God is not, a wall is like a spider's web." So, too, you and I shall one day walk out of death's dark cave completely intact! For more information, see *Kindred Spirit Magazine*, Summer 1986.
9. Stuart Townsend, "How Deep the Father's Love for Us," copyright 1995 by Kingsway's Thankyou Music.
10. C. S. Lewis, *Reflections on the Psalms*, quoted in John Piper, *Desiring God* (Portland: Multnomah Press, 1986), p. 17.
11. Arnold Dallimore, *George Whitefield* (Carlisle, PA: Banner of Truth Trust, 1989), pp. 123, 124.

Scripture Index

General Index

Index of
Sermon Illustrations

Aldous Huxley quote: "I had motives for not wanting the world to have a meaning," 249–250

Repentance

Mortimer Adler quote: "if one converts by a clear conscious act of the will, one had better be prepared to live a truly Christian life," 258

Scoffers

Peter's accusers compared Peter's gospel teaching on the Second Coming to myths and fairy tales, 212–215

Unlike the boy in Aesop's fable, "The Shepherd's Boy," Peter was not crying "Wolf, Wolf!" as the scoffers accused him of concerning the Second Coming, 244

Second Coming

Peter reminds readers of three of Jesus' parables to warn readers to prepare for the Second Coming: the ten virgins, the ten talents, and the separation of sheep and goats, 247

Peter compares the suddenness of the Second Coming to a thief coming in the night. The analogy of street robberies and how the victims never saw the thieves coming takes the point further, 259

The need to prepare for the Second Coming is compared to the Japanese attack at Pearl Harbor on December 7, 1941, which also was sudden. The Americans were completely unaware of the impending attack until it was too late, 259

Sin

Søren Kierkegaard's parable of a wild duck who continually visited tame ducks in a barnyard illustrates the dangers of failing to leave a way of life behind, 131

Quote by C. S. Lewis: "the only way in which I can make real to myself what theology teaches about the heinousness of sin," 131–132

In *The Holiness of God,* R. C. Sproul tells how Billy Graham's presence irked a non-Christian golfer, 133

Analogy: "Love takes the oxygen out of sin the way a blanket chokes the air from one caught on fire," 141

William E. Gladstone was plagued by the secret sin of pornographic reading: "I read sinfully, although with disgust . . . with a prurient curiosity against all the rules of pious prudence," 349

Soul's Homesickness

In a Martyn Lloyd-Jones quote, *hiraeth* is used to illustrate the soul's homesick. The "elect exiles of the dispersion" experienced this longing, 29–31, 35

For Christians "grounded" by the soul's homesickness, the remedy for *hiraeth* is the hope gained through the resurrection of Jesus, 31

Kyle Dugdale used architecture to discuss the soul's homesickness in this post-Edenic world: "Architecture has struggled to mitigate the effects of the fall," 75

Stability (The Firm Foundation of Faith)

A structural engineer writes: "Most people readily think of vertical stability and can quickly relate that to the need for securing solid foundations," 207

Stone Images

Daniel interpreted King Nebuchadnezzar's dream about a statue of gold, silver, bronze, iron, and clay that a stone destroyed, 73

Isaiah wrote about a chosen, precious cornerstone, 73

A psalmist wrote about the cornerstone that would bring salvation but would be rejected, 73–74

Jesus identified himself as the cornerstone spoken of by the prophet Isaiah, 74

Peter described Christians as "living stones," 74

Submission

To understand why Peter spoke of slavery as he discussed submission, a doctoral candidate in philosophy considered the differences between slavery in the Bible and American slavery, 94

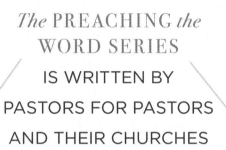

The PREACHING *the*
WORD SERIES

IS WRITTEN BY

PASTORS FOR PASTORS

AND THEIR CHURCHES